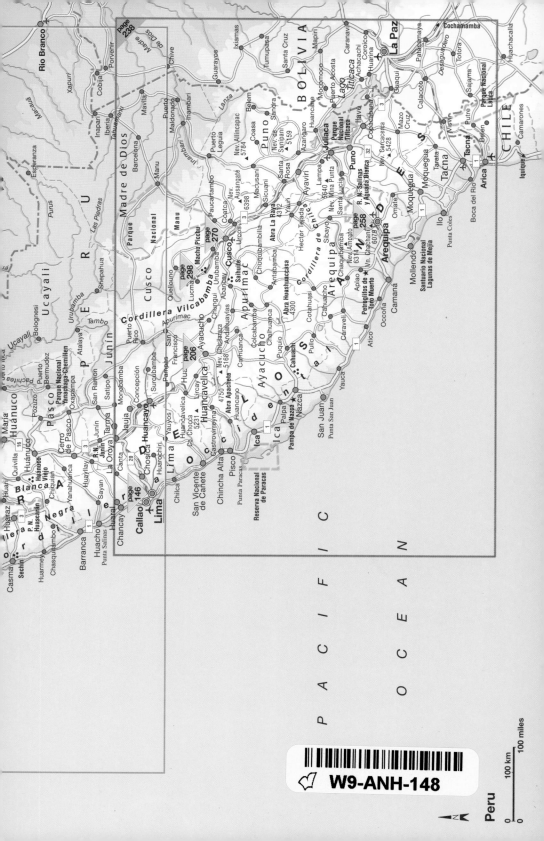

Peru

# INSIGHT GUIDES
# PERU

# APA PUBLICATIONS L
Part of the Langenscheidt Publishing Group

# PERU

*Insight Guide*

## Editorial

*Project Editor*
**Rachel Lawrence**
*Series Editor*
**Dorothy Stannard**
*Picture Manager*
**Steven Lawrence**

## Distribution

*United States*
**Langenscheidt Publishers, Inc.**
36–36 33rd Street 4th Floor
Long Island City, NY 11106
Fax: 1 (718) 784 0640

*UK & Ireland*
**GeoCenter International Ltd**
Meridian House, Churchill Way West
Basingstoke, Hampshire RG21 6YR
Fax: (44) 1256 817988

*Australia*
**Universal Publishers**
1 Waterloo Road
Macquarie Park, NSW 2113
Fax: (61) 2 9888 9074

*New Zealand*
**Hema Maps New Zealand Ltd (HNZ)**
Unit D, 24 Ra ORA Drive
East Tamaki, Auckland
Fax: (64) 9 273 6479

*Worldwide*
**Apa Publications GmbH & Co.**
**Verlag KG (Singapore branch)**
38 Joo Koon Road, Singapore 628990
Tel: (65) 6865 1600. Fax: (65) 6861 6438

## Printing

**Insight Print Services (Pte) Ltd**
38 Joo Koon Road, Singapore 628990
Tel: (65) 6865 1600. Fax: (65) 6861 6438

**CONTACTING THE EDITORS**
We would appreciate it if readers
would alert us to errors or out-
dated information by writing to:
**Insight Guides, P.O. Box 7910,
London SE1 1WE, England.
Fax: (44) 20 7403 0290.
insight@apaguide.co.uk**

**www.insightguides.com**

# ABOUT THIS BOOK

The first Insight Guide pioneered
the use of creative full-colour
photography in travel guides in
1970. Since then, we have
expanded our range to cater for our
readers' need not only for reliable
information about their chosen destination but also for a real understanding of the culture and workings
of that destination. Now, when the
internet can supply inexhaustible
(but not always reliable) facts, our
books marry text and pictures to
provide those much more elusive
qualities: knowledge and discern-
ment. To achieve this, they rely
heavily on the authority of locally
based writers and photographers.

## How to use this book

This book is carefully structured to
convey an understanding of Peru's
people and culture, and guides readers through its cities, national parks,
and Andean towns and villages.

◆ The **Best of Peru** section at the
front of the guide helps you to pri-
oritize what you want to do.

◆ The **Features** section, indicated
by a pink bar at the top of each
page, covers the natural and cultural
history of the country and includes
illuminating essays on Andean
Adventures, Music and Dance, Peoples of the Amazon, and Daily Life in
the Andes.

◆ The main **Places** section, indicated by a blue bar, is a complete
guide to all the sights and areas
worth visiting. Places of special
interest are coordinated by number
with the maps.

◆ The **Travel Tips** listings section,
with a yellow bar, provides full information on transportation, hotels,
shopping, activities from culture to

**LEFT:** the Uros Islands on Lake Titicaca.

1971. He also contributed the chapters on The Incas and Machu Picchu, and revised the chapter on Andean Adventures. Peter has lived in Cusco for many years and is the author of several books on South America, including *Exploring Cusco* and *Machu Picchu Historical Sanctuary*, as well as the *Pocket Guide to Peru* and the *Pocket Guide to Ecuador and the Galápagos*, both published by Insight Guides.

The Places and Travel Tips sections were updated by **Gabi Mocatta**, a freelance journalist who writes and photographs for newspapers, magazines, and travel guides. She first fell in love with South America volunteering on eco-tourism development projects in Venezuela. She's since traveled extensively in Peru, and currently works with remote Andean communities on sustainable development projects. Gabi also contributed the features on Jungle Lodges, the Cordillera Huayhuash, and Climbing Huascarán.

This new edition builds on previous editions written and updated by **Nick Caistor, Mary Dempsey, John Forrest, Jane Holligan, Kim MacQuarrie, Lynn Meisch, Julia Meyerson, Robert Randall, Mike Reid, Katherine Renton, Michael Smith, Simon Strong, Lesley Thelander, Betsy Wagenhauser, Barry Walker, Adriana von Hagen**, and **Diana Zileri**.

The principal photographer was **Abraham Nowitz**, but many other talented photographers contributed their work, including **Eric Lawrie, Gabi Mocatta**, and **Peter Frost**.

This book was proofread by **Neil Titman** and indexed by **Isobel McLean**. Thanks also go to **Paula Soper**.

to sports, an A–Z section of essential practical information, and a handy Spanish phrasebook. An easy-to-find contents list for Travel Tips is printed on the back flap, which also serves as a bookmark. ◆ The **Photographs** are chosen not only to illustrate the beauty of Peru's varied landscape, but also to convey its cultural diversity.

### The contributors

This new edition was commissioned and edited by **Rachel Lawrence**, Insight Guides' South America editor, and builds on earlier editions produced by **Tony Perrotet**, **Andrew Eames**, and **Pam Barrett**.

The Introduction, History, and Features sections were updated by **Peter Frost**, a writer, photographer, and independent scholar who has been exploring the Andes since

## Map Legend

| | |
|---|---|
| ━ ━ ┈ | International Boundary |
| ┈┈┈┈ | Province Boundary |
| ━ ∙ ━ | National Park/Reserve |
| ┈┈┈┈ | Ferry Route |
| ✈ ✈ | Airport: International/Regional |
| 🚐 | Bus Station |
| Ⓜ | Metro |
| ❶ | Tourist Information |
| ✝ ✝ ✝ | Church/Ruins |
| ✝ | Monastery |
| ∴ | Archaeological Site |
| ∩ | Cave |
| ⬙ | Statue/Monument |
| ★ | Place of Interest |
| ⚑ | Beach |
| ⌁ | Lighthouse |

The main places of interest in the Places section are coordinated by number with a full-colour map (e.g. ❶), and a symbol at the top of every right-hand page tells you where to find the map.

**BELOW:** grinding quinoa into flour.

# Contents

**LEFT:** the ancient ruins of Chan Chan.

Maps

**LEFT:** Chimu pottery.
**BELOW:** Statue of Liberty, Trujillo.

## Travel Tips

# THE BEST OF PERU: TOP TEN SIGHTS

From ancient ruins to colonial gems, and sandy beaches to majestic mountains, here is a rundown of Peru's most spectacular attractions

△ Twice as deep as the Grand Canyon, Peru's **Colca Canyon** is one of the world's great natural wonders. From the Mirador del Condor, Andean condors can be seen gliding on the air currents high above the valley floor. *Page 262*

△ The high-altitude city of **Cusco** was known to the Incas as "the navel of the earth." It is home to some of colonial Peru's most impressive buildings, built directly on top of stones laid by the Incas. *Pages 269–81*

▷ The **North Coast** is home to Peru's best beaches, including Máncora, Punta Sal, Playa La Pena, and Huanchaco, famous for its *totora* reed boats. *Pages 170–9*

△ The ancient city of **Machu Picchu** lay hidden under jungle for centuries. Perched on a hilltop high in the Andes, it is an architectural marvel. *Pages 292–303*

△ Cut off from the outside world until 1970, the **Monasterio de Santa Catalina** is an oasis of calm amidst the hustle and bustle of Arequipa's busy streets. *Pages 259–60*

▷ Giant etchings of animals and geometric figures created many thousands of years ago, the **Nazca lines** are one of the world's greatest archeological mysteries. *Pages 250–3*

▷ The incredible floating islands of **Uros** on Lake Titicaca date back to pre-Inca times and are made of *totora* reeds which must be continually replaced as they rot away. *Page 311*

△ Lima's **Plaza Mayor** lies at the heart of the "City of Kings" founded by Francisco Pizarro in 1535. It is overlooked by the Cathedral, the Archbishop's Palace, and the Government Palace. *Pages 153–4*

△ The **Cordillera Blanca** offers some of the best trekking in South America. *Pages 193–201*

▷ Peru is home to four types of **cameloid**: llamas, alpacas, guanacos, and vicuñas.

# THE BEST OF PERU: EDITOR'S CHOICE

With its astounding natural variety, eclectic blend of cultures, and outdoor adventures of all kinds, Peru is endlessly surprising. Here are the editor's top tips for making the most of it

## BEST NATURAL WONDERS

● **The Rainforest**
Covering some 50 million hectares, home to some of the greatest biodiversity on the planet, and storehouse of traditional medicine. *See pages 216–27.*

● **The Andes**
The highest mountain range outside the Himalayas, and snow capped for much of the year. *See pages 192–203.*

● **The Volcanoes**
Near Arequipa, many are over 6,000 meters (19,000 ft) high, their craters filled with boiling mud. *See page 257.*

● **The Northern Beaches**
The Northern Beaches of Punta Sal, Máncora, and around Tumbes: sparkling clear water, white sands and palm trees. *See pages 178.*

● **Lake Titicaca**
The highest navigable lake in the world. *See pages 306–15.*

● **The Coastal Desert**
So dry that in places it has received only 3 cm (1 inch) of rain in the past 30 years. *See pages 250–4.*

● **The Colca and Cotahuasi Canyons**
The deepest river canyons in the world. *See page 262.*

● **Hot Springs**
The Baños del Inca in Cajamarca and the hot springs at Chivay. *See pages 189 and 262.*

## BEST ADVENTURE TOURISM

● **Trekking**
Trekking in the Cordillera Blanca and the Cordillera Huayhuash, near Huaraz.

● **The Inca Trail**
The hard – and scenic – way to reach Machu Picchu.

● **Climbing**
Climbing some of the highest mountains in the world, like Huascarán 6,760 meters (22,200 ft), Peru's tallest peak.

● **Whitewater rafting**
Whitewater rafting on the Urubamba and Apurímac Rivers near Cusco.

● **Mountain biking**
Mountain biking in the Cordillera Negra, the ranges near Cusco, or the trails of the Colca and Cotahuasi Canyons near Arequipa.

● **Kayaking**
Kayaking the clear waters of Lake Titicaca and visiting its unique islands.

● **Surfing**
Surfing the waters of the Pacific Ocean which offer some the best surf breaks in the world. *See Andean Adventures, pages 120–9, for details of adventure sports in Peru.*

**LEFT:** Lake Titicaca. **ABOVE:** camping in the Cordillera Blanca.

## BEST NATIONAL PARKS

● **Parque Nacional Manu** Covering 1,716,295 hectares of rainforest, this is the largest national park in Peru and one of the largest on the planet. It is home to 800 species of bird, 200 types of mammals, and seven distinct indigenous tribes. *See pages 229–31.*

● **Parque Nacional Huascarán** Some 340,000 hectares

**ABOVE:** macaws in Manu National Park.

protects some of Peru's best high-altitude environments. *See page 198.*

● **Reserva Nacional Pacaya-Samiria** Two million hectares of lakes, rivers, and semi-submerged rainforest, territory of the rare manatee, pink dolphins, and giant anacondas. *See page 226.*

● **Parque Nacional Cordillera Azul** Protects the northern cloud forests between the Andes and the lowland rainforest. Little visited, home to indigenous communites. New species of birds have recently been discovered here. *See page 187.*

## BEST FOR FAMILIES

● **Train to Machu Picchu** The passenger train from Cusco is a spectacular way to travel to Machu, especially for kids who are too young to walk the Inca Trail. *See page 297.*

● **Islas Ballestas** Take a boat out to the Islas Ballestas, Peru's answer to the Galápagos, to see penguins, sea lions, seals, and pelicans. *See page 245.*

● **Parque de las Leyendas** Lima's zoo in Pueblo Libre offers a great way to learn more about Peru's wildlife and is

divided into coast, mountain, and jungle zones. It also has a children's playground. *See page 159.*

● *Yavari* **steamship** This restored Victorian steamship is now a floating museum. Tour the ship and discover how it was transported in pieces from England. *See page 310.*

**ABOVE:** La Virgen de la Candelaria festival in Puno.

## BEST FESTIVALS

● **La Virgen de La Candelaria** In early February in Puno, thousands of people in traditional dress participate in dances, songs, parades, folkloric plays, and fireworks to celebrate the city's patron saint. *See page 309.*

● **Inti Raymi** The Festival of the Sun. This yearly occasion on June 24 in Cusco is perhaps the biggest and most colorful festival in

Peru, and celebrates the return of the sun after the winter solstice. *See page 279.*

● **Carnival** Celebrated throughout Peru in mid-February, most wildly in Cajamarca. *See page 186.*

● **Semana Santa** This festival in March or April is marked with solemn religious processions in the streets. One of the best is in Ayacucho. *See page 206.*

● **Independence Day** Celebrated on July 28 and 29 throughout the country.

● **El Señor de los Milagros** Held on October 18, 19, and 28 in Lima, a huge procession in honor of the city's patron saint *See page 157.*

## Best Food and Drink

● **Pisco**
Peru's national drink is a powerful type of brandy. Pisco Sour is the national cocktail made with Pisco, lemon juice, sugar syrup, and egg white.

● **Ceviche**
Raw fish and mixed seafood marinated in lemon juice, garlic, and spices.

● *Anticuchos*
Marinated beef heart kebabs.

● *Humitas* **and** *tamales*
Corn meal dumplings cooked in corn or banana leaves, sometimes with a savory filling.

● **Pachamanca**
An Andean specialty of spiced meat, potatoes, and corn, cooked in the ground on hot rocks.

● *Pollo a la brasa*
Roast chicken is one of Peru's favorite meals and lip-smackingly good.

● **Potatoes**
Peru has some 400 varieties of potatoes, or *papas*. They are the key ingredient for numerous dishes, including the delicious *papa a la huancaína*, a creamy dish with eggs.

● *Aji*
A hot, spicy sauce made with chilis and garlic that is the ubiquitous accompaniment to meals, particularly in the highlands.

● *Chicha morada*
A sweet, deep purple non-alcoholic drink made from corn which is surprisingly refreshing.

● *Cuy* Although not to everyone's taste, roasted or fried guinea pig is a Peruvian specialty.

**ABOVE:** Isla Amantaní on Lake Titicaca.

## Best Cultural Experiences

● **The Island of Amantaní**
On this island in Lake Titicaca, visitors can stay as guests in villagers' homes and share the meals they prepare. *See pages 312–3.*

● **The Uros Islands**
Titicaca's amazing floating islands of reeds. *See page 311.*

● **Handicraft shopping**
Shop in one of Peru's many craft markets, such as Pisac near Cusco. *See page 287.*

● **Visiting a market**
Food markets are found in larger towns and offer an impressive range of Peruvian produce, including unusual fruits and vegetables.

● **Session with a shaman**
Learn about your future or drink the powerful Ayahuasca in Chiclayo or the Amazon. *See page 221.*

● **Trekking with llamas**
Walks organized by villagers from the Callejón de Huaylas that use llamas as pack animals. *See page 202.*

**LEFT:** Peruvian spirit.

## BEST HISTORICAL SITES

● **Machu Picchu**
Peru's most iconic site; one of the New Seven Wonders of the World. *See pages 292–303.*

● **Kuélap**
Little visited ruined citadel in Peru's north, spectacular enough to rival Machu Picchu. *See page 190.*

● **Chan Chan**
The ancient ruins of the Moche civilization, and the largest adobe city in pre-Columbian America. *See pages 175–6.*

● **The Nazca lines**
Mysterious etchings on the desert floor, of vast magnitude and only visible from the air. *See pages 250–3.*

● **Cusco**
Ancient capital of the Inca empire, overlaid with Spanish colonial buildings. *See pages 268–281.*

● **Huaca Pucllana**
This recently restored pre-Inca site in Miraflores, Lima, dates back to AD 400 and was the administrative center of the Lima culture. *See page 162.*

● **Huacas del Sol y de la Luna**
Ancient temples just outside Trujillo were built over several generations of the Moche people and were once covered with brightly-colored murals. *See page 175.*

**ABOVE:** visiting the Huaca Pucllana in Lima.

## BEST MUSEUMS AND GALLERIES

● **Museo de los Santuarios Andinos**
In Arequipa, exhibits include a fascinating display on Inca human sacrifice, and a mummified body of one of the victims. *See page 261.*

● **Qoricancha**
Now the Iglesia Santo Domingo, the Qoricancha, or Temple of the Sun in Cusco, was the Incas' most sacred building. *See page 275.*

● **Monasterio de San Francisco**
In Lima with its religious art and amazing skull-filled catacombs. *See page 155.*

● **Museo de Arte Precolumbino**
A wonderful collection of textiles, pottery, and gold in Cusco. *See page 279.*

● **El Museo Brüning**
This fascinating museum near Chiclayo contains gold treasures from the Tomb of Lord Sipán. *See page 177.*

**ABOVE:** traditional Peruvian hats made from llama wool.

## TRAVELERS' TIPS

● **Go with the flow**
Don't expect everything to go to plan. Things change with astounding frequency in Peru. Be flexible and don't get angry when your plans need to be altered.

● **Keep your change**
Always carry toilet paper, bottled water, and small change in Peru. Outside the biggest tourist spots, you can rarely pay small amounts with large denomination notes.

● **Make friends**
You may have been warned to be careful, but don't let this stop you enjoying people's generosity and kindness. Peruvians are endlessly hospitable and always keen to communicate with visitors.

● **Travel light**
Arrive with your suitcase half empty: you can buy almost anything you need here, and clothes are stylish and cheap.

● **¿Habla español?**
Even if you aren't a linguist, be sure to learn a few phrases in Spanish. The effort will be appreciated and will make for a more fulfilling trip.

# ANCIENT AND MODERN

Inca ruins, Amazon jungle and fascinating tribal customs make Peru a top destination for travelers interested in landscape and culture. But it is also has a modern, urban side that looks to the future rather than the past

**D**espite its rugged and often inhospitable landscape, Peru ranks among the world's great centers of ancient civilization. The sun-worshiping Incas are the last and most famous in a long line of highly developed cultures that thrived thousands of years before the arrival of Europeans. Their remains fascinate travelers and archeologists alike. Along with the stunning Inca ruins near Cusco and the great city of Machu Picchu, Peru is home to the Nazca lines etched on its coastal deserts, the Colla burial *chullpas* near Lake Titicaca, the enormous adobe city of Chan Chan, the great Moche adobe pyramids and burial sites near Trujillo and Chiclayo, and the massive stone citadel of Kuélap near Chachapoyas. These cultures left no written records, just mysterious and beautiful works in gold, silver, and stone.

But ancient ruins are only a fraction of the story. Although the traditional American world was shattered by the bloody Spanish conquest in the 1500s, the legacy of ancient cultures is very much alive. Roughly half of Peru's 27 million people are of indigenous origin; often living in remote mountain villages, they still speak the Quechua or Aymara tongue of their ancestors, and many of their beliefs and customs are a mixture of traditional Andean ways and the culture imposed by the Spanish conquistadors. There are also more than 50 ethnic groups who live in Peru's Amazon region, some of whom still shun contact with the outside world.

Peru is also one of the most spectacular countries on earth. Its variety is astonishing: scientists have ascertained that of 101 possible ecological zones, Peru has 84 within its borders. As a result, the country can offer virtually every conceivable scenic attraction: the Peruvian Andes draw

trekkers and mountain climbers from all over the world, over half of Peru lies within the Amazon jungle, and the world's driest desert runs the entire length of its coast.

In the 21st century, Peru is still being formed as a modern nation. Separated by geographical differences and an often violent past, Peruvians today are justly proud of their heritage and their country's riches. Peru is one of the world's great travel destinations. ❑

**PRECEDING PAGES:** Virgen de la Candelaria festival, Puno; coastal mist in Lima; sunset on the beach at Máncora. **LEFT:** a dancer in traditional dress at one of Peru's many festivals. **ABOVE:** stallholder in Lima. **RIGHT:** on Pimental beach.

# LAND OF EXTREMES

**Mountains, deserts, and jungle combine to make the Peruvian landscape a varied and breathtaking one, where nature is firmly in control**

**B**ordered to the north by Ecuador and Colombia, to the east by Brazil and Bolivia, to the south by Chile, and to the west by the waters of the Pacific, Peru is the third-largest country in South America. Ask Peruvians about their homeland and they will cut it into geographical slices – coastal desert, highlands, and jungle – pointing out that theirs is the only South American nation which contains all three. It is this challenging geography that has given Peru its varied legacy of ethnic cultures, foods, music, and folklore.

Peruvians often use superlatives to describe the country's features. They include Lake Titicaca, the world's highest navigable lake at 3,850 meters (12,720 ft) above sea level, and Mount Huascarán, Peru's biggest Andean peak and South America's fourth-highest mountain at 6,760 meters (22,200 ft). The River Amazon, the world's greatest river system, has its source in the far south of Peru and, along with its rainforest namesake, makes up much of the country.

*Peru is home to two of the world's deepest canyons, which both lie just outside Arequipa. Twice as deep as the USA's Grand Canyon, the Colca Canyon has a depth of 3,180 meters (10,600 ft), while Cotahuasi is even deeper at 3,500 meters (11,480 ft).*

Settled among those wonders are 27 million Peruvians, 8 million of them crowded into Lima and the surrounding area. About 45 percent of the population is indigenous – mostly Quechua-speakers, with a small proportion of Aymara-speaking peoples. Some 37 percent are mestizos (of mixed white and native blood), 15 percent are of European extract, and 3 percent are descendants of black slaves brought to work the cotton and sugar plantations, Chinese indentured laborers shipped in during the 19th-century guano boom, or later waves of Japanese immigrants. Spanish and Quechua are the official languages. Some 90 percent of the country's residents are Roman Catholic, although the religious rites they practice bear traces of pre-Christian religions.

## Barren beaches

The Spanish conquistadors' first glimpse of Peru was along its 2,500-km (1,500-mile) coastal desert – one of the driest in the world. Visitors familiar with South America's Caribbean coast find Peru's

**LEFT:** Mount Ampato and Mount Sabancaya in the Colca valley. **RIGHT:** the dense Amazon rainforest.

sandy beaches unsettling, with their harsh backdrop of dunes or cactus-covered cliffs. But when conquistador Francisco Pizarro arrived in 1532 the coast was less desolate. The native peoples had developed sophisticated irrigation systems, and fields of vegetables and grains were grown in the desert. Today, agricultural settlements still flourish around the oases formed by rivers running down from the Andean slopes, creating fertile valleys in the otherwise bare terrain.

At the southern end of the coast, Chile's appropriation of some of this desert land more than a century ago in the War of the Pacific (1879–83) meant the loss of a hidden treasure – tracts rich

fog that causes havoc with air traffic and covers Lima for much of the year with a gloomy mist known as *garúa*. The exceptions to the rainless norm are the freak showers, and sometimes floods caused by El Niño *(see opposite)*.

## Mountain and jungle

Above all, it is the highlands that are associated with Peru. Here Quechua-speaking women weave rugs and garments, condors soar above the Andes, and wild vegetation camouflages Inca ruins. Although breathtaking to look at, the Sierra seems brutally inhospitable: the thin, cold air here combines with a rugged landscape to make the Andes an obstacle to

in the nitrates sought for fertilizers and explosives. Still, the coast has brought wealth to Peru despite its inhospitable landscape and dearth of water (only a cup of measurable precipitation every two years is recorded in some areas). Fish stocks are plentiful in the coastal waters, making Peru one of the world's foremost exporters of fishmeal, a livestock feed derived from anchovies.

It is the cold, fish-bearing current running along the hot coast from the south that keeps rain away from the desert. So little moisture accumulates above the Humboldt Current (named for the 19th-century German explorer Alexander von Humboldt) that ocean winds heading toward the mountains rarely carry condensation. What they do bring to the land, however, is a thick, dense

transportation, communication, and development.

Nevertheless, nearly half of Peru's population is scattered across the Sierra. Between the harsh mountain ranges where alpaca herders and potato farmers eke out a living, lie warmer, fertile valleys where irrigated crop terraces have produced abundant corn and vegetable harvests since Inca times.

Three-fifths of Peru is jungle, divided into the hot, steamy Lower Amazon and the so-called High Jungle, or *ceja de la selva* (eyebrow of the jungle). The latter is the area where the mountains meet the Amazon, a subtropical expanse where coffee, tropical fruits – and much of the world's coca crop – are grown.

Peru has a policy of protecting the rainforest through legislation and by designating virgin areas as national parks. Extending from the Andean foothills to the east of Cusco into the low jungle is the Parque Nacional Manu, which has one of the world's most impressive concentrations of wildlife; more than 850 bird species alone have been spotted from the park's research station. A few hours away by river from Puerto Maldonado is the Reserva Nacional Tambopata, which contains more than 1,110 butterfly species and a quantity of insects that are found nowhere else on earth.

The presence of oil and natural gas beneath the Peruvian rainforest, plus a new Trans-Oceanic highway from Brasil through southeastern Peru, places protected areas under constant threat. In late

quake struck the coast 160 km (100 miles) south of Lima, causing massive damage in Pisco, Chincha, and Ica, killing more than 500 people, and leaving upwards of 100,000 homeless.

The broad range of weather conditions across the country makes labels such as "winter" and "summer" of little practical use. Lima residents refer to their hot sunny months (December to April) as summer, and the rest of the year, when the fog sets in, as winter. In the Sierra, winter is the rainy months (November to April). Snow is uncommon in inhabited highland areas, although the highest Andean peaks are snow-covered throughout the year. The jungle, meanwhile, is hot and humid all year.  ❑

2007, Peruvian and international conservationists succeeded in stopping – for now – a projected law to shrink the Tambopata reserve by 20 percent, opening a highly sensitive area to oil exploration.

## Land of earthquakes

Nature has dealt this country many cruel blows. Peru straddles the Cadena del Fuego (the Chain of Fire), a geologic fault line running the length of the continent. The line passes along the coast, cutting directly through Arequipa which, over the centuries, has borne the brunt of the seismic damage.

In August 2007 a violent 8.0-magnitude earth-

**LEFT:** Titicaca, the world's highest navigable lake.
**ABOVE:** Peru's arid coastline.

### EL NIÑO

Every few years, Peru's climate is affected by an unusual phenomenon whereby a warm current traveling from the equator pushes southward, displacing the cold Humboldt Current, with potentially destructive effects. Known as El Niño, meaning "The Christ-Child," it gained its name because it arises around Christmas.

Centuries ago its disruptive effects brought down an entire ancient civilization, the Moche. More recently, in 1982–3, and again in 1997–8, unusually fierce currents spread the effects across the globe and brought the phenomenon to international attention. Peru's northern coast in particular suffered very badly from the floods and mudslides brought on by heavy rainstorms.

# DECISIVE DATES

**10,000–3000 BC**

**Human settlement, based on** marine resources and rudimentary floodplain agriculture, appears on the Peruvian coast.

## COTTON PRECERAMIC PERIOD

**3000–1800 BC**

First known urban settlement of the Americas established on the coast at Caral. Simple cotton textiles appear.

## INITIAL PERIOD

**1800–800 BC**

Irrigation agriculture appears on the coast, together with maize cultivation and pottery.

Settlements move inland to control supply of water.

## EARLY HORIZON PERIOD

**800–300 BC**

Chavín culture rises on strategic trans-Andean trade route. Innovations in textiles, metallurgy, and stone carving appear.

## EARLY INTERMEDIATE PERIOD

**300 BC–AD 650**

Nazca and Moche cultures flourish on the south and north coast, developing distinctive ceramic styles. The Nazca lines are drawn on the southern desert and the Moche build huge adobe pyramids. El Niño weather events provoke collapse of the Moche civilization.

## MIDDLE HORIZON PERIOD

**AD 600–1000**

Wari people initiate terrace agriculture in the central highlands, and the Tiwanaku develop intensive raised-field cultivation on the shores of Lake Titicaca. The Sicán culture thrives in the Lambayeque valley, producing superb gold, silver, and copper objects.

## LATE INTERMEDIATE PERIOD

**c.1000–1470**

Numerous regional cultures emerge; most important are the Chimu, the Chachapoyas, the Ica, the Huanca, and the Incas. The Chachapoyas people build the huge walled citadel of Kuélap; successive kings of Chimu build the adobe city of Chan Chan.

## THE INCA EMPIRE

**1438**

According to later Inca mytho-history, Pachacutec launches an imperial expansion across a vast swathe of the Andes. The Incas absorb the crafts and technologies of assimilated peoples, and deploy their own genius for agricultural engineering, architecture, and large-scale organization.

**1527–32**

The death of Huayna Capac leaves the empire divided between his sons, Huascar and Atahualpa. Civil war erupts, and Atahualpa emerges victorious.

## THE SPANISH CONQUEST

**1532**

Spanish conquistadors arrive in Tumbes and march to meet Atahualpa at Cajamarca. The Inca emperor is tricked and captured, and offers a huge ransom in exchange for his life.

**1533**

The Spaniards execute Atahualpa, then march on Cusco and loot the city's treasures. Manco, another son of Huayna Capac, is installed as puppet ruler.

**1535**

Francisco Pizarro founds Lima, which will later become the seat of the Spanish Viceroyalty.

**1536**

Manco rebels against the Spanish, but is defeated at Sacsayhuamán. The following year he retreats to Vilcabamba.

**1538**

Diego de Almagro, Pizarro's original partner, leads an opposing faction. Civil war breaks out. Almagro is defeated and garroted.

**1541**

Pizarro is assassinated by Almagro supporters.

**1544**

Manco is murdered by Almagrist allies at Vitcos.

---

**FAR LEFT TOP**: artifact from the tomb of the Lord of Sipán. **FAR LEFT BOTTOM**: Huaca del Dragón. **LEFT TOP**: Sechín mural. **LEFT BOTTOM**: pre-Columbian vessel. **ABOVE**: Atahualpa. **RIGHT**: Francisco Pizarro. **FAR RIGHT**: Charles III of Spain.

**1570s**

Viceroy Francisco de Toledo invades Vilcabamba and executes Manco's son, Tupac Amaru, ending Inca resistance. Toledo establishes *reducciones*, the forced resettlement of native populations, and formalizes the *encomienda* system, whereby Indians provide tribute to their Spanish masters, and co-opts the *mita*, an Inca taxation-through-labor system.

**Early 1600s**

A Catholic campaign to stamp out native religions results in many indigenous beliefs and rites being given a Christian veneer.

**1700–13**

The War of the Spanish Succession in Europe sees the Habsburg dynasty replaced by the Bourbons, who try to improve the economy and reduce corruption.

**1759**

Charles III ascends the throne of Spain and opens up trade in Peru.

**1767**

The powerful Jesuit Order, influential in securing fairer

treatment of natives, is expelled from the New World.

**1780**

Indigenous rebellion against the Spanish led by José Gabriel Condorcanqui, known as Tupac Amaru II, who is defeated and executed in 1781.

**1784–90**

Viceroy Teodor de Croix institutes reforms, setting up a court to deal with indigenous claims.

**1814**

An indigenous uprising led by Mateo García Pumacahua captures Arequipa and wins Creole support before being put down by royalist troops.

**1820**

After liberating Chile, the Argentinian General José de San Martín invades Peru, helped by the recently formed Chilean navy under British command.

## MODERN HISTORY

**1821**

San Martín enters Lima and proclaims Peruvian independence on July 28, although royalists still control most of Peru.

**1824**
Independence armies headed by General José de Sucre crush royalist forces at the Battle of Ayacucho.

**1824–6**
Bolívar presidency, after which a period of turmoil ensues, with 35 presidents in 40 years.

**1840**
First guano and nitrate fertilizer contracts with Britain, which come to control Peru's economy.

**1851**
Lima–Callao railroad inaugurated.

**1854**
President Ramón Castilla abolishes slavery and "Indian tribute" taxation.

**1866**
Spain attacks the port of Callao, failing in a last desperate bid to recover her strategic colony.

**1869**
Spain recognizes Peruvian independence.

**1877**
Foreign debts bankrupt Peru.

**1879**
War of the Pacific over nitrate deposits in southern Tarapacá province begins.

**1880**
Chile occupies the provinces of Tacna, Arica, and Tarapacá.

**1881**
Chileans sack Lima and occupy Peru.

**1883**
Treaty of Ancón cedes Tarapacá to Chile.

**1911**
Hiram Bingham announces discovery of Machu Picchu.

**1924**
Exiled Victor Raúl Haya de la Torre founds Alianza Popular Revolucionaria Americana (APRA).

**1925**
First major El Niño weather event of the 20th century.

**1931**
Haya de la Torre is allowed back to Peru to contest elections, but is defeated.

Numerous *apristas* are killed in the subsequent uprising.

**1941–2**
Border war with Ecuador ends in victory for Peru. Rio de Janeiro Protocol establishes a new border.

**1948**
Military coup brings General Odría to power.

**1962**
Another military coup heads off a probable APRA election victory.

**1963–8**
President Belaúnde initiates modest land reform, but is swept from power in another military coup.

**1968**
General Juan Velasco introduces land reforms and nationalization. Quechua is recognized as the second language.

**1970**
Massive earthquake strikes northern Peru, killing some 70,000 people.

**1972**
Second major El Niño event of the 20th century.

**1975**
Centrist policies follow a palace coup by General Morales Bermúdez, but economic woes pile up.

## 1980
Belaúnde returns to power in democratic elections. Terrorist organization Sendero Luminoso (Shining Path) becomes a serious threat.

## 1983
Third major El Niño event causes disastrous flooding.

## 1985
APRA takes power for the first time, under youngest-ever president Alán García. His policies cause hyperinflation, shortages, and chaos, while nationwide terrorist violence spirals out of control.

## 1990
Unknown Alberto Fujimori defeats novelist Mario Vargas Llosa to win presidency.

## 1992
Fujimori suspends Congress and Constitution and

introduces tough economic and anti-terrorist measures. Sendero Luminoso leader Abimael Guzmán is captured.

## 1995
Border clashes lead to major military conflict with Ecuador, ending in ceasefire. Fujimori is re-elected, and his supporters gain a majority in Congress.

## 1996–7
Members of armed Tupac Amaru hostage-taking group killed after four-month siege at Japanese ambassador's residence. All but one of 72 hostages survive.

## 1998
Peace treaty with Ecuador leads to final settlement of border dispute.

## 2000
Fujimori wins third term amidst opposition boycott and widespread charges of vote-rigging. Leaked videos of high-level bribery trigger mass protests. Fujimori flees to Japan and faxes his resignation.

## 2001
Outsider politician Alejandro Toledo wins elections and takes office as first elected indigenous president of Peru. His term is marred by strikes, protests, and the rise of ultra-nationalist opposition politics, but also sees high prices for Peru's export commodities, and vigorous macro-economic growth.

## 2006
Alán García achieves political resurrection, claiming to have learned from disastrous presidential mistakes in the 1980s and promising economic stability; he narrowly wins a second term.

## 2007
Ex-president Fujimori is extradited from Chile after a failed attempt at political comeback in Peru. On trial in Lima, he receives six years in prison for abuse of power and faces more serious human rights charges. In August an 8.0-magnitude earthquake hits the coastal region of Ica, killing more than 500 people, and leaving some 100,000 homeless.

**FAR LEFT TOP**: 19th-century guano workers. **MIDDLE LEFT**: Hiram Bingham. **LEFT**: President Belaúnde. **ABOVE**: APRA victory in 2006. **RIGHT TOP**: Alberto Fujimori on trial. **RIGHT**: earthquake damage in Pisco.

# LOST EMPIRES:
# PERU BEFORE THE INCAS

More than a millennium before the Incas ruled Peru there were societies creating adobe cities, woven garments, and exquisite objects of gold and silver

Civilization in the Andes has long been equated with the Incas. Almost every account of Peru by 16th-century Spanish chroniclers told of fabled Inca wealth, and lauded their achievements in architecture and engineering, inevitably comparing them to the feats of the Romans. However, archeologists working on the Peruvian coast and highlands have since shown that the origins of Peruvian civilization reach back more than four millennia, some 4,000 years before the Incas emerged from their highland realm to forge Tahuantinsuyu, their enormous empire of the four quarters of the world *(see page 40)*.

Not until the mid-19th century did early scientific observers begin to suspect the true antiquity of Peruvian civilization. No one imagined at the time that civilization in the New World could be almost as ancient as that of the Old. Data emerging from Peru, however, shows that the earliest monumental architecture is roughly contemporary with the pyramids of Egypt and pre-dates the large-scale constructions of the Olmec in Mesoamerica by more than 1,000 years.

## The beginnings of civilization

The first traces of human settlement in Peru have been found along the coast, where some 41 river valleys, running off the western slope of the Andes, slice through the desert, creating fertile oases interspersed by arid expanses of sand. In the years 3000–1800 BC, a time known to archeologists as the Cotton Preceramic, small communities thrived along the coast, harvesting the rich Pacific Ocean for its bounty of shellfish, fish, and marine mammals. On river floodplains they culti-

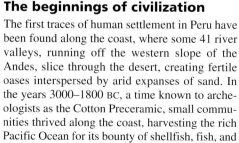

vated cotton and gourds and hunted for deer. In the *lomas*, lush belts of fog vegetation located a few miles inland, they gathered wild plants. Before the introduction of true weaving, they created twined and looped textiles of cotton and sedge, some decorated with intricate designs that attest to technological and esthetic skills.

Toward the end of the Cotton Preceramic, larger settlements emerged, such as that of Paraíso just north of Lima, which covered 58 hectares (143 acres). Over 100,000 tons of quarried stone were used here to build monumental platforms. At Aspero in the Supe valley, 145 km (90 miles) north of Lima, the largest mound, comprising rubble and stone blocks, is 10 meters (33 ft) high and measures 30 by 40 meters (98 by 130 ft) at

---

**LEFT:** the ancient walls of Chan Chan, near Trujillo.
**RIGHT:** a restored mural at Sechín.

its base. Both of these centers were surrounded by sprawling residential areas containing burial grounds and thick midden, or waste, deposits.

## The Initial Period

Some time around 1800 BC, at the beginning of what is known as the Initial Period, these fishing communities began to move inland. Although the majority of sites documented from this time average only 20 km (12 miles) from the coast, they were far enough up-valley to tap the rivers and construct irrigation canals, substantially increasing the ancient Peruvians' subsistence base. Evidence from the middens indicates that in addition to

cotton and gourds they grew squash, peppers, lima and kidney beans, peanuts, and avocados, and supplemented their diet with marine products. Maize, which would become an Andean staple, was introduced somewhat later, possibly from Mesoamerica where it was first domesticated.

Two further revolutionary inventions belong to this period: the introduction of pottery and of simple weaving techniques.

In the Casma valley, 275 km (170 miles) north of Lima, large Initial Period settlements flourished at sites such as Moxeke-Pampa de las Llamas. Located 18 km (11 miles) inland, the complex once covered an area of 2.5 sq km (1 sq mile),

### THE OLDEST URBAN CENTER

The recently excavated site of Caral, 190 km (114 miles) north of Lima, is a residential and ceremonial complex dating from the very beginning of the Cotton Preceramic period – around 2700 BC. Apparently the center of an area featuring numerous large truncated pyramids, Caral has been identified as the earliest known urban center of the Americas. Around 3,000 people lived there, dedicated to commerce and pleasure, and living – most unusually – without warfare of any kind.

dominated by two mounds. The 27-meter (90-ft) high pyramid of Moxeke, excavated in the early 20th century, is decorated with awesome adobe friezes of snarling felines and human attendants, which are painted red, blue, and white. The temple facade has been reconstructed at Lima's Museo de la Nación.

Facing Moxeke lies Huaca, or Mound A – once almost 6 meters (20 ft) high and 135 meters by 135 meters (450 ft by 450 ft) wide. Here, access to storage areas was controlled by wooden doorways, and the images of two fanged felines guard one of two entrances.

These architectural monuments, with U-shaped platforms and sunken circular courtyards, have been documented from sites just south of Lima to the Moche or Trujillo valley, 595 km (370 miles) north of Lima. Near Trujillo stands the Huaca de los Reyes, which also contained elaborate adobe friezes of felines, once painted red, yellow, and cream, long faded by the desert sun. The arms of the U-shaped temple point upriver, toward the Andes and the source of water, a constant preoccupation on the rainless coast.

The Initial Period also saw the construction of sites such as Sechín, which is in the Casma valley too, and was first excavated some 80 years ago by Julio C. Tello, a renowned Peruvian archeologist. Here, carved on stone monoliths surrounding an adobe temple, a macabre procession of victorious warriors and their dismembered victims commemorates a battle – although who the victors or the vanquished were is still uncertain.

## Sierra cultures

The emergence of complex societies on the coast was paralleled by developments in the highlands, where archeologists have documented the rise of ceremonial architecture at sites such as Huaricoto in the Callejón de Huaylas, 250 km (155 miles) northeast of Lima. Unfortunately, preservation of organic matter is not as good in the highlands as it is on the arid coast, and so the archeological record for this area is not as complete.

Nonetheless, excavations have unearthed ceremonial structures with fire-pits, where offerings were burned. Llamas had already been domesticated by this time, serving both as beasts of burden and as an important food source. Llama caravans carried highland produce – potatoes and other Andean tubers and grains – to the coast, where they were exchanged for goods from the warm coastal valleys: dried fish and shellfish, seaweed, salt, cotton, peppers, and coca leaves, to supplement the heavy inland diet. The guinea pig (cuy), an Andean delicacy, was probably also domesticated about this time.

## The Early Horizon Period

In the highlands, construction began around 800 BC at the ceremonial center of Chavín de Huantar, near Huaraz (see page 199). Perhaps one of the most famous sites of ancient Peru, Chavín was believed until recently to have been the inspiration for the similar art style that spread throughout much of coastal and highland Peru. The period

(approximately 800–300 BC) is often referred to as the Chavín Horizon.

However, research over the past 35 years has shown that Initial Period developments on the coast (including U-shaped temples, circular sunken courtyards, stirrup-spout ceramics, and an elaborate iconography featuring fanged felines and snarling gods) culminated at Chavín, and did not originate there as some had thought.

Perhaps because the culture was based midway between the coast and the jungle, Chavín iconography even incorporated jungle fauna into its elaborate system. The Tello Obelisk, on view at Lima's Museo de la Nación, features a fierce caiman.

### TREASURES IN STORE

Many of the ancient sites really should be seen, in order to appreciate their atmosphere and sheer size. But to see most of their treasures you must go to one of the museums where the finds are kept. The Tello Obelisk and many other Chavín carvings, as well as weavings from Paracas, are now in the Museo de la Nación in Lima. To see treasures from Sipán, and a variety of Moche and Chimu finds, pay a visit to the excellent Museo Brüning and the spectacular new Royal Tombs of Sipán in Lambayeque.

**LEFT:** wall carvings at Sechín depicting decapitation and human sacrifice. **RIGHT:** Chimu textile.

The spread of the Chavín cult brought with it innovations in textiles and metallurgy, and coastal sites contemporary with the Chavín temple were perhaps branch shrines of a powerful Chavín oracle. Painted cotton textiles found at Karwa, near the Bay of Paracas, about 170 km (105 miles) south of Lima, for example, depict deities reminiscent of those carved on stone slabs at Chavín de Huantar.

The weavings found buried with mummy bundles at Paracas and dated to about 300 BC are perhaps the finest ever produced in ancient Peru. Because of the hundreds of mummy bundles buried in stone-lined pits, this is sometimes known as the Necropolis Phase. By this time almost every

weaving technique known today had been invented by the Peruvians. Evidence for a far-flung trade network is also visible at Paracas: obsidian from the highland region of Huancavelica; cameloid fiber, probably alpaca, also from the highlands; and feathers of tropical birds used to adorn fans, which probably came from the jungle. Traces of the use of cameloid fiber in north-coast weavings, again probably alpaca, also appear at this time.

Metalworking techniques, such as soldering and repoussé, and gold-silver alloys were first used by ancient Peruvians on the north coast during the Early Horizon Period. The Moche were to add to the repertoire of metalworking skills a few centuries later.

## The Nazca and Moche cultures

The decline of Chavín influence led to the emergence of regional cultures in river valleys on the coast and in highland valleys during a time known as the Early Intermediate Period, which lasted until about AD 600. In the Nazca valley, weavers and potters followed the Paracas tradition, but instead of producing painted and incised pottery, they began to make ceramics decorated with a variety of vividly colored mineral pigments, some showing scenes of domestic life.

On an arid plain north of modern-day Nazca, the Nazca people etched giant images by brushing away surface soil and stones to reveal the lighter-colored soil beneath. Images of birds, some measuring 60 meters (200 ft) across, predominate, but they also drew killer whales, a monkey (90 meters/300 ft across), and a spider (45 meters/ 150 ft long). All these creatures feature on Nazca ceramics. The straight lines and trapezoids appeared a few hundred years later.

There are numerous theories about why the lines were drawn. Maria Reiche, who spent much of her life studying the phenomenon (see opposite), believed they formed part of an astronomical calendar; Erich von Daniken attributes them to visitors from outer space – a theory given little credence by archeologists. More recent theories suggest that the geoglyphs were paths linking sacred sites or a surface map of underground aquifers, or that they were linked to mountain worship and fertility. Indeed, many of the animal images can be tied to Andean fertility concepts, and some of the lines point to the mountains in the distance, the source of valuable water.

The ancient Nazca lived in settlements

---

### A TEXTILE AGE

By the beginning of the Common Era, virtually every textile technique ever invented was already used in Peru. The first Europeans encountered natives using weaving techniques to make roofs, bridges, armor, slingshots, accounting devices, and of course cloth, woven from cotton, llama, alpaca, and – as the highest privilege – the finest vicuña wool. Soldiers were paid in cloth, and the coded symbols in the tunics of the nobility displayed a rich store of social and cultural information.

dispersed around the Nazca drainage area. They worshiped at the ceremonial center of Cahuachi, downriver from the modern city of Nazca.

On Peru's north coast, the Moche people flourished in the Moche or Trujillo valley, known in ancient times as Chimor. From their early capital at the Huacas del Sol y de la Luna (Temples of the Sun and the Moon) south of Trujillo, the Moche held sway over 400 km (250 miles) of desert coast. The Temple of the Sun, one of the most imposing adobe structures ever built in the New World, was composed of over 100 million mudbricks.

The Moche built irrigation canals, aqueducts, and field systems that stretched for miles, con-

Peru, they perfected an electrochemical-plating technique that gilded copper objects.

## The Lord of Sipán

The discovery in 1987 of the tomb of a Moche lord at Sipán, near the modern city of Chiclayo some 800 km (500 miles) north of Lima, has provided much new data on the ancient Moche, including evidence that most valleys under Moche influence had their own powerful regional governors. The lord had been buried with hundreds of pieces of funerary pottery, as befitted his status, but also with an astonishing amount of gold and silver *(see pages 177, 180–1)*. Discoveries at Sipán also link

necting neighboring valleys, and cultivated maize, beans, squash, peanuts, and peppers. In their *totora* reed boats they fished and hunted for sea lions, and captured deer along the rivers. They kept domesticated dogs and traded for luxury goods such as turquoise from present-day Argentina and lapis lazuli from present-day Chile, which they crafted into jewelry, and exotic seashells from the Gulf of Guayaquil.

Famed for their ceramics, Moche potters created realistic portrait heads and fine line drawings of gruesome sacrificial ceremonies. The most imaginative and skilled metalsmiths in ancient

**LEFT:** a gold artifact found in the tomb of the Lord of Sipán. **ABOVE:** the Huaca del Dragón.

### QUEEN OF THE DESERT

Maria Reiche, the German mathematician who dedicated her life to studying the Nazca lines, initially went to Peru in the 1930s, where she worked as a translator for Paul Kosok, an irrigation expert who first spotted the lines from the air. She spent years taking measurements and making charts, and, having concluded that the lines were part of an astronomical calendar, wrote a book about her findings: *Mystery on the Desert*. Reiche was awarded the Order of the Sun – the country's highest honor. She died in 1998.

its metalwork to similar pieces looted from the site of Loma Negra near Piura, on the far north coast.

Sometime in the period AD 650–700 the Moche Kingdom came to an end. It is thought that the El Niño phenomenon – when the warm waters flowing from the equator replace the cold waters of the Humboldt Current – could have produced torrential rains and destroyed irrigation canals, causing widespread famine.

## The Middle Horizon Period

With the fall of Moche in the north and the decline of Nazca to the south, a powerful southern highland kingdom exerted its architectural and artistic influ-

ence over large areas of Peru between AD 600 and 1000, wiping out the styles of the conquered peoples in the process. The capital of this empire was Wari (or Huari), a large urban center near the modern city of Ayacucho. Archeologists have excavated Wari military sites at Piquillacta near Cusco, at Cajamarquilla near Lima, and at Marca Huamachuco, which is in the highlands to the east of Trujillo.

The Wari style is strongly reminiscent of the ceramics and sculpture from the Bolivian Altiplano site of Tiahuanaco, which flourished between 200 BC and AD 1200. Situated at the southern end of Lake Titicaca at 3,856 meters (12,725 ft) above sea level, Tiahuanaco was the highest urban settlement in the New World. Its people employed an ingenious cultivation system that archeologists estimate could have sustained a city of some 40,000 people.

Tiahuanaco farmers cultivated potatoes, *oca*, and *olluco* (Andean tubers), as well as quinoa and *cañiwa* (grains) on raised fields known as *camellones* in Spanish, formed by digging lake-fed canals and heaping up the resulting soil to construct raised fields about 10 meters (33 ft) wide. During the day the sun heated the water in the canals, which radiated its warmth at night to protect the crops from frost. Recent experiments have shown that crops which were grown in this way could have produced harvests that were seven times greater than the average yield.

## The Sicán discoveries

With the decline of Wari influence, regional cultures again flourished in the coastal valleys. In the north the Lambayeque or Sicán culture appears to have been centered some 50 km (30 miles) north of Chiclayo. Here a team of archeologists have used radar techniques to assist in excavating a number of tombs. These elaborate burial sites have yielded fascinating evidence of the Sicán culture.

The burial chamber of one important male was surrounded by numerous female skeletons, thought to be weavers, who may well have been sacrificial victims. The remains of a richly decorated expanse of cloth were also unearthed. Scores of gold, silver, and copper masks and vessels were discovered, including an exquisite gold-alloy mask with emerald eyes, which suggest that the site was an important metalworking center. The size of the complex also suggests that it was the capital of what must have been an extremely wealthy and powerful culture. However, the complex appears to have been abandoned in about AD 1100. The remnants

of the population moved a few miles south to Túcume, where they constructed 26 large, flat-topped adobe pyramids and numerous smaller structures.

## Heyerdahl's project

The Túcume pyramids were excavated by a team under the direction of Norwegian explorer Thor Heyerdahl, best known for his *Kon-Tiki* voyage. Unlike most pre-Columbian sites, Túcume has eluded looters because the Spanish conquerors spread the rumor that it was haunted. So ingrained was the belief that Heyerdahl had to have a purification ceremony performed before the dig could begin in 1987.

Although he recorded numerous graves containing silver figurines and textiles worked in tropical feathers, Heyerdahl showed most enthusiasm over artifacts that supported his theory that ancient Americans were capable of long-distance navigation and were the first settlers in Polynesia. Chief among such finds were a wooden oar and a balsa raft frieze on a long section of wall at the site. Túcume was conquered by the Chimu people a few centuries later, and subsequently used by the Incas.

## The Chimu culture

It was probably around 1300, during the period known to archeologists as the Late Intermediate (c.1000–1470), that construction began at Chan Chan (near Trujillo), the Chimu capital near the ancient Moche site of the Temples of the Sun and the Moon. It seems that Chan Chan was then continuously occupied by the Chimu dynasty until it fell to the powerful Inca armies of Tupac Yupanqui in about 1464.

Rising to prominence in the north while the Incas gained power in the south, the Chimu realm stretched 965 km (600 miles) along the coast, from the Chillon valley in the south to Tumbes in the north. Spanish chroniclers of the 17th century recorded a Chimu myth of the arrival on a balsa raft of the dynasty's legendary founder, Taycanomo. Details of his life are largely mythical, but he probably did exist. The legend spoke of 10 Chimu kings, who ruled for about 140 years, which gives the early 14th-century date for the founding of Chan Chan.

There are nine rectangular compounds at Chan Chan, the largest adobe city in the world, each corresponding to a Chimu monarch. Each compound

served as an administrative center as well as a palace, a royal storehouse, and, on the king's death, his mausoleum. The succeeding monarch then built a new one, and the deceased ruler's compound was maintained by his family and loyal retainers.

Around the royal compounds, in small, crowded dwellings, lived a population of about 50,000, chiefly weavers, potters, and metalsmiths, who supplied the royal storehouses. Today the sprawling mudbrick capital of Chan Chan is a bewildering labyrinth of ruined adobe walls, some 7.5 meters (25 ft) high and stretching for 60 meters (200 ft). At its height in 1450 the city covered 23 sq km (9 sq miles). The eighth compound,

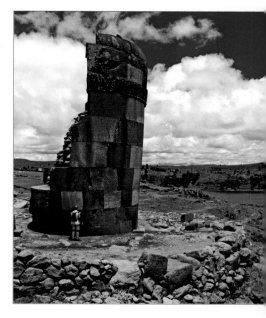

or Tschudi Complex, has been partially restored and gives some idea of what the capital must have been like. Remains of adobe friezes showing patterns of waves, fish, seabirds, and fishing nets, all vital to the survival of these coastal people, can still be seen adorning some of the walls.

## The Chachapoyas culture

Contemporary with the Chimu was the Chachapoyas culture (AD 1000–1470), which flourished in the northern highlands. The remains of Kuélap, a huge stone city, stand above the River Utcubamba, but apart from the fact that the people who built such massive, fortified structures must have felt under threat, we have little information about them. ❑

**LEFT:** the adobe city of Chan Chan.
**RIGHT:** pre-Inca Colla burial *chullpa* at Sillustani.

# THE INCAS

The Peruvian empire of the Children of the Sun was short-lived but brilliant. It spread rapidly from the Central Highlands, bringing order, material abundance, and a sophisticated culture

eru's pre-Hispanic history is a long one, filled with the marvels of ancient civilizations that fed multitudes by irrigating deserts, wove textiles so fine they cannot be reproduced even today, and built adobe cities that have survived millennia of earthquakes. Some, like the Chimu, Moche, Nazca, Wari, and Chavín, left behind traces that have allowed archeologists and scholars to reconstruct pieces of their societies. Others may always remain nameless and obscure. However, no group is as well known, or perhaps as astounding, as the Incas – the magnificent culture dominating much of the continent when the Spanish conquistadors arrived.

The Inca nation – the Children of the Sun – was a small regional culture based in the central highlands. Like the Chimu, Chancay, Ica, and other groups, they exerted local autonomy over large population centers and had distinct styles of textiles and pottery. But in the early 1400s, under the reign of Pachacutec, the Incas began an expansion – one of the greatest and most rapid that has ever been recorded.

In little more than 50 years, Inca domination was extended as far north as modern Colombia and south to present-day Chile. Groups that resisted were summarily vanquished and relocated as punishment. Others, through peaceful negotiaions, joined the kingdom with little loss of regional control provided that they were prepared to worship Inti, the sun, as their supreme god, and paid homage to the Inca leaders.

As each regional culture fell, Inca teachers, weavers, builders, and metallurgists studied the conquered people's textile techniques, architecture, gold-working, irrigation, pottery, and healing methods. As a result, they quickly accumulated massive amounts of information more advanced than their own.

By the time the Spanish arrived, Cusco, the Inca capital, was a magnificent urban gem; irrigated deserts and terraced mountainsides were producing bountiful crops, storehouses of food had eliminated hunger, and Inca military might had become legendary.

Although the accuracy of Spanish chronicles are suspect, and the Incas themselves left no written records, scholars, anthropologists, and archeologists have managed to piece together fragments of a magnificent world.

**LEFT:** the Inca citadel of Machu Picchu.
**RIGHT:** Inca terracing is still in use today.

## A strict world order

Inca society was clearly hierarchical and highly structured, but not necessarily tyrannical or repressive. Everyone had a place and a part to play. Food and resources were stored and distributed so that all were fed and clothed. There was no private property, and everything was communally organized. It may have been a society in which the majority accepted their role without feeling exploited.

The Inca polity was a pyramidal system of government, with the ruling Inca (as the emperor was called) and his *coya*, or queen, at the apex. Under him stood the nobility, the "Capac Incas," supposedly the true descendants of Manco Capac, the

founding Inca, and belonging to some 10 or 12 *panacas*, or royal houses. Each emperor founded a *panaca* when he came to power, so the current ruler's was the only one headed by a living man. The other *panacas* centered their lives and cults around the mummified remains of a former Inca. The city of Cusco was filled with the huge palaces built by Inca rulers to house their personal retinue, their descendants, born to their many wives and concubines, and, finally, their own mummy.

The *panacas* of Cusco coexisted with a similar number of *ayllus* – large kinship groups – of lesser nobility, the so-called "Incas-by-privilege," who were early inhabitants of the Cusco region, predating the Incas. They held lands, had ritual and economic functions, and many other aspects of

life in common. The *panacas* and noble *ayllus* belonged to two separate divisions, Upper and Lower Cusco, whose relationship was both competitive and complementary.

> *The royal mummy, housed in the* panaca, *was attended to as royalty after the death of the ruler as during his lifetime. It received daily offerings of food and drink, and at certain festivals it was paraded around Cusco.*

Below these two groups stood the regional nobility, who were not Incas at all but held aristocratic privileges along with intricate blood relationships and with reciprocal obligations to the ruling caste. Everyone in the empire was bonded to the whole by such connections, except for one large, amorphous group, the *yanacona*, who were a domestic class serving the *panacas*. They received no formal benefits and, although they could reach a high status, their loyalty was usually negotiable. Many of them defected to the Spaniards after the Inca Atahualpa's capture in 1532.

## The privileges of power

The nobility reserved many privileges for themselves, granting them selectively to outsiders. Polygamy was common, but exclusively aristocratic. Likewise, chewing coca leaves and wearing vicuña wool were privileges of the ruling caste. Noble males wore huge, ornate gold plugs in their pierced ears. Their beautifully woven tunics carried heraldic symbols called *tokapu*. All citizens wore the clothes and hairstyles befitting their station and ethnic group. The streets of Cusco were colorful, for hundreds of groups were represented in the city, each with its own distinctive costume.

Scores of local languages existed, but the lingua franca of the empire was Quechua, a language spoken today from northern Ecuador to southern Bolivia. Its origins are obscure, but the Incas are believed to have acquired it from some other group. The nobles also used a private language, possibly a "high" chivalric dialect with elements of both Quechua and the Aymara language of the Lake Titicaca region.

The ruling lords were fond of hunting, and a royal hunt was a spectacular affair. Animals were not slaughtered indiscriminately, but culled. Young females of most species were released for future reproduction. The myth of power within the Inca state held that the emperor was a divine being unlike ordinary mortals, descended from the sun via his founding ancestor, Manco Capac. He gave voice to the desires and intentions of this deity.

The sun may have become the supreme Inca deity after the rise of the ninth emperor, Pachacutec; before that, the supreme deity was Viracocha, an almighty creator also worshiped by other cultures. Inca religion was not confined to the sun and Viracocha. Cusco's great temple, the Coricancha, or Court of Gold, contained shrines to the moon, lightning, the Pleiades, Venus, and the rainbow. There were also shrines to scores of local deities – idols or sacred relics brought to Cusco by

Cusco. The *panacas* and *ayllus* had care of individual *huacas* and groups of *ceque* lines.

## Heart of the four quarters

The young Inca nobles were educated by *amautas*, scholars who transmitted cultural knowledge, often in the form of mnemonic songs and verses. Music and poetry were respected arts among the nobility, as was painting. An immense "national gallery," called Puquín Cancha, was destroyed during either Pizarro's conquest or the preceding civil war.

The Inca calendar featured an array of important festivals, which marked stages of life and the agricultural calendar. The summer and winter solstices

innumerable regional peoples. The Incas did not attempt to erase local religions but included their gods in an ever-expanding pantheon.

Beside local and celestial deities there were the *apus* – the spirits of great mountains – and the *huacas*: stones, caves, grottoes, springs, and waterfalls, believed to contain spirit powers. More than 300 *huacas* existed around Cusco, many of them housing the mummies of lesser nobles, and all of them connected by imagined lines that radiated from Coricancha like the spokes of a wheel. This system of sacred geography, known as the *ceque* system, was closely linked to the ritualistic and economic life of

**LEFT:** the Incas developed complex irrigation systems.
**ABOVE:** a 12-angled stone in Cusco.

### CHOSEN WOMEN

A special place in Inca high society was occupied by the *acllas*, or chosen women. The Spanish drew a simplistic parallel between them and the Roman Vestal Virgins, labeling them Virgins of the Sun. Some may have been virgin devotees of certain deities, but chastity was not a major preoccupation of the Incas, and young people were not expected to be sexually abstinent.

The *acllas* were selected for their talents and beauty, and many were concubines of the Inca. Others served the main temple, producing weavings and foods whose destination was the sacrificial fires of the Coricancha. It is also likely that some belonged to a caste of astronomer-priestesses associated with the cult of the moon.

were the greatest celebrations, held with numerous sub-festivals. The *Capac Raymi* summer solstice, for example, also featured the coming-of-age celebrations for the new crop of young nobles. The males underwent trials, including ritual battles, and a death-defying race. Another great ceremony was *Sitwa*, in September, when foreigners had to leave Cusco, and the Incas engaged in a ritual of purification, casting out sickness and bad spirits.

Cusco itself was a holy city as well as the administrative capital of the empire. It was the centre of Tahuantinsuyu – the formal name of the Inca empire, meaning the four quarters of the world. The great royal roads to the four *suyus* began at

the main square. Here all things came together, and soil from every province was ritually mingled with that of Cusco.

The four *suyus* corresponded to the cardinal points. The northern quarter was the Chinchaysuyu – northern Peru and modern Ecuador. The south was the Collasuyu – Lake Titicaca, modern Bolivia, and Chile. The Antisuyu was the wild Amazon forest to the east. The Kuntisuyu was the region west of Cusco, much of it also rugged country, but including the south and central Peruvian coast.

## A rural empire

Tahuantinsuyu was not significantly urbanized. There was the great complex of Chimu on the north coast and, of course, Cusco. And there were a few

> *Everyone from the highest to the lowest was involved to some degree in working the land. Even the emperor ritually tilled the soil with a golden foot-plow, to inaugurate the new planting season.*

large administrative centers along the spine of the Andes, housing a mainly transient population, which mustered and distributed the resources of entire regions. But most of the population lived in small rural communities scattered across the land.

The complex organization of the Inca state rested on a foundation of efficient agriculture. It is notable that virtually any Inca ruin, no matter what its original function, is surrounded and penetrated by agricultural terraces and irrigation channels. Fields of corn stood in the very heart of Cusco.

Corn was the prestige crop. The great irrigated terracing systems whose ruins we see today were mainly devoted to its cultivation. Other Inca staples were potatoes and some other indigenous Andean root crops, plus beans, quinoa – a species of the beet family – and the related amaranth. The huge altitude range of the tropical Andes allowed the Incas to enjoy a great variety of foods, but it also required them to develop many localized crop strains for particular microclimates. This they did, with typical thoroughness, at several experimental agriculture centers, whose ruins survive today.

The Incas' great food surpluses enabled them to divert labor to a variety of enterprises. They created a vast road network – so expertly laid that much of it still exists – and built astonishing structures of stone, so finely worked and of blocks so large that they required staggering amounts of time and effort. The Incas employed thousands of artisans to produce works of gold and silver, pottery, and fine textiles. They also raised great armies, able to march thousands of miles without carrying provisions, so extensive was their network of storehouses.

The system that made these works possible was called *mita*. It was a kind of community tax, paid in labor. Every community sent some of its able-bodied young men and women for a limited period into the service of the state.

The period varied according to the hardship of the work – mines, for example, were a tough assignment, and accordingly brief. Working in a state pottery was easier, and correspondingly longer. Some communities – such as the famous one which rebuilt the Apurímac suspension bridge, Q'eshwachaca, each year – rendered their *mita* in a specific task. One *ayllu* provided the emperor with inspectors of roads, another with inspectors of bridges, and one supplied the state with spies.

The life of a transient *mita* worker was rewarded by institutional generosity and punctuated by public festivals of spectacular drunkenness. Peasants who were otherwise tied to their villages for life mingled with groups from exotic locations worlds away, and caught a glimpse of the dazzling world of the Inca nobility. It was probably the most exciting time of their lives. Later the Spanish took over this institution and turned it into near slavery in their *encomienda* system.

## Binding the Andes to Cusco

About every 10 km (6 miles) along the great skein of roads that knitted the empire together stood a *tambo*, a kind of lodge, with storage facilities for goods in transit and communal quarters for large groups of people. Closer together were little huts that served as relay stations for the *chasquis*, the relay message-runners, who could allegedly cover the 2,400 km (1,500 miles) between Quito in Ecuador and Cusco in 10 days.

Every major bridge and *tambo* had its *quipucamayoc*, an individual who recorded everything that moved along the road. Their instrument was the *quipu*, a strand of cord attached to color-coded strings, each carrying a series of knots tied so as to indicate a digital value. The *quipucamayocs* were the accountants of the empire. *Quipus* may also have served as a means of sending messages, with certain types of knot being assigned a syllable value, so that a row of knots formed a word.

Crimes of property were rare; stealing was regarded as an aberration and dealt with ruthlessly when it occurred. Offenders suffered loss of privileges, with public humiliation and perhaps physical punishment. Serious or repeated crimes were punished by death, the victim being thrown off a cliff or imprisoned with poisonous snakes and dangerous animals.

A combination of techniques sustained the growth of the Inca empire. Military conquest played a part, but so did skillful diplomacy; some of the most important territories may have been allied confederates rather than subordinate domains. The glue holding the empire together

was the practice of reciprocity: ritual generosity and favors to local rulers on a huge scale, in exchange for loyalty, labors, and military levies, women for the Inca nobility, products specific to the region, and so on. The emperor maintained fabulous stores of goods to meet his ritual obligations and create new alliances.

## The path to power

The Incas were perhaps not imperialist, in our sense of the word, at the outset. There was an ancient Andean tradition of cultural influences, spreading out by means of trade and pilgrimage from important religious centers such as Chavín,

**LEFT:** poncho worn by a person of high status.
**RIGHT:** Inca ruins at Pisac in the Sacred Valley.

and later Tiahuanaco. It is likely that Cusco started in this way, too; later the Incas extended their sway in southern Peru by means of reciprocal agreements and blood alliances.

Then, in 1438 came the pivotal war of survival against the Chancas, a powerful group from the north. The historical existence of the Chancas has never been confirmed by archeology, but the Inca version was that the man who took the title Pachacutec – "transformer of the world" – defeated the invading Chancas at the gates of Cusco. Subsequently he transformed Inca culture, and launched the expansion which would be continued by his son, Tupac Yupanqui, and grandson, Huayna Capac. As

the Incas extended farther from their center, they confronted groups with ideas and identities increasingly different from their own. Thus, continued expansion increasingly required the use of force.

When the Incas used military force they used it sparingly. Many opponents surrendered without a fight when they saw the size of the army sent against them. The Incas still preferred to cut off an enemy's water supply, or starve him into submission, rather than confront him directly in battle.

War and warriorhood were an important part of Andean life from early times, yet they surely cannot have been of paramount value to the Incas. If they had, then military tactics and technology

### BROTHERS AT WAR

Ironically, it was Huayna Capac's desire to unite his domain through marriage which achieved the opposite result and led to civil war. He had married the daughter of Duchicela, king of Quito, and the son of this marriage, Atahualpa, became the Inca's favorite. But his other son, by a different queen, Huascar, was descended from Inca lineage on both sides and was therefore the legitimate heir.

When Huascar ascended the throne in 1527, a civil war broke out which lasted for five years. Eventually Atahualpa emerged victorious and established his capital at Cajamarca, shortly before the arrival of the Spanish conquerors.

would have been at their peak, whereas in fact their weapons and methods of warfare were still extremely primitive – far inferior to their attainments in administration, architecture, agriculture, and engineering – and had not evolved since the earliest times of Andean culture. They fought with clubs, stones, and all-wooden spears. Even the bow and arrow, though known to them, was not widely used in battle. The gulf between their fighting capacity and that of the steely Spanish conquistadors was tragically wide.

Many groups the Incas had conquered, such as the Huanca from Peru's central highlands, resented Inca domination. They had to be held in place by threat of force, and later they happily deserted to fight with the Spanish.

In the years just before the Spanish invasion, Pachacutec's grandson, Huayna Capac, was far from his homeland, fighting in the mountains along the present northern frontier of Ecuador with Colombia. Quito, the base from which the campaigns were launched, had become a de facto second capital, and a northern aristocracy had formed. On the death of Huayna Capac the two groups fell into violent conflict, resulting in civil war between Huascar and Atahualpa *(see opposite)*.

## Artists in stone

Like other peoples of the New World, the Incas had not discovered how to smelt iron ore, but their use of other metals was quite sophisticated. They had mastered many techniques for working gold and silver, and created bronze alloys of varying types for different uses.

None of these metals was much use for working stone, which was one of the glories of the Inca civilization. Modern research shows that the finely fitted stones were primarily cut and shaped using hammer-stones of harder rock. This process was laborious, but not as slow as we might imagine. The Incas' vast manpower and their reverence for stone enabled them to persevere through the many years it took to complete such astounding structures as Machu Picchu and Sacsayhuamán.

Despite their wondrous skills, the Incas never invented the wheel, nor a form of writing. Andean terrain is extremely steep, and the Incas' only draft animal was the small, lightly built llama, unable to pull a load exceeding 45 kg (100 lb). So the absence of a wheel is understandable. Thus, lacking the first reason to devise a wheel, the Incas never discovered its other uses, such as making pots. They did, however, inherit the distaff spindle for spinning thread, which has been used in the Andes for thousands of years.

Another invention the Incas lacked was the arch. To span great gaps they built sturdy suspension bridges. In buildings they used the trapezoidal aperture. This shape – tapering upwards, with a stone or wooden lintel across the top – will take a fair amount of weight from above. All four walls of almost every Inca building also leaned slightly inward, making them very stable. This technique, combined with the brilliantly interlocking joins of their stonework, made

their buildings almost earthquake-proof – a useful feature in Peru.

The absence of any form of writing is harder to explain. The *tokapu* textile symbols and the *quipus* were the closest they came. Quechua is full of ambiguities, puns, and multiple meanings, relying heavily on context for its true sense. It is the language style of an oral culture, but whether this is the cause or the effect of having no written language is impossible to say. While the Incas lacked certain things we take for granted, this did not prevent their creating a sophisticated civilization, whose echoes still reverberate throughout the Andes. ❏

## MOVING MIGHTY BOULDERS

The mystery of how the Incas moved and fitted enormous stones has been patiently investigated by the US architect Vincent Lee. He has demonstrated a possible method, within the technical capabilities of the Incas, by maneuvering stones onto massive log sleds, which were then levered along stout wooden rails. Fitting might have been done by trial and error, although Lee believes a simple plumb line and pantograph device was used to project the profile of a finished stone onto an uncut block.

**LEFT:** the mighty fortress of Sacsayhuamán, just outside Cusco. **RIGHT:** a rope bridge much like the ones the Incas constructed.

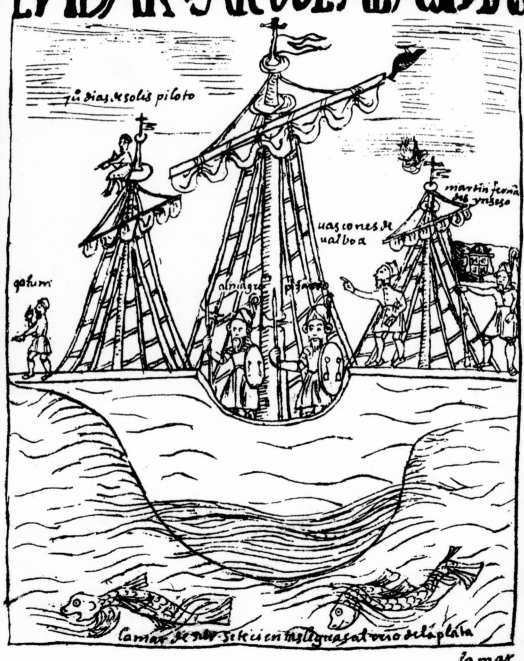

gu dias de solis piloto

martin fernā del ynoeso

uascones de ualboa

almagro pisarro

go tum

la mar de sur se cien mil leguas al uerso de la plata

la mar

# THE CONQUEST

Lust for gold, fueled by rumors of glittering temples and fabulous treasures, made the Spanish conquest of Peru one of the bloodiest episodes in the history of empire

It was in 1532 that a motley collection of Spanish conquistadors first appeared on the fringes of the Inca empire, the largest and most powerful empire that South America had ever known. In the months to come, these 62 horsemen and 106 foot soldiers commanded by a professional soldier named Francisco Pizarro would march to the heart of Peru and brutally seize control of the Inca throne. Within a decade, a glittering Andean world would be firmly in the grip of the Spaniards, its glories stripped and its people virtually enslaved.

Few historical events have been as dramatic or cruel as the conquest of Peru. Although only a handful in number, the invading Spaniards had on their side an astonishing streak of good luck, complete technological superiority, and a lack of principle that would have made Machiavelli shudder. Apparently experiencing no emotions other than greed and fear, they were repeatedly able to trick their way into the confidence of the Inca rulers and nobility, only to betray them. By the time the Incas realized the ruthlessness of their foes, it was too late.

## The invasion of America

Cautiously marching into Peru's coastal desert, Pizarro and his men were in the front ranks of Spain's explosion into the New World. It had been only four decades earlier, in 1492, that Christopher Columbus had landed in the West Indies – the same year that Castile drove the last Moors from European soil. With no foe inside its boundaries and a need to bolster national pride and replenish the royal coffers, Spain soon

**LEFT:** the conquistadors set sail for the New World.
**RIGHT:** Francisco Pizarro, their Spanish leader.

directed the violent energies of its soldiers across the Atlantic. In 1519, Hernán Cortés, with 500 men and 16 horses, conquered the fabulously wealthy Aztec empire in Mexico. Panama was settled, and conquistadors were soon looking toward the newly found Pacific Ocean as a route to even further riches.

Although the existence of Peru was still no more than a rumor at that time, it was only seven years later that two already relatively wealthy soldiers from Spain's barren Extremadura region, Francisco Pizarro and Diego de Almagro, led two expeditions down the west coast of South America before stumbling on the city of Tumbes and gathering information about the Inca empire. Intoxicated by the prospect of conquering a new

Mexico, Pizarro went back to Spain, where he gained permission from the Spanish Crown to undertake the conquest. He then recruited a band of adventurers from his home town, Trujillo, before setting sail again.

By the time Pizarro returned to Tumbes in 1532 with his 168 men, it was in ruins. In a stroke of fortune that would determine the fate of Peru, the Spaniards had found the Inca empire in an unparalleled crisis, weakened for the first time by a bitter civil war. Several years earlier, a virulent disease – probably smallpox, spreading like wildfire among the Indians from European settlements in the Caribbean – had struck down the supreme Inca, Huayna Capac, together with his son and designated heir. Two other sons who survived the epidemic, the half-brothers Huascar, who was based in the capital city of Cusco, and Atahualpa, the commander of the imperial armies in Quito, fought a bitter war for the succession. The civil war ended with Atahualpa victorious, but the empire was rocked and badly weakened by the struggle *(see page 42)*.

When Pizarro landed, Atahualpa had only just become the undisputed Inca. He was heading in triumph south from Quito to the capital when news arrived that a group of tall, bearded men had entered his lands. Atahualpa was camped

not far from the Spaniards' route of march and on hearing the news the Inca decided that he would meet the strangers himself.

## Into the Andes

Pizarro and his force turned away from the barren coast to climb the rough road into the Andes. Although exhausted by the thin, high-altitude air, the conquistadors marveled at the first signs of the Inca civilization: steep valleys were lined with rich terraces of maize, shepherds stood by with flocks of ungainly llamas, and powerful stone fortresses overlooked the Spaniards' path. But the Inca warriors and their subjects watched the advancing strangers impassively: Atahualpa had given orders that they should not be hindered.

### MUTUAL DISTRUST

One contemporary chronicler recorded the Spaniards' surprise and awe at the sight of Atahualpa's army and entourage in the valley outside Cajamarca: "Nothing like this had been seen in the Indies up to then. It filled all us Spaniards with fear and confusion. But it was not appropriate to show any fear, far less to turn back. For had they sensed any weakness in us, the very Indians we were bringing with us would have killed us."

One can only speculate about how the Inca leaders and their soldiers felt on seeing the Spanish soldiers for the first time, clad in armor and mounted on strange, unknown beasts with "golden shoes" upon their four feet.

Finally Pizarro arrived at Cajamarca. Stretching into the valley beyond were the tents of the Inca's army and entourage. Pizarro entered the near-deserted town and sent his brother Hernando with

> The Incas were mystified by the conquistadors' lust for gold. Manco Inca, who came to the throne in 1533, observed "Even if all the snow in the Andes turned to gold, still they would not be satisfied."

a group of horsemen to meet Atahualpa. The Inca received the envoys with all the pomp and splendor of his magnificent court. When permitted to speak, the Spaniards used a translator to convey that Pizarro "loved [the Inca] dearly" and wished to meet him. Atahualpa agreed to a meeting in Cajamarca the following day.

Only that night did the Spaniards fully appreciate what they had got themselves into. Pizarro had no definite plan, and the conquistadors heatedly debated what should be done. They were several days' march into an obviously huge empire. Outside, the camp fires of the Incan army lit up the surrounding hillsides "like a brilliantly star-studded sky." They were terrified, but the lust for gold was even stronger than fear.

## The capture of the Inca

Next morning, the Spaniards prepared an ambush. Hidden in Cajamarca's main square, the soldiers waited tensely all morning without any sign of movement in Atahualpa's camp. Many began to suspect that their treacherous plan had been detected and they would all be slaughtered outright. It was not until nearly sundown, after Pizarro had once again sent envoys to promise that "no harm or insult would come to him," that the Inca decided to pay his visit.

Atahualpa and his nobles arrived in full ceremonial regalia. "All the Indians wore large gold and silver discs like crowns on their heads," one observer wrote. Atahualpa himself wore a collar of heavy emeralds and was borne on a silver litter by 80 blue-clad nobles. Surrounding him were "five or six thousand" men, either unarmed or carrying clubs and slings. But Atahualpa found no Spaniards in the square, and called out impatiently: "Where are they?"

LEFT: Atahualpa is carried on his throne to meet Pizarro. RIGHT: Atahualpa asks Pizarro if the Spaniards eat gold (Huaman de Poma de Ayala).

Friar Vicente de Valverde emerged from the darkness with a translator and a copy of the Bible. What happens next is confused by the chroniclers, but has been pieced together by John Hemming in his classic *Conquest of the Incas*. It appears that Valverde began to explain his role as a priest. Atahualpa asked to look at the Bible, never having seen a book. "He leafed through [the Bible] admiring its form and layout. But after examining it he threw it angrily down amongst his men, his face a deep crimson." This "sacrilege" was all that the Spaniards needed to justify their actions. Valverde began screaming: "Come out! Come out, Christians! Come at these enemy dogs who reject the things of God!"

Pizarro gave his signal. Cannons blasted and the Spaniards piled into the plaza with their battle cry of "Santiago!" Cavalry crashed into the horrified Indian ranks and began a wholesale slaughter: the natives "were so filled with fear that they climbed on top of one another – to such an extent that they formed mounds and suffocated one another."

Retreat had been blocked, and none of the entourage escaped alive. Pizarro himself hacked a path straight for the Inca and grabbed his arm. He suffered the only wound to befall the Spanish troops, inflicted by one of his own men who went to stab the Inca. Pizarro deflected the blow, cutting his hand. Atahualpa was rushed away from the carnage and locked, ironically enough, in the Temple of the Sun.

## The royal prisoner

The Spanish could hardly believe their luck in capturing Atahualpa. The Inca empire, already divided by the civil war, was now without its absolute leader. On the instructions of the Spaniards, Atahualpa issued orders from captivity, and his stunned people could only obey.

The conquistadors took whatever they wanted from the surrounding camp. Inca soldiers looked on as Hernando de Soto demanded men as porters, women as slaves, llamas for food – and, naturally, as much gold, silver, and jewelry as his squadron could carry. Atahualpa, seeing that the Spaniards were interested above all in precious metal, assumed that they must either eat it or use it as a medical remedy (as depicted in drawings by the 16th-century indigenous chronicler Huaman Poma de Ayala). Atahualpa offered a ransom for his freedom: a room of 88 cubic meters (3,100 cu. ft) in size would be filled once over with gold and twice with silver.

The Spaniards were amazed at the offer, and Pizarro hastened to agree – summoning a secretary to record the details as a formal pledge and give a stamp of legality to the deal. In return, Pizarro promised to restore Atahualpa to Quito. It was a blatant lie, but one that served the conquistadors' purpose brilliantly: the whole Inca empire was mobilized to supply them with booty.

Llama trains from Quito to Lake Titicaca were soon starting out, loaded down with precious statues, jugs, and dishes.

## Abuse and murder

Meanwhile, a small group of Spaniards went to Jauja, where Atahualpa's greatest general, Chalcuchima, was stationed. Trustingly, the general agreed to accompany the Spaniards back to Cajamarca, thus giving Pizarro the only other man who might have led a coordinated resistance to his invasion. Having treated the general well until his arrival at Cajamarca, they then tortured him to obtain more information about gold, and set about burning him at the stake. He was released "with his legs and arms burned and his tendons shrivelled."

---

### A TRUE LEADER

While awaiting the arrival of the promised treasure, the Spaniards became impressed by their royal prisoner. One of Pizarro's men later wrote that "Atahualpa was a man of 30 years of age, of good appearance and manner, although somewhat thickset... He spoke with much gravity, as a great ruler."

The Inca possessed an incisive intellect, grasped Spanish customs quickly, and learned the secrets of writing and the rules of chess. During the time he remained a prisoner, Atahualpa's servants and wives maintained the royal rituals, bringing the Inca his cloaks of vampire-bat skin and burning everything that he touched or wore.

Atahualpa now realized that he had made a grave mistake in cooperating with the invaders, and that they had no intention of releasing him or leaving his empire. In mid-April 1533, Pizarro's partner, Diego de Almagro, arrived from Panama, with 150 Spanish reinforcements, before leaving again for Spain with news of the conquest and booty for Holy Roman Emperor Charles V. The influx of treasure into Cajamarca turned it into an undisciplined boom town and made the Spaniards bolder. But rumors began that Inca forces were massing to rescue their leader.

Many Spaniards became convinced that they were in danger so long as Atahualpa remained

instructing him through an interpreter in the articles of our Christian faith… The Inca was moved by these arguments and requested baptism… His exhortations did him much good. For although he had been sentenced to be burned alive, he was in fact garroted by a piece of rope that was tied around his neck."

News of the execution horrified Atahualpa's supporters, especially when it was learned that there was no Inca column advancing on the city. When news arrived in Europe, educated opinion was equally appalled. Even Holy Roman Emperor Charles V was upset about the execution, protesting that it offended the divine right

alive. Others saw the value of the Inca as a prisoner, and argued that it would be difficult to justify an execution. Chroniclers record that a captured native claimed to have seen an Inca army marching on Cajamarca. Pizarro panicked and called an emergency council. It was obvious that the Inca could no longer be counted on to support Spanish rule. The council quickly decided that he should die.

Pizarro's secretary coldly recorded the sordid proceedings. The Inca was "brought out of his prison… and was tied to a stake. The friar [Valverde] was, in the meantime, consoling and

---

**FAR LEFT:** gold Inca tunic. **LEFT:** Atahualpa in chains.
**ABOVE:** the death of Atahualpa.

### GOLD FEVER

The Spaniards waiting in Cajamarca for Atahualpa's treasure heard endless rumors of Cusco's magnificence. Cusco's holiest site, the Qoricancha, was covered in gold sheets and its Sun Temple sported a golden disk studded with jewels. This sacred building was flanked by a field filled with plants and animals crafted in precious metals.

Atahualpa, anxious to regain his freedom, urged Pizarro to send men to loot this imperial treasure. Three illiterate soldiers were dispatched, and they stripped the Qoricancha with their own hands. Thus no educated Spaniard ever saw it in its glory, and the memory of its full splendor was lost forever.

of kings upon which his own rule – and that of all contemporary monarchs – was based. But by then the Spanish Crown's share of booty was arriving from Peru, and such scruples could be overlooked. The priceless art and sculpture of the great Inca empire went straight to the smelters of Seville.

## Onward into the heartland

In August 1533, the Spaniards marched on Cusco. It seems an audacious project, but it is important to realize that a large part of the Inca empire's population, especially around the southern Sierra, welcomed the news of Atahualpa's death. To those

gave the conquistadors mobility and allowed them to strike downward on their opponents' heads and shoulders, while the strange animals also created fear and confusion amongst the Incas.

The Spaniards' steel armor was almost impenetrable to the natives' bronze hand-axes, clubs, and maces. And Pizarro's men were some of the most experienced fighters Europe had to offer. Again and again the invaders would use their technological advantage to press home victories against apparently overwhelming odds.

Pizarro founded Jauja as the new Peruvian capital and pressed on. What followed was a desperate race to cross the several rope bridges spanning

who had backed his brother Huascar in the civil war, Atahualpa was a usurper and his troops from Quito an enemy occupying force. It should also be remembered that the invaders were not dealing with a united people, but with a collection of disparate groups, some of whom were happy to be part of the Inca empire, while others still resented the Inca yoke and were willing to fight on the side of the Spaniards. Realizing this, Pizarro was now ready to pose as the liberator of the Andes.

At Jauja, a contingent of Atahualpa's army tried to make a stand. The Spanish cavalry charged and routed them immediately. This first armed clash of the conquest revealed a pattern that would be repeated: the native foot soldiers were no match for the mounted and well-armored Spaniards. Horses

the Andean gorges before the Quitans could destroy them. On one occasion the Indians attempted an ambush, and managed to kill several Spaniards in hand-to-hand battle. Pizarro decided that the captured general Chalcuchima had planned the attack and ordered him to be burned alive. But the attack had been to no avail: there was a final pitched battle in the pass before Cusco, and the Quitans' morale broke. They slipped away from the Urubamba valley under cover of night and left the Inca capital to the invaders.

## Dividing up the spoils

Pizarro and his men marched unopposed into the nerve-center of the Inca world, the "navel of the universe," Cusco. "The city is the greatest and finest ever seen in this country or anywhere in the Indies," Pizarro wrote back to Charles V. "We can assure Your Majesty that it is so beautiful and has such fine buildings that it would be remarkable even in Spain." But the invaders barely had time to marvel at the precise Inca masonry and the channels of water running through every street before installing themselves in various Inca palaces and starting on the serious business of pillaging the city.

Pizarro realized that his small force would not survive a true popular uprising, and so attempted to keep the looting of Cusco relatively orderly – at least until reinforcements arrived. He offered his men tracts of land and the right to the unpaid labor of the local population. This attempt to induce the Spaniards to become settlers, and to produce rather than destroy, would later become institutionalized in Latin America as the *encomienda* system. After "founding" the city in the name of the Spanish king, Pizarro rode back to the barren coast of Peru and created his colonial capital, facing the sea: modern-day Lima, where his statue stood until it was finally removed in 2004.

Pizarro had also accepted the offer of the 20-year-old Manco, another of Huayna Capac's sons, to become the new Inca. Manco wanted the Spaniards to restore him to his father's crown, and the conquistadors were happy to have him as a puppet leader in the southern Sierra. He was installed as leader in Cusco while two groups of Spaniards headed toward Quito to take on the retreating imperial army that remained loyal to Atahualpa's memory.

## The reality of conquest

Under Manco Inca's nominal rule, Cusco seemed tranquil enough. But it wasn't long before the puppet ruler began to see the Spanish "liberators" in their true colors. Their greed and brutality grew in proportion with their confidence; they were obviously in Peru to stay.

Manco was distressed to see the Inca world crumbling before his eyes. The natives of Cusco refused to obey him, while many of his subject tribes began to assert their independence. The swelling ranks of Spaniards began forcing the locals into press-gangs, extorting gold from nobles

and raping Inca women. They harassed Manco Inca for treasure, captured his wife, and pillaged his property.

Manco could tolerate no more and announced his intention to rebel. Vast numbers of native soldiers were mobilized, and Manco slipped away from Cusco into the mountains. It was 1536, and the great rebellion had begun.

## Incas on the offensive

Manco's troops quickly took Sacsayhuamán, the great fortress overlooking Cusco whose massive stone blocks still awe visitors today. Chroniclers record that the Inca force was about 100,000

---

**FAR LEFT:** the Plaza de Armas in modern-day Cusco. **LEFT:** the Inca rebellion. **RIGHT:** Manco Inca on the throne (Huaman de Poma de Ayala).

### TOWERS OF POWER

Sacsayhuamán, outside Cusco, gained renown as a fortress after the battle fought there between the Incas and the Spaniards, but it was actually a combined Inca administrative center, temple, and storehouse. Dominated by three tall towers, it was an expression of Inca power, initiated by the emperor Pachacuti and continued under successive rulers, but never completed. All but the mightiest walls were later demolished, and the stones were used to build the churches and mansions of Spanish Cusco.

strong against the Spaniards' 80 cavalry and 110 foot soldiers, commanded by Francisco Pizarro's brother Hernando. Their defenses were bolstered by large contingents of native forces, but the outlook for the Spaniards was grim: Cusco was surrounded and, for all they knew, they might have been the last Spanish outpost in Peru.

The Inca attack finally began with slingshot stones, made red-hot in campfires, hailing down onto Cusco's thatched roofs, which immediately set them alight. But black slaves extinguished the flames on the roof of the building where the main body of Spaniards were sheltering. Even so, Manco Inca's forces captured the majority of

the city. In retaliation the Spaniards decided on a desperate plan: to counter-attack the strategic fortress of Sacsayhuamán.

*The Spaniards' behavior toward each other was a source of amazement to the Incas. Not only were the all-powerful conquerors falling out among themselves, they had shown themselves capable of stealing from one another – a severely punishable crime in the Inca empire.*

Another of the Pizarro brothers, Juan, led 50 horsemen in a charge straight at the native lines. Despite their overwhelmingly superior numbers, the Incas still did not have a weapon that could

seriously injure the Spanish cavalry. Although Juan Pizarro was killed, the conquistadors forced their way to a safe position on the hill opposite Sacsayhuamán. They prepared a night attack using medieval European siege tactics, and took the outer terrace of the fortress.

## The Spanish hold on

The capture of Sacsayhuamán was the key to Cusco's defense. Although the city remained surrounded for another three months, the Incas found it impossible to take. Fighting continued with extraordinary cruelty. Captured Spaniards had their heads and feet cut off. Indian prisoners were impaled or had their hands chopped off in Cusco's main square.

The rebellion was more successful in other parts of the empire. Francisco Pizarro organized several relief expeditions from Lima, but the Incas had learned to use geography against the Spanish. One group of soldiers was caught in a narrow gorge by a hail of rocks; most were killed, the remainder captured. Another force was trapped, and their heads sent to Manco Inca. Now the victorious natives marched on Lima.

The attack on the town came from three sides, but in the flat coastal plains the Spanish cavalry proved invincible. A determined charge routed the main native force, and the commanding general was cut down in his tracks.

Meanwhile the Spaniards went on the offensive in Cusco, with an attack on Manco in the nearby terraced fortress of Ollantaytambo. Manco cunningly diverted the nearby river to flood the approaches, incapacitating the deadly Spanish cavalry. The rebel Inca was seen riding a captured horse along the heights, directing his troops with a lance, as rainforest archers and warriors wielding captured Spanish weapons claimed the lives of several Spaniards. The conquistadors beat a hasty retreat and the siege dragged on – but the tide had turned.

## Reconquering Peru

Spanish governors from other parts of the Americas were quick to come to Pizarro's aid. Reinforcements soon arrived from Mexico and Nicaragua, while Diego de Almagro returned with troops from a failed expedition to Chile. When Almagro relieved Cusco in April 1537, Manco Inca decided that his cause was lost and retreated with his forces into the remote Vilcabamba valley. The Spaniards chased him as far as Vitcos, but became distracted by looting. The Inca escaped under cover of darkness, carried in the arms of 20 fast runners. The Spaniards would have time to regret their greed: deep inside the subtropical valley, behind an almost impenetrable series of narrow gorges and suspension bridges, Manco created an Inca court-in-exile that would survive in various forms for another 35 years.

By now there was a new twist to the complicated politics of the conquest: Almagro and Francisco Pizarro, the original partners in the invasion, had never reached agreement on how the empire should be divided between them, so the plotting between the two former allies plunged Peru into civil war.

occasionally harassed Spanish travelers from his jungle hideaway, was firmly under Spanish control. He possessed fabulous wealth and had been made a marquis by the grateful Spanish Crown. But on June 26, 1541, Pizarro's past caught up with him: he was surprised in his Lima palace by a group of supporters of his murdered partner, Diego de Almagro. He was able to kill one of his attackers before being hacked to death. His corpse was thrown into a secret grave.

Pizarro's ally Bishop Vicente de Valverde – the priest who had first attempted to convert Atahualpa – tried to escape to Panama, but the ship was wrecked off the island of Puna, and it is

No sooner had Manco Inca fled than the three surviving Pizarro brothers united against Almagro, pitting Spaniard against Spaniard on Andean battlefields. Eventually, in 1538, the Pizarrist faction defeated Almagro outside Cusco, and the general was garroted.

## Victory and revenge

At 63 years of age, Francisco Pizarro was at the peak of his bloodstained career. Although no longer active on the battlefield, he was undisputed governor of a Peru which, although Manco Inca still

**LEFT:** the capture, trial, and execution of Diego de Almagro. **ABOVE:** the Iglesia de Santo Domingo, which stands on the site of the Inca temple of Qoricancha.

believed that cannibalistic natives devoured the hypocritical cleric.

The deaths of Pizarro and Valverde seem a fitting end to the first stage of the conquest. But the era that was beginning would be no less brutal. Now that most of the easily appropriated Inca treasures had been seized and distributed, the Spanish began to exploit the population mercilessly. The conquistadors who had received land and the right to native labor under the *encomienda* system became the elite of the new colony. They extorted tribute in the form of grain, livestock, and labor, and forced the native peoples into a brutal form of feudalism.

In 1542 a new viceroy arrived from Spain to impose order. Fearing for their own interests, some

Spaniards mustered behind Gonzalo Pizarro, who marched into Lima in 1544 and was declared governor of Peru. But unrest continued, and two years later the viceroy was killed in battle against Gonzalo's troops. When this news reached Spain, Pedro de la Gasca was sent to rule the troublesome colony. Gonzalo initially held his own but in 1548, deserted by his own men, he was forced to surrender, and was put to death, another victim of the greed and disorder that characterized the conquest.

## The last Incas

While this infighting was going on, Manco Inca had maintained his court in Vitcos, teaching his

troops Spanish military techniques in order to wage a guerrilla war. Manco's fatal mistake was to spare a group of pro-Almagro Spaniards who had fled to Vilcabamba. The refugees grew bored with exile and, believing they would be pardoned by the Pizarrist faction if they murdered the Inca, they fell on their host and stabbed him. They paid with their lives for their treachery, but the Inca leader was irreplaceable; with his death, any real resistance to the Spanish virtually collapsed.

As the Spaniards consolidated their rule, Manco Inca's son Titu Cusi maintained the Vilcabamba court. The Spanish understood that, as long as any legitimate royal figure stayed free, there would always be some faint hope for Indian freedom. Long negotiations were aimed at drawing the Inca out to live in Cusco, but to no avail. Then, in 1569, two Augustinian friars entered the secret Inca nation and attempted to convert the Inca to Christianity.

In 1570, Friar Diego Ortiz became a close companion to Titu Cusi, and when Titu became ill, Friar Diego Ortiz prepared a healing potion which he hoped would save him. Unfortunately, the Inca died as soon as he drank it. His horrified troops, believing their leader had been poisoned, immediately killed Friar Diego Ortiz. The other friar was dragged along the ground for three days by a rope driven through a hole behind his jaw, before being dispatched by a blow to the skull from a mace.

This "martyrdom" gave the Spanish a pretext to invade Vilcabamba yet again. This time the conquistadors gathered an irresistible force. The new Inca, Tupac Amaru, put up a spirited defense against the invading column, but the Spaniards captured first Vitcos and then Vilcabamba.

Tupac Amaru tried to escape into the thick Amazon jungle, but his progress was slowed down by his wife, on the verge of giving birth, and a local chief betrayed the party's movements. Finally, a pursuing team of Spaniards spotted a campfire in the rainforest and pounced on the Inca, capturing him and bringing him back to Cusco with a golden chain around his neck.

With all resistance ended, and no leader to rally dissident spirits, the Spaniards were left in total control of the vast empire. But there was no time to rest on their laurels: they were already beginning to discover that governing the country was going to be just as difficult a task as subduing it had been. ❑

### DEATH OF AN EMPEROR

Viceroy Francisco de Toledo was determined to destroy the Inca royal lineage, along with its prestige. He had rebel generals tried and hanged and, ignoring all appeals for clemency, had the last emperor swiftly converted to Christianity, tried for the deaths of various Spaniards in Vilcabamba, and sentenced to beheading in Cusco's main square. On the scaffold Tupac Amaru recanted his native faith, proclaiming his conversion to Christianity and denouncing the Inca religion as a sham.

In September 1572, 40 years after Pizarro's capture of Atahualpa in Cajamarca, the wailing of thousands of conquered Indians announced the death of the last Inca.

# Looking for the Past

The birth of American archeology in the late 19th century brought explorers to Peru in search of "lost cities" such as Vilcabamba, to which the last Incas had retreated.

One of the first archeologists to explore Peru was Hiram Bingham, who visited many important ruins, discovering Machu Picchu in 1911, which he declared was Vilcabamba. He also found the Inca ruins at Espíritu Pampa, but dismissed them as unimportant. In 1963 another American, Gene Savoy, who described himself as "a non-professional archeological explorer," and who had already made important discoveries of pre-Inca civilizations in the northern coastal valleys, turned his sights on the southern jungles, intent on disproving the widely held belief that Machu Picchu was the lost city.

Basing his work on his interpretations of the texts of the same Spanish chroniclers as used earlier by Bingham, Savoy took a closer look at Espíritu Pampa. It is a large site containing at least 60 buildings and some 300 houses, but unspectacular and overgrown with rainforest vegetation. Some buildings had been roofed with Spanish-style terracotta tiles, proving that they were constructed after the Spanish conquest. This evidence, coupled with location and topographical details, clinched the identification of Espíritu Pampa as the site of Vilcabamba the Old.

Savoy made two more expeditions to the area, uncovering more Inca sites and remains of roads, then switched his attentions farther north in search of the ancient cities of the Chachapoyas, a pre-Inca tribe that ruled much of the northern Peruvian Andes (c. AD 1100–1400). In the remote Pajaten

region, at the southern edge of the empire, he discovered a vast complex with large circular structures, decorated with stone reliefs depicting carved animal and human heads, suggesting that the site had ceremonial as well as defensive functions.

In the late 1960s Savoy explored many other known ruins in the Chachapoyas area, including Kuélap, an impressively defended fortress, perched on a mountain ridge high above the left bank of the River Utcubamba. He also publicized, for the first time, the existence of remains at Monte Peruvia (Purunllacta). He estimated that this site, some 155 sq km (60 sq miles) in extent and spread across more than 30 hilltops linked by roadways, was one of the great cities of the Chachapoyas culture eventually conquered by Inca Tupac Yupanqui.

In 1969 Savoy changed direction again. Fascinated by the legend about the founder of the Chimu culture who arrived by sea, he hoped to prove that early Peruvians traded across the Pacific. To this end, he constructed a *totora* boat and sailed up the South American coast to Panama.

The Chachapoyas region was the scene of another major discovery in 1997, when superbly preserved cliff-face tombs filled with Inca and Chachapoyan mummies were found at Laguna de los Cóndores, near Leimebamba.

Savoy, Bingham, Thor Heyerdahl, and Maria Reiche are just a few of the foreign explorers who have been drawn to Peru; there is something about its ancient cultures which continues to inspire the imagination today.     ❏

**LEFT:** Tupac Amaru. **ABOVE:** Gene Savoy in the 1960s.
**RIGHT:** Machu Picchu shrouded in mist.

# FROM COLONY TO REPUBLIC

From early colonial mismanagement, through the battles
for independence, to 20th-century coups, Peru has
known little stability on its path to
becoming a modern state

The chaotic years of early colonial administration were to change with the arrival in 1569 of Francisco de Toledo, Peru's fifth viceroy. A brutal but efficient ruler, Toledo consolidated Spain's command over the former Inca empire. After finally crushing the rebel bastion of Vilcabamba and dealing with a revolt by dissatisfied conquistadors, he set about ordering every aspect of colonial life.

## Spain's iron fist

The effects of Toledo's decrees were to alter the face of the Andes for ever. One of his most drastic measures was the establishment of *reducciones*, the forced resettlement of indigenous people into Spanish-style towns complete with a central plaza, church, town hall, and prison – the symbols of Spanish authority. *Reducciones* facilitated the collection of tribute from the Indians and their conversion to Christianity.

The new viceroy also formalized the *encomienda* system, whereby Indians provided labor and tribute to an *encomendero*, their Spanish landlord. The premise of the *encomienda* was completely alien to the Andean way of life, which was a system based on reciprocity and redistribution. In addition, the large tracts of land that formed the *encomiendas* ignored the Andean concept of verticality, whereby an ethnic group living near, say, Lake Titicaca, had access to land and produce – cotton, fish, and hot peppers – from the warm coastal valleys. Under the colonial order, distribution of goods went in only one direction: from tribute payer to local ethnic lord (*curaca*), and thence to *encomendero*.

**LEFT:** 16th-century map of Peru.
**RIGHT:** a colonial altar.

---

### THE FAT OF THE LAND

The *encomienda* system ensured a life of ease and luxury for the landowners. Contemporary records show that one group of tributaries in Conchucos in the north-central highlands were obliged to provide their *encomendero* annually with 2,500 pesos of gold, the harvest of over 1,500 hectares (3,700 acres) in wheat, maize, barley, and potatoes, 30 sheep, 12 kg (26 lb) of candle wax, 25 donkey-loads of salt, and 45 pairs of grouse. They also had to give their master 20 eggs every Friday.

Because *encomenderos* rarely traveled outside the towns where they lived, it was usually the *curacas* who collected the tribute. Terrorized by the Spanish, they in turn terrorized their own people into fulfilling their tribute obligations. They soon learned Spanish and borrowed the trappings of colonial nobility, dressing in Spanish-style clothing, carrying firearms, and riding on horseback.

## Squeezing Peru dry

The Spanish colonial economy was essentially based on coercion and plunder. The treasures of Cusco had already been distributed, but there were other sources. In the north-coast city of Trujillo,

named after Pizarro's birthplace in Spain, the Spanish Crown granted licenses for the pillage of the ancient *huacas* (temples).

Once the Spanish had exhausted tombs to plunder, they turned to mines, a quest that led to the discovery in 1545 of Potosí. Today a bleak tin-mining city in the Bolivian highlands, 4,070 meters (13,350 ft) above sea level, in its heyday in the 17th century Potosí was the richest and largest city in the world, with a population of 150,000 people. Potosí's silver filled the coffers of the Spanish Crown with the necessary cash to finance battles across Europe. The town's coat of arms read: "I am rich Potosí, treasure of the world and envy of Kings."

But the discovery of Potosí brought with it renewed hardship for the indigenous peoples. In 1574 Toledo legalized the *mita*, the traditional Inca system of enforced labor on a rotational basis. It was another example of an Andean institution twisted to suit Spanish needs; under the Incas the system had involved young people working in the service of the state for a limited period, depending on the task involved. In return, the transient workers had received hospitality from the local community as well as a look at the world outside their own village. Under the Spanish version of the system, Indian workers were force-marched hundreds of miles to Potosí, where two out of every three died as a result of the appalling working conditions, since miners were forced to remain below ground for six-day stretches.

Even more horrific were the mercury mines in Huancavelica – one of which, Santa Barbara, soon became known as the "mine of death." Thousands of people from neighboring provinces died in the mines, asphyxiated by lethal fumes of cinnabar (sulphide of mercury), arsenic, and mercury.

The traditional chewing of coca leaves had initially been condemned by the Catholic Church until it was realized that the Andean peoples could not survive the brutal mining *mita* without it. The leaf was soon touted by the Spanish as a cure-all to ward off hunger, thirst, and fatigue. The trade was organized and controlled: thousands of local highlanders, unadapted to life in the torrid jungle, died working the coca fields. Llama caravans carried coca leaves from Cusco, the center of production, to Potosí, 1,000 km (620 miles) away. The Church also reaped the benefits of the lucrative trade, collecting a tithe on each full basket.

Francisco de Toledo also initiated the *mita de obrajes* (textile workshops). Working under harsh factory conditions, workers were forced to weave

### THE DIABOLICAL HERB

Although some authorities tried to limit the production of coca, too many fortunes were made from the trade. "There are those in Spain who became rich from this coca, buying it up and reselling it and trading it in the markets of the Indians," wrote Spanish chronicler and soldier Pedro Cieza de León, who traveled through Peru in the 1540s.

"Without coca there would be no Peru," noted another contemporary observer. This terse statement has a familiar ring today, as the multi-billion-dollar cocaine industry threatens the country's stability.

for their Spanish masters, producing cloth for local consumption and export.

Toledo tried to limit the wealth of the *encomenderos* by ensuring that their land reverted to the Crown after a couple of generations, to be replaced with *corregimientos*. But this system had few advantages for the native peoples, as the *corregidores* (or co-regents) were also charged with collecting tribute and providing workers for the *obraje* and mining *mitas*.

## Christians on the march

The early 1600s saw a far-flung campaign against idolatry, spurred on by a revival of native religion

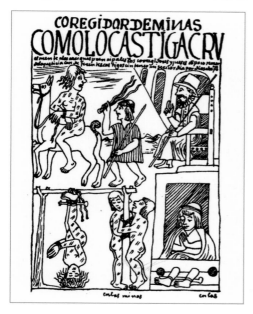

in 1565. The renewed religious zeal of the Catholic Church led to a push to stamp out native beliefs once and for all. At the same time, this crusade gave rise to valuable dictionaries and accounts that are still being studied by historians today. Priests visited outlying provinces, collecting information on cults and sometimes torturing villagers to reveal the whereabouts of idols and *huacas*.

In many ways, the Catholic campaign served to entrench native faiths; rather than taking over, Christianity formed a thin veneer over traditional cults and beliefs, many of which still exist today.

**LEFT:** the horrendous conditions in the Potosí mines.
**ABOVE:** punishments inflicted by the Spanish.
**RIGHT:** the San Francisco monastery library in Lima.

This syncretism, in which traditional beliefs dominate, led to the replacement of Andean pilgrimage centers and festivals by superficially Catholic ones.

> By the early 1700s, the colonial system was firmly established throughout the Andes. At is height, the viceroyalty of Peru was 15 times the size of Spain, and for two centuries ruled from Panama to Argentina.

Under the prevailing system of mercantilism, which promoted exports and restricted imports and goods produced for local consumption, the

elite grew rich, while the mass of people remained impoverished. Spain decreed that all trade from South America should pass through Lima, ensuring a massive influx of taxes. Lima, the opulent "City of Kings," was crammed with magnificent churches and mansions.

In Spain, meanwhile, the end of the War of the Spanish Succession (1700–13) saw the Habsburg dynasty replaced by the Bourbons, who reigned until Napoleon occupied Madrid in 1808. Efforts by Bourbon monarchs to improve the colonial economy and stem corruption were to little avail.

## Indigenous uprising

During the 18th century, exploitation of the indigenous population sparked off various rebellions, from Quito in present-day Ecuador to La Paz (capital city of today's Bolivia). The most serious of these was the uprising instigated by José Gabriel Condorcanqui, also known as Tupac Amaru II, as he claimed to be descended from the renegade Inca Emperor killed in 1572 *(see page 54)*. Born in Tinta, south of Cusco, Tupac Amaru II studied in Cusco at a school for Indians of noble birth. It was not his intention to rid Peru of the Spanish yoke; rather, he fought against the tyranny of the *corregidores*, the miserable conditions at the haciendas, mines, *obrajes*, and coca plantations, and the subsequent malnutrition and disease. Increasingly, he lobbied for indigenous

*audiencia*, or royal court, in Cusco to deal with indigenous legal claims. Meanwhile in Spain, Charles III, who had come to the throne in 1759, ordered that commerce be opened up, allowing ports other than Lima to conduct trade. He banned the *repartimiento*, the forced sale of inferior goods to native peoples at inflated prices, and ended the *corregimiento* system. He also divided the viceroyalty into seven intendancies under royal rule, paving the way for the regionalism that would break South America into its present patchwork of republics.

Not all the Spanish government and clergy exploited the indigenous population. One clergy-

rights, demanding that the mine *mita* be lifted and the power of the *corregidores* limited.

In 1780 he had Tinta's hated *corregidor*, Antonio Arriaga, taken prisoner and hanged in the public square. It was the start of a public revolt that spread throughout the Peruvian highlands. Spanish reinforcements were sent from Lima to quell the uprising. At a decisive battle in Checacupe, in 1781, the Spaniards dispersed Tupac Amaru II's men and captured the rebel leader and his wife. Tupac Amaru II, like his ancestor before him, was executed in Cusco's public square, and forced to witness the execution of his family before he was drawn and quartered. As a result of the rebellion, the viceroy Teodoro de Croix (1784–90) began to institute long overdue reforms. He set up a special

man, Don Baltasar Jaime Martínez de Compañón y Bujanda, stands out. Appointed bishop of Trujillo in 1779, he spent his years traveling around a vast diocese covering the northern third of Peru. In a letter to Charles III dated 1786 he described the "wretchedness" he encountered everywhere.

## The push for independence

On the eve of Napoleon's march on the Iberian peninsula, Spain's hold on its colonies was already waning. Despite the best endeavors of the authorities, news of the French Revolution (begun in 1788), as well as the United States' War of Independence from Britain (1775–83), had filtered through to the colonies – at least to the criollos (American-born Peruvians of European descent) –

and inspired hopes for self-determination. When Napoleon forced Charles IV to abdicate in 1808, and then placed his own brother Joseph on the Spanish throne, there were rebellions in many parts of South America. Declarations of independence in Upper Peru (now Bolivia) and Quito (Ecuador) in 1809 were followed by uprisings in the Peruvian cities of Huánuco and Cusco. But freedom from Spain was not so easily won: royalist troops regained control in many parts of the continent, and bloody wars were waged for the next 15 years.

There were many Peruvians who supported the colonial system, since Lima was still its wealthy

declared their independence. General San Martín entered Lima in 1821, proclaiming independence for all Peru on July 28.

His first move was to abolish the tribute system, the mining *mita*, and the *corregimiento*, reforms which had been attempted earlier by Charles III. He even went so far as to ban the term "Indian" and proclaimed the descendants of the Incas to be citizens of Peru.

But Peru was not prepared for self-rule. San Martín opted for a new monarchy to replace Spanish rule and searched for a European prince to rule the former colony. In the subsequent tumultuous months, the monarchical plan was

administrative capital. Peru became the strongest bastion of pro-Spanish feeling, and other newly independent countries could not feel secure until it, too, was liberated.

After Argentinian General José de San Martín's successful invasion of Chile in 1819, a rebel navy commanded by the British admiral Lord Cochrane sailed from the Chilean port of Valparaíso and landed in Paracas, on Peru's south coast. The following year the armada attacked Lima, dispersing royalist troops, who fled to the central and southern highlands. Meanwhile, the northern cities of Trujillo, Lambayeque, Piura, and Cajamarca

**LEFT:** Lima's Plaza Mayor in 1680. **ABOVE:** Tupac Amaru II. **RIGHT:** Simón Bolívar, "El Libertador."

### THE PROGRESSIVE PRIEST

Fascinated by natural history and colonial life, the bishop of Trujillo, Martínez de Compañón, and his team of artists produced over 1,000 drawings, plans, and maps in ink and watercolor covering antiquities, flora and fauna, customs, music, and costumes of northern Peru. The 18th-century cleric is considered by many to be the grandfather of Peruvian archeology: he collected some 600 pre-Columbian artifacts for shipment to the Spanish king, who founded a "Cabinet of Natural History and Antiquities" in Madrid.

scuttled following the election of a parliament. The seven viceregal intendancies became departments headed by prefects, modeled on the French system of government.

## Freedom and chaos

In 1822 San Martín sailed to Guayaquil (Ecuador), where he met Venezuelan statesman Simón de Bolívar, El Libertador. A far-sighted political thinker influenced by the ideas of the Enlightenment, Bolívar had liberated his home country, and wanted San Martín's help to establish Gran Colombia, comprising Venezuela, Colombia, and Ecuador (which lasted only from 1823 to 1830).

San Martín needed troops to root out the last Spanish royalist forces in the Andes and offered Peru's leadership to Bolívar. During his brief presidency (1824–6) Bolívar advocated republicanism. He commanded troops at the Battle of Junín in 1824, but it was not until the Battle of Ayacucho later that year that rebels headed by Venezuelan General José de Sucre crushed the royalist troops.

Bolívar's departure for Colombia in 1826 created a power vacuum, and the congress elected José de la Mar as president. San Martín's promises to abolish the tribute system, *mita*, servitude, and to recognize Quechua as an official language, were never followed through. The wars of independence had left the country ravaged, crops unattended, and food scarce. Instead of indigenous peoples being granted equal status as citizens of a republican Peru, an all-out assault on indigenous landholdings began.

Between 1826 and 1865, 35 presidents, many of them military officers, governed Peru. Chaos reigned. Charles Darwin, who visited the capital during his journey of scientific discovery in the 1830s, recalled: "Lima, the City of Kings, must formerly have been a splendid town." But he found it in a "wretched state of decay; the streets are nearly unpaved, and heaps of filth are piled up in all directions, where the black *gallinazos* (vultures) pick up bits of carrion."

## Economic boom

Despite the political chaos of the early republican years, the economy grew, with large cotton and sugar estates developing on the coast. In 1849 Peru began to import Chinese labor to work the fields. In 1865 Spain, hoping to regain a foothold in its former colony, occupied the Chincha guano islands. A year later President Mariano Prado declared war on Spain and, after the Spanish navy bombarded the port of Callao, Peru decided to revamp its fleet, buying arms in Europe. Using the guano concession as a guarantee for the vast sum of 20 million pesos, Peru acquired the *Huascar* and *Independencia* warships from Britain.

The guano boom also initiated an era of railroad construction in the 1870s. The US railroad entrepreneur, Henry Meiggs, won the bid for the Callao–La Oroya line, an engineering feat of tunnels and bridges that began at sea level and rose over 5,000 meters (16,400 ft) to the mining town of La Oroya. In 1877, unable to pay its British creditors, the Peruvian state became bankrupt. Worse was to come.

---

### THE RED AND WHITE FLAG

According to the legend, the colors of Peru's republican flag were inspired by the red and white feathers of the flamingoes General José de San Martín saw upon landing at Paracas.

The full flag also includes the national coat-of-arms, incorporating famous symbols of the wealth and history of Peru. It represents the animal, vegetable, and mineral realms, and features a vicuña, a quinine tree, and a cornucopia spilling out gold coins.

## War breaks out

In 1879 Chile declared war on Peru and Bolivia over a dispute concerning sodium nitrate and borax deposits in the province of Tarapacá. The War of the Pacific (1879–83) found the armed forces of Peru and Bolivia woefully unprepared. Chilean troops occupied southern Peru and then bombarded Callao, occupying Lima and cutting off the capital from the hinterland. Following the peace treaty of 1883, Peru ceded Tarapacá to Chile.

The war brought economic chaos. The tribute system was reinstated and a salt tax levied. In 1886, British bond-holders began negotiations: Peru's debt was canceled in exchange for a 66-

began belching fumes of arsenic, lead, and zinc into the atmosphere, ravaging the country; and fishmeal began to be exported from Peru's abundant anchovy plants.

Workers in the mines, coastal factories, and urban sweatshops began to form unions. But it was on the north coast, where laborers on the sugar haciendas began to organize, that a new class-consciousness found political expression. In 1924, while exiled in Mexico, a popular activist named Victor Raúl Haya de la Torre formed the Alianza Popular Revolucionaria Americana (APRA), with a loose platform based on anti-imperialism and nationalization that attracted

year control of the major railroads and 2 million tons of guano. The Peruvian Corporation was set up in 1890 to manage their interests.

By 1900, US interests were beginning to replace the British in controlling the Peruvian economy. Following the Spanish-American War over Cuba in 1898, US expansionists had begun to show an interest in Latin America. Many businessmen, seeing their domestic market as saturated, were looking for new outlets.

US investors set up the Cerro de Pasco Mining Company, which soon controlled all the mines in the central Sierra. In 1922 a smelter at La Oroya

**LEFT:** an Indian worker in a tungsten mine.
**ABOVE:** crossing a canyon in La Oroya in the 1920s.

### RICH PICKINGS

By 1830 Peru had discovered a new resource that replaced minerals as the country's main export: guano. The rich piles of bird droppings deposited on Peru's offshore islands were much sought after in Europe as fertilizer and fetched enormous prices.

The first guano contract was negotiated with a British company in 1840. Indigenous people worked in appalling conditions at the guano stations, where ammonia fumes shriveled the skin and often caused blindness. By 1849, Peru's economy was almost entirely in the hands of two foreign firms, one based in London, the other in Paris, which between them shared exclusive guano marketing rights.

middle-class voters who felt neglected by the oligarchical rule. Haya de la Torre was allowed back to contest the 1931 elections, but was defeated in what *apristas* denounced as a fraud. Party members rebelled in Trujillo, killing 60 military officers. In reprisal, the military executed over 1,000 *apristas* in the ruins of Chan Chan.

## Urban drift

For the next 50 years, APRA was kept out of power as Peru oscillated between Conservative and military regimes. Manufacturing industry developed, and thousands of *campesinos* (subsistence farmers) flocked into Lima. Pressure for land reform

and some redistribution of wealth grew. The first government of Fernando Belaúnde (1963–8), who promised some cautious progressive measures, was a failure, and, after widespread disgust at tax concessions given to the International Petroleum Company (a subsidiary of Standard Oil of New Jersey), yet another coup occurred. Belaúnde was marched out of the Presidential Palace in his pyjamas, and into exile. But General Juan Velasco, who headed the new junta, was not a typical military ruler, and went on to champion many of the radical APRA reforms.

Velasco's measures were drastic. They included sweeping agrarian reform, expropriating vast landholdings, and turning family-run estates into cooperatives. Petrol, mining, and fishing industries were nationalized at a stroke. Food for the urban population was subsidized by the state. And, in a profound symbolic gesture, Peru was recognized as a bilingual country, with Quechua as the second language.

## A bloodless coup

Well intentioned Velasco's measures may have been, but they were not backed by sound economic planning. The newly nationalized industries were badly managed and lacked the necessary finance, and the country was already slipping into economic chaos well before the 1973 international oil crisis. The military split into factions, and in 1975, Morales Bermúdez, heading an alliance of Conservative and reformist officers, staged a bloodless coup against Velasco, who died soon afterwards.

The new military government soon proved incapable of running the country. Debt soared, and inflation ran out of control. A wave of industrial unrest culminated in a general strike in 1977, which marked a turning point. A constituent assembly was elected, and its president, Haya de la Torre, lifted the last barrier to adult suffrage, giving 2 million illiterate adults the right to vote.

Peru returned to civilian rule in 1980, when President Belaúnde was elected to a second period in office. Ironically, this also marked the emergence of the Sendero Luminoso (Shining Path) guerrilla group, when its members burned ballot boxes in Ayacucho. The following decade was marked by the single-minded violence of this group and the state's response to it. ❑

### RUBBER BARONS

The Peruvian rubber boom lasted from 1880 to 1912. The existence of latex in the rubber trees of the Amazon was common knowledge, but it was only after Charles Goodyear discovered the process of vulcanization, which kept rubber firm in high temperatures, that its commercial possibilities were realized. The rubber barons of Iquitos in Peru and Manaus in Brazil lived in luxury until an Englishman smuggled the seeds from the Amazon to Asia (via Kew Gardens in England) and the monopoly came to an abrupt end.

**LEFT:** General Juan Velasco.

# The "Covered Ones"

**Friction between Peru's Spanish-born residents and its upper-class mestizos did more than spark the independence revolution. It gave Lima its most scandalous fashion.**

Spanish women in 18th-century Lima enticed men in traditional fashion, showing off their tiny waists and wafting elaborate fans. Not to be outdone, the *mestizas* created an alluring look of their own by covering their faces with Arab veils – except for one eye which peeked out. They were known as the *tapadas* or "covered ones."

Although veiled, the *tapadas* were far from modest. Their skirts were hiked shamelessly up to show feet tinier than those of their Spanish rivals, and necklines were lowered, while the fairer-skinned Spaniards remained covered under Lima's strong sun, this being long before the European craze for finding a suntan attractive.

When the European women squeezed their middles even more, the thicker-waisted *mestizas* scrimped on the fabric encircling their ample hips. As a result, skirts in the 1700s became so tight that their wearers could take only the tiniest of steps. But one part of the costume remained constant throughout these changes: the veil hiding all but one eye, with which a great deal could be said.

"This costume so alters a woman – even her voice since her mouth is covered – that unless she is very tall or very short, lame, hunchbacked or otherwise conspicuous, she is impossible to recognize," wrote early French feminist Flora Tristan. "I am sure it needs little imagination to appreciate the consequences of this time-honored practice which is sanctioned or at least tolerated by law."

The *tapadas* spent their afternoons strolling, and the "consequences" of their tantalizing fashion ranged from playful flirting to sinful trysts. Ironically, it was said that some of them even caught out their own husbands. So scandalous was the behavior the costume permitted that the archbishop attempted to condemn it, but the *tapadas* refused to serve their husbands, attend their families, or carry out church duties while the sanction was in effect.

Conspiracy was endemic in the early 19th century, and many *tapadas* used their afternoon walks

**RIGHT:** the scandalous fashion of the "covered ones."

to pass messages to organizers of the revolution, thus playing an important part in forming the nation. The site for this romantic and political intrigue was the Paseo de Aguas – a walkway of reflecting pools and gardens built for a woman who inspired one of South America's most famous romances.

By stealing a viceroy's heart, *mestiza* Micaela Villegas placed herself firmly in history and legend. Count Amat y Juniet built her Lima's finest house, bought her a gold and silver coach and, although in his sixties when they met, fathered her only child.

Villegas was known as "La Perrichola," Amat's mispronunciation of *perra chola*, literally "half-breed bitch," an epithet he threw at her during a heated

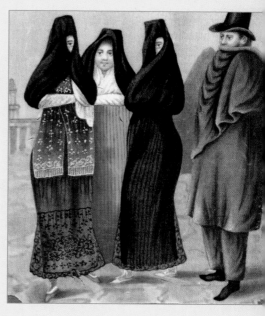

argument. Despite the harshness of this name, Amat adored the actress, who had first caught his eye on a Lima stage. Their love inspired Jacques Offenbach's 1868 opera *La Périchole*.

But the Perrichola story has a sad ending. Inconsolable when her aged lover was ordered back to Spain (where, in his eighties, he married one of his nieces), La Perrichola vowed that she would never love again. She gave her considerable wealth to the poor, and entered a convent.

A Cristal beer factory now stands on the site of the opulent mansion, but the Paseo de Aguas survives in the Rímac district north of the river, behind the Presidential Palace and next to the Convento de los Descalzos. The latter is worth a visit in itself for its collection of colonial paintings. ❑

# DEMOCRACY AND CRISIS

**Peru has become a democracy, the battle against terrorism has been won, and inflation is under control, but the rural-urban divide has still to be bridged**

Peruvian politics appeared to have turned full circle when Fernando Belaúnde Terry was elected president for a second time in 1980. But he returned to a country that had changed a great deal after 12 years of military regimes, with a high level of popular frustration and the beginnings of violent armed opposition aimed at toppling the state.

Belaúnde brought with him a free-market-oriented economic team that hastily undid some of the Velasco legacy *(see page 64)* by returning some state companies to private control, and trying to increase competition and lower tariffs. They also turned their back on the experiment to kick-start a Peruvian industrial base, focusing instead on capitalizing on the country's rich natural resources.

External forces did much to disrupt their efforts. From 1982 raw material export prices slumped, while in 1983 a powerful El Niño current triggered flooding and natural disasters that devastated fishing and agriculture. Meanwhile, Belaúnde, known for his high rhetoric, continued to build roads into the jungle and colonize eastern

*Tens of thousands of people are thought to have died in "the years of violence" under the Belaúnde government. Most lived in the Andean highland regions of Ayacucho or neighboring provinces.*

Peru, thus ensuring that public spending remained high. The Latin American debt crisis also undercut the economy, causing credit lines to dry up, leaving Peru faced with the choice of defaulting or strangling any hopes of economic advance.

**LEFT:** police presence in Lima's Plaza Mayor.
**RIGHT:** Fernando Belaúnde Terry.

As popular discontent continued to grow, the Belaúnde government became increasingly repressive, responding to strikes and protest marches with tear-gas and riot police. The government badly misjudged the Sendero Luminoso revolt in the Andes, ignoring early signs of activity, then allowing counter-insurgency forces to act with indiscriminate violence against the indigenous population.

## Hopes dashed

The first-ever Peruvian president from the ranks of the mass Alianza Popular Revolucionaria Americana (APRA) party, the youthful Alán García, represented the country's hopes for unity and economic relief. García retreated from the previous government's ties with the IMF. In July 1985 he dropped a bombshell on the foreign banks, announcing that Peru would limit its foreign debt payments to 10 percent of its export earnings, with the result that international bankers and lending agencies refused to offer any more credit to Peru.

> In the last years of García's presidency inflation soared at around 40 percent a month, people's savings were wiped out, and food shortages ensued. Shock austerity measures left many with no option but the ollas comunes (soup kitchens).

The policy fanned domestic consumption and started a two-year spurt of growth. Yet this ran out of steam as foreign reserves tumbled and credit lines dried up. Inflation romped ahead and the value of wages slumped. The economy tumbled into chaos. Central bank coffers had been emptied by the chaotic early exchange-rate controls, followed by the raging inflation. The García administration ended its days amid allegations of widespread extortion and corruption.

## Jockeying for power

García also failed to find a way of containing the threat from Sendero Luminoso and the smaller pro-Cuban Movimiento Revolucionario Tupac Amaru (MRTA), with the former moving its atten-

tion from the Andes to the capital. His reputation as a man of the masses suffered as he appeared incapable of reining in the tactics of the military, who were determined to put down insurgency in the Andes. Thousands continued to be killed or "disappeared" by brutal attacks from rebels and the military. In Lima, the massacre of hundreds of rioting *senderistas* at two top-security prisons in July 1986 undermined García's human rights record. There was a growing sense of anarchy as a third of the country came under emergency rule.

One of García's legacies was popular disgust with all traditional parties. That disillusion turned into a tidal wave of support for a former agri-

cultural university rector, Alberto Fujimori, in the 1990 elections. At first, no one took any notice of the engineer of Japanese descent campaigning in shantytowns on the back of a tractor, but Fujimori began creeping up the opinion polls.

The front-runner, well-known novelist Mario Vargas Llosa, made the crucial mistake of accepting an alliance with the old rightist parties, including Belaúnde's AP (Popular Action Party), which sparked voters' concerns that he was a Trojan horse for the same old political elite. The popular perception of Vargas Llosa – who had lived much of his life in Europe – as a haughty intellectual, far removed from the grit of daily life in the shantytowns, also worked against him. Rejecting the *blanquitos* (the white elite), people turned to a candidate they related to more easily: Fujimori. The little-known candidate of the Cambio 90 Party romped to victory against Vargas Llosa. The novelist left shortly afterwards and took up Spanish nationality, a move that further alienated him from his home country.

## The reign of Fujimori

No one made a bigger impact on the Peru of the 1990s than Alberto Fujimori. He seized power with both hands and ruled with an instinctive sense of the popular mood, which he at first expertly manipulated. He began by breaking electoral promises and adopting the economic shock

The main achievement of Fujimori's first term (1990–5) was not an economic one. In September 1992, the capture of the Sendero Luminoso leader, Abimael Guzmán, who had gained almost mythical status, dealt a fatal blow to the rebel organization. Shown to the press in a huge circus-size cage, dressed in a striped prison suit, Guzmán was seen to be just an aging man. Although Sendero remained active for a while, the capture of Guzmán and other top members destroyed its organization.

Peru's economy began to climb back out of a decade-long trough, as confidence returned to a community that had been shaken by bombings in

programs championed by the defeated Vargas Llosa. The economic measures he introduced began with price rises and currency devaluation, which hit Peruvians hard. He combined these with a radical program of privatization, cutting tariffs, and simplifying taxes.

The Fujimori administration set its sights on returning to the international financial community, in order to win IMF approval. Gradually the economy appeared to recover, but the sale of state enterprises led to thousands of job losses, and workers' wage rates declined in real terms.

**FAR LEFT:** Alán García's first election victory.
**LEFT:** Abimael Guzmán, leader of Sendero Luminoso.
**ABOVE:** the 1995 Peru–Ecuador border dispute.

### WAR IN THE NORTH

In January 1995 an old wound reopened, when Peruvian and Ecuadorean troops clashed in a disputed area of the remote rainforest frontier. Each side accused the other of igniting the conflict. Fighting upslope in dense jungle against well-defended and concealed Ecuadorean positions, Peru took heavier casualties, losing scores of soldiers, and some warplanes and helicopters. Exact losses have never been independently confirmed.

Fujimori acquired some domestic prestige by standing firm, and the bitter fighting ended in an uneasy brokered ceasefire. But the seriousness of the conflict led both sides to modify their previously intransigent positions, and in 1998 a border treaty finally settled the centuries-old dispute.

the country and cities. Fujimori's autocratic style at first found an echo in a society that had been on the brink of chaos. Backed by army tanks, his decision in April 1992 to dissolve parliament and sack top judges met with majority support. He claimed he needed to bypass a corrupt parliament and judiciary. Further radical measures followed, with the decision to try alleged terrorists in "faceless" military courts, where the judge's identity was kept secret, and the repentance law that encouraged rebels to turn themselves in and receive pardon or lower sentences if they denounced others. In practice, that measure led to hundreds of innocent people being jailed for years on the say-so of others.

Yet Fujimori weathered criticisms, and the election of a constituent assembly in 1993 persuaded the US government to lift a suspension on aid. The economy began to expand, and by 1993 Peru's growth rate was among the highest in the world.

## La Cantuta murders

The darker side of Fujimori's authoritarian regime was seen in the killings of La Cantuta. A death squad of intelligence agents murdered nine students and a professor from the university and buried their bodies in sand dunes outside Lima. Several agents were tried and sentenced, but the Amnesty Law, passed in 1995, gave immunity to

### THE DARK LORD

During the Fujimori years, Vladimiro Montesinos presided over the national intelligence services as the embodiment of unchecked power, menace, and corruption. No fiction could improve on his sinister, infinitely complicated resumé: ex-army officer, cashiered for forging his commanding officer's signature; a law degree earned while doing time in a military prison; onetime CIA agent; drug- and arms-trafficker, death-squad overseer – above all, master of political chicanery.

His debut in national politics was to cause to "disappear" the court files on a criminal case charging presidential candidate Alberto Fujimori with fraudulent property deals. Thereafter, it seems, he also ensured the records in Japan "disappeared" that would have proved Fujimori was born

there and could have invalidated his constitutional right to be president of Peru. After Fujimori won the presidency in 1990, Montesinos acquired extraordinary power as the president's right-hand man, while amassing a huge illegal fortune. He subverted democratic institutions and spread a web of organized corruption. In hundreds of private meetings he cajoled and bribed public officials, congressional deputies, journalists, judges, and generals. And secretly, he videotaped them all.

After Fujimori's rigged election for a third term in 2000, some of the "Vladivideos" were smuggled out and shown on national TV, unleashing an uncontrollable scandal. Montesinos was first to fall. He now resides in a maximum-security prison which, ironically, he himself ordered built.

members of security forces who had taken part in human rights abuses since 1980, and freed those convicted of the killings.

By the end of his first term, Fujimori was credited with almost eliminating the twin evils of the 1980s: inflation and terrorism. In gratitude, Peruvians not only voted him back in with a 64 percent majority in 1995, but also gave his Cambio 90–Nueva Mayoría alliance a majority in Congress. His main challenger, former UN Secretary-General Javier Pérez de Cuellar, lacked the popular touch.

Fujimori's resounding victory in what independent observers termed a generally fair and free election meant he recovered international political legitimacy. Yet hopes that he would relegate army and intelligence service to less important roles proved unfounded. The unofficial head of the intelligence services, Vladimiro Montesinos, became increasingly powerful.

Furthermore, Fujimori appeared to focus on finding a way to stand for a third term, even though the Constitution allowed only two consecutive terms of office. In many people's eyes, the business of government began to take second place to the push for re-election in the year 2000. The pro-Fujimori Congress suggested he could stand again, as his first election victory, in 1990, preceded the new Constitution. When three judges on the Constitutional Tribunal ruled that such a re-election was unconstitutional, Congress sacked them. The National Magistrates Council, charged with appointing and sacking judges, later resigned after its powers were cut.

## Job shortages

Equally, the privatization program that the Fujimori government embarked on began to falter in his second term. Public discontent with the cost of privatized services like telephones and electricity seemed to have sparked indecision on the part of policy-makers. In 1998, with Peru in the third year of an IMF program, the fund's team was expressing praise for the meeting of macroeconomic goals, and growth in 1997 had been a healthy 7.4 percent.

Yet most Peruvians were perplexed that the figures were not reflected in an improvement in their standard of living. "If the economy is doing so well, why am I doing so badly?" was the front-

cover headline of the weekly magazine *Caretas*, echoing the popular sentiment, with the main complaint being the shortage of properly paid jobs.

## The siege

Fujimori's second term faced its greatest crisis at the end of 1996, when a group of masked and well-armed rebels of the Movimiento Revolucionario Tupac Amaru (MRTA) blasted their way into a reception at the Japanese ambassador's residence in Lima and took hundreds of guests hostage. The 126-day hostage crisis put massive international pressure on Fujimori's government, because dignitaries of many nationalities were among the captives.

The siege came at a time when most Lima residents believed that terrorist attacks were a thing of the past. For the MRTA, an organization that grew out of far-left groups in the early 1980s, the siege was a last-ditch attempt to save the movement, whose support had dwindled to around 100 armed rebels, and to push for the release of hundreds of members then in prison.

During the stand-off that ensued through the hot Lima summer, several groups of hostages were released from the besieged residence, until there remained a core group of 72, including Foreign Minister Francisco Tudela and Fujimori's brother, Pedro.

While the International Red Cross mediated, and talks to discuss the rebels' demands began, Fuji-

**LEFT:** Alberto Fujimori on trial in Lima, in 2007.
**RIGHT:** soldiers help hostages escape from the Japanese ambassador's residence in 1997.

mori took a gamble. Miners were drafted in to dig a warren of tunnels under the residence, and on April 22, 1997, a commando unit blasted its way in and rescued the hostages. One hostage, two commandos, and all 14 rebels were killed – according to some reports, after they had surrendered. Fujimori claimed credit for the successful rescue operation, and his popularity ratings soared. But this success could not halt popular discontent, especially when Fujimori pushed for a third term in office in the 2000 elections. When he was declared the victor over his closest rival, Alejandro Toledo, there were claims of widespread fraud, and thousands protested during his inauguration in Lima.

Venezuela, he was captured and returned to Peru to stand trial. He faces charges ranging from organizing death squads to involvement in illegal drugs-trafficking. He has so far been convicted on corruption, abuse of power, and arms-trafficking charges, and is serving a 20-year sentence.

A caretaker government under the veteran politician Valentín Paniagua took over. It had three main tasks: to organize fresh elections, to guarantee continuity in economic affairs, and to investigate the corruption of the Fujimori regime and the human rights abuses committed in the struggle against the armed opposition groups over 20 years since 1980.

Even so, Fujimori might have held onto power had it not been for the "Vladivideos." The secretly filmed tapes incriminated both Montesinos *(see page 70)* and scores of public figures, and when they began to appear on television the scandal overwhelmed the Fujimori government.

Fujimori and Montesinos fled the country. Fujimori went to Japan, where his parents had been born, and faxed his resignation as president. The Peruvian Congress stripped him of his office for "moral incapacity." Deploying his dual Peruvian-Japanese citizenship, he installed himself in a luxury apartment outside Tokyo, while the Japanese government refused Peru's requests to extradite him.

Montesinos was less fortunate. After spending several months in hiding in neighboring

## Truth and reconciliation

In 2001, the government set up the Truth and Reconciliation Commission, not only to look into the "years of violence" between 1980–2000, but to establish responsibilities, and also to pave the way for reparations *(see opposite)*.

The Paniagua administration also established an independent electoral commission, which organized fresh presidential and congressional elections for April 2001. The front-runners in the first round were center-left economist Alejandro Toledo and former president Alán García. Despite

**ABOVE:** trade union protest in Lima against the free-trade agreement with the US. **RIGHT:** Alán García speaking at the White House in 2007.

only having returned to Peru a few months earlier, García and his APRA party made a surprisingly

> The Truth and Reconciliation Commission's report concluded that 69,000 people had died as a result of attacks by Sendero Luminoso and other extremist groups, the majority of them innocent peasants.

strong showing, but Toledo was the winner in a second round of voting.

Alejandro Toledo, the shoeshine boy who went on to graduate from Stanford and Harvard, took office in 2001. Despite his reforms aimed at

many were seeing little benefit from the country's economic success.

## Today's challenges

Today, as García struggles to fulfill his pledges of improved government services, especially in health and education, various wild cards have been tossed into the political deck. Astonishingly, ex-president Fujimori forsook his comfortable Japanese exile and surfaced in Chile in a doomed bid for political resurrection. Extradited to Peru, he has been sentenced to six years in prison for abuse of power, and still faces more serious human rights charges. Meanwhile, in Congress an

reducing poverty and restoring faith in the country's corrupt institutions, his presidency was marked by strikes and scandals. In the mountain town of Andahuaylas, an insurrection led by Antauro Humala, brother and cohort of the ultra-nationalist politician Ollanta Humala, claimed five lives and rocked the government.

Nevertheless, in 2006 Toledo presided over orderly elections and handed over a buoyant economy to the new president, a resurgent Alán García. García's first term in the 1980s had taken Peru into economic meltdown, but his main opponent, Ollanta Humala, was seen by most Peruvians as an even riskier choice. Humala's political strength came from the impoverished and rebellious highlands where

unruly faction of Fujimori supporters, led by his daughter Keiko, threatens political repercussions.

A major earthquake on the south coast in August 2007 has become a political scandal, owing to the slow pace of reconstruction. And a maritime border dispute with Chile has inflamed nationalist anti-Chilean grievances dating back to the 19th century. The US–Peru free-trade treaty, negotiated under Toledo and ratified in 2007, has been controversial and divisive. While coastal regions and mining enclaves thrive, poverty and social unrest persists in the mountains. Nationalist anti-business groups, encouraged by President Hugo Chávez of Venezuela, stand to gain from these undercurrents if they continue unabated through the next national elections, scheduled for 2011. ❑

# A CHANGING SOCIETY

**Almost 500 years of foreign settlement and interracial mixing have produced a complex blend of indigenous Peruvian, European, and African cultures**

Since pre-Columbian times, Peruvians have been divided by geography. There are three main geographical regions: the arid *costa* (coastal strip); the Andean Sierra or highlands; and, to the east of the mountains, the Amazon basin. Almost half of Peruvians live in the coastal region, some 8 million of them in the capital, Lima. It is a city of extremes, with the richest and most Europeanized Peruvians living not far from the poorest shantytowns, where mestizo migrants from the provinces have come in search of work or to escape the violence that has marked Peru in recent years.

From the arid deserts of the coast, the Andean Sierra rises up to more than 6,000 meters (19,700 ft) above sea level. For the modern nation state, this mountain mass poses major problems for development and integration into a single society. The huge natural barrier severely limits the penetration of motorized transport and telecommunications, while frequent earthquakes and landslides further complicate the already arduous terrain. The result is dramatic regional diversity, and considerable inequalities in services and living standards.

*The highlands comprise a quarter of Peru's territory, but are home to half the population. Social anthropologist John Murra described the Andes as an archipelago, a series of island-like pockets of isolated communities, which is an apt description.*

Health, education, and law-enforcement programs are unevenly distributed across Peru. About a third of the country has no conventional medical services:

**PRECEDING PAGES:** Catholic priests leading a religious procession in Puno, southern Peru. **LEFT:** watching the world go by. **RIGHT:** city life.

people rely on the *curanderos* – healers who use a variety of natural and spiritual remedies.

## Many worlds

Over the past 470 years, there has been a long process of inter-cultural mixing, creating the mestizo – a mixture of indigenous and European heritage. Today the majority of Peruvians fall into this category, and it is possible to become mestizo by choice as well as by birth. Anyone assuming Western dress in the rural highlands is usually referred to as mestizo or sometimes *cholo*. Peruvian social divisions are culturally, as much as racially, defined.

There are two large ethno-linguistic groups in the Andes: the larger of the two speaks Quechua, the language of the Inca empire; the smaller group speaks Aymara and is settled around Lake Titicaca and in neighboring Bolivia. The Quechua language is far from uniform, and someone speaking the dialect of Huancayo might not be fully understood by a Quechua-speaker from Cusco.

Beyond these broad distinctions, other complexities arise. There are "white" ethnic groups, like the Morochucos of Pampa Cangallo (Ayacucho) who have light-colored eyes and hair, speak Quechua, and see themselves as *campesinos* (subsistence farmers). The *misti*, the dominant social class in the Andes, speak Quechua and share other cultural traits but enjoy access to education and some of the luxuries of modern life. To the east,

the Andes mountains fall away to the River Amazon system. The *selva alta* (higher slopes) were colonized by *campesinos* only in the second half of the 20th century. Some of the valleys here are where most of Peru's coca crops are grown. The lower foothills of the Andes gradually give way to the vast Amazon river system and its *selva baja* (low-lying jungle). It is here that the 53 ethno-linguistic indigenous groups (some 5 percent of Peru's population) live, although their lands are increasingly being encroached upon by settlers.

Until the trade was banned in the 19th century, landowners brought in black Africans to serve as slaves on their haciendas and frequently used

them to repress the local Indians. Black influence on the music and dance of Peru has been extensive *(see page 108)* and has also made an impact on the country's cuisine. Today, Afro-Peruvians are prominent in sport, but noticeably absent in political life, and still suffer discrimination.

Lima has a strong Anglo community, while in the high jungle, around Oxapampa, there are descendants of German and Austrian immigrants, mainly coffee growers, who still retain firm links with their countries of origin.

## The urban-rural divide

Peruvian culture is sharply divided between indigenous and colonial societies, between the mountains and the city. There are elite white criollos, most of whom live in Lima, who trace their blood-lines back to the Spanish conquest of 1536. They are joined by incomers from Italy, Spain, and other European countries. A surprising number of politicians have Arabic surnames, as there was an influx of Palestinian refugees to Peru after 1948. The criollos and other "gringos" enjoy the cultural legacy of colonialism, and their eyes are firmly fixed on Europe and the United States.

North American mass culture, from Reebok to Disneyland, is an integral part of their children's upbringing, and shopping trips to Miami for clothes and consumer goodies are quite common. Most of these products can now be found in the mega shopping centers of Lima, but they still cost a lot more. A visitor from Europe or the USA will feel a comfortable familiarity in Lima's cafés, department stores, and supermarkets.

Rural communities now also aspire to ownership of televisions and jeans, but this comes into conflict with their traditional values. Heirs to awe-inspiring pre-Columbian cultures, the people of the Andes are maintaining the traditional practices of their ancestors in a rapidly changing world. Their livelihood continues to be based on family-owned fields, or *chacras*, which are farmed by hand or with the help of draft animals.

The social organization of communities in the Andes differs greatly from that of Europeanized criollo culture. Work, marriage, and land ownership are centered on a complex extended family organization – called the *ayllu* in Quechua – which dates back at least to Inca times. One of the main functions of *ayllus* is to organize reciprocal work exchanges. These often take the form of group projects like roof raising or potato harvesting, which are usually made more festive and enjoyable by communal meals and plentiful supplies of *chicha* (homemade corn beer).

The Quechua- and Aymara-speaking peoples of Peru inhabit some 5,000 peasant communities located throughout the Andean Sierra. These communities are based on an agricultural economy, but families frequently supplement their incomes with labor-intensive cottage industries in which they produce the distinctive handicrafts found on the tourist trail, in addition to foodstuffs such as bread, cheese, and honey.

A large majority of highland people live a marginal and impoverished existence. While retaining a fierce loyalty to their ancestral heritage, the poor of the Andes are nevertheless eager to share in the benefits of a modern lifestyle, which include educational opportunities, electricity, sewage systems, and clean water.

## Growth of a monster

Many Andean communities suffered greatly during the 20th century, and between the 1960s and the 1980s Lima seemed like a promised land to the rural poor. Thousands of migrants from as far afield as Ayaviri, Bambamarca, and Huaraz gradually filled the city with a huge Andean population. Added to endemic poverty in the highlands,

**LEFT:** women play an important role in rural communities. **RIGHT:** a young *limeña*.

### LANGUAGE OF THE MOUNTAINS

It is thought that Quechua probably originated somewhere in the central highlands, later becoming the common language of Andean traders. When the Incas adopted it, Quechua acquired new power and status as the lingua franca of the empire.

With an estimated 8 million speakers today, it has official language status and is the most widely spoken indigenous language of the Americas. Yet, despite this, Quechua is endangered. For those migrating from rural communities to the cities, Quechua becomes a social handicap, while millions of children nationwide receive Spanish education, and parents cease to teach them Quechua.

there were various other reasons for the influx: President Velasco's agrarian reform in the early 1970s was unsuccessful, as the *campesinos* did not know how best to work the land they were allotted, while in the 1980s and early 1990s Sendero Luminoso guerrillas terrorized the rural poor, the very people in whose interests they claimed to be fighting.

Urban authorities were unable to satisfy the basic needs of these migrants, and thus the multitude of *pueblos jóvenes,* or shantytowns, surrounding Lima came into being, as there simply was no place within the city for all these people to go *(see page 160)*.

With the end of rural violence, migration to the capital has slowed. But Lima still receives a huge proportion of Peru's resources and services, and has the greatest population mix of the entire country, with groups from the interior often concentrated in their own neighborhoods.

Many people in recent years have returned to their villages, with help from a state repopulation program. But when the state aid runs out, some trickle back to the cities before they can reap a harvest, and their children, used to a degree of urban living, find it difficult to settle in the inhospitable *puna*. It is unlikely that the trend to move to the cities will be reversed.

## Middle-class Peru

The most difficult social area to define is that of the middle classes. Until the 1960s, it was the poor cousin of the oligarchy, providing clerks, merchants, and civil servants. Once modernization started in earnest in the 1970s, the middle class came into its own, both in Lima and in provincial cities. This was due to the diversification of the economy and to the expansion of the Peruvian state, both as a purveyor of public services and as an employer.

However, middle-class prosperity was short-lived, as these were the very same people who suffered most under García in the 1980s, when hyperinflation wiped out their savings and diminished the buying power of their salaries. Many professionals, teachers among them, were forced to eke out a hand-to-mouth existence. Their situation is somewhat better now, but, as recent history has demonstrated, the middle class is vulnerable because it depends for its lifestyle on a disposable income.

## Improvements in education

The latter half of the 20th century saw a dramatic rise in the number of people receiving an education. *Campesinos* and their recently migrated cousins in the cities sacrificed a great deal to get an education so that they could gain access to status and income. Schooling represents a great lifestyle change for rural people, as children traditionally work on the farms and tend the livestock.

It also represents a new expense, as the communities themselves often fund the schools. In the Río Tambo area dedicated young teachers are working in one-room schools in remote rainforest villages, largely funded by local communities. These added expenses, together with the loss of child labor on the farms, obviously complicate

### KEEPERS OF THE INCA FLAME

Q'eros, a remote, mountainous area of southeastern Peru, caused a minor stir in the 1950s, when anthropologists discovered that its people maintained traditions and beliefs almost untainted by European influence. The Q'eros people claimed to be descendants of Incas who had fled from the Spanish invasion and thus preserved their way of life and customs.

These people still cling to their remote homeland, marry among themselves, and maintain a powerful mystique. Their music and dress are distinct from other Quechua-speakers, and their traditional shamans are frequently called upon by both city dwellers and tourists to perform healing rituals and offerings.

*Thousands of poor Andean communities have built one-room schools with dirt floors, benches, and painted blackboards. The communities bore the cost of constructing the schools, and they also pay the wages of the teachers.*

rural education programs. Although the Fujimori government made building new schools a priority, there are still about 1 million school-age children in Peru who receive no state education.

But progress is being made, and in many villages the sharpest students are sent off to the cities

The state is still regarded with suspicion and fear by many rural Peruvians, who cling to their traditional social structures and practices. The idea of democratic rule is recent – it was only in the 1980 elections that some 2 million Peruvians who could not read or write were given the vote.

Even the Roman Catholic Church, a pillar of the old order, has changed tremendously in recent decades, with consequences for Peru's predominantly Catholic population. Since the late 1960s, there has been increasing tension between the conservative Catholic Church hierarchy and the so-called "liberation theologists" who argue that the Church must fight to reduce poverty and injustice

to finish their schooling, as their parents realize that learning to read and write can mean gaining full citizenship.

## Haphazard development

Westerners often take for granted the progress achieved in the 20th century. In Peru, material progress has caused many problems in a poor, mainly rural society. It is only in the past 25 years that many remote regions have come into contact with the outside world, with the building of roads, the spread of electricity, and the modernization of agriculture.

---

**LEFT:** college students hanging out in Miraflores.
**ABOVE:** Peru, a country of contrasts.

in this world. They have encouraged Masses in Quechua, Aymara, and other languages, and helped lead social protest movements. But today the counter-revolution championed by leaders calling for the Church to focus on its spiritual message has been largely won, with the archbishop of Lima and most other Peruvian bishops now belonging to the ultra-conservative Opus Dei movement. In recent years there has also been a big increase in evangelical sects, particularly among the groups newly arrived in the cities from the country areas.

## A woman's place

The shake-up of Peruvian society that came with the terror of the Sendero Luminoso years in the 1980s brought a sudden change in the role of women. Although in pre-conquest Andean Peru women had rights and obligations on a more equal footing than in the colonial era, that standing had gradually been eroded in a society best described as *machista,* where women generally took traditional wife-and-mother roles. In many ways, the 1980s marked a shift. In the Andes, and later in the Amazon, the disruption of normal life by Sendero Luminoso attacks and migrations often left the women in charge of reorganizing life; some 78 percent of migrant families had a woman head of household at one point. In Lima shantytowns, where economic chaos left many impoverished, it was women who were the backbone of daily

life, holding the family together with the *vaso de leche* (glass of milk) breakfast clubs and the ubiquitous *clubes de madres* (mothers' clubs). The community soup kitchens the women organized were vital to feed their families, and the work of organization brought forward many female community leaders at a time when other popular organizations like trade unions and local political parties were falling apart because of rebel and military threats.

Divorce is not uncommon, but can be hard to obtain. Many married men openly take lovers, and in this predominantly *machista* society this is accepted without much fuss. In many rural com-

### MOUNTAIN EXPORTS

Alarmed by the widening economic gulf between highlands and coast, the Peruvian government signed a free-trade treaty with the US in 2007 with the aim of encouraging the cultivation of non-traditional export crops such as blueberries and quinoa, a protein-rich grain.

Bread enriched with potato flour is being promoted locally, in order to boost consumption of Peru's mountain-grown staple. The program is in its infancy, but its success or failure could seriously affect the country's political future.

munities the attitude toward women is still extremely traditional: in societies like that of the Ashaninka in the central Amazon jungle, men still take two or more wives. Women do most of the work in the fields, while men restrict themselves to hunting and fishing. In rural Peru illiteracy rates are much higher among women (43 percent) than among men (30 percent).

In urban Peru, women are starting to shake off the restrictions of the *machista* society, with the numbers of students going to university now almost equal between the genders, and women starting to have a presence in professional ranks as judges, academics, and bankers. In public life, women occupy ministerial posts, and a prominent political party is led by Lourdes Flores Nano, who has been a viable candidate in two presidential elections.

The wide-reaching family-planning program given priority by Fujimori in the early 1990s has meant a decline in births, with population growth now down to around 1.8 percent a year. That same program came in for some serious criticism, including allegations that many thousands of poor uneducated women were being sterilized without sufficient information or after-care. Large numbers of them died as a result – an indication of the disregard for the well-being of rural peasant women. A lack of health services in many parts of Peru means that maternal mortality is still high, with 261 deaths of mothers for every 100,000 births. Life in Peru still revolves largely around the family. For economic reasons young people usually live with their families until they marry, and many continue to do so afterwards.

## Law and order

Terrorism has been almost eradicated, apart from a few incidents in the remote Andes. Although there are reports of assaults and muggings in the larger cities, pickpocketing or bag-snatching is the most commonly encountered crime.

The power of the military was greatly diminished following revelations of its involvement in the corrupt Fujimori regime. The Toledo government subsequently made efforts to cut the military budget and began a reform of the police and the judicial system. However, bribery still occurs frequently.

As a sign of Peruvians' renewed confidence after the fear of the 1990s, there have been many street protests against government measures. Most of these have been quickly brought under control by the police, although there was considerable violence during demonstrations in the southern city of Arequipa in 2002.

## The black economy

One striking feature of contemporary society is the massive scale of the informal or underground economy, in which some 40 percent of the nation's population are involved. However, the *ambulantes* (street vendors) who once crammed the streets of Lima have been swept away, and many of the vendors have now been reorganized in markets and given tax ID numbers.

The informal sector is epitomized by the so-called *combi* culture, a result of large-scale government lay-offs which led to an explosion of independent *combi* (minibus) and taxi drivers attempting to replace jobs lost in the state sector. Cars and *combis* would be bought with severance pay and launched into direct competition with existing transport services.

Such examples are common, and are not confined to the poorest sectors. As full-time jobs and careers have become scarce, more and more middle-class and professional Peruvians also work at two or three jobs in order to survive. Everyone is looking for a *chamba* – a way to make money and stay afloat in an uncertain world.  ❏

### BLACK MARKET INNOVATIONS

Now that most of the *ambulantes* have been moved off the streets of Lima, those remaining tend to be the more desperate and most needy people, wandering the city streets with bags of chewing gum, sunglasses, hairclips, or trinkets.

Among the more inventive people working in the informal economy these days are those who set up stalls outside the prisons and hire out the long skirts and low-heeled shoes that female visitors are required to wear; and those who wait at traffic lights, not to clean your windshield as you might expect, but to waft a herb called *ruda* over your car, to bring you good luck in exchange for a small sum of money.

---

**LEFT:** many religious customs are a fusion of ancient and Christian beliefs. **RIGHT:** a hotel worker; many Peruvians have more than one job to make ends meet.

# DAILY LIFE IN THE ANDES

Traditional hospitality and hard work remain the norm in
Andean villages, where the fabric of life – from marriage
and community work to cooking and clothing – has
barely changed for centuries

The route to most villages in the Peruvian Andes is a narrow, graded-earth road, baked concrete-solid under the fierce sun of the dry season, and awash with torrents of rain, slick with mud, narrowed or closed by rockslides, during the rains. The villages reached by these roads are mostly inhabited by Quechua-speaking descendants of groups once ruled by the Incas. These resilient people have adapted, whenever it was inevitable or advantageous, to the alien Spanish culture forced on them, creating a distinctive version of the ardent Catholicism of their conquerors, and incorporating introduced crops and livestock into their agrarian repertoire.

The Spanish peasant costume of the 16th century was adopted, and in derivative form is still worn to this day. The fundamental outline of highland rural life today more resembles that of a medieval European village than the lifestyles of the Information Age.

Houses are typically made of adobe bricks or stone, with packed-earth floors and thatch roofs, and an occasional flash of corrugated steel indicating some source of cash income. The open rafters inside are blackened from years of cooking over an open hearth or clay oven in the corner.

Communities often consist of farmhouses scattered about the mountainside, whose center is a soccer pitch, and perhaps a schoolhouse. The landscape is stitched with precarious stone walls, built more for removing rocks from the soil than for setting boundaries.

Larger Andean villages often reveal a markedly different plan. These were the *reducciones*, forced settlements created by the Spanish in the 1570s, as

**LEFT:** a woman leading her livestock. **RIGHT:** alpacas are bred throughout the highlands for their wool.

### THE CUP THAT CHEERS

The fermented corn beer called *chicha* plays a vital role in Andean life. It is both a mildly alcoholic social lubricant and a nutritious component of the daily diet. When visiting a village one is almost obliged to sample it. The beige-colored liquid is more like soup than beer in appearance and has a sour taste.

*Chicha* is home-brewed in large batches and, once prepared, must be consumed within a day or two. The householder therefore sells off the surplus to neighbors for a few cents per enormous glass.

they swept scattered communities into organized towns, the better to control, tax, and evangelize the native population. The orderly grid-pattern streets, with main squares fronting a church, town hall, and police station, are often crumbling and semi-abandoned, as many inhabitants have drifted back to their native communities.

## High-altitude living

The essence of rural life is the ruling fact of altitude and the necessity of having access to lands from the high *puna*, where animals graze, through lower slopes where beans and potatoes are grown, on down to warmer valleys where maize and vege-

tables thrive, and often even lower, into the tropical regions of avocado, fruits, and coca. The need to control these different ecological zones has been a driving force in everything from inter-village rivalry to trans-Andean trade and the rise of empires.

Fundamental to traditional village life is the *ayllu* – the extended kinship group, of which there might be several in one village – and the social glue of *ayni*, a reciprocal work obligation whereby everyone gathers to help build someone's house, for example. *Minka* is community work such as cleaning irrigation channels, whereby everyone benefits.

In the midst of all this, some families have more or better land, and others are worse off. Though

### THE FREEZE-DRIED HARVEST

When the potato harvest is over, the task of preparing part of the bounty for long-term storage begins. The *papas* are spread out on the ground and allowed to freeze during the winter night. Next day, as they thaw beneath the warm Andean sun, the farmers trample on them barefoot, squeezing out as much moisture as possible. This process is repeated for two or three nights until the potatoes are completely dry. The dark little nuggets, called *chuñu*, have an earthy flavor when cooked and can be stored indefinitely.

actual wealth is rare, and most farming is for subsistence, the better-off can sell some of their livestock or produce in the markets and perhaps buy a battery-operated radio or CD player. Electrification has now reached many rural areas which barely had candles 20 years ago, along with clean water from communal taps and a growing variety of processed foods and factory-made goods.

As families increase, land often becomes too scarce to support the numbers living off it, and younger people migrate seasonally or permanently to the cities, in search of paid work. Their urban lives usually begin with the discarding of their

**LEFT AND ABOVE:** taking pigs and sheep to market.
**RIGHT:** a traditional highland wedding ceremony.

traditional clothes, Quechua language, and Andean values. City life can be harsher in its way than the highland village, and the typical migrant starts out selling candy on street corners.

## Agricultural cycle

The highland agricultural cycle begins in August and September, when the Andean winter – a succession of warm, cloudless days and stunningly clear, frigid nights – begins to draw to a close. The crops are generally planted from low altitude to high altitude, and harvested in reverse order. Summer, the growing season, is also the rainy season. During these months the fields are hoed and weeded, and the earth of the fallow fields is turned in preparation for the coming year's crops, often under most unpleasant conditions such as rain, hail, and mud. The potatoes are harvested in May, when the rains have ended.

Later the grains and beans are cut and allowed to dry for threshing, and lastly the maize is harvested. After the harvest has been threshed and stored, the community turns to the dry-season activities of weaving, pottery-making, building, and repairing the damage done by the rains.

From their ancestors the Quechua people have inherited tireless devotion to a ritual calendar bound to the annual cycle of life. Every village

### COCA – THE CONTROVERSIAL LEAF

Millennia before a 19th-century European scientist isolated the "active principle" in the coca leaf – cocaine – ancient Peruvians were chomping on wads of leaves, while busily creating sophisticated and powerful civilizations.

Modern scientists have discovered beneficial substances, such as vitamins, in the leaf, along with a complex of complementary alkaloids. They have also documented its ability to stabilize heart-rate and blood-sugar levels, which may account for its fame as an enabler

of hard physical effort. It is also used to combat the symptoms of altitude sickness.

Coca chewing persists in Andean society to this day, infusing village life with decorous and sociable exchanges of leaves (somewhat less decorous during fiestas). The leaves are also used in medicinal applications for assorted maladies, in the form of serial wads for hard labor and long journeys, and as sacramental offerings in ceremonies. Many things make Andean culture what it uniquely is, and coca is certainly one of them.

celebrates a series of Catholic saints' days, each of which seems to have absorbed some aspect of the old pre-Christian festivities. After the celebration of Mass comes ritual drinking and feasting, and often the attendance of masked dancers in elaborate costumes with bands playing raucous music. Libations are preceded by careful "feeding" of the earth with ritual drops of liquor and, in a back room away from the eyes of the priests, village shamans make symbolic offerings to the earth and the mountain deities.

The fiestas are organized by a rotating series of sponsors known as *carguyocs*, whose contribution denotes their status in the social organization of the village. Every family of some status – that is, with a broad circle of family and associates whom they can call on for support – passes through an ascending hierarchy of *cargos* during their lifetime, which establish their prestige and authority in the community.

Marriage is seen as just one step in a long period of mutual relationship which began in the fields, continued under the roof of one set of parents, and has already produced at least one child. The formal wedding is often undertaken on the occasion when the couple is fulfilling an important religious *cargo*, when it is deemed auspicious to get married in church. ❑

## PAYING THE EARTH

The persistence of Andean religion is most evident in the ceremony known as *pago a la tierra*, or "payment to the earth." Every significant event in an Andean village is preceded by a ritual offering to Pacha Mama (Mother Earth), which is carried out by a trained specialist.

A package containing tiny wrappers of llama fat, sugar, candy, and dozens more items, is laid out in combination with multiple *k'intus* – clusters of three coca leaves, and huayruro seeds. These offerings are accompanied by prayers and invo-

cations, then sprinkled with wine and alcohol, burned, and buried in a special place.

The specialist is usually a *pampamisayoc* – one known for his skill in performing the rituals – but on rare occasions the officiator might be an *altomisayoc* – one who communicates directly with the *apus*, the mountain spirits. These individuals acquire their vocation through dreams or vision quests, bathing in icy mountain lakes, and in special cases, being struck by lightning three times.

# A Day in the Village

**In order to appreciate Andean village life, imagine spending a full day with a family, from the early morning *mate* to a glass of *chicha* at the end of the day.**

**A** typical day begins in the darkness well before the first cockcrow, when someone stirs and turns on the radio. In the south central highlands around Cusco it will be tuned to Radio Tawantinsuyu, whose disk-jockeys broadcast their programs in Quechua and Quechua-Spanish and play *wayno* and *marinera*, the country music of Peru.

The woman of the family rises from her bed, a pallet of heavy, handwoven woolen blankets laid over a pile of sheepskins on the earthen floor of the adobe hut or, in more fortunate households, on a wooden bed-frame with a mattress fashioned of bundles of reeds. Her first task is to stir up the embers of yesterday's fire in the hearth and add a few sticks of firewood, to fetch water and put on a kettle for *mate*, a heavily sugared herbal tea. Breakfast, eaten at or before dawn, consists of *mate* with bread or with *mote* – boiled dried corn, one of the basic dishes of Quechua cuisine.

*Almuerzo* (lunch) is eaten before the men set out for their day's work, at an hour when most people would be having breakfast. It is usually a rich soup of vegetables and rice, served with boiled potatoes and perhaps a hot pepper sauce and a glass of *chicha*, a homemade corn beer. The man of the household is assisted by his sons and grandsons, and by neighbors who may owe him a day's work in exchange for one he has spent helping in their fields. The entire complement of laborers gathers in the kitchen to be fortified with bowls of soup and glasses of *chicha*.

As they leave the house, the woman begins cooking the third meal of the day, which comprises two or three dishes, with meat and potatoes and *mote*. This meal is a gesture of gratitude toward the men assisting her husband. At the same time, she tends to the children and animals, feeding children, chickens, and pigs, and milking the cow before it is led to pasture by one of the children, along with the sheep. Depending on the task being performed in the fields, she may be assisted by the wives of the men working with her husband, or perhaps only by her daughters and small children.

At midday, she carries the meal, and sometimes a bottle or two of *trago* (cane liquor) for the men, to the fields.

As the men plow or hoe the last rows of the field, the women may help, though more often they sit and watch, talking among themselves and sipping cups of *chicha*. At the end of the day, everything is gathered up and they all begin the walk home, with the children driving home the cattle and herds of sheep and goats. At home, the adults have another glass of *chicha* warmed over the fire, or a cup of *mate*. Eventually the fire is allowed to die, the pallets are laid out, and everyone settles down for a well-deserved night's sleep. ❑

**LEFT:** corn harvest. **ABOVE:** chopping firewood.
**RIGHT:** a mother and son in the highlands.

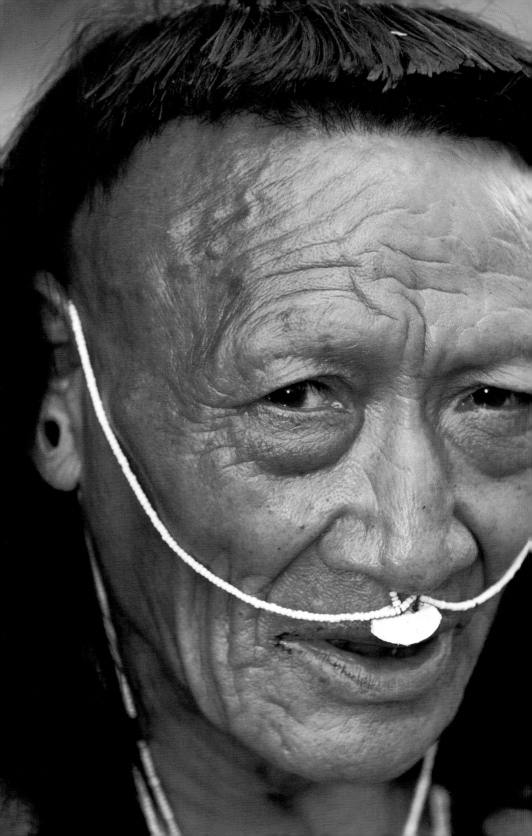

# PEOPLES OF THE AMAZON

Over the centuries Amazon peoples have faced many threats to their way of life, from bounty hunters and missionaries to oil companies and globalization. Miraculously, however, "uncontacted tribes" still exist

The indigenous peoples of the Amazon have long played a part in Peruvian history. According to Inca oral history, hordes of native Amazonians, known as Antis, were said to have climbed over the Andes and sacked the Inca capital of Cusco several times. The Inca fortress of Pisac is thought to have been an outpost protecting the capital from attack by jungle tribes to the east.

When the Incas and the Antis were not warring, trade was carried out between them, the former trading cloths, manufactured goods, and bronze axes in return for gold, feathers, exotic fruits, woods, animal skins, and medicinal plants.

## The lure of gold

After the collapse of the Inca empire, the Spaniards concentrated on mining wealth from the Andes and from coastal areas, and generally left the indigenous people alone. The few expeditions mounted into the jungle generally met with disaster. In some cases, such as among the Jivaro people then living in northern Peru, the Spaniards did establish towns and attempt to tax the Indians increasing quantities of gold.

*The Incas referred to the eastern quarter of their 4,500 km- (2,800 mile-) long empire as Antisuyo, and to the tribes who inhabited its jungles as the Antis – from which the name Andes derives.*

In 1599, however, the Jivaro people staged a massive revolt, burning and sacking the cities and slaughtering thousands of people. They then captured the Spanish governor, who was on a tax-collecting mission.

"They stripped him naked, tied his hands and feet and while some amused themselves with him, delivering a thousand castigations and jests, the others set up a large forge in the courtyard, where they melted the gold. When it was ready in the crucibles, they opened his mouth with a bone, saying that they wanted to see if for once he had enough gold. They poured it little by little, and then forced it down with another bone; and bursting his bowels with the torture, all raised a clamor and laughter," wrote one colonial chronicler.

Such victories were few for the indigenous peoples, however. As elsewhere, their greatest nemesis was not so much Spanish military force

**LEFT:** Yaminahua man. **RIGHT:** a Machiguenga woman prepares food for a celebration.

as the introduction of European diseases: their immune systems were totally unprepared for European pathogens. In the Inca empire there are thought to have been about 7 million *indígenas* at the time of the Spanish conquest, but 50 years later there were fewer than 2 million. The same pattern was repeated in the jungle, beginning in the zone of greatest contact – the Amazon and its major tributaries – and gradually working its way into deeper parts of the forest.

Slave-raiding, which started on Brazil's coast in the 16th century, gradually worked its way further into the Upper Amazon and Peru. Within 100 years of Francisco de Orellana's first descent *(see*

*below)*, the "teeming Indians" who had once thronged the Amazon's banks were nowhere to be seen. Tribes that hadn't been captured or wiped out by disease simply retreated further into the interior of the jungle.

The biggest incursion into Peru's Amazon, however, didn't occur until the rubber boom in the late 19th century. Almost overnight, the most isolated jungle rivers and streams were overrun by rubber tappers who carried the latest Winchester carbines. Rubber trees were few and far between – hence rubber-tapping demanded intensive labor. Entire villages were sacked to capture indigenous people for slave labor. In the case of especially hostile tribes, *correrías*, or armed raids, were carried out, in which villages were surrounded and their inhabitants slaughtered by the employees of the great rubber barons. Whole areas of the Amazon were thus wiped clear of native populations in a matter of decades. But in 1912 the rubber market began to collapse and, almost overnight, the rubber tappers withdrew. The remaining tribes were left alone except for occasional visits by missionaries.

## The bulldozers arrive

In the 1960s, Peru's government became concerned about the numbers of peasants moving from the Sierra to the coastal cities, yet was unwilling to enact the land reforms which might have kept them in their villages. It therefore chose the easier alternative, encouraging these people to move into the vast, unsettled Amazon that makes up two-thirds of the country. A north–south highway was partially bulldozed through the jungle to encourage settlement, and soon impoverished Peruvians began to pour in. New communities, some of them organized by religious sects anxious to make new converts, were established.

The systematic extraction of hardwood trees – mahogany, cedar, and caoba – repeated the pattern of the rubber boom, as day laborers bankrolled by wealthy patrons moved into the virgin forest looking for quickly extractable wealth. Gradually, one by one, isolated tribes were contacted by missionaries, woodworkers, or oil-drillers. At the start of the 20th century there were some 40 uncontacted tribes in the Peruvian Amazon, and there are now estimated to be 15 such tribes left, two on the northern border with Ecuador, and the remainder in the southeastern rainforest. Today most of Peru's 200,000 native Amazon peoples exist in varying stages of acculturation.

---

### FIRST CONTACT

The first of the conquistadors to get close to Peru's Amazonian tribes was Francisco de Orellana, who was part of Gonzalo Pizarro's expedition which left Quito in 1540 in search of El Dorado.

He later recalled: "We saw coming up the river a great many canoes, all equipped for fighting, gaily colored, and the men with their shields on, which are made out of the shell-like skins of lizards and the hides of manatees and of tapirs… they were coming on with a great yell, playing on many drums and wooden trumpets, threatening us as if they were going to devour us." Orellana survived and even learned enough words to talk to the native Amazonians.

## Indigenous cultures

In the 16th century there was considerable discussion in Europe as to whether the native peoples of the New World were "the sons of Adam and Eve," and hence deserving of the rights of real human beings. Finally, in 1512 a Papal Bull decreed that Amazonian Indians did, indeed, possess souls.

Alexander von Humboldt (1769–1859) was the most famous of the scientists who made exploratory trips into the Amazon; and eventually anthropologists began living among different tribes and recording a bewildering variety of cultures. The Amazon jungle is characterized as hav-

But tribes on the *varzea* – the more limited floodplain areas where the soil is renewed annually – did not fight among themselves, and instead had permanent villages running into thousands of inhabitants. Although battles were sometimes fought with the terra firma tribes in order to take slaves for work in *varzea* fields, population control did not exist. The necessity for carefully monitoring seasonal planting patterns and river fluctuations gave rise to an infrastructure which eventually came to include temples and priests, as well as complex systems of rules and food storage. And although the *varzea* tribes were the first to be hit by European contact and disease, Orel-

ing extremely poor soils, and game animals which, while diverse, are few and far between.

As a result, Amazon villages on the terra firma – the immense areas of land between the large rivers – are typically small (25 to 100 people), mobile, and widely spaced due to the jungle's low bioproductivity and the rapid exhaustion of the soil. In addition, these tribes almost universally practiced contraception techniques or infanticide in order to keep their populations down. Thus, the Jivaro penchant for head-shrinking was simply a variation on trophy head-taking and warfare patterns widely practiced throughout the Amazon.

**LEFT:** Yagua man with blowpipe. **ABOVE:** traditional weaving techniques of the Campa people.

lana's men, back in the mid-16th century, reported numerous *varzea* tribes living in towns with temples and roads leading off into the interior.

As a result of their similar habitats, the Amazon tribes had other features in common. Almost invariably, they viewed their forest and the animals in it as sacred and imbued with spirits. Most Peruvian tribes took hallucinogenic drugs such as *ayahuasca*, the "vine of death," which allowed them to see and interact with the powerful spiritual world. The forest was their provider – their mother – and was not to be abused.

Even today, most scientists concede that no one understands the jungle better than the remaining tribes. For thousands of years they have lived there harmoniously, and while they do not possess our own far more powerful technology, they have an understanding of, and reverence for, this most complex habitat on earth which the rest of the world lacks.

## A people left in limbo

Currently there are some 200,000 indigenous people in the Peruvian Amazon, who are divided into 53 different ethnic groups, speaking languages from 12 different linguistic families. Some groups, such as the Toyeri in southeastern Peru, were said to number several thousand at the turn of the 20th century but are composed of only a couple of individuals today. Others, such as the Machiguenga and Campa, living in the jungles north and east

of Machu Picchu, number tens of thousands.

Unlike Brazil, which has a governmental entity (FUNAI) to regulate indigenous affairs, Amazonian tribes in Peru have little governmental support. Legislation allowing indigenous communities to possess land was only finally passed in 1974. In the last two decades over 30 native organizations have sprung up to defend their rights.

Despite increasing organization, Peru's Amazon peoples continue to exist in a social and legal limbo. At best they are seen as a hindrance to a government whose goal is to "develop" the Amazon. The native peoples' limited territorial rights have not been helped by the government's threat to sell off state land that it considers "unculti-

vated." Indigenous groups have been encouraged to reject their own culture and become, in effect, rootless Peruvian citizens. Because of the Peruvian government's lack of interest in its people's history, foreign missionary groups have taken on

> *Different indigenous groups have gradually realized that only if they put aside historical enmities and organize themselves can their rights be defended or secured.*

the job of contacting and integrating Peru's Amazonian tribes into the national culture.

A US Protestant missionary group, the Summer Institute of Linguistics (SIL), has worked with dozens of tribes over the past 50 years, giving their languages a written form into which they hope to translate the Bible. Although SIL has nursed a number of tribes through contact-induced epidemics, it has been widely criticized for contributing to the destruction of cultural identities, and it now has a much lower profile.

Some cultures seem to withstand or assimilate acculturation better than others. The Shipibo people living along the River Ucayali have, despite long historical contact, maintained much of their traditional culture. They operate their own cooperative store (Maroti Shobo), where they sell and export their exceptionally high-quality weavings and pottery decorated with striking geometric designs using traditional materials and methods. In 1990 the Ashaninka tribe living on the Ene River retaliated fiercely against Sendero Luminoso guerrillas who had killed their chief. Other tribes, however, have less resistance to change and have lost their cultures within a very few generations.

## Contemporary problems

The greatest new pressure on indigenous groups comes from oil and gas exploration. Reserves in the northern jungles, which have been exploited for over three decades, are declining, and the Peruvian government has begun auctioning off new prospecting blocks along the eastern flanks of the Andes, including the Upper Amazon basin.

In Madre de Dios during the 1990s, a consortium headed by Mobil Oil attracted strong international criticism for entering the remote Las Piedras region, home to uncontacted native groups.

At that time Mobil also explored the Candamo valley, one of the most biodiverse areas known on Earth, finding significant, but at that time uneconomic, natural gas deposits. Mobil abandoned the concession, and the area was incorporated into the new Bahuaja-Sonene National Park. In 2007 the government attempted to remove this vital section from the park and lease it for drilling. National and international protests forestalled the initiative, but the incident demonstrated that the existence of national parks guarantees nothing.

To the west of the Parque Nacional Manu, where uncontacted Machiguenga and Yaminahua groups live, lies the enormous Camisea natural gas deposit. The pipelines that would run to the Peruvian coast, and possibly across to Brazil, could also prove to be a potential source of conflict.

Biological prospecting is another threat. Several large pharmaceutical companies have visited the region to assess the biological potential. Due to one of their discoveries, huge quantities of *uña de gato* (cat's claw), known to alleviate some symptoms of cancer and Aids, have been harvested in an uncontrolled manner and sold to outsiders.

On a more positive note, the land-titling program for indigenous communities proceeds apace, especially in central and northern Peru, with several million hectares titled in recent years.Change is inevitable, but it must be handled carefully, in partnership with the indigenous peoples, so that their culture is protected. ❏

In northern Peru the Achuar, a Jivaro-speaking group, have maintained their reputation as a fiercely independent people and refused to allow oil workers into their territory. Despite government threats and new laws stating that indigenous lands no longer belong to them by right, the impasse remains.

One notable success for local people was the exclusion of oil companies from the Pacaya-Samiria protected area. Native representative groups are having to learn fast how to deal with multinationals and persuade them to respect their lands and offer fair compensation.

---

**LEFT:** Shipibo craftswomen making items to sell to tourists. **ABOVE:** commercial logging poses a grave threat to the Peruvian Amazon and its people.

### No Contact

According to Survival International, there are an estimated 15 uncontacted indigenous groups in remote regions of the Peruvian Amazon. They are so rarely seen that the government agency overseeing petroleum resources has suggested that they were invented by conservationists to block oil exploration. However, in 2007 members of one such group were spotted and photographed from an aircraft in the Río de las Piedras region of southeastern Peru.

Contact with outsiders is potentially fatal for these people with no immunity to contagious diseases. Although protected by international law, their homelands are under threat from illegal loggers, and the government wants to open them up to oil and gas exploration.

# HOW CRAFTS HAVE ADAPTED

**Many of Peru's crafts have pre-Columbian origins, yet have incorporated new designs and contemporary motifs**

Long before the Incas, Peru was a land of craftspeople. Fine weaving found in the funeral bundles at Paracas, gold pieces worked by the Chimu people in northern Peru, and startlingly realistic Moche ceramics pay testimony to a people for whom work done with the hands was always important. In the Inca empire, specially chosen women dedicated their lives to such tasks as weaving delicate capes from the feathers of exotic birds. Metallurgy was also a high-status occupation long before the Spaniards arrived in the New World.

Fortunately, these artistic traditions were not obliterated by the European conquest, and today there are few places in Peru where handicrafts – some little changed from those of centuries ago, others modified for the tourist market – cannot be found.

## Ancient artifacts

Handicrafts played multiple roles in indigenous cultures that had no written language. Moche ceremonial cups were not simply for drinking: they told stories – depicting everything from festivities to

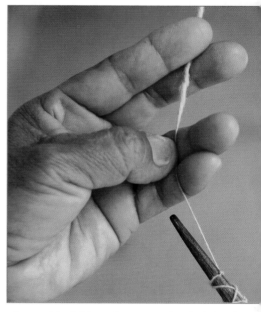

*Artisan stores in Lima stock a variety of handmade items of the highest quality, from every geographical region of Peru. Arrangements can be made for shipping, and prices are quite attractive.*

daily events. Through these finely detailed ceramics archeologists have identified diseases afflicting the Moche people, discovered that pre-Columbian soci-

eties punished thieves by amputating their hands (then fitted the reformed criminals with prosthetic limbs), and determined that they practiced rudimentary birth control. Likewise, the patterns on clothes woven in the highlands have unraveled some of the secrets of how the Aymara people lived.

The designs used in some clothes depicted the status of the wearer; other garments were used only for special fiestas, and still others had woven into them motifs that were important to the community. (Nowadays the designs include airplanes and other modern inventions.) After the Spanish conquest, handicrafts began to fuse the old and new ways, as Indian woodcarvers whittled statues of the Virgin Mary dressed like a *campesina*, or angels with Indian faces.

**PRECEDING PAGES:** crafts from the Uros Islands.
**LEFT:** handicrafts stall in the Colca valley.
**RIGHT:** making cotton thread the traditional way.

Some handicrafts are found all over the country, but in different colors and designs, such as the popular wall-hangings displayed in outdoor markets. Other items come from only one community or region. The decorative gilt-edged mirrors sold in Peru generally originate in Cajamarca; authentic ceramic Pucara bulls are crafted in Pupuja, near Puno; real Yagua jewelry comes only from the jungle area near Iquitos; but artisanal items from all over the country can be picked up in Lima. Some of the goods on sale, such as the Christmas tree ornaments and *arpilleras* – embroidered and appliquéd scenes – are produced by women's cooperatives in Lima's shantytowns. Visitors can find gold- and silver-rimmed goblets, carved leather bags, woolen goods of all kinds, jungle blowpipes, ceramics carrying both modern and antique designs, and a wealth of jewelry (*see Travel Tips, pages 336–7 for further information*). Bargaining is traditional here, and prices may be comparable with those in Cusco or the jungle.

Lima's Miraflores neighborhood is full of handicraft boutiques. Hand-knitted llama- and alpaca-wool sweaters and ponchos in modern styles, as well as carved wood and leather furniture, grace the store windows. This is also the best place to buy indigenous paintings, jewelry, and traditional gold and silver items.

## Gold and silver

Chile has its lapis lazuli and Colombia its emeralds, but the item most associated with Peru is gold, with silver and copper running close seconds. The 16th-century chronicles of Garcilaso de la Vega tell of the Europeans' first glimpse into the courtyard of Coricancha, the Temple of the Sun, in Cusco. Before them was a life-size scene in blindingly brilliant gold, perfect in detail down to the tiniest butterfly. Worked in gold were llamas, corn stalks, flowers, and birds. What remains in the Lima museums and the Museo Brüning in Lambayeque is but a fraction of the treasure that once existed. Today, gold and silver items, ranging from silver-rimmed crystal glasses to fruit bowls and candelabras, are available from a large number of boutiques in Lima (*see Travel Tips, page 337*).

The Spanish conquerors also found skilled craftsmen working gold and silver into finely turned jewelry and adornments. This tradition has not been lost, as evidenced by the intricate gold filigree produced in Catacaos outside Piura in the northern desert. These complicated pieces, which try an artist's patience and imagination, dangle from the ears of the townswomen, who claim that gold shines even brighter under the desert sun. These are the big, drooping earrings that women dancing the *marinera* wear. In San Jerónimo, near Huancayo in the central highlands, silver filigree is tooled into peacocks, fighting cocks, and doves.

Jewelry made from out-of-circulation coins is sold in the Plaza San Martín in Lima and around the Plaza de Armas in Cusco. Popular items are earrings, necklaces, and bracelets made from leather, and *sol* coins bearing the image of a llama. Informal jewelry-makers also sell jewelry made from chrysocolla (Andean turquoise) and hand-painted ceramic. But Peru's best-quality hand-painted ceramic jewelry is designed by the Association of Artisans of **Pisac Virgen del Carmen** in Pisac, about an hour outside Cusco.

## Woven tales

Although much of today's *artesanía* is more practical than illustrative and is geared toward tourists, some items still tell stories. Delicately woven belts sold in the Sunday market at Huancayo carry designs of trains, a tribute to the metal monster that connected that isolated highland city to the rest of the country. The wide belts are worn both for decoration and for support by the women who trudge the highlands with their children on their backs. Colors in the textiles and knitted goods on Taquile, the distinctive weavers' island in Lake Titicaca, can indicate the wearer's marital status or community standing. Some colors are used only on certain holidays.

Everywhere you go on Taquile Island you will see men knitting the distinctive woolen hats which they habitually wear. Legend has it that the rainbow Kuyichi, angered by the Taquile people, took away their color and left them in a world of grays and browns, but the people used their fingers to weave color back into their lives.

Taquile goods can be purchased from the co-operative on the island. Knitted items are available from a number of shops in Cusco, and some of the best bargains (although the quality is hit and miss) come from the women selling their wares in the bazaars in the streets off the main square of that city. Be wary of assurances as to whether the item is made of wool from sheep, llama, or alpaca (usually, they say it is baby alpaca, which local guides cynically refer to as "maybe alpaca"). Stop at some of the upmarket shops and feel the difference between wools from the three animals before starting your shopping.

Woolen cloth which is purported to be antique usually is not, as the damp highland climate does not allow wool to last indefinitely. Many weavers now use dark colors and ancient designs to give the impression that the textile has been around for centuries, but such cloth is no more antique than are the rustic-looking dolls that some unscrupulous sellers claim have come from ancient graves.

Knitted and woven goods are definitely the purchases most popular with visitors. Highland markets – including the big Sunday market in Pisac outside Cusco – abound with alpaca sweaters, llama rugs, small woolen bags called *chuspas* that are used to carry coca for chewing, blankets, and cotton cloth. In Cajamarca, native women in layered

**FAR LEFT:** an intricately embroidered hat.
**LEFT:** embroidered bands. **RIGHT:** jewelry made from shells and stones.

skirts called *polleras* walk down the streets with drop spindles dangling from their fingers.

The quality of woven items ranges from those made with crude wools still embedded with flecks of thistle, to the fine yarns and modern designs found in Lima's boutiques. Brilliant dyes made from seeds, herbs, and vegetables are often used to produce the typical vivid colors. Cloth may come from the Andean highlands, particularly Cusco, Puno, and Cajamarca, or from the jungle where the Conibo and Shipibo peoples weave cotton with designs incorporating serpents and Christian crosses.

Crafts from the Amazon region can be obtained in the Lima suburb of Miraflores, at the Antisuyo

store, or from the South American Explorers' Club (*see pages 122 and 348*).

## Basketware

From frigid Puno to the hot desert near Chiclayo, Peru is proud of its basket weavers. On Lake Titicaca, *totora* reed baskets and miniature boat souvenirs are produced by the indigenous people, who live in reed huts on reed islands. In the port of Huanchaco, on Peru's northern coast, the fishing boats themselves are woven from reed; tourists can purchase miniature versions. This coastal region is also known for its finely woven straw hats, similar to Panamas, and known as *jipijapas*. These hats, and white cotton ponchos, make up the traditional dress of the northern cowboys, or *chalanes*.

## Religious scenes

A very different kind of handicraft are the colorful *retablos*, originally made in Ayacucho, which derive from the small portable shrines brought to Peru by the conquistadors. Usually smaller nowadays, and tucked into decorated wooden boxes or the hollow of a reed, these depict busy scenes that may be solemn or comical in mood, depending on the artist's inclination. The subject matter used always to be religious, and often still is, but even the scenes showing religious processions are turned into rollicking fiestas, overflowing with figures made of wood, plaster, papier mâché, or clay, which may include a snoozing drunk, disruptive children, and wayward animals, or even artisans making hats or weaving cloth.

Superb *retablos* fashioned of hollow gourds are still a specialty in Ayacucho, as well as the traditional wooden ones, some tiny, some as much as 1 meter (3 ft) high. Wooden *retablos* may be found in most outdoor markets, but the most delicate ones – carved from the white and gray Huamanga stone some call Peru's marble – are found only in boutiques and cooperatives such as Artesanías del Perú. Actually a type of soapstone, Huamanga is carved into anything from matchbook-sized Nativity scenes to oversized chess sets – with figures of Incas and llamas replacing traditional kings and knights. Incidentally, much of what appears to be marble in Peru's churches is actually Huamanga stone.

Outside Lima and Cusco, the best places to purchase crafts are usually cooperatives or outdoor markets. In markets you are usually expected to bargain, and you generally get a good price. Depending on the size and vitality of the town, the markets may last only from pre-dawn to mid-morning once a week, or they may go on for days at a time. ❑

### FORBIDDEN GOODS

Beware of unscrupulous merchants selling antiques from grave sites: they are almost certainly fakes, and it is illegal to buy or take pre-Columbian antiques out of the country in any case. Much the same goes for goods made from vicuña. If the item really does contain vicuña fibers, which is unlikely, it may have been made in violation of international law. Don't even consider buying souvenirs made from the feathers, skins, or shells of rainforest creatures, many of which are endangered species.

# Pottery Culture

**As far back as 1500 BC, the ancient civilizations of Peru produced fine pottery in many different styles.**

The first major center of pottery production was the Chavín culture in the central Andean region from around 1000 to 300 BC. The pots they produced are often in the shape of images of the jaguar god and other mythical animals. Others show that the Chavín potters were masters in the use of subtle colors, producing geometric patterns in reds and browns. It was this early group which had already begun to make the typical "stirrup-spout" pottery, where handles from twin vessels rise to form one central spout.

From a similar period on the south coast come the wares produced by the Paracas culture. Here geometric designs predominate, and the colors used are much more vivid, with patterns made from incisions into the fired clay. Other pots show a wide range of fruits, vegetables, and plants that are of use to humans, suggesting they were symbolic food for the dead.

But the most astounding Peruvian pottery comes from the Moche people, who thrived on the northern coast from AD 100 to 700. Moche pottery is extraordinarily realistic, especially in the pots known as "portrait-head effigies," which display individual characteristics, emotions, and even diseases, as well as scenes from their mythology.

The most popular Moche pottery takes realism to even greater lengths in its *huacos eróticos* (erotic vessels) showing every combination of the sexual act. The Rafael Larco Herrera Museum in Lima has a particularly good collection *(see page 161)*. So realistic are these pots that they are also used by anthropologists to study the sexual behavior of the ancient Peruvians, and they are thought to be ceremonial rather than pornographic in intent. The Moche were also the first group in Peru to mass-produce their pottery thanks to the use of molds.

A very different style of pottery was produced to the south by the Nazca people. They were master potters, producing highly colored vessels with stylized geometric forms. Farther inland, the harsh mountain conditions often meant that the pottery traditions were not so developed. But the Huari people near Lake Titicaca produced some pots with remarkably realistic portraits and highly skilled ceremonial ware.

The Chimu people (AD 1000–1470) learned the secret of making black pottery by reducing the oxygen during firing. These were often burnished before firing to give them a characteristic silver sheen.

Inca pottery production was minimally sculpted and tended to employ repetitive geometric patterns with few naturalistic motifs. As with many things in

their empire, utility was the most important factor, so their most typical pottery is the large water containers or *aryballos* that could be strapped onto people's backs. The arrival of the Spaniards meant that much of this production was smashed, particularly anything considered idolatrous, and the old traditions and culture were lost. But for the tourist, some of the colonial wares are also very beautiful pieces, to be appreciated in their own right. ❑

**LEFT:** decorative hair clip. **ABOVE:** replica Moche tiles from Huaca de la Luna. **RIGHT:** ornate Moche jug.

# MUSIC AND DANCE

**The harps and pipes of the Andes are joined in a musical melting pot by African rhythms on the coast and salsa in the cities**

Whether we are aware of it or not, many of us became acquainted with Andean music in the late 1960s when Paul Simon and Art Garfunkel released a recording called *El Cóndor Pasa*, accompanied by a group called Los Incas. Its English lyrics were new, but the melody, with its haunting native tonalities, was written in 1913 by the Peruvian folk composer Daniel Alomías Robles. Los Incas, who later called themselves Urubamba, were in the vanguard of a movement to preserve the indigenous culture of the Andes, to present it proudly to the world beyond the borders of its native countries. Now this music is played by *conjuntos folklóricos* in settings – dimly lit restaurants and European theaters – which would be inconceivable to the indigenous peoples for whom it is simply a part of daily life.

The music can also be heard on the street corners, played by native musicians who depend on their talents – sometimes extraordinary – and other people's appreciation of them to gain a meager living. It can also be heard, far from the nightlife of the cities, in villages, where a less well-rehearsed group of musicians may accompany the private celebration of a wedding or a public dance performance during a festival, or where a lone shepherd might play a melancholy song to keep himself company on the mountainside.

## Ancient tradition

The instruments, the forms of the songs, and the lyrics have constituted a linked tradition of oral poetry in a culture that until recently had no written language. Its roots lie deep in Peru's pre-Columbian history. In the ruins and ancient

---

**LEFT:** dancers at the Virgen de la Candelaria festival in Puno. **RIGHT:** a marching band in Trujillo.

graveyards on the Peruvian coast you can still find small broken clay pan pipes and whistle-like flutes which produce pentatonic or diatonic scales, and sometimes other exotic scales that defy description by Western musical notation. They are tossed aside by *huaqueros* (grave robbers) in search of the fine textiles and pottery buried in the tombs. The Incas inherited an astonishing variety of wind instruments, including flutes and pan pipes of all types and sizes. Inca musicians also played conch-shell trumpets, and drums made from the skin of the Andean puma.

*Quenas* are notched end-blown flutes with a fingering style similar to that of a recorder. *Quenas* were often made of llama bone, but are now usually carved of wood. They produce a pentatonic scale which, to ears trained to a European musical tradition, has a distinctly melancholy tone to it. *Quenas* vary in size and pitch, so that each has its own reedy voice.

The pan pipes, called *antaras* or *zampoñas*, also vary in size, and there may be one set of four or five pipes, or three or four joined sets of eight or ten pipes, each of a different octave, to be played by a single musician with astonishing dexterity. *Antaras* or *zampoñas* are played by blowing across the end of the pipes, a technique which gives a breathy sound which may be as high-pitched as a bird call or almost as deep as a bassoon. They are often played in complex duets, with musicians alternating single notes of a quick, smooth-flowing melody, never missing a beat.

## Hispanic influence

To this ensemble the Spanish introduced strings, which native musicians readily adopted, inventing

> *Music accompanies most aspects of life in the Peruvian highlands, from mundane activities to solemn rituals and jubilant celebrations. Quechua people say that all new clothing is "for dancing."*

new, uniquely Andean instruments such as the *charango* (a small mandolin, scarcely the size of a violin, the body made from the shell of an armadillo), and the Andean harp with its great, boat-like, half-conical sounding-box. The instruments melded together perfectly; an ensemble of *quenas* and *zampoñas* weaves a rich tapestry of windy pentatonic harmony, and into this fabric are woven, like golden threads, the bright, quick sound of the *charango* – which may be strummed or plucked – and the voice of the harp.

The Andean harp has 36 strings spanning five octaves of the diatonic scale, though it is usually played in a pentatonic mode. Its deep sounding-box gives it a full, rich sound and a powerful bass voice, so that a bass line is usually played by the left hand while a melody or harmony is plucked by the right. Percussion is provided by a simple, deep-voiced frame drum – a *tambor* or a *bombo* – played with a stick with a soft, hide-covered head, or by an even simpler instrument called the *caja*, which, as its name implies, is a wooden box with a sound hole for reverberation, upon which the player sits to thump out a rhythm with the hands.

These, essentially, are the instruments which are played today – joined occasionally by a violin or accordion – though the drums now are more likely to be covered with goat than puma skin, and the eerie, wind-like call of the conch-shell trumpet may be heard only in the most traditional highland villages. There is also an element of improvisation – the composition of a village group may depend on who is available at the time.

The effect is magical, utterly characteristic of the Andes, evocative of high, windy passes, of the breeze blowing through the reeds of Lake Titicaca, of the dwarfing immensity of the mountains on a clear, bright, winter day.

The indigenous chronicler Huaman Poma de Ayala, in his massive descriptive history of life

### SORROWFUL LAMENT

The 16th-century chronicler Huaman Poma de Ayala offered the words of a song which he called a *huanca*: "You were a lie and an illusion, like everything which is reflected in the waters… Perhaps, if God approves, we shall one day meet and be together forever. Remembering your smiling eyes, I feel faint; remembering your playful eyes, I am near death…"

These lyrics are typical of the genre. Huaman Poma's example of the *yaravi* reveals the same universal themes of love, loss, and loneliness.

under both Inca and Spanish rule (*Nueva Crónica y Buen Gobierno*, written between 1576 and 1615), listed the names of a number of song forms, which are the ancestors of contemporary Andean music: the *yaravi*, the *taqui*, the *llamaya*, the *pachaca harahuayo*, the *aimarana*, the *huanca*, the *cachiva*, and the *huauco*.

Many of these he attributed to particular characters or activities – a shepherd's song (the *llamaya*), a song for victory in war, or for a successful harvest, or to accompany work in the fields. Of these names only the *yaravi* (or *haravi*) seems to have survived in common usage, but the lineage of contemporary Andean music can be

records, cassette tapes, and CDs, and played on the radio. The recording artists, like pop musicians and vocalists everywhere, become household names, and their careers are followed attentively, especially by the young. They come into fashion, then disappear, like groups anywhere in the world.

The primary form of popular music which has evolved from those traditional forms is the *wayno* (or *huayno* in its Spanish spelling, and pronounced "wino" in both), which constitutes a rich complex of poetry, music, and dance. The *wayno* is a rural music, a bit like bluegrass, and each region has developed its own characteristic variation. It is fundamentally dance music and is typically played in

traced back to at least the 17th century, and probably to pre-Columbian origins, perhaps the very songs named by Huaman Poma.

## Popular revival

Music never stands still, however. The traditional music, which has survived in relatively pristine form among native musicians, and in the past few decades enjoyed a renaissance as folklore, has also evolved a parallel, popular form. Today this is not only performed in the *chicherías* or *cantinas* frequented by both urban and rural Quechua-speakers, but is also recorded in sound studios on

**LEFT:** playing the *quena* (flute).
**ABOVE:** drummers at a festival in Puno.

### SALSA FEVER

Alongside its traditional music, Peru has a pop culture, although most of it is imported. Rock, pop, and reggae – both original and translated versions of US, British, and Spanish songs – are heard on the radio and in clubs, bars, and discos. Most popular of all, though, is salsa, which originated in the Caribbean but is now heard throughout the continent – and beyond. Go to a *salsateca* and watch Peruvians dancing to this infectious music, or shed your inhibitions and try it for yourself.

2/4 time with an insistent, infectious rhythm; the dance is usually performed by couples, their hands joined, with much stamping of the feet to cries of "*Más fuerza! Más fuerza!*" ("Harder! Harder!").

But the *wayno* is also a literary form, representing a tradition of oral poetry which goes back at least to the time of the Incas. The *wayno* is essentially a love song, but a melancholy and melodramatic one: a song of love found and lost or rejected, a song of rivalry and abandonment, and of separation and wandering in strange lands far from home. The modern *wayno* is clearly a direct descendant of the songs of Huaman Poma's day.

Melodramatic as they may be, however,

## Música criolla

Peruvian music cannot be fully understood without looking at the contributions made by the country's black population. The first black people to arrive in the Americas came on Christopher Columbus's first voyage, in 1492. They were brought to the New World as servants of the conquistadors and at first enjoyed a measure of liberty. But by the end of the 16th century, shiploads of blacks were being brought in from various regions of Africa as slave labor.

In Peru – where slavery was not as pervasive as it was in some other parts of Latin America – Africans were brought in to raise the *plantaciones*

anthologies of lyrics disclose a sophistication of poetic form and poetic voice, ranging from tragic to ironic to comic, which is remarkable in a completely oral tradition. *Waynos* to this day are learned and preserved within a social context, transmitted informally and usually anonymously, from musician to musician, in the setting of private celebrations or great religious festivals in every village of the Peruvian Sierra.

The *wayno* will certainly continue to evolve; today an urbanized form of this fundamentally rural music is developing, in which the traditional naturalistic motifs are being replaced by abstract, more universal terms. But, in the light of its long history, it seems pretty safe to guess that this music will survive for nearly as long as the Andes themselves.

(crops) of cotton, sugar cane, and grapes grown on the central coast. They were concentrated mainly in places like Lima, Chincha, and Cañete, where there are still significant black populations today.

Their masters, not content with working them for punishingly long hours in the fields, made their slaves entertain them at parties and other social occasions, by playing instruments or dancing. Because the slaves came from different parts of Africa, their music thus became a mixture of these different regional forms, gradually blended with Andean and Spanish rhythms, to emerge as *música criolla*.

**LEFT, ABOVE, AND RIGHT:** dancers at the Festival de la Marinera in Trujillo.

Slavery in Peru lasted until the republican period, in the mid-19th century, when President Ramón Castilla granted slaves their freedom. But although they were legally free, blacks were still marginalized. They lived in what were known as *palenques* (an Antillan name which means "an inaccessible place"): isolated villages which became focuses of resistance to the abuse that their people still suffered. Athough geographically isolated, the *palenques* were linked to the city markets, establishing interaction between the outcasts and society.

This interaction helped the Afro-Andean population to develop a musical culture. Their music was a way of expressing resistance, and asserting themselves in a situation where they were otherwise dominated and suppressed. Music was also the practice of an art and, just as importantly, a way of having fun. The *panalivio*, or "bread relief," was a musical form with a lamenting tone, in the vein of the black music of the southern United States, which reflected the social conditions under which the blacks of the time lived, and which ended in an upbeat tempo. From this music arose other rhythmical variations such as the *festejo* and the *resbalosa*.

## Dance variety

Dance, naturally, grew up alongside Afro-Peruvian music. The *zamacueca* stands out as the unmistakable precursor of the stately and elegant *marinera*, which has become the national dance, with *limeña* and *norteña* versions. In and around Trujillo, you may well stumble across one of the frequent *marinera* dance competitions. The Festival de la Marinera in January is the biggest one.

Varieties of black music and *zapateo* (a form of rhythmic tapping) can often be seen and heard in various parts of Lima and in Chincha, where it is especially popular. (Chincha's Fiesta Negra in February is a good time to hear all kinds of Afro-Peruvian music.) The guitar, the *cajón* or *caja*, sometimes a donkey's jawbone and other instruments combine to create rhythms that accompany the *zamacueca* and the *festejo*.

Another typical dance is *El Alcatraz*, in which dancers holding lighted candles attempt to inflame their partners. A *conjunto* called Perú Negro is one of the most popular dance groups in the country, while black singers such as Susana Baca and Eva Ayllón have gained numerous fans since the 1990s. ❑

# FESTIVALS AND FUSION

**Peru's festivals are a fusion of Catholic, Inca, and early agricultural rites, celebrated with high spirits and a fitting sense of drama**

In any Andean community at any time of the year, you may stumble on a village fiesta. These local events are colorful occasions, always accompanied by music, dance, vivid dress, and large quantities of food and *chicha*. Coastal festivals can also be lively, especially in Chincha, where the black population stages the Fiesta Negra in February with Afro-Peruvian music and dance. Major festivals, like the Fiestas Patrias in late July, commemorating Peru's Independence, are celebrated nationwide. Others are specific to one location, like Lima's celebration of El Señor de los Milagros, which sees thousands of people following a procession headed by a black figure of Christ on the Cross.

One of the reasons Peru's festivals are so exciting is that they blend the rites of the Catholic Church with those which go back much farther – to Inca times or the veneration of Pacha Mama, Mother Earth. A good example of this is the Inti Raymi celebration in Cusco. The Festival of the Sun had been a huge event under the Incas, and Catholic leaders, realizing it could not be stamped out, nudged it to June 24, the day of John the Baptist, and everyone was happy.

Pre-Lent Carnival, which was grafted onto pagan celebrations in Europe, is widely celebrated, very noisily, with lots of water hurling. La Virgen de la Candelaria (Candlemas), in February, is another event where Catholic and pre-Columbian rites mingle, particularly in Puno, where the *diablada*, a devil dance involving grotesque masks, is the main event.

**ABOVE**: the Virgen de la Candelaria festival is known for its grotesque masks and dancing devils.

**ABOVE:** during the Virgen de la Candelaria festival, local people dance in honor of Mamacha Candelaria, the patron saint of Puno.

**BELOW:** the Inca Festival of the Sun, or Inti Raymi, is celebrated every year in Cusco on June 24. The Inca Sapa is carried on a golden throne from Qoricancha to the fortress of Sacsayhuamán followed by an entourage of priests, noblemen, and soldiers.

## LORD OF THE EARTHQUAKES

Celebrated on the Monday of Holy Week, this is a major event in Cusco. Our Lord of the Earthquakes (Nuestro Señor de los Temblores), the image of Christ on the Cross which hangs in the cathedral, is credited with saving the city from destruction during a major earthquake in 1650. The statue is carried through the streets on an ornate silver litter. Red flower petals, symbolizing the blood of Christ, are scattered in its path and thousands of *cusqueños* join the procession, along with civic leaders, priests, nuns, and military representatives.

When a severe earthquake rocked the city in 1950, the image was set up in the Plaza de Armas, while townspeople begged the Lord to stop the tremors. Like many other festivals, this is a mixture of superstition, genuine religious feeling, and enjoyment of ritual for its own sake, and it is a splendid occasion.

**Above:** each May thousands of people, some dressed as bears, make the pilgrimage to Quoyllur Riti, a sacred glacier in the Cordillera Vilcanota. Pilgrims leave miniature models of things they desire in the hope that the Lord of the Snow Star will help them realize their dreams.

**Left:** a festival dancer wearing brightly-colored shawls and a traditional multi-layered skirt known as a *pollera*.

# FUSION OF FLAVORS

From the fish-based cuisine of the coast to the substantial, spicy dishes of the highlands and the fruits of the jungle, Peruvian cooking offers plenty of tempting tastes

Peru's different geographical regions, its varied climates, and its mixture of peoples combine to provide a cuisine that is among the most extensive and interesting in South America. This food appears not only on dining tables but is also immortalized in pre-Hispanic pottery, which sometimes takes surprisingly realistic forms of fruits and vegetables, in the centuries-old weavings found in many of the burial grounds that have been excavated, and in wall paintings.

## Fruits of the sea

The best dishes in Lima and other coastal cities are based on the abundant seafood available. The collision of the Humboldt and other currents means the Peruvian sea is full of the plankton that larger fish eat, providing fishermen and cooks with a great variety to choose from.

The most typically Peruvian dish is *ceviche*, a plate of raw white fish in a spicy marinade of

*The Paracas area is known for its fresh seafood, used in dishes such as* chupe de camarones, *a thick shrimp stew, and* tacu tacu, *an invigorating mix of different shellfish with rice and beans.*

lemon juice, onion, and hot peppers. Each restaurant has its own marinade recipe, and when the fish is freshly caught, *ceviche* can be delicious. It is best to avoid buying the cheaper versions sold in the street, however. *Ceviche* is traditionally served with corn and sweet potato, and there are many variations on the basic formula, often with the addition of shellfish in *ceviche mixto.*

**LEFT:** oysters fresh from the Pacific. **RIGHT:** delicious fruits are grown in the Peruvian *selva* (jungle).

Among the best shellfish are *camarones* (shrimp), *calamares* (squid), and *choros* (mussels), all of which are prepared in a number of ways. Any dish listed as *a lo macho* means it comes with a shellfish sauce.

Another cold fish recipe is *escabeche de pescado*, cold fried fish in a sauce of onions, hot peppers, and garlic, adorned with olives and hard-boiled eggs. The king of fresh sea fish is the *corvina* or white sea bass, together with another excellent white fish, the *chita,* and the *lenguado* or sole. These are usually served *a la plancha* (grilled) or with any number of sauces.

In Cusco and other towns of the highlands, *trucha* or rainbow trout is very plentiful, as they are farmed in many rivers and lakes. Less common but more distinctive is *pejerrey* or kingfish, served steamed with potatoes and yucca.

In the jungle region, the main ingredient of many dishes is fish from the Amazon and its tributaries. The most succulent is the prehistoric looking *paiche* fish, with its abundant soft white flesh. Broiled or grilled, it may be accompanied by *palmito* (strips of soft palm heart that look like ribbons of pasta), yucca, and fried bananas; or it may be wrapped in banana leaves and then baked on coals to make a dish known as *patarashca*. Other fish worth trying in the jungle region are the *zúngaro* and even the *piranha*, which despite their vicious reputation are soft and tender on the plate.

As well as the seafood, the cities and towns of the coastal desert region offer hearty dishes with chicken, duck, or goat. A favorite on the northern coast is *seco de cabrito* (roasted kid goat), often cooked with fermented *chicha* and served with beans and rice. A similar recipe is used to cook lamb, which becomes *seco de cordero*. A popular way of serving chicken is *ají de gallina,* a rich concoction of creamed chicken and a touch of hot peppers served on boiled potatoes.

In Lima, especially during the gray winter months, the *limeños* often prepare a thick vegetable stew called *sancochado* served with meat. Another hearty meal common in the capital is *cau cau*, tripe cooked with beans and potatoes and served with rice.

## Spicy peppers

Hot peppers are grown all over the country and are used to add spice to everything from fish to stews. On the north coast, where fish is an important part of the diet, sauces of hot peppers and onions are heaped on top of the main dish or offered as accompaniment in small side bowls. In the Amazon, where the food tends to be less spicy, people dip jungle vegetables and yucca into fiery pepper sauces.

But it is in the highland region where *picante* (as the hot, spicy taste of peppers is known) reaches an art form. The degree of spiciness depends on the type of *ají* or chile pepper used. These can vary from the moderately sharp taste that novices can tolerate to the screamingly hot *rocoto* peppers whose fire-engine red is not only decorative but a warning signal. Tourists beware: as in Mexico, locals love to confuse newcomers with the strength of the *picante*, which can destroy your tastebuds for the rest of the day.

It is thought that early farmers in Peru grew about five species of hot peppers, which were transported over the years to Central America, the Caribbean, and Mexico. Christopher Columbus, who was searching for the black pepper of the eastern isles when he came upon hot chiles in the Caribbean, may be responsible for their English name. "There is much *axí,* which is their pepper, and it is stronger than pepper, and the people won't eat without it for they find it very wholesome," he wrote in his journal in 1493. The hot peppers he brought back were an immediate success in Spain and the rest of Europe.

Restaurants in Arequipa vie with each other to serve their version of *rocoto relleno* (stuffed peppers), which are delicious with fresh local cheese.

### GOLDEN GRAINS

A pre-Columbian legend describes the dismemberment of the god Pachacámac. His teeth were changed into grains of corn, and his genitals into yucca and sweet potatoes, thus providing the earth with food, so that his people would not go hungry. Another legend tells the story of an Inca noble who fell into a well while walking. His father, the sun god, looked down sadly on his imprisoned son, but could not intervene to save him. The sun god's tears of gold reached the earth, irrigated it, and made the fields flourish.

However, tourists unaccustomed to hot spices should beware: eating too much *picante* can cause a kind of diarrhea known as *jaloproctitis*; this is why Peruvians do not serve it to small children, nursing mothers, or the infirm.

## A world staple

The small subsistence farms of the Peruvian highlands are home to a vegetable now found all over the world: the humble *papa* or potato. Several hundred varieties are cultivated, including the yellow *limeña*, the small purple potato, and the dried *chuño*, which is frozen in the harsh climate around Puno and Lake Titicaca. These potatoes can be

*estofado* (a stew of chicken, corn, carrots, and tomatoes) as well as the ever-present *lomo saltado* (strips of beef with onions, tomatoes, and fried potatoes). The *papa amarilla* (yellow potato) is considered the best.

Peru's highland soil also produces other tubers that form part of the national cuisine. There is the *olluco* vegetable, which can range in colour from red to orange, and has a taste like new potatoes. It is often shredded and served with dried llama meat or *charquí* (beef jerky) in a stew. In a few places you may find *oca* or *arracacha* served instead of the usual potato. The sweet potato or *camote* is also plentiful and full of taste.

stored for up to four years. In some areas around the lake, the Aymara still ritually stuff potatoes with coca leaves and bury them as a tribute to the earth mother, Pacha Mama, in the hope of a bountiful next harvest.

Potatoes are an essential part of most of the filling one-pot dishes common in highland cuisine. A famous dish named after them is *papas a la huancaína*, a creamy concoction of potatoes, peppers, and boiled eggs. Or they can be served with a peanut sauce in *papa ocopa*, or simply stuffed with meat, onions, boiled eggs, and raisins for *papa rellena*. They also take their place in

**LEFT:** a demonstration of Peruvian cooking.
**ABOVE:** making *ceviche mixto*.

### NEW WAVE FROM THE ANDES

The experimental and evolving trend of *novoandino* cuisine has fueled Peru's current "gastronomy boom." Highland ingredients once disdained as "Indian food" have been discovered by the Lima elite, gourmet tourists, and health-food cognoscenti. Upscale restaurants now serve such delights as the high-altitude quinoa grain, along with small and delicious highland potatoes, *aguaymanto*, an acid wild Andean fruit, and alpaca meat, esteemed for its low fat and cholesterol content.

## Ritual food

Corn was introduced to Peru from Central America many hundreds of years ago. It was the most sacred food for many of its peoples before the Spanish invasion, and is found in nearly as many colors and varieties as the potato. The fermented corn drink *chicha* is made into a cloudy and extremely strong beer that is ceremoniously poured onto the ground during planting and harvest festivals, and then drunk in enormous quantities. Purple corn is converted into a refreshing non-alcoholic drink known as *chicha morada*, and turned into the purple dessert called *mazamorra morada*.

Corn is cooked and presented in many ways. *Choclo*, boiled large-grained ears of corn, are sold on every street corner, usually with slices of cheese and *picante* sauce. Corn kernels are also part of stews such as *chicharrón con mote,* with pork and tomatoes. Fried corn kernels called *cancha* are a common snack served before meals, or to nibble with beer or *pisco.*

Before the arrival of the Spaniards, the different highland civilizations in Peru cultivated many other grains. Some of them, including the purple-flowered *kiwicha* and the golden quinoa – both kinds of amaranth – were banned by the Vatican on religious grounds, and disappeared from the Peruvian diet for several centuries. They are now being rediscovered as healthier variants to the potato, and are being used once more in breads, cookies, soups, and salads.

## Jungle fare

As well as the plentiful fish of the Amazon and other tropical rivers in Peru, the jungle area offers many other culinary delights. There is *jabalí* or wild boar, and other game. There are the *juanes* – a kind of *tamale* stuffed with chicken and rice – and turtle soup. In the Amazon, bananas replace potatoes as the staple, with many different kinds for frying, boiling, or eating fresh. The other staple is yucca, which accompanies most meals, and is also fermented to make a strong alcoholic drink called *masato.*

## Acquired tastes

There are two dishes served throughout Peru which are very popular, although visitors are often taken aback when offered them. Every street corner and many restaurants offer *anticuchos* – skewers of meat which were originally grilled cattle and pig hearts, but can now include even pieces of fish and vegetables. If you are invited to a Peruvian barbecue, this is more than likely what you will be served. Around Cusco, a choice delicacy is the *cuy* or guinea pig. This is often presented deep-fried like Southern chicken, and the taste is somewhere between chicken and rabbit.

## Sweet teeth

Peruvians love to finish a meal with a sweet dessert. Often this will be something that is part of the culinary tradition brought over from Spain. Favorites include *manjar blanco*, a kind of fudge made from boiled milk and sugar; *cocadas* (coconut macaroons); or the typically Spanish

---

### RESTORATIVE DISH

Fish is traditionally believed to have rejuvenating powers, and *aguadito* – a thick rice and fish soup – was traditionally served to all-night revelers after the three-day wedding celebrations once common along the coast. An *aguadito* may also be served to those guests who just won't go home after a party that continues into the wee hours of the morning. At vendors' kiosks in working-class areas of Lima, a sign promising *aguadito para recuperar energía* (*aguadito* to recuperate energy) can often be found.

*churros*, pastry dough similar to donuts fried and eaten with honey or chocolate.

During the October celebrations honoring the Lord of Miracles (El Señor de los Milagros) another Spanish delicacy, *turrones,* are sold everywhere. In the summer months, cones of crushed ice *(paletas)* flavored with fruit syrups (and optionally topped with condensed milk) are sold on street corners – but be careful with them, as the water used to make the ice may upset travelers' stomachs.

Other common sweets include *yuquitas,* deepfried yucca-dough balls rolled in sugar; *picarones,* donuts coated in honey; and *tejas,* a sweet biscuit filled with *manjar blanco.* One of the oldest traditional desserts is the crunchy cookie known as *revolución caliente,* which dates from the independence era in the early 19th century. Street sellers call out: "*Revolución caliente, música para los dientes*" ("Hot revolution, music for the teeth").

As well as these sweet concoctions, Peru has a wonderful variety of fruit, served fresh or as juices *(jugos).* Passion fruit or *maracuyá* is perhaps best as a juice, but the jungle region also provides mangoes, papaya, and other tropical fruit. *Lúcuma,* a small brown fruit found only in Peru, has a strong, nutty, exotic taste, and is used in ice creams and sorbets. Another delicate tropical fruit is the *chirimoya,* or custard apple, while the highlands supply *tuna,* the fruit of the prickly pear cactus, which can be eaten alone or as part of a salad.

## Thirst-quenchers

As with other Latin American countries, it was the Spanish missionaries who first established vineyards in Peru. But until recently the Peruvian wine industry has not been as developed as those of Argentina and Chile, and only a few of the vineyards around Ica – the Tacama, Tabernero, and Ocucaje labels for example – are of any note. Most of the grapes are used instead for making *pisco,* which in turn is the basic ingredient for the Peruvian national drink, *pisco sour.* This cocktail is a mixture of *pisco,* egg whites, lemon juice, and sugar, plus a few drops of bitters. The result seems innocuous, but can be explosive. So important is *pisco* to national identity, that in 1988 the Peruvian government declared it to be part of the "cultural heritage of the nation."

*Mate de coca,* tea made from coca leaves, is

served in hotels and restaurants throughout the highland region as an antidote to altitude sickness. *Manzanilla* or camomile tea is also a popular way to finish a meal. Coffee usually comes as a concentrated liquid known as *esencia,* which is then diluted with boiling water. High-quality coffee is grown in Peru; the best is from Chanchamayo, and one of the best brands is Café Britt.

Carbonated drinks are called *gaseosas,* and the extremely popular local one is known as *Inca Kola.* There are many lager-type beers *(cerveza),* including brands such as Pilsen, Cristal, Arequipeña, and Cusqueña – the last generally considered by connoisseurs to be the best in Peru. ❑

### CHINESE FOOD, PERUVIAN STYLE

Nineteenth-century Chinese immigrants brought their cooking style to Peru, and it is now embedded in the Peruvian gastronomic repertoire. Even the ubiquitous *lomo saltado* is derived from a Chinese dish. Chinese restaurants are known as *chifas,* and they are found all over the country. Choosing a dish can be bewildering, as many *chifa* menus list their offerings in Chinese. *Arroz chaufa,* sautéed rice with chopped meats and vegetables, and *wantan cam lu,* a sweet, sour pork-based dish, are reliable choices.

**LEFT:** hot peppers and bags of *salsa picante.*
**RIGHT:** mixing a *pisco sour.*

# ANDEAN ADVENTURES

**Peru offers superb opportunities for outdoor activities, such as trekking, mountaineering, horseback riding, and river-rafting, with organized excursions to suit a range of abilities, time frames, and budgets**

Few places in the world allow you to drive by car in one day across almost rainless deserts near sea level, climb 5,000 meters (16,500 ft) to frigid regions of permanent snow, and then descend again to hot and dense tropical rainforests. But this is Peru.

In an area about the size of Britain, France, and Spain combined, Peru contains 84 of the world's 101 known ecological life zones. With so much geographical, cultural, and biological diversity, and with wild rivers, huge coastline, and a country where much of the mountain landscape is open, unfenced, and criss-crossed with trails, the range of possible adventure experiences is almost limitless.

Trekking is the nation's first and foremost adventure activity, the headline hike being the incomparable Inca Trail to Machu Picchu, but with dozens of other popular routes scattered across the country and winding their way across the high passes and astounding scenery of the tropical Andes. Major areas for trekking are the Cusco region and the Cordillera Blanca, with Arequipa and the Colca canyon, Chachapoyas, and mountain areas closer to Lima also growing in popularity.

Rafting and kayaking are well-established and exciting options on some of the dramatic Amazon tributaries, such as the Apurimac and the Tambopata, or on some of the Pacific watershed rivers, such as the deep Cotahuasi canyon, or the easier waters of the Rio Cañete near Lima.

Mountain biking has mushroomed in popularity in recent years, especially in the Cusco region, while horseback riding, paragliding, and mountaineering all have their devotees and favorite

areas. Certain spots on the coast have some of the world's finest waves, worshipped by congregations of devoted surfers.

Two main climate patterns reign in Peru: the coastal cycle, and the mountain/rainforest cycle. The southern-hemisphere winter brings low cloud and drizzle to Lima and the central coast from about April through November, when the ocean is cold with stiff winds most of the way to the border with Ecuador. December brings warmer weather and sunshine, and city dwellers take to the beaches. In the mountains winter (May to October) is dry and sunny, though cold at night, and this is the season for most adventure activities. November and December bring on the highland rains, which grow intense from January through

---

**PRECEDING PAGES:** surfer off Máncora beach.
**LEFT:** camping in the Cordillera Huayhuash.
**RIGHT:** kayaking through one of Peru's many canyons.

March. Some trekking on the better-maintained trails is possible during these months, but stay away from the remoter areas, or be prepared for highway washouts, mud-clogged trails and major delays. The rainforest is always hot, but with much less rain in the winter months.

## Trekking

Adventurers should be very aware of altitude as a potential cause of suffering, disappointment, and occasionally serious problems. Andean trekking routes often cross high passes ranging from 4,000 to 5,000 meters (13,200 to 16,500 ft). Before you set out, know what altitudes you will

be facing, and above all, take time to acclimatize and exercise gently at a high-altitude locations such as Cusco or Huaraz before beginning any strenuous activity.

The condition that trekkers often suffer, Acute Mountain Sickness, known locally as *soroche*, features headaches, nausea, insomnia, and shortness of breath. At higher altitudes this can sometimes turn into pulmonary edema or cerebral edema, when fluid collects in the lungs or brain respectively. Both of these are dangerous and potentially fatal conditions. Symptoms are a dry, persistent cough, excessive fatigue, cyanosis (purple lips and fingernails), mental confusion, incoherence, and lack of coordination. Group members should look out for these signs in others, since the victim is usually unaware of the problem. Any appearance of these symptoms should be treated as an emergency, and the victim must be evacuated to a significantly lower altitude immediately.

No skill is required for trekking, but some degree of fitness is recommended. Hat, sunblock, sunglasses, raingear, flashlight, extra batteries, insect repellent, layers of both lightweight and warm clothing, a good pair of walking shoes or boots, and a good sleeping bag are essential items to take with you. Need for a tent and multi-fuel or camping gas stove (wood fires are both impractical and unecological) and a first-aid kit, depends on whether or not you decide to sign up with one of the numerous agencies offering trekking services. These vary a lot in price and quality of service. As a rule of thumb, if time is your constraint, sign up with an outfitter; if money, go independent, although this is not an option on the Inca Trail.

Most essential trekking equipment can be bought or rented in Cusco or Huaraz, but not elsewhere. When hiring equipment be sure to assemble, check, and test every item thoroughly before setting out. In Cusco brand-name lightweight trail boots can be purchased at Molinopampa, a sort of smuggler's supermarket near the airport.

Trekking food can be bought in the large towns and cities, but is not readily available on trails, so carry all you need for your trek. Packet soups, pasta, and noodles can be purchased in stores and markets, along with dried fruits and grains. Most common spices are also available.

All drinking water should be sterilized with purification tablets, iodine solution, or a filtering pump. Powdered flavorings to disguise the unpleasant taste of treated water are available in stores.

### SOUTH AMERICAN EXPLORERS' CLUB

For independent travelers planning more than a week or two in Peru, this valuable non-profit information and support network is highly recommended. Their clubhouses in Lima and Cusco have an invaluable stock of maps, guidebooks, and trail reports. The staff are friendly and more than willing to give advice both to beginners and experts.

SAE members receive a quarterly magazine, use of the library, and other perks, such as gear-storage facilities. *(See page 348 for contact details.)*

## The Cusco region

The **Ausangate Loop** is a well-known high-altitude classic of dramatic mountain scenery and cultural encounters with traditional Quechua alpaca and llama herders, making a full circle around Ausangate (6,380 meters/20,930 ft), the highest mountain in southern Peru. Beginning and ending with glorious open-air hot springs, no campsite is much below 4,000 meters (13,200 ft), and two of the passes are at around 5,000 meters (16,500 ft). Huge glacial moraines, raw cliffs and slopes in multicolored mineral shades, and lakes in intensely varied blues make this an unforgettable five-day journey. The road from Cusco to

*All popular trekking routes are served by villagers offering mules, horses, or portering services. Horses are forbidden on the Inca Trail, however, where all groups use porters.*

## The Inca Trail

The **Inca Trail** to Machu Picchu *(see pages 292–303)* was for years *the* hike to do in Peru. Nothing else can compare with the startling variety of scenery, Inca ruins, and ecological zones, packed into three or four days of exquisite hiking. There is also a popular short one-day ver-

sion of the trail that feeds in from the railroad near Machu Picchu.

However, the overwhelming numbers of hikers on these ancient paths have forced authorities to restrict access, raise costs, and impose strict regulations. Today would-be trekkers must reserve months ahead and sign up with a licensed operator. Though only the fortunate few can do the Inca Trail these days, the new limits have had one fortunate side effect: hikers are spreading out into undeveloped and unrestricted areas, and discovering scores of less well known but wonderful treks.

**LEFT:** trekking in the Cordillera Blanca.
**ABOVE:** the ancient Inca Trail.

the trailhead at Tinqui is part of the new Trans-Oceanic highway to Brasil, and is much improved, taking only about four hours.

The back-door route to Machu Picchu, from **Salcantay to Santa Teresa**, was promoted by local guides when Inca Trail permits grew scarce. It has some of the glory of the Inca Trail, and crosses a higher, more spectacular mountain pass between Humantay and Salcantay (6,270 meters/20,570 ft), two of the highest peaks in the Cordillera Vilcabamba. Starting at Soraypampa after a three-hour drive from Cusco, you cross the high pass on the first day of this three- or four-day trek, and the rest is downhill, descending from frigid wasteland through grasslands, dwarf forest, and tropical cloud forest as it descends the Santa Teresa valley. From here there are road and rail links to the town of Aguas Calientes, near Machu Picchu. A variant adds an extra day over an Inca highway through the ruins of Patallacta, with spectacular views eastward to Machu Picchu.

Both the Ausangate region and the Salcantay route now offer the option of lodge-to-lodge hiking – the latter a rather high-end private service, the Ausangate a mid-level cooperative effort involving local communities.

A comparatively recent offering, **Choque-quirao** is a spectacular five-day round-trip journey to an Inca site which rivals Machu Picchu

It is possible to continue this hike northward into the Vilcabamba region, over the Minas Victoria pass, then either east over Puerto Yanama (4,700 meters/15,400 ft) to Machu Picchu or north following imposing Inca stone highways over the Choquetacarpo pass (4,600 meters/15,080 ft) to Huancacalle and the ruins of Vitcos: about 10–12 days in total, in either case. If trekking only to Choquequirao, using pack-horses, you must retrace your steps to Cachora. Brave souls carrying their own backpack or using porters can take the steep route out via San Ignacio and Huanipaca.

North of Cusco, beyond the Urubamba valley,

for its setting. The journey begins with a scenic five-hour drive west from Cusco across the Apurimac River to the trailhead at the canyon-rim town of Cachora, with optional visits (which add time) to fascinating Inca sites at Limatambo and Sayhuite along the way. A nearly 1,800-meter (6,000-foot) descent into the hot semi-desert floor of the Apurimac canyon is followed by a 1,500-meter (5,000-foot) ascent to the cloud forest site of Choquequirao. Thought to have been a royal estate of the emperor Topa Inca, this is a sprawling, well-preserved site, with superb, massive terracing features, including a set of terraces inlayed with 22 large llama figures in white stone. Terrain is very steep, and a measure of fitness is called for.

lies a broad region of mountains known as the **Lares region**, where traditional Quechua people herd their llamas and alpacas. At the eastern end lies Lares, locally famous for its superb hot springs, and to the west lies Ollantaytambo, jumping off spot for Machu Picchu. Several hiking routes cross the mountains northward into this area from the Sacred Valley, or one can drive to Lares and trek westward to Ollantaytambo.

For those who prefer short overnight treks or camp-free day hiking, there are several short hikes around Cusco, including the route from Tauca, near Chinchero, to the stunning and little-visited Inca site of Huchuy Cusco, which overlooks the Sacred Valley at Lamay. It can be done in one rather long day (with a very early start), or with an overnight camp at the ruins. Possible day hikes around Cusco include climbs of nearby mountains Mama Simona, Huanacauri, Senca, and Picol.

## The Cordillera Blanca

Eight hours north of Lima by bus, the city of **Huaraz** is the starting point for an array of spectacular treks among Peru's highest mountains. The Cordillera Blanca is home to the country's highest peak, **Huascarán** (6,760 meters/22,200 ft) and 30 other summits above 6,000 meters (19,700 ft), and a maze of trails climbing between them from two parallel north–south valleys, the

**Olleros–Chavín** route, which ends at the ancient ruins of Chavín de Huantar. In Huaraz, the Casa de Guías can provide the latest information on trails and mountain conditions, along with names of porters and mule-wranglers. The main street of Luzuriaga sports dozens of trekking outfitters and equipment rental stores, along with an array of discos, *peñas*, and bars for winding down after strenuous trekking.

## The Cordillera Huayhuash

This stunning, more remote region of high peaks is reached from Huaraz via **Chiquián**, a small town at the north end of the range. For serious

Callejón de Huaylas and the more remote Callejón de Conchucos to the east. Routes range from day hikes out of Huaraz, to lengthy two-week circuits encompassing most of the Cordillera. The most famous route is the five-day **Llanganuco– Santa Cruz** trek, but many other scenic hikes carry less traffic. At least one short acclimatization hike out of Huaraz – such as the **Laguna Churup** trail – is advisable, since most of the Cordillera Blanca trails cross passes of at least 4,400 meters (14,430 ft).

Huaraz is also the jumping-off point for the less scenic, but popular and relatively easy

**LEFT:** Parque Nacional Huascarán.
**ABOVE:** contemplating the climb ahead.

### RESPONSIBLE ADVENTURES

Conservation and fair practices boil down to one thing: respect – for the land and its people. It's hard to know, until after a trip, how well a company treats its staff and the environment, but one thing is clear: both will suffer if visitors haggle excessively.

Make sure your company is packing out garbage and not burying or dumping it en route, and not contaminating water supplies. Avoid disposable plastic water bottles – boil or purify water instead. See that your outfitter treats its crew properly, providing them proper food, shelter, and medical attention when needed, and not overloading porters. When trekking independently with a hired crew, remember that those concerns are your responsibility.

and fit trekkers only, a 12-day circuit of the entire range, with at least one very high pass every day, starts here. Still steep, but much shorter at four days, is the round-trip from Chiquián to Jahuacocha, a lake with stunning views of the highest peak, Yerupajá (6,634 meters/21,760 ft). **Cajatambo** at the south end of the Cordillera is a possible exit point to Lima for a shorter circuit, and also provides access for excellent shorter hikes in the vicinity.

## Around Arequipa

Although not a famous trekking area, the capital of the south offers hiking out of **Cabanaconde** at the western end of the Colca canyon, down into one of the world's two deepest canyons, Colca or Cotahuasi. It's also possible to ascend the summit of Misti, the enormous active volcano that looms over the city of Arequipa. But be warned – although technically easy, this three-day climb peaks at 5,820 meters (19,000 ft). Arequipa is too low for acclimatization, so it's essential to spend time in Cusco, Puno, or the Colca area immediately before this ascent.

## Northern Sierra

More isolated and less known than Peru's major trekking areas, this region of mountainous cloud

forest filled with hilltop ruins and cliff tombs also offers many superb routes, accessed from the towns of **Chachapoyas** and **Leimebamba**, northwest of Cajamarca.

## Mountain biking

The sport has taken off in recent years, and the 2007 Megavalanche downhill marathon near Cusco really put Peru on the mountain biking map. Cusco is the major center, with lots more options out of Huaraz, Arequipa, and even Lima. Stupendous scenery, wide open country, a multitude of trails, and from Cusco, major day-long downhill runs are the attractions.

Blanca. Arequipa is a good jump-off point for biking in the Colca and Cotahuasi canyons, and shorter day runs around the city. Lima also has access to big downhill runs from the mountains to the beach.

Rentals and tours are available in all cities. Check bikes carefully, and make sure the fee includes gloves, a good helmet, and a repair kit. Tours should always provide a support vehicle.

## Mountain climbing

The Peruvian Andes have some famous climbing areas, first and foremost the Cordillera Blanca, out of Huaraz, with some 30 summits above 6,000

A classic one-day outing near Cusco is the Maras–Moray plateau route, which is both easy and scenically dramatic. Great downhills include the aforementioned Málaga pass, whose western slope route can be planned to end with a hike into Machu Picchu from Santa Teresa. A staggering descent from frigid grassland at Tres Cruces into the steamy eastern rainforest can run one or two whole days, and another one-day downhill run from the Lares pass near Calca follows an Inca road.

Huaraz has spectacular tours from one to three or four days, into the heart of the Cordillera

meters (19,680 ft), among them Peru's highest mountain, **Huascarán** (6,760 meters/22,200 ft). The adjacent Cordillera Huayhuash is also a stellar climbing area, though more difficult and remote. You find everything from walk-ups to extreme technical climbs in this region, but the altitudes make acclimatization a major consideration *(see page 122)*.

A popular acclimatization warm-up climb is the **Nevado Pisco** (5,800 meters/19,000 ft). This has a steep yet rapid ascent, offering spectacular views from the saddle, and there is a mountain refuge at the base of the mountain. The Cordillera Blanca is the only area in Peru with a system of mountain refuges, accredited guides, and mountain rescue services.

**LEFT:** en route to the Cordillera Blanca.
**ABOVE:** the annual Megavalanche mountain bike race outside Cusco.

The Arequipa region has both walk-ups and harder peaks, and Cusco has some hard technical climbs with longer approaches. These areas have little support for mountaineers, although there are one or two companies in each city which provide guiding and equipment services.

## Horseback riding

One of the draws for horse lovers is the Peruvian *paso* horse, a local breed which has been developed for its unique gait, and is famously comfortable to ride. Traditionally they are more adapted to coastal conditions, but today some companies offer *paso* treks in the mountains, while other outfits prefer the sure-footed mountain horses.

Around Cusco a variety of horse treks set off from the Sacred Valley into and across the spectacular Cordillera Urubamba, along with easier one-day journeys on the nearby Maras plateau. For a fun outing near Cusco itself, horses can be rented behind the Inca site of Sacsayhuaman, just outside the city. But be sensitive: some (not all) outfits mistreat their horses, and if these are thin, with saddle sores and in poor condition, do not encourage these practices by renting them. The Cordillera Blanca also has good horseback riding options, as does the popular Colca canyon near Arequipa.

## Paragliding

In Lima steady coastal winds rising off the cliffs fronting Miraflores offer some paragliding excitement in reliable conditions. Cliffside outfits will take you on a tandem high above the beach, soaring past the balconies of shiny high-rise hotels and apartment blocks.

Paragliding in the mountains is more problematic, due to unpredictable air currents, but intrepid souls who ride paragliders above the Sacred Valley near Cusco are rewarded with stunning views of mountains, remote villages, and Inca ruins. ❑

### TOUCHING THE VOID

In 1985 British climbers Simon Yates and Joe Simpson were descending from the summit of Huayhuash peak Siulá Grande (6330 meters/20,800 ft) when Simpson slipped and broke his leg. Yates's attempt to lower him to safety ended with a crippled Simpson dangling over an abyss. Unable to move, Yates finally cut the rope. Simpson survived the fall, and crawled out alone to their base camp. His book about the experience, *Touching the Void*, became a best-seller and an award-winning film.

**ABOVE:** horseback riding along the beach at Máncora in northern Peru.

# Running the Andes

**Virtually all rafting in Peru offers stunning and varied scenery. Colossal rivers run off the Andes, not least the Amazon, which is called the Apurimac at these latitudes.**

Just hours from Cusco by road, the four-day Apurimac run through a deep and spectacular canyon is one of the most exciting short rafting trips anywhere. Class Four-plus rapids generate the full-adrenaline experience, along with stretches of dreamy floating where wildlife such as torrent ducks, foxes, otters, condors, and even mountain lions may be seen.

Rafting experience is not essential, but travel with a reputable company which takes time for training and safety sessions, and therefore beware of cheaper three-day trips. The highland weather timetable applies to most trips, with the rivers being run mainly from May through October.

The Urubamba valley, close enough to Cusco for day-rafting excursions, has lost its luster due to water pollution from the mushrooming city of Cusco. However, upstream of Cusco the river is still clean, and here the Chuquiqawana to Cusipata section makes a boisterous and scenic full-day trip, runnable most of the year.

Also starting from Cusco, the remote upper Tambopata River affords a world-class cloud-forest rafting adventure, a week-long ride down a mighty Amazon tributary, with frequent wildlife sightings. As the river flattens out, other highlights kick in: a clay-lick teeming with macaws and parrots, and remote rainforest lodges offering last nights of comfort before Puerto Maldonado, and a flight back to Cusco.

**ABOVE:** a whitewater rafting excursion.
**RIGHT:** a river valley near Huaraz.

Arequipa features a fun and easy rafting trip, the half-day Río Chili run. At the other extreme, the Cotahuasi claims to be the planet's deepest canyon, and connoisseurs rate this run among the world's top ten. The trip begins with hiking down Inca trails, and lasts for six stunning days, with camping in seldom-visited Inca ruins. The nearby Colca canyon is only for hard-core rafters, but its lower section, known as the Río Majes, has some easy rafting, with the nearby petroglyphs of Toro Muerto adding interest to a day's outing.

Near Lima, the Río Cañete can be run during the summer months from December to April. It's short and easy rafting, usually in warm, sunny weather, out of the resort town of Lunahuaná.

Further north, out of Huaraz, the Rio Santa, running along the Callejón de Huaylas, has good, moderate rafting with stupendous views.

River running can be dangerous. Regulation is scant, so anyone can set up a company; meanwhile hard-bargaining budget travelers drive down prices, compromising safety. The cheapest deal, with the shortest time on the river, means overworked, underpaid guides; a tendency to run, instead of walk around, dodgy rapids; no safety kayak; spiffy-looking life-vests, sporting new outer fabric but worn core material lacking buoyancy; beat-up helmets, etc. So choose carefully, inspect equipment, and ask for the guide's Swiftwater Rescue Technician credential, and Wilderness First Aid certificate. ❑

# WILDLIFE OF THE SIERRA

From cameloids and condors to wooly monkeys and spectacled bears, the Peruvian Andes and the cloud forest are home to an amazing variety of wildlife

The Andes of Peru have been heavily populated by wildlife for thousands of years. In Inca times all types of Andean wildlife enjoyed a form of protection, and although periodic hunts occurred, these were few, and the privilege of the ruling class. After the Spanish conquest and the breakdown of the Inca infrastructure, wild animals were hunted indiscriminately and consequently suffered a population decline that was further advanced by the cutting of high Andean woodlands, which provide essential cover for many animals.

Today the persecution of wild animals continues, in some cases because of damage caused by animals to crops, in most cases because of misconceptions. The careful observer, however, can still find a wide variety of Peruvian fauna while traveling in the Andes.

## Endangered species

The most conspicuous animals encountered by a visitor to the Peruvian Andes are the cameloids. There are two wild cameloids in the country: the vicuña and the guanaco, from which llamas and alpacas were domesticated many centuries ago.

The vicuña, reputed to have the finest wool of any animal, has been brought back from the verge of extinction through concerted conservation efforts. Special areas have been established for the species, such as the Pampas Galeras reserve in south-central Peru. They are now to be found in quite large numbers in many areas, but are still considered vulnerable. In Inca times, vicuña wool was obtained by running the animal to the ground, picking its fleece by hand and then releasing it. This not only assured a regular supply of wool each year but also maintained population levels.

The modern illegal hunter resorts to firearms, the primary cause of the vicuña's demise. Prosecution is rare, however, since the people who possess guns are often influential, and therefore above the law.

The other wild cameloid, the guanaco, reaches its northernmost limit in the highlands of central Peru, and from here extends down the Andean chain to the southern tip of South America – Tierra del Fuego. In Peru the guanaco is most likely to be seen in the departments of Tacna, Moquegua, Arequipa, and Puno, and is to be found in isolated rocky ravines with bunch grass. Guanacos are

**LEFT:** vicuñas in the Reserva Nacional Salinas y Aguada Blanca. **RIGHT:** guanaco crossing.

wild relatives of the llama and alpaca, but they are instantly distinguishable from their domesticated cousins by their bright tawny coloration, similar to that of the vicuña.

The precise relationship between the domestic llamas and alpacas and the wild guanacos and vicuñas is not entirely clear. All possible crosses of the four cameloids have been accomplished, and the offspring of all crosses are fertile. Most taxonomists now agree that the domestic llamas and alpacas are a product of the cross-breeding of guanacos and vicuñas. Whatever the exact relationships, the domesticated cameloids are to be found throughout the Peruvian highlands.

The only natural enemy of the cameloids is the puma or mountain lion. This large, tawny, unspotted cat was much revered by the Incas as a symbol of power and elegance.

Unfortunately, after the conquest, Andean people lost the conservationist outlook of the Incas, and the puma has suffered dramatically as a result of indiscriminate hunting. The puma's habit of picking off an unwary llama has not endeared it to the local people, and these days it is possible only to catch a fleeting glimpse of this magnificent cat as it crosses remote Andean valleys or stalks mountain vizcachas – sturdily built, burrowing members of the rodent family.

## Rare cats

Two smaller members of the cat family are also to be found in the high Andes. Both species are shy, and little is known of their status and habits. The pampas cat *(Felis colocolo)* is typically an animal of the intermontane Andean valleys, although it does occur close to the coast in northern Peru and in the high cloud forest of the eastern slopes of the Andes.

The Andean cat *(Felis jacobita)* is rarer still and in Peru is limited to the southern highlands. This is a high-altitude species, mostly nocturnal, and seems to prey on mountain vizcachas. Tracks of this species can be seen at the snow line nearly 5,000 meters (16,000 ft) above sea level, but for the short-term visitor to the Andes an encounter with any of the Peruvian wild cats is a rare event indeed.

## Woodland creatures

More conspicuous, and more commonly seen by backpackers in the highlands, are the two species of deer. Both species were once more common than they are now, and the principal causes of their demise are hunting and the cutting of the high Andean woodlands that provide essential cover. The white-tailed deer is still relatively abundant in more remote areas where hunting pressure is low, since this species shows a remarkable adaptability to various habitat types. It occurs from the coastal

is a primary source of fuel at high altitudes. Consequently, the barrel-chested, short-legged *taruka* is on the decline. If encountered, it is easily distinguished from the white-tailed deer by its two-pronged antlers (the white-tailed deer has one prong only). It is still possible to find this species on the Inca Trail to Machu Picchu.

Easiest of all to see while hiking through the highlands of Peru are the rodents and omnivores. The Andean fox is ubiquitous in all parts of the Andean region, and can be found at all altitudes up to 4,500 meters (14,800 ft). This species of fox is larger and longer-legged than its North American and European counterparts and commonly in-

plain (in zones of sufficient vegetation) to 4,000 meters (13,000 ft) above sea level, and then into the cloud forest of the eastern slopes of the Andes, down almost to the Amazon basin at 600 meters (2,000 ft). It is quite common for a hiker in the Andes to encounter this animal.

Its much rarer relative, the Andean huemul (or *taruka* as it is known in Peru), is harder to see. The *taruka* is a species in danger of extinction and is found at extremely high altitudes. Its presence is governed by the availability of cover, mostly small isolated patches of woodland. This type of woodland is disappearing at an alarming rate, as it

**LEFT:** mountain vizcacha.
**ABOVE:** the elusive Andean huemul.

vestigates any empty cans or leftover food outside tents. The Andean fox is everywhere regarded as a dangerous stock killer, especially of sheep. The stomachs of these animals often contain quantities of vicuña wool, but it is not known whether it is a predator of this species or only a carrion eater. Whenever possible, the Andean fox is killed by the local people, yet it remains common.

While walking along stream banks or drystone walls, the observant hiker will notice a large number of small rodents, ranging from the typical house-mouse type familiar to all of us, to mice with a striking color combination of chocolate-brown and white. It is not that there are a greater number of mice-like creatures in the Andes, but simply that, because of very low temperatures at night, most Andean rodents are diurnal. They are also the principal food source of a variety of predators, including the Andean weasel *(Mustela frenata)*, a vicious mustelid that will tackle prey twice its size. The abundance of diurnal rodents also accounts for the high density of birds of prey, such as the red-backed and puna hawks, the cinereous harrier, the black-chested buzzard-eagle, and the aplomado falcon.

The guinea pig, or *cuy* as it is known in Peru, is domesticated extensively in the Andes, and wild ones are also fairly common along stony banks and drystone walls, where they live in colonies. Any Quechua household will have its

## The cloud forest

On the eastern slope of the Andes the environment is dominated by humid, temperate forest. Where left undisturbed by humans, the forest continues from 3,600 meters (11,800 ft) down to the tropical rainforest of the Amazon basin. The type of forest above 2,500 meters (8,200 ft) is commonly known as "cloud forest," a name derived from the fact that for most of the year the trees are shrouded in mist. Indeed, most of the moisture needed by the forest is captured from the enveloping clouds. The cloud forest grades into high grassland at about 3,400 meters (11,200 ft) and harbors many exotic animals.

colony of guinea pigs living in the kitchen area, as the animal is regarded as a delicacy.

The last two conspicuous animals of the Andes are the hog-nosed skunk and the mountain vizcacha. The former, which may be familiar to visitors from North America, is mostly nocturnal and can often be picked up in car headlights. The latter is a sociable creature commonly found in rock screes and boulder fields. Very well camouflaged, it often betrays its presence with a high-pitched whistle. Looking like a cross between a chinchilla and a rabbit, the mountain vizcacha (the prey of large carnivores) can be seen sunning itself on boulders in the early morning and late afternoon. They can often be seen in the ruins of Machu Picchu.

### CONFLICT OVER CONSERVATION

The spectacled bear is a good example of the conflict between conservation and, for the poor, self-preservation. Although an important animal in Andean folklore, the bear has a very poor reputation among small farmers due to its habit of raiding maize crops at the edge of hill forests.

Unfortunately for the bear, its fat is much sought-after and its body parts have medicinal uses. None of this bodes well for the bear's survival, and it is being hunted to the extent where population levels are becoming dangerously low.

The spectacled bear is perhaps the most impressive animal of the zone, with a total body length of up to 183 cm (6 ft). This animal is a true omnivore, eating a wide variety of foods such as fruits and berries, large insects, succulent plants, and, at high elevations, the lush hearts of terrestrial bromeliads. The spectacled bear will also eat small mammals and rodents when given the opportunity.

Other shy inhabitants of the cloud forest include two species of small deer. The larger of the two is the dwarf brocket deer. About half the size of the white-tailed deer, it is found to a height of 3,300 meters (10,800 ft) in the departments of Puno and Cusco. The other is the pudu, the size of a small

a wide variety can be seen right up to the snow line.

The bird that first comes to mind when one is writing of the Andean peaks is the Andean condor.

> *The Andean condor is the largest flying bird in the world, with a wing span of up to 3 meters (10 ft). It covers huge distances in search of the carrion on which it feeds.*

This huge member of the vulture family is a carrion feeder, but is not averse to starting its meal a little prematurely. The condor is not a hunter and is incapable of grasping or carrying prey, having

dog, difficult to see and mostly nocturnal. It is relentlessly hunted with guns and dogs and must be considered vulnerable at present. Occupying the same habitat as the pudu is the wooly monkey, found in small family groups where hunting pressure is low and can still be found in cloud forest beyond Paucartambo in the department of Cusco.

## Diversity of birdlife

Southeast Peru has a greater diversity of birdlife than any other area on the planet. The majority of these species occur in the cloud forests and lowland rainforests of the eastern Andean slopes, but

**LEFT:** the unpopular Andean fox. **ABOVE:** an Andean condor soaring above the Colca canyon.

feet not unlike those of a chicken. (Sensational reports in newspapers of condors carrying off unattended babies must therefore be dismissed.) The sight of a condor sailing effortlessly against the backdrop of ice-capped Andean peaks is one that will not be forgotten quickly.

The condor is still a familiar sight throughout the high country, but far more commonly seen are the smaller songbirds such as sierra finches, cinclodes, miners, and seedsnipes. At the limit of the cloud forest, the number of species increases, and the birds are more brightly colored. Anyone taking a stroll here in the morning will see mixed-species flocks of colorful mountain-tanagers and flycatchers, as well as various species of hummingbird, flitting between the moss-festooned branches. ❏

# PLACES

A detailed guide to the entire country, with
principal sites clearly cross-referenced
by number to the maps

**M**apping out an itinerary for Peru might seem a daunting prospect. The country is three times as large as California, and many times more varied, with the Andean mountain range and Amazon jungle creating imposing barriers to travel. Yet journeys that were all but impossible 50 years ago are now everyday events. Peru's major cities are linked by air, while long-distance buses and trucks connect towns and villages. These days, the threat from Sendero Luminoso (Shining Path) guerrillas has receded, and most areas are regarded as safe.

Most travelers to Peru begin their journeys in Lima. As the former center of Spanish South America, it retains some fine colonial architecture, and treasures from all over the country can be found in its impressive museums. The Panamericana highway runs the length of the coast: to the north it leads to the ancient Chimu site at Chan Chan and relaxed coastal cities like Trujillo, and to the south, it takes you to Nazca, whose plains are etched with gigantic drawings made by a mysterious pre-Inca culture.

A 40-minute flight from Lima takes travelers straight into the heart of the Andes, to the Inca capital, Cusco. Apart from its own attractions, Cusco serves as a base to visit the Urubamba valley and the most famous site on the continent: Machu Picchu. The southern city of Arequipa is one of Peru's most elegant colonial cities, set in the shadow of the snow-capped Volcán

Misti, and renowned for its intellectual life. From Cusco and Arequipa, many travelers fly or take the popular railway journey to Puno, by the shores of Lake Titicaca. The world's highest navigable lake is populated by fascinating indigenous communities, who still ply its waters in *totora* reed canoes.

Increasing numbers of travelers are visiting an area that takes up over half of Peru's landmass: the Amazon basin. The northern city of Iquitos is the place from which to begin an Amazon adventure, while in the south there is the Parque Nacional Manu, possibly the purest section of rainforest in South America. ❏

**PRECEDING PAGES:** ruined church at Juli; Pimental; Plaza Mayor, Lima.
**LEFT:** view from Amantaní Island. **ABOVE:** Máncora; Palacio Torre Tagle; Sillustani.

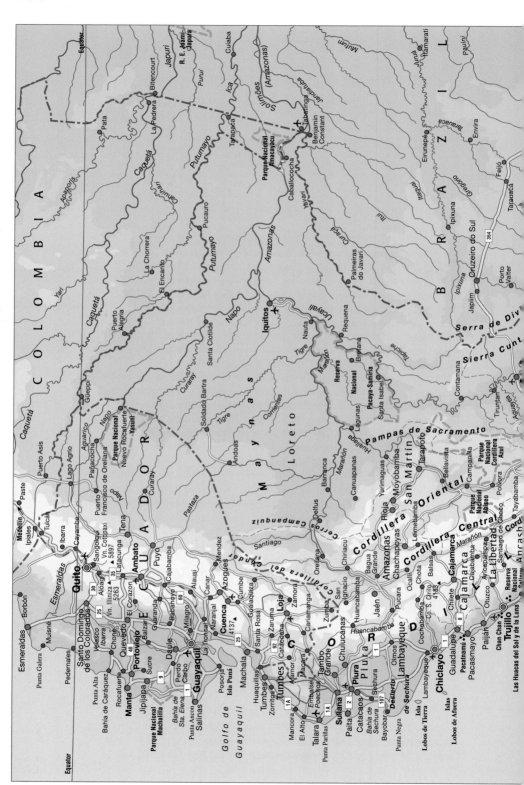

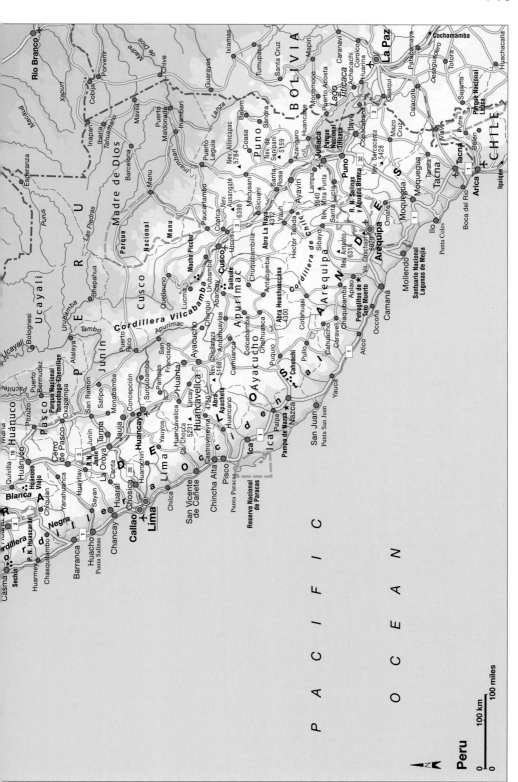

**Peru**

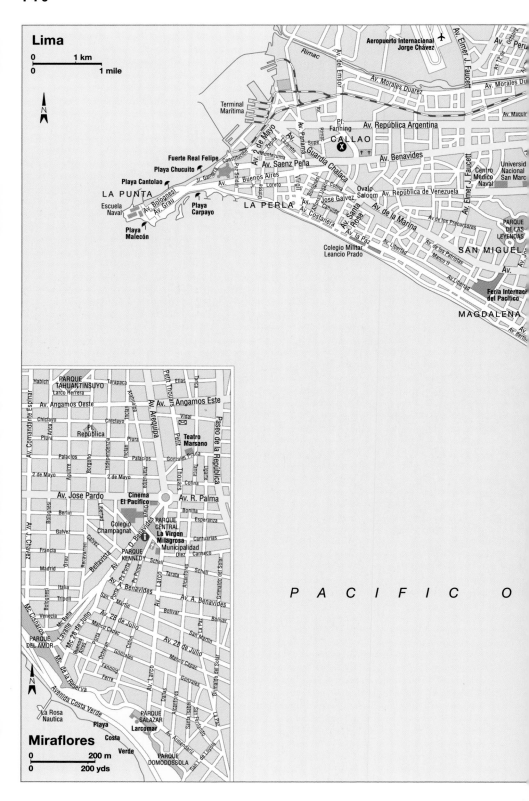

## Lima

0 — 1 km
0 — 1 mile

N

Rímac

Aeropuerto Internacional
Jorge Chávez

Av. Elmer J. Faucett

Av. Peru

Av. del Emsor

Av. Morales Duarez

Av. Morales Du

Terminal
Marítima

Av. Maquir

Pl.
Fanning

Av. República Argentina

CALLAO

Av. 2 de Mayo

Av. Panamá

Guardia Chalaca

Av. Benavides

Av. Saenz Peña

Zepita

Buenos Aires

Montezuma

Jr. Loreto

Jr. Garcia

Construcción

Paz Soldán

Av.

Universid
Nacional
San Marc

Centro
Médico
Naval

Av. Elmer J. Faucett

Fuerte Real Felipe

Playa Chucuito

Playa Cantolao

LA PUNTA

Escuela
Naval

Av. Bolognesi

Av. Grau

Playa
Carpayo

Playa
Malecón

Av.

Virgil

Colina

Bolognesi

Jose Galvez

Canuto

Ovalo
Saloom

Av. República de Venezuela

Santa Rosa

Av. de la Marina

Av. de los Precursores

PARQUE
DE LAS
LEYENDAS

SAN MIGUEL

LA PERLA

Av. Costanera

Av. la Paz

Av. Libertad

Av. de los Patriotas

Manco II

Colegio Militar
Leancio Prado

Av.

Av. Libertad

Feria Internaci
del Pacífico

MAGDALENA

Av. Beri

## Miraflores

PARQUE
TAHUANTINSUYO

Habich

Larco Herrera

Tarapaca

Petit Thouars

Elias

Tarca

Av. Comandante Espinar

Av. Angamos Oeste

Av. Arequipa

Av. Angamos Este

Paseo de la República

Chiclayo

Arica

Plura

Pl.
República

Chiclayo

Piura

Vidal

Petit

Teatro
Marsano

Palacios

Independencia

Borgoño

Palacios

Gonzales Prada

Tarca

Ugarte

2 de Mayo

Aguirre

Arequipa

2 de Mayo

Tarata

Colina

Av. Jose Pardo

Cinema
El Pacífico

Av. R. Palma

Bolognesi

Berlin

Libertad

O. Benavides

Bonilla

Esperanza

Galvez

Colegio
Champagnat

PARQUE
CENTRAL

La Virgen
Milagrosa

Cantuarias

Av. J. Chávez

Francia

Grau

Recavarren

Bellavista

PARQUE
KENNEDY

Municipalidad

Diez

Canseco

Madrid

Italia

Schell

Schell

Grimaldo del Solar

Tripoli

San Martin

Av. A. Benavides

Bolivar

Bolivar

San Martin

Venecia

Av. 28 de Julio

Mc. Belle

Manco Capac

Paz

Mc Cisneros

PARQUE
DEL AMOR

Mc. 28 de Julio

Lavalle

Buenos Aires

Porta

Av. 28 de Julio

Manco Capac

Mc. de la Reserva

Ocharan

Gonzales

Fanning

Av. Larco

Gonzales

Santa Isabel

La Paz

Avenida Costa Verde

Ferra

Dallas

Alcanfores

San Fernando

La Rosa
Nautica

Playa

Costa

Verde

PARQUE
SALAZAR

Larcomar

PARQUE
DOMODOSSOLA

San J. de Loyola

0 — 200 m
0 — 200 yds

N

P   A   C   I   F   I   C   O

# LIMA

Major urban renewal schemes have given Lima back some of its former splendor. But it remains a sprawling city with many different faces, from the old colonial heart to modern Miraflores

Lima

**H**erman Melville (the 19th-century American author of *Moby Dick*) called **Lima** ❶ "the saddest city on earth." Many visitors have agreed with him, while some residents have been even less complimentary – "Lima the horrible" was how writer Sebastián Salazar Bondy described his native city in the 1960s. But tourists who take such descriptions – and their own first impressions – at face value risk missing out on a city of rare fascination and unexpected pleasures.

While locals may gripe, most have an enduring love-hate relationship with their paradoxical city. Lima has both decaying colonial splendor and the teeming vitality of an oriental bazaar; melancholy, cloudy winters and warm, breezy summers; impoverished urban sprawl and quiet, elegant corners among ancient buildings where the night air is scented with jasmine.

## The City of Kings

Lima was founded by the Spanish conquistador Francisco Pizarro on January 18, 1535. The foundation was planned for January 6 – Epiphany, or the Day of the Kings – and despite the delay the capital was still known as La Ciudad de los Reyes or "The City of Kings." Pizarro traced a grid of 13 streets by nine to form 117 city blocks on the site of an existing indigenous settlement beside the southern bank of the Río Rimac (from which the name Lima was derived). But he had no great army of workers: the city's first inhabitants numbered fewer than 100.

Pizarro had originally made his capital at Jauja, in the Andes. The rapid switch was determined by a strategic need to be close to his ships – his only lifeline in a rebellious, still largely unconquered country. The Rimac valley provides the best line of communication through the Andean peaks to the interior of central Peru, while the rivers Chillón and Lurín also reach the sea within the present-day boundaries of the city, making the site one of the best-watered in the coastal

**LEFT:** Jirón de la Unión. **BELOW:** clowning around in Plaza San Martín.

*If you are wondering why some street names include the word "Jirón," they are the major thoroughfares, made up of several blocks. Each individual block may have a different name.*

desert. Several *huacas*, or funeral mounds, along with other pre-Columbian ruins, survive in greater Lima as testimony that the area was populated before the conquest. The most important pre-Inca religious site in coastal Peru was nearby at Pachacámac.

The only drawback was the future city's microclimate. Because of a meteorological phenomenon known as thermal inversion, Lima is often draped in a damp blanket of low cloud – the *garúa* – from May through October, although the summer months can be agreeable. And though the visitor may often forget the fact, seeing exuberant gardens of yellow amancaes or purple bougainvillaea (the product of careful irrigation), rainfall rarely amounts to more than a few nights of drizzle, insufficient to wash the desert dust from the facades of buildings that require frequent repainting.

## Capital of the New World

For two centuries after its foundation, Lima was the political, commercial, and ecclesiastical capital of Spanish South America, and the seat of the Inquisition as well as of the viceroys. But its beginnings were modest, and gave little clue to its later splendor. The mestizo chronicler Garcilaso de la Vega described it as having "very broad and very straight streets, so that from any of its crossroads the countryside can be seen in all four directions," adding that the houses were roofed with reeds rather than tiles.

But by the early 17th century, Lima's population had risen to about 25,000, the majority of whom were indigenous

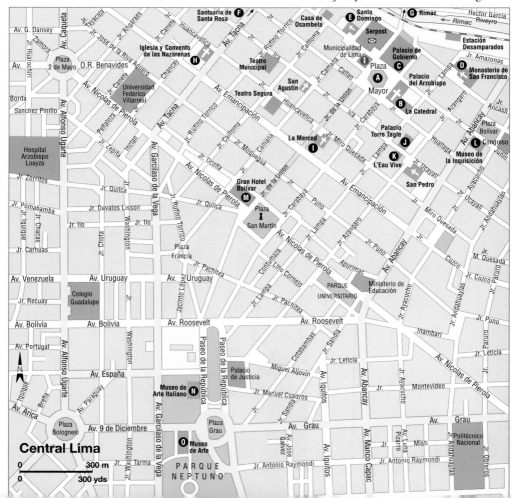

Central Lima

*Recommended Restaurants and Cafés on pages 164–5*

people working as servants or artisans, and African slaves. In the 1680s a protective wall with 12 gateways was built around the city, because of fears of raids by English privateers. The wall was demolished in the 1870s, although fragments can still be seen beside the railway line in the Barrios Altos. Despite being frequently damaged by earthquakes, the city was rich as well as powerful. The most powerful earthquake, in 1746, destroyed much of the city, and the palaces, churches, mansions, and monasteries we see today were subsequently rebuilt and expanded. Across the Río Rimac, pleasure gardens for the aristocracy were carefully laid out.

Lima's gradual decline from preeminence began in the late 18th century, as new viceroyalties were created in Bogotá and Buenos Aires, and the city's monopoly on trade between Europe and South America was broken. As would be expected of a royalist city, independence from Spain was initiated from outside. Expeditionary forces, first from Argentina under General José de San Martín and then from Colombia under Venezuelan Simón de Bolívar, "The Liberator," oc-cupied the city. Installed as republican Peru's first president in the suburb of Magdalena, even the austere Bolívar was affected by Lima's sybaritic elegance. It was at a ball in the city that he met and fell in love with Manuela Saenz, the Ecuadorian wife of a British doctor, who was to become his lifelong companion. Bolívar's presidency lasted only from 1824 to 1826, and when he left for Colombia a period of political instability and economic chaos ensued.

*Statue of General José de San Martín in Plaza San Martín.*

## Bursting its boundaries

After an initial turbulent period, the city's development resumed in the mid-19th century. The first railway in South America opened between Lima and its port of Callao in 1854, followed swiftly by further lines to connect the city with the growing coastal villages of Miraflores and Chorrillos. But setbacks followed, as Lima was occupied and partially sacked by Chilean troops in 1881 during the disastrous War of the Pacific. It was only in the early 20th century that the city burst its 17th-century Spanish limits and embarked on a process of change and growth that has lasted to the present

**BELOW:** living on the edge: Lima seen from Barranco.

*Inside Lima's cathedral there is a gallery of religious art that can be visited free of charge.*

**BELOW:** the austere interior of the cathedral.

day, the product of both massive migration from the Andean hinterland and the decline of the upper classes as Peru moved falteringly toward democracy. The outline of the modern city dates from the beginning of this period. Industry began to spread westward along the Callao railway, and up the central highway to Vitarte in the east.

The building of Paseo Colón and Avenida Nicolas de Piérola or La Colmena (begun in 1898), and of Plaza San Martín (1921), created new arteries and a new central focus to the south of Pizarro's Plaza de Armas, which was revamped in 1997 and renamed the Plaza Mayor. The rising urban upper-middle class moved away from the crowded center to the spacious south, toward Miraflores and the new district of San Isidro, laid out as a leafy garden suburb. Working-class suburbs sprang up over the river in Rimac, in El Agustino to the east, and in La Victoria to the southeast. By 1931, Lima's population had reached 280,000, having doubled in little more than two decades.

In the years since then, two trends have given Lima its present urban structure. Infill development of middle-class suburbs has completed a triangle enclosing the area between the city center, Callao, and Chorrillos. Outside this triangle, Andean migrants made their homes in sprawling, self-built shantytowns stretching north, south, and northeast, occupying the vacant desert sands in the shadow of the Andean foothills. The shantytowns now contain half the city's estimated population of over 8 million. They started as squatter settlements of rush-matting huts, but decades of hard work have turned some into pleasant districts. Many others remain desperately poor, lacking electricity, piped water, or paved streets. But the migrants and their children have changed the character of the city irrevocably. Many of them came to Lima during the 1980s, when the violence of the Sendero Luminoso movement and the military, of which *campesinos* (subsistence farmers) were often the innocent victims, made rural life intolerable. As the city swelled with rural migrants, the old downtown area fell into decay, and businesses and hotels took flight, re-establishing themselves in better-run districts like San Isidro, Miraflores, and La Molina. Street vendors, drug-pushers, prostitutes, and pickpockets took over the city center. Successive mayors have since imposed a clean-up campaign which moved the street vendors – *ambulantes* – from the historic center. This was accompanied by a certain amount of strife, but has proved successful. Many of the vendors are now operating in organized markets, and have found that the move has also brought commercial success.

## Plaza Mayor

A major program of urban renewal is in progress in the historic center of the city. Under the auspices of Unesco it has been declared part of "the Cultural Heritage of Mankind," and there have been spectacular changes in both architectural restoration and street cleanliness and security. The usual starting point for

exploring Lima is **Plaza Mayor** Ⓐ (formerly Plaza de Armas), which has benefited greatly from recent renovation. Stand in the middle of this handsome square, by the 17th-century bronze fountain, and you are at the city's historic heart. Look out for the Angel of Fame on the fountain: it's a copy of the original which, it is said, flew away in 1900. Most of the buildings are 18th-century reconstructions, but the spirit of the conquistadors permeates the square.

The eastern side of the square is dominated by the **Catedral** Ⓑ (open Mon–Sat 9am–4.30pm; entrance fee) on a site chosen by Francisco Pizarro, but reconstructed several times after earthquakes. The present building was begun in the 18th century, after the almost complete devastation of the previous one in the 1746 earthquake. Much of the exterior has been painted in yellow-ochre, as part of a successful policy to brighten up dusty facades with colors used in the colonial period.

Inside, the cathedral is large and unusually austere. Notable are the 17th-century wooden choir stalls. To the right of the entrance is a small side-chapel dedicated to Pizarro, where his skeleton lies in a sealed wooden coffin. Found in 1977 during excavations in the Cathedral crypt and put on display in 1985, to mark Lima's 450th anniversary, it replaced the remains of an anonymous conquistador, long mistakenly thought to have been Pizarro.

Next door to the Cathedral is the **Palacio del Arzobispo** (Archbishop's Palace), rebuilt in the 1920s with an impressive wooden balcony. Opposite stands the **Municipalidad de Lima** (City Hall), built in the 1940s after fire destroyed its predecessor. The pleasant interior includes a fine library. Next to it on the square is the headquarters of the **Club de la Unión**, a lunchtime haunt of politicians and professionals. Between them at the mouth of Pasaje Santa Rosa is a monument, in the form of a large chunk of rough-hewn stone, to Taulichusco El Viejo, the last *cacique* (chief) of pre-conquest Lima, which was unveiled in 1985 as a belated antidote to the ghost of Pizarro.

On the north side of the plaza is the **Palacio de Gobierno** Ⓒ (Government Palace; open Mon–Fri 8.30am–1pm and 2–5pm; free admission; or a free two-hour guided tour – take a copy of your

**BELOW:** Plaza Mayor.

*The Central Post Office building, which now houses Serpost, is regarded as a national monument.*

**BELOW:** Changing of the Guard at the Presidential Palace.

passport at least one day before, 2–5pm), built on the site of Pizarro's palace, where he was assassinated in 1541 – the first Latin American coup d'état. The present building was completed in 1938, and suffers from the taste for grandiose French baroque which afflicted dictatorial leaders of the time. Much of the ground plan at the rear of the building remains the same as in Pizarro's day. At 11.45am, every day except Sunday, you can catch the Changing of the Guard, performed in the front courtyard by goose-stepping troops from the Hussares de Junín regiment, dressed in the red-and-blue ceremonial uniforms and ornamental helmets of the independence period. To arrange a guided tour of the palace go to the office of Relaciones Públicas in the same building to make an appointment, or tel: (01) 311 3908.

In a small side square, between the palace and the Municipalidad, stands an equestrian statue of the ubiquitous Pizarro, somewhat disregarded these days,

although a plan to have him removed altogether was unsuccessful. Behind him, the building topped with antennae houses an office of Peru's National Intelligence Service. To the left is the Café Conquistador, with tables on the pavement – a good place for a coffee and a rest while sightseeing. Nearby stands the Central Post Office, now called **Serpost**, its offices grouped around a handsome open-air neo-classical arcade, recently restored.

Farther up toward the river are a couple of splendid old hat shops, where you can acquire a felt stetson or a Panama for around US$12–15. This is where the booming contraband market of **Polvos Azules** used to be, but the street vendors and shop-owners have been moved to the old industrial area just outside the center. Thieves abound here and in the city center generally, and visitors should take great care of their valuables while exploring the streets of Lima. Until you become accustomed to the city, you would also be best advised not to wander alone in the center by night.

Doubling back into Plaza Mayor again, on a charming street corner (the intersection of Jirón Carabaya and Jirón Junín)

you will find the oldest building in the square, **La Casa del Oidor**. Dating from the early 18th century, it has the wooden balconies in the form of enclosed galleries projecting from the first floor that were colonial Lima's most graceful feature. Farther up Carabaya, past several shoe shops (hand-stitched cowboy boots made to measure), is the **Desamparados Station**, a neoclassical building dating from 1908. This is the terminal for the spectacular journey to Huancayo, along the highest rail track in the world, via Ticlio, which reaches 4,800 meters/16,000 ft above sea level *(see page 210)*. With the removal of the street vendors, a new promenade, the Paseo Chabuca Granda, has been created behind the Presidential Palace on the southern bank of the Río Rimac. Many *limeños* (the people of Lima) like to stroll here at the weekends, and the municipality organizes concerts and theater performances in specially constructed arenas.

## Monasterio de San Francisco

Turn right along Jirón Ancash and you will come to the **Monasterio de San Francisco** ❹, the jewel of colonial Lima. Even if you are not a fan of colonial churches, don't miss this one. The church faces a small paved square, full of pigeons and portrait photographers. The outside is attractively painted in colonial yellow, but it is the interior that is fascinating; much of it is decorated in the geometrical *Mudéjar* (Andalusian Moorish) style. Established soon after the foundation of Lima, it has suffered earthquake damage over the years, but has been sensitively restored in the original style. Its outstanding features include the 17th-century library, with 25,000 leather-bound volumes and 6,000 parchments dating from the 15th to the 18th century. The cupola has a superb *Mudéjar* carved wooden ceiling of Panamanian cedar, dating from 1625. In a gallery above the nave of the church are 130 choir stalls and 71 panels with carvings of Franciscan saints, made of the same wood. Restoration work has exposed (under eight layers of paint) 17th-century murals in the cloister and adjacent chambers (open Mon–Sun 9.30am–5.30pm; guided tours; entrance fee).

The monastery's collection of religious art includes paintings from the workshops of Rubens and Zurbarán and, in the refectory, a *Last Supper* painted in 1697 by a Flemish Jesuit priest. San Francisco has probably survived more recent earthquakes because of the solid base provided by its catacombs, which were used as Lima's cemetery until 1810. A network of underground chambers, which are open to the public, contains hundreds of skulls and bones, stored in racks according to type. A secret passage (now bricked up) led from here to the Government Palace.

There are many other colonial churches in the center. To reach the **Iglesia de Santo Domingo** ❺ (open Mon–Sat 9am–12.30pm and 3–6pm, Sun 9am–1pm; entrance fee) retrace your steps along Ancash, past the Post Office, to the corner of Jirón Camana. The church, which has a pleasant cloister with tiling from Seville, contains the tomb of San Martín de Porres, a black saint who lived and died in Lima and is venerated

**ICE CREAM**

For mouthwatering Italian ice cream, head to Heladería 4D, Angamos Oeste 408, in Miraflores. There is also a branch of Ben and Jerry's in the Larcomar shopping center.

**BELOW:** colonial buildings just off the Plaza Mayor.

*One of the catacombs
in the Monasterio de
San Francisco.*

**BELOW:** feeding the
birds outside the
San Francisco
monastery.

throughout Latin
America. There is
also an urn here
which holds the
ashes of Santa
Rosa de Lima, the
patron saint of the
New World and the
Philippines as well
as the city of Lima.
To reach the **San-
tuario de Santa
Rosa** continue
along Conde de
Superunda and
turn right on Avenida Tacna. The sanctuary, a modest hut built in the 16th century on the site of the saint's birthplace
and now set in a pleasant garden, contains relics of Santa Rosa (open daily
9am–1pm and 3–6pm; free admission).

As you walked along Conde de Superunda, between Santo Domingo and the
Santuario, you may have noticed that this
is one of several streets in the center with
good colonial balconies. Since the city
council's "Adopt a Balcony" campaign
many balconies – previously in a sad
state of decay – have been restored by

private investors. The **Casa de Osambela** (Jirón Conde de Superunda 298, tel:
01-427 7989; open Mon–Fri 9am–5pm;
free admission) is open to the public and
well worth visiting. A late 18th-century
mansion with an ornamental cupola,
beautifully restored in the 1980s, it
houses a small art gallery and the offices
of various cultural institutions.

## Across the river

At this point, make a small detour. You
could cross the Puente Santa Rosa here
or, better, return to the little bridge
behind the Palacio de Gobierno, the
**Puente de Piedra** (Stone Bridge), built
in Roman style in 1610 (its mortar reputedly bound with thousands of egg whites
for strength), which leads over the river
to **Rimac** , once the playground of the
aristocracy and now a lively working-
class district. The Hatuchay Peña (a
nightclub with Peruvian music and dancing), popular with both tourists and
locals, is in Jirón Trujillo, as soon as you
cross the bridge.

Turn right and you will come to **Plaza
de Acho**, the oldest bullring in the Americas. The **Museo Taurino** (open Mon–
Fri 9am–6pm, weekends by appointment
only; tel: 01-481 1467) has a collection
of bullfighting memorabilia and, notably,
some Goya engravings. There is a
panoramic view of the city from Cerro
San Cristóbal. Organized tours visit the
Rimac district and this hill several times
a day. Buses leave from the main plaza,
and the tour includes a visit to the bullfighting museum.

At the foot of the hill is the **Alameda
de los Descalzos**, laid out in 1610 as a
pleasure garden with statues and
wrought-iron railings, but now rather
run-down. It leads to the **Monasterio de
los Descalzos** (Monastery of the Barefoot Friars; open Tue–Sun 10am– 6pm;
entrance fee), recently restored and well
worth the walk to get there. To the right
is the **Paseo de Aguas**, another pleasure
garden created in the 18th century by
Viceroy Amat for his famous mistress,
La Perrichola (*see page 65*), but also
sadly in need of repair.

## Churches and miracles

On the south side of the River Rimac, on the corner of Avenida Tacna and Jirón Huancavelica, stands the **Iglesia y Convento de las Nazarenas Ⓗ**, which houses the image of El Señor de los Milagros (The Lord of Miracles), the black Christ painted by a freed African slave that has become the most important focus of popular religious feeling in Lima. The miracle was that the wall on which the painting appeared was the only part of a 17th-century shantytown to survive an earthquake. In October the image is borne around the city center for several days (October 18, 19, and 28) by teams of men wearing the purple robes of the brotherhood of El Señor de los Milagros. Hundreds of thousands of people turn out to accompany the image in what is one of the largest public gatherings in South America. The church can be visited (open Mon–Sat 7am–noon and 4–8.30pm; free admission), but the convent is a closed Order.

Leaving Las Nazarenas, go to the next corner and turn left down Avenida Emancipación for four blocks, then left again on Jirón de la Unión, which brings you to the **Iglesia de la Merced ❶**. This church, which, like most in Lima, suffered severe earthquake damage and was rebuilt in the late 18th century, is built on the site of the first Catholic Mass celebrated in the city, in 1534 (open daily 8am–noon and 4–8pm; free admission).

Leaving La Merced, go down Jirón Quesada, then turn left on Jirón Azangaro and you will reach the **Iglesia de San Pedro** (open daily 9.30–11.45am and 2–5pm; free admission), another baroque church with *Mudéjar* influences, which was consecrated in 1638.

## Colonial mansions

The city center contains several fine examples of secular colonial architecture. Outstanding is one on Jirón Ucayali, close to San Pedro: the **Palacio Torre Tagle ❶** (Jirón Ucayali 323, tel: 01-311 2400; open Mon–Fri 9am–4.30pm by appointment only; free admission) was completed in 1735 and gives a good idea of the opulence of Lima in its colonial prime. It now houses the Foreign Ministry, but visits are allowed to the courtyard, from where you can see the finely carved wooden balconies. Opposite

*One of the ornate balcony grills of Palacio Torre Tagle.*

**BELOW:** the opulent Palacio Torre Tagle.

*Making traditional ham sandwiches at Bar Cordano, a Lima institution.*

**BELOW:** the open air Pasaje de la Casa de Correos by the Central Post Office.

Torre Tagle, in another colonial mansion, is **L'Eau Vive Restaurant** *(see page 164)*, run by French-speaking nuns. They serve excellent, reasonably priced French food. Customers are encouraged to join them in singing the Ave Maria at 3pm and 9pm.

From here make a slight detour to the **Museo de la Inquisición** (Museum of the Inquisition; open daily 9am–5pm; free admission), on Jirón Junín. This is the building where generations of alleged heretics were tortured and tried. You can visit the main hall (with a fine 18th-century wooden ceiling) and the sinister, underground dungeons and torture chambers. The stocks are original, and there are mock-ups of other torture techniques. Between here and the river is a huge daily market, and an archway proclaiming that this is Lima's **Chinatown**.

## Republican Lima

South of the Plaza Mayor, the largest square is the **Plaza San Martín**, the hub of the modern city center. If you approach the square from Plaza Mayor, you should take the pedestrianized **Jirón de la Unión**, once Lima's most elegant shopping street.

As recently as the 1940s it was considered scandalous for women to stroll along Jirón de la Unión without wearing a hat. Now it is a teeming mass of shoppers and fast-food joints.

The colonnaded Plaza San Martín, recently restored and repainted and brightly lit, is an important gathering place for political meetings. In the center is an equestrian statue of General José de San Martín, Peru's Argentinian independence hero. On its west side is the **Gran Hotel Bolívar** , built in the 1920s. Though now it often seems to have more elderly waiters and bellboys than guests, the hotel retains much of its former atmosphere. A Palm Court trio serenades people drinking afternoon tea in the domed lobby, and its giant *pisco sours* (called *catedrales*) remain justly famous. Even if you are not staying here, the Bolívar is the perfect place to stop and rest during a city tour; the decor and ambience make the high price of the drinks worthwhile.

Next to the Bolívar is **Jirón Ocoña**, the center of Lima's street foreign exchange market, where money-changers buy or sell dollars round the clock. The

market is sophisticated and in times of high inflation, rates change hourly. Across La Colmena from the Bolívar is the **Club Nacional**. Though it is no longer the watering-hole of Peru's once all-powerful oligarchy, it has recently taken on a new lease of life, with the revamping of the city center. The clients now are a blend of old-money families and prominent members of the business community.

## Touring the museums

Lima has a wealth of museums, some of them displaying the best of the pre-Columbian treasures unearthed from sites around the country. It is a very large city and the museums are scattered around it, but transport is not hard to find. The Tourist Office will be able to help you find the best routes between places of interest. Taxis are inexpensive and there is no shortage of them. They come in all shapes and sizes, some smart, some very dilapidated, and they don't have meters, so try to fix a price in advance. Then, armed with a map, you can pick and choose among Lima's cultural offerings.

Leaving Plaza San Martín, head south down Unión (which becomes Belén) to the Paseo de la República and the **Museo de Arte Italiano** (open Mon–Fri 10am–5pm, Sat–Sun 11am–5pm; entrance fee). There is a good selection of Italian and other European paintings from the early 20th century, and the neoclassical building itself is worth seeing for its fine mosaics.

On the other side of Avenida 9 de Diciembre (usually called Paseo de Colón) is the **Museo de Arte** (open daily except Wed 10am–5pm; free on Mon), containing an extensive collection of Peruvian art from the conquest to the present. The Filmoteca here is a cinema club that shows films for a low admission price. It has two auditoriums where concerts are given, and is surrounded by a very pleasant public park.

From the museum, take the Avenida 28 de Julio, then turn right down Avenida Aviación to the San Luis district. Here, on

Avenida Javier Prado Este in San Borja, you will find the **Museo de la Nación** (National Museum; open Tue–Sun 9am–6pm; entrance fee), which has a wonderful collection of artifacts from the Chavín culture, including an ingenious replica of a Chavín stela, woven articles found at Paracas, and ceramics from Nazca, among other things, making it one of the best museums in the city.

In 1998 it was discovered that a large proportion of the exhibits at the **Museo de Oro** (Gold Museum; Av. Alonso de Molina 1100; open daily 11.30am–7pm; entrance fee) were modern replicas. However, the museum also has a collection of genuine textiles, stone carvings, and ceramics on display.

The next stop on the museum tour is the **Museo Nacional de Arqueología, Antropología y Historia** (National Museum of Archeology, Anthropology, and History; http://mnaah.perucultural.org.pe; open Tue–Sat 9am–5pm, Sun until 6pm; entrance fee), in (another) Plaza Bolívar in the suburb of Pueblo Libre. Although some of the exhibits have been moved to the Museo de la Nación, it is still one of the most interesting museums in the

**KIDS**

Lima's zoo is located in the Parque de las Leyendas in Pueblo Libre. It is split into the three geographical regions of Peru: the coast, mountains, and jungle, and also has a childrens's playground.

## Lima's Magic Fountains

One of Lima's favorite new attractions is the **Circuito Mágico del Agua** in the Parque de La Reserva. Thirteen spectacular fountains make an incredible display of music, water, and light. Visit at dusk and you'll see them come to life in a kaleidoscope of spotlit colors. There's a tunnel of water which you can walk through (and stay relatively dry) and a fountain in which you can attempt to dodge the timed water spouts (and end up soaking wet).

The **Fuente Mágica** spouts 80 meters (260 ft) into the air, reaching its climax with an orchestral crescendo which you can watch from a classical folly nearby. The fountains reportedly cost US$13 million to build, which provoked rumblings of discontent over "frivolous" spending, but they have proved a hit with *limeños* and visitors alike. The delight on the faces of fellow visitors is almost as wonderful as the fountains themselves. The fountains (open Wed–Sun 4–10pm; entrance fee) are located on the corner of Av. Petit Thouars and Jr. Madre de Dios, to the south of of the Estadio Nacional.

# Oasis of Hope

**There is a side of Lima very different from the affluent streets of Miraflores and San Isidro. Like many of Lima's barrios, Villa El Salvador started as a squatter camp and evolved into an officially recognised suburb.**

V illa El Salvador is more than just another shantytown formed by aspiring Andean migrants. Tucked behind sand dunes not far from the Inca shrine of Pachacamac, about 30 km (20 miles) south of Lima, it was founded in 1971 by an initial wave of 10,000 migrants who had fled from the mountain areas around Huaraz in the wake of an earthquake. Today it is home to around 350,000 people, and is a prototype of self-determination by Peru's marginalized Andean majority.

The settlement's success has brought international recognition. It has been nominated for the Nobel Peace Prize, won Spain's prestigious Prince of Asturias award for social achievement, and been designated by the United Nations as a Messenger of Peace. Its key factor is the Andean tradition of community organization centered on the family unit.

Each block of houses, or *manzana*, comprises 24 families; 16 blocks make up a residential group, and 22 of these form a sector. Health centers, communal kitchens, and sports grounds bond the groups together. Education is prioritized, and illiteracy in Villa El Salvador is minimal, unlike in other similar shantytowns. Most of the houses are built of adobe bricks or concrete, and have drainage, mains water, and electricity. The community is criss-crossed by roads and dotted generously with shady poplar, eucalyptus, pomegranate, and banana trees.

Clever irrigation, worthy of the residents' Inca forebears, has converted hundreds of hectares of sandy desert into arable land, using the community's own treated sewage. Fruit and cotton are grown in the fields, as are corn and fodder crops for the thousands of privately and communally owned cattle whose milk and cheese are sold locally.

Villa El Salvador's first martyr was Edilberto Ramos, who was killed resisting police attempts to expel the original settlers. It was his death that forced the government to hand over the land. But the powerful sense of local identity, forged by such bravery and collective action in combating poverty, was shaken by terrorist infiltration during the early 1990s.

In 1992, popular community leader and deputy mayor María Elena Moyano was shot dead in front of her children by Sendero Luminoso guerrillas. Later that same year the mayor of Villa El Salvador was wounded in a terrorist attack after criticizing Moyano's killers. These deaths helped to strengthen the sense of community in Villa El Salvador, and to reinforce local political development.

The town's libraries, community radio station, and written bulletins demonstrate the determination to communicate, and the belief that education genuinely brings self-advancement and change. The industrial park, created in 1987, provides much-needed local employment and exports products to many parts of the world.

The community continues to flourish despite enormous problems of malnutrition and continuing underemployment. It is an oasis that has tapped a spring of hope from beneath the desert floor.

While there are no official tours to Villa El Salvador, it's often possible to arrange a visit through your hotel. If you do go, be respectful (and careful) with your camera. ❏

**LEFT:** the market place in Villa El Salvador.

country, with a superb collection of pottery and textiles from all the main cultures of ancient Peru. It is well laid out, in chronological order, and the curators have resisted the temptation to swamp visitors with too many exhibits.

Close by on Avenida Bolívar is the **Museo Larco** Ⓢ (www.museolarco.org; open daily 9am–6pm; entrance fee), which has a vast collection of pre-Columbian ceramics, gold and silver objects, and some interesting textiles. A small annex holds a fascinating collection of erotic pottery from the Moche period. Few of the exhibits are labeled, but they are impressive for their fine quality.

## The modern capital

It's time now to leave museums behind for a while and have a look at modern Lima. Two main arteries, the Avenida Arequipa and the Paseo de la República expressway, link the city center with the business district of **San Isidro**, where you might take a look at another museum: a very special private collection called the **Enrico Poli** (Lord Cochrane 466; open daily, tel: 01-422 2437 for an appointment, call one or two

days before; entrance fee). It's well worth a stop to see the School of Cusco paintings and silver and gold work from colonial and pre-Columbian times.

These two long avenues lead to **Miraflores** ⓣ, the main area for restaurants, cafés, nightlife, and some shopping. Avenida Larco used to be the main shopping area, but in recent years new commercial centers like Centro Comercial Larcomar, Caminos del Inca, and Jockey Plaza Shopping Mall have become the places for those born to shop. A good selection of handicrafts is sold at hundreds of shops and stalls on **Avenida Petit Thouars** in Miraflores. Be sure to do some (respectful) bargaining, as prices here are higher than elsewhere in Peru.

Miraflores is really a place for the here and now, but there is one museum worth a look, the **Museo Amano** (Retiro 160, 11th block of Av. Angamos; tours Mon–Fri at 3, 4, and 5pm; tel: 01-222 5827 – call two or three days before for

*Shoeshine in Miraflores.*

**BELOW AND LEFT:** views from the Larcomar complex.

**TIP**

One of the best ways to see Lima's beaches and to get a perspective on the city from above is to take a paraglider flight. There are tandem flights for beginners, and one-day and multi-day courses. Contact Aeroxtreme, Av Tripoli 350, Dpto 302, Miraflores, tel: (01) 242 5125, email: mike@aeroxtreme.com.

an appointment; free admission, donations welcome). The museum displays a beautiful collection of textiles, mostly from the Chancay culture.

Close to Avenida Arequipa is the massive pre-Inca adobe pyramid site called the **Huaca Pucllana**. This has been cleared in recent years, and there are frequent guided tours (open Mon, Wed–Sun 9am–1pm and 2.30–5pm; entrance fee). There is also a small museum, and an excellent bar and restaurant.

At the top end of Larco is the **Parque Kennedy**, where artists sell paintings at the weekend. Here, next to the Pacífico Cinema, is the Café Haiti, a prime spot for people-watching. Round the corner, in Ricardo Palma, is the more upmarket Vivaldi Café. Walking down Diagonal, you will find export-quality coffee in the trendy Café Café or the Café Olé, and a little farther on, a pedestrianized side street crammed with pizzerias with open-air tables. Continue down the Diagonal and you reach the cliffs overlooking the Pacific, laid out with gardens – a lovely place to watch the sunset. A cobbled road leads down a gully to the sweep of beaches called the **Costa Verde**. This

beautiful part of town is safer than it used to be, although it is advisable not to walk here alone or after dark. *Limeños* flock here in their thousands to bathe on summer Sundays, but the sea is polluted. The resorts to the south of the city are better for swimming.

But the Costa Verde is an attractive place, for the coast road sweeps on round (with fine views of the city) to the isolated beach of **La Herradura** , a popular spot to eat *ceviche* (fish marinated in lemon juice with onion and hot peppers) while watching the Pacific breakers. Closer to Miraflores are two superb fish restaurants (with international prices) – the Costa Verde on the beach, and the traditional Rosa Náutica *(see page 165)*, built on a pier surrounded by the ocean.

From Playa La Herradura, the road doubles back through a tunnel, leading to **Chorrillos** ⓥ, an area of mixed social composition, high on the sandy cliffs. Down on the beach is a fishing wharf, where small boats can be hired.

The road now loops back toward Miraflores and takes you to **Barranco** ⓦ, a beautiful district of colonial and

**BELOW:** the pre-Inca Huaca Pucllana. **RIGHT:** the official tour.

19th-century housing, much of which has been recently restored. This romantic neighborhood is the home of many bohemians, writers, and artists, and is celebrated in Peruvian waltzes. It has become the center of the city's nightlife, with a score or more of *peñas* (folk clubs) and bars where music of all kinds is played. The bar La Noche (Av. Bolognesi 307) is a popular place for a beer, and it's recommended for a night out in Barranco *(see Travel Tips, page 340)*. For a more traditional evening, go to Juanito's (Av. Grau 274), an old Italian-run bar on the plaza and a popular haunt of generations of *barranquiños*.

Opposite the attractive main square is the wooden **Puente de Los Suspiros** or Bridge of Sighs, a traditional meeting place for lovers, set among gardens overlooking the Pacific. Cross the bridge, follow the path by the church, and you'll find several small bars where *anticuchos* (cured and marinated beef-heart kebabs) are served. From the bars right at the end you have a good view of the Costa Verde. On Saturday evening you can sample *anticuchos* the traditional way, from the stalls that are set up

outside the church. For a touch of culture, visit the **Museo Pedro de Osma**, a private museum containing colonial art (Pedro de Osma 421; open Tue–Sun 10am–1.30pm and 2.30–6pm; entrance fee).

## The Pacific port

Now joined to the capital, the port of **Callao** ✪ was originally a settlement apart, some 15 km (9 miles) west of the city. Though Callao is poor and run-down, it has several points of interest. The **La Punta** area is one of them. There the Club Universitario restaurant, the Rana Verde (Green Frog; Plaza Gálvez; tel: 01-429 8453) is open to visitors at lunchtime. Permission is required to enter the docks, but from the neighboring wharf launches take passengers for trips round the bay. Nearby is the 18th-century **Real Felipe Fort**, the last royalist redoubt in Peru. It was captured by Bolívar's forces in 1826 after a year-long siege. It now contains a military museum – the **Museo Militar** (open daily 9am–4pm; entrance fee). ❑

*Taking a siesta in the gardens in Barranco.*

**LEFT:** path down to the sea.
**BELOW:** strolling through leafy Barranco.

# RESTAURANTS AND CAFÉS

## Restaurants

Prices are per person for a two-course meal, excluding wine:
**$** less than US$10
**$$** US$10–20
**$$$** more than US$20

### Chinese

**Chifa Capon**
Ucayali 774
Tel: (01) 427 2969
Traditional restaurant in downtown Chinatown. **$**

**Chifa Kun Fa**
San Martín 459, Miraflores
Tel: (01) 447 8634
Typical Peruvian-style Chinese cuisine. **$**

**Chifa Lung Fung**
Av. República de Panamá 3165, San Isidro
Tel: (01) 441 8817
One of the city's best Chinese restaurants. **$**

### Criolla

**Las Brujas de Cachiche**
Bolognesi 472, Miraflores
Tel: (01) 446 6536
Good criolla food. **$$**

**Huaca Pucllana**
Gral. Borgoño Cdra. 8 s/n
Tel: (01) 445 4042
This excellent restaurant overlooks an ancient adobe pyramid. The menu features new twists on classic criolla cooking. **$$**

**Manos Morenas**
Av. San Pedro de Osma 409, Barranco
Tel: (01) 467 0421
*Peña* with a well-deserved reputation for criollo food and live music (Thur–Sat from 10pm). **$$**

### French

**Le Bistrot de mes Fils**
Av. Conquistadores 510, San Isidro
Tel: (01) 422 6308
A real French bistro serving great food. **$$$**

**L'Eau Vive**
Ucayali 370
Tel: (01) 275 612
Fine provincial dishes prepared and served by nuns. The sky-lit inner courtyard is one of Lima's most pleasant settings for lunch (the nuns – and customers – sing Ave Maria nightly at 9pm). **$$**

### International

**Ambrosia**
Hotel Miraflores Park Plaza, Malecón de la Reserva 1035, Miraflores
Tel: (01) 242 3000
Tempting gourmet cuisine in classy surroundings. **$$$**

**La Gloria**
Calle Atahualpa 201–5, Esq. 2 de Mayo, Miraflores
Tel: (01) 445 5705
Delicious Mediterranean food – the quality is commensurate with the price. **$$$**

### Italian

**La Trattoria**
Manuel Bonilla 106, Miraflores
Tel: (01) 446 7002
Delicious homemade Italian pasta. **$$**

**Valentino**
Manuel Bañón 215, San Isidro
Tel: (01) 441 6174
Excellent Italian cusine. **$$**

### Japanese

**Matsuei Sushi Bar**
Manuel Bañón 260, San Isidro
Tel: (01) 422 4323/ 442 856
Excellent Japanese food. **$$$**

### Peruvian

**Astrid y Gastón**
Calle Cantaurias 175, Miraflores
Tel: (01) 242 5387
Arguably Lima's best restaurant, offering exquisite *novoandino* dishes. **$$$**

**El Bolivariano**
Pasaje Santa Rosa 291, Pueblo Libre
Tel: (01) 261 9565
If you want to eat traditional Peruvian fare, this is one of the best places to come in Lima. **$$**

**LEFT:** *ceviche mixto.* **RIGHT:** an exquisite dessert.

### Junius

Jirón Independencia 125, Miraflores
Tel: (01) 617 1000, ext 278
Great Peruvian food, a flamboyant floorshow, and handicrafts for sale. **$$$**

### El Señorio de Sulco

Malecón Cisneros 1470, Miraflores
Tel: (01) 441 0183
Exquisite Peruvian cuisine on the quay-side. **$$$**

### Las Tejas

Diez Canesco 340, Miraflores
Tel: (01) 444 4360
Excellent *anticuchos* (kebabs) plus live criollo music (Thur–Sat). **$$**

## Seafood

### Cevicheria Barranco

Av. Panamerica Sur 270, Barranco
Tel: (01) 467 4560
This little restaurant is easy to overlook, but it serves a great-tasting *ceviche limeño*. **$**

### La Costa Verde

Playa Barranquito
Tel: (01) 477 5228
A good choice for both food and atmosphere. **$$$**

### Punto Azul

Calle San Martin 595, Esq. Alcanfores, Miraflores
Tel: (01) 445 8070
Punto Azul serves some of the best ceviche in Lima. It is one of several branches in the city. **$$**

### La Rosa Naútica

Espigón 4, Costa Verde, Miraflores
Tel: (01) 447 005
Lima's most famous seafood restaurant. Located at the end of an ocean boardwalk with great Pacific views. **$$$**

## Steakhouses

### La Carreta

Rivera Navarrete 740, San Isidro
Tel: (01) 442 2690
Excellent Argentine beef. **$$**

### Cuarto y Mitad

Commandante Espinar 798, Miraflores
Tel: (01) 446 5229
A great place for a grill. **$$**

### La Tranquera

Av. José Pardo 285, Miraflores
Tel: (01) 447 5111
Good steaks in a kitsch ranch-style dining room. **$$**

## Vegetarian

### Bircher-Benner

Av. República de Panamá 3615, San Isidro
Tel: (01) 422 8918
Inexpensive, good food; Lima's best option for vegetarians. **$**

### Restaurante Vrinda

Av. Javier Prado Este 195, Miraflores
Tel: (01) 592 2486
Excellent vegetarian food served in salubrious surround-ings. **$$**

## Cafés

### Bohemia

Santa Cruz 805, Ovalo Gutiérrez, Miraflores
Tel: (01) 445 0889/ 446 5240
Good salads, sand-wiches, and mains. **$$**

### Café Café

Larcomar, Av. Malecón de la Reserva 610, Miraflores
Tel: (01) 445 9499
A great spot for coffee and cakes, overlooking the Pacific. There is another branch at Már-tir Olaya 250. **$$**

### Café de las Artes

Camino Real 1075, San Isidro (Centro Cultural PUCP)
Tel: (01) 222 6899
A hangout for the young, hip, and arty in a univer-sity cultural center. **$**

### Café Haiti

Diagonal 160, Miraflores
Tel: (01) 446 3816
Favorite hangout for writers and artists. **$**

### Café Olé

Pancho Fierro 115, San Isidro
Tel: (01) 440 1186
Smart café serving good coffee and snacks. **$$**

### Mangos Café Restaurant

Larcomar, Av. Malecón de la Reserva 610, Miraflores
Tel: (01) 242 6779
Pleasant café with a terrace. **$$**

### La Tiendecita Blanca – Café Suisse

Av. Larco 111, Miraflores
Tel: (01) 445 9797/ 445 1412
Excellent tea shop. **$$**

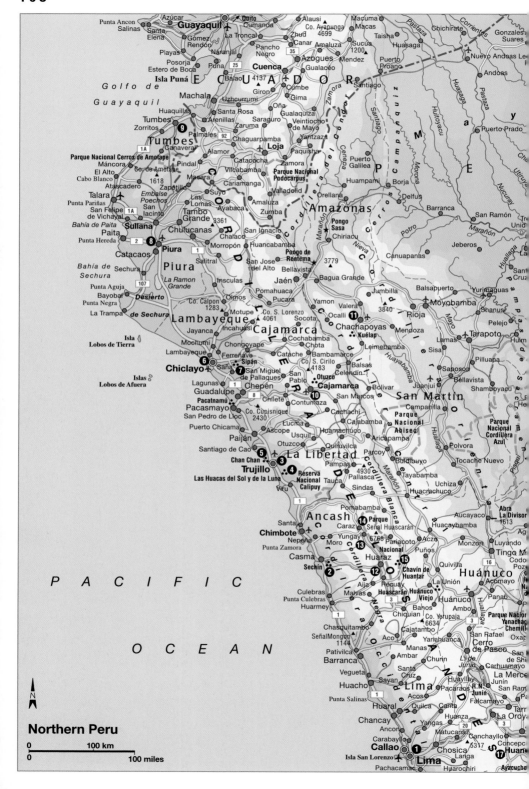

Northern Peru

0        100 km

0        100 miles

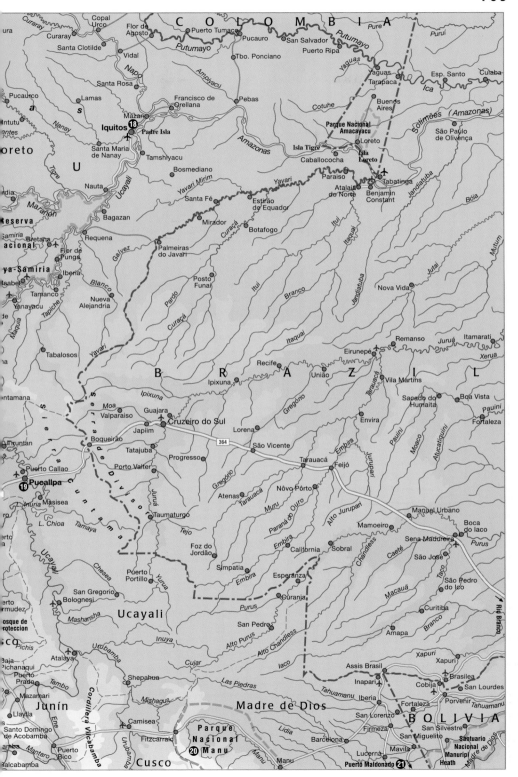

*Recommended Restaurants on page 179*

# THE NORTH COAST

The colonial city of Trujillo, a wealth of archeological digs,
Peru's best beaches, and a witchcraft market are some of
the highlights along the north coast

Lima

he north coast of Peru is not visited as much as the area farther south, but it has much to offer, including a wealth of archeological sites, the colonial city of Trujillo, and the port of Chiclayo. Regular buses ply the Panamericana north from **Lima ❶** to the border with Ecuador. The first stop after Lima for most people is **Sechín ❷**, an ancient archeological site decorated with extraordinary wall carvings showing bellicose warriors and their hapless, dismembered victims. The first excavation work here was done in the 1930s by the eminent Peruvian archeologist J.C. Tello. The site is still under excavation, but much of it can be seen, and there is an informative museum on the site (open daily 9am–5pm; entrance fee). The site is believed to date to the end of the Initial Period (*c*.1000 BC), but nothing is known about the people who built it. You can get to Sechín by taking one of the frequent buses from Lima (about 350 km/220 miles) to the small town of Casma, from where you can get a taxi or a *colectivo* to the ruins.

## Colonial-style Trujillo

The next stop along the coast is at **Trujillo ❸**, Peru's most important northern city (and the second-largest in the country, with a population of 1.2 million). Charming, formal, and simple, this is the perfect spot from which to explore Peru's gentle but fiercely patriotic north. Founded in 1535 and named after Francisco Pizarro's birthplace in Spain, Tru-

jillo was the resting place for Spaniards journeying between Lima and Quito. It soon merited the title "Lordliest City," and its well-preserved colonial homes with intricate wooden Andalusian-style balconies and window grills pay testimony to an elegant past.

Although European ways were firmly planted here, *trujillanos* eschewed blind loyalty to the Spanish Crown. In December 1820, it became the first Peruvian city to proclaim its independence from Spain, and liberator Simón de Bolívar, moving down the coast from Ecuador,

**Main attractions**
SECHÍN
COLONIAL TRUJILLO
HUACAS DEL SOL Y DE LA LUNA
CHAN CHAN
HUACA DEL DRAGÓN
HUANCHACO
MERCADO DE BRUJOS
MUSEO BRÜNING
MÁNCORA

**PRECEDING PAGES:**
the Huaca del Sol.
**LEFT:** fishing boat.
**BELOW:** Trujillo's
town hall.

*The Statue of Liberty in Trujillo's Plaza de Armas.*

set the seat of his revolutionary government here. From Trujillo he prepared his campaigns for the decisive battles of Junín, Pichincha, and Ayacucho. At the last battle, on the plain bearing the same name, soldiers under Mariscal José de Sucre turned back the royalist troops once and for all.

A century later, political fervor coursed through Trujillo when the city gave birth to the progressive political party APRA, the American Popular Revolutionary Alliance. But the ideas of its founder, Victor Raúl Haya de la Torre, were too radical for the government of the day; the party was outlawed and forced to operate in secret. Government repression and torture of *apristas* (as APRA party members were called) culminated in 1932 in the brutal "Trujillo Massacre." After a rebellious crowd of party followers attacked an army post and killed the officers in charge, 1,000 people were executed by military firing squads among the adobe walls of Chan Chan.

Over the following decades, the *apristas* were the most strident opposition party, but never came to power. In 1962, Haya de la Torre, by then aged 67, won the elections for APRA, only for the military to refuse to recognize his victory. It was not until 1985 when Alán García won a landslide that APRA finally governed Peru – but Haya de la Torre himself had been dead for six years. Even today, on the anniversaries of Haya de la Torre's birth and death, his grave with its eternal torch and inscription "Here Lies the Light" is piled high with flowers. The mention of his name sparks perhaps more outpourings of love – and hatred – than that of any other Peruvian.

Another of Trujillo's militant *apristas*, the writer Ciro Alegría, was exiled to Chile, where he published the first of the trilogy, based on his childhood and *campesino* (subsistence farmer's) life, that made him one of the continent's most acclaimed authors. He won literary attention with *La Serpiente de Oro (The Serpent of Gold)*, but is best-known for *El Mundo Es Ancho y Ajeno (The World is Wide and Foreign)*.

## Around the Plaza de Armas

These tumultuous days of exile and bloodshed seem distant now in Trujillo, where formality and turn-of-the-20th-

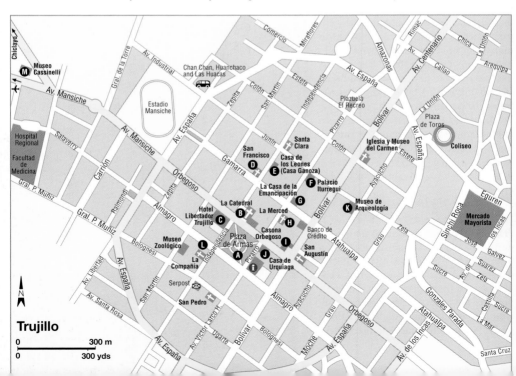

**Trujillo**

0       300 m

0       300 yds

*Recommended Restaurants on page 179*

century charm hang in the air. The best way to see this city is on foot, and the best place to start is the huge **Plaza de Armas Ⓐ**, at the center of which is a statue of a running winged figure – Liberty, whose face closely resembles Simón Bolívar's – holding a torch. This landmark stands on disproportionately short legs, designed to appease officials who feared the monument would end up taller than the Cathedral facing it.

The plaza is dominated by the **Catedral Ⓑ** (open Mon–Fri 8am–12.30pm and 4–8pm, Sat 8am–1pm, open Sun for Mass only), dating from the mid-18th century. The Cathedral once had elaborate metal adornments and railings, like many of the colonial houses, but they were melted down for armaments during the War of Independence. The **Hotel Libertador Trujillo Ⓒ**, housed in a beautiful colonial-style building, stands on the northwest corner of the square. Even if you are not staying in the hotel (it's about the most expensive in Trujillo), try to have breakfast or lunch in its small-windowed dining room looking out onto the plaza. From this vantage point one can see the comings and goings of the city's elderly men who stake out shady benches to read their morning newspapers, the young mothers carrying their market baskets with toddlers in tow, or uniformed schoolgirls huddled together sharing secrets.

Two blocks from the square, on Jirón Independencia, is the colonial **Iglesia San Francisco Ⓓ** (open daily Mon–Sat 7–9am and 4–8pm, open Sun for Mass only). Almost opposite stands the attractive **Casa de los Leones Ⓔ** (open Mon–Fri 9am–1pm and 2–6pm, Sat 9am–1pm), also known as the Casa Ganoza Chopitea, which houses a small art gallery as well as an office of the Policía de Turismo. It got its name from the statues of lions that guard the front door. Most of Trujillo's mansions have been elegantly restored by national banks or other private enterprises, and are well worth visiting if you can get inside. If not, you must be content with the view from outside of the detailed window grills and intricately carved wooden bal-

conies, which are synonymous with this city. The window grills are purely decorative; over the centuries their simple designs became increasingly elaborate as the colonial *trujillanos* tried to outdo one another. The balconies, on the other hand, had a practical purpose: they allowed upper-class women to look down onto the street, but prevented interested menfolk from looking in.

From Casa de los Leones, turn right on Junín, then right again on Jirón Pizarro, to see the **Palacio Iturregui Ⓕ** (open Mon–Sat 9am–7pm; free admission), a neo-colonial building where Trujillo's unilateral independence from Spain was declared in 1820. It is now the home of the rather smart Club Central, which runs a small ceramics museum (open daily 11am–6pm; entrance fee). Rather oddly, it is not this building but another one nearby that is called **La Casa de la Emancipación Ⓖ** (House of the Emancipation; open Mon–Fri 10am–6pm). This mansion is typical of those constructed in the 16th and 17th centuries, and is one of the few containing its original furniture. Like many of Peru's most elegant colonial mansions, this is now the property of a

*The once exclusive Club Central is now home to a ceramics museum.*

**BELOW:** Trujillo's Plaza de Armas.

*Colonial opulence in La Casa de la Emancipación.*

**BELOW:** Palacio Iturregui.

bank, the Banco Continental, and the staff are happy to show visitors where earthquakes and remodeling over the centuries have changed the building's original lines. Back towards the Plaza Mayor you will find the **Iglesia de La Merced** ❶, where a small crowd of visitors can often be found peering upward at the intricately carved dome. The next stop, on the corner of Orbegoso and Bolívar, is the **Casona Orbegoso** ❶, a stately colonial mansion, no longer open to visitors, but impressive for its grand exterior. Almost opposite is the Iglesia de San Agustín, the oldest church in the city.

Back on the Plaza de Armas is the elegant colonial **Casa de Urquiaga** ❶, which belongs to the Banco de la Nación (open Mon–Fri 9am–3pm, Sat 10am–1.30pm; free admission), said to be where the liberator Simón Bolívar stayed when in Trujillo.

A block away from the Plaza de Armas, on Jirón Pizarro, lies the **Museo de Arqueología** ❶, the museum of the National University of Trujillo (open Mon–Fri 8am–2.45pm; entrance fee). Among the artifacts here are fine pieces of Moche and Chimu pottery and copies of some of the wall paintings found at the Huaca de la Luna *(see opposite)*. Turn left into the square (along Almagro) and you'll come to **La Compañía** ❶, another notable colonial church, which is now used as an auditorium by the University of Trujillo. Close to the church is the Museo Zoológico (open Mon–Fri 8am–7pm, Sat until 1pm; entrance fee), but the stuffed exhibits are not very exciting. For an interesting experience you could then get a taxi to the western outskirts of the city, in the direction of Chiclayo, to one of the most unusual museums you are likely to find. The **Museo Cassinelli** ❶ (open Mon–Sat 9am–1pm and 2–6pm; entrance fee) is housed in the basement of the Cassinelli gas station and holds a fascinating private collection of Moche and Chimu ceramics.

## Trujillo's dancing horses

*Trujillanos* are proud of their *caballos de paso*, a fine breed of horses with a tripping gait that has made them known worldwide. Another legacy of the conquest, since there were no horses on the continent before the arrival of the Spaniards, these horses have been immortalized in

Recommended Restaurants on page 179

Peruvian waltzes. In particular, composer Chabuca Granda, for whom a monument is erected in the bohemian neighborhood of Barranco in Lima, wrote of the *chalanes* or riders in their *jipijapa* sombreros upon their honey-colored mounts. These riders still compete in their own form of the *marinera* dance – smoothly guiding their horses through the steps. The best of these trotters are bred in and around Trujillo, and buyers from around the world congregate to see them shown at the annual Spring Festival – *Festival de la Primavera*. Don't forget, though, that Peru's spring is the northern hemisphere's fall, and this festival takes place in September.

The *Festival de la Marinera* is celebrated in the last week of January, when dancers from all over the country compete for the title of *Campeones de la Marinera*. It's a spectacular show, and the whole town has a party atmosphere, particularly during the finals on the last weekend. The *marinera* is a graceful dance rooted in African and Spanish rhythms; some say its steps mimic the strutting of a rooster courting a hen. Women in ruffled lace skirts seductively flit toward white-garbed men in ponchos before quickly pulling away. The men attempt to win back their attention, tossing up hats and catching them in mid-fall.

## Nearby temples

About 10 km (6 miles) southeast of Trujillo lie the **Huacas del Sol y de la Luna** (Temples of the Sun and the Moon) ❹. You can get there by minibus from Trujillo, or go with a guide on an organized tour. These two pyramidal temples were built by the Moche people (100 BC–AD 850) over several generations. The Huaca del Sol (arguably the largest pre-Columbian building in the Americas) is currently being excavated, but at the smaller Huaca de la Luna, years of archeological work have begun to unveil a series of temples superimposed on one another to form a pyramid covered in beautiful, brightly colored murals (open daily 9am–4.30pm; entrance fee).

To the northwest of Trujillo (take one of the frequent minibuses or *colectivos*

from Trujillo) are the ruins of **Chan Chan** ❺ (open daily 9am–4.30pm; entrance fee), possibly the world's largest adobe city. Laid out over 20 sq km (7½ sq miles) just 600 meters/yards from the ocean, its seven citadels are enclosed by a massive adobe wall. Chan Chan was the capital of the Chimu empire and was once home to some 100,000 people. Its citizens fished and farmed, worshiped the moon, and had no written records – leaving it to archeologists to unravel their secrets. An echoing silence surrounds visitors to this ancient city, whose walls bear carvings of fish, seabirds, fishing nets, and moons.

Aided by sophisticated aqueduct and irrigation systems, the Chimu turned the arid wasteland around them into fertile fields of grain, fruits, and vegetables supporting a population that may have reached 35,000. When conquered by the Incas, the Chimu were not forced to change their ways – except for the addition of the sun to their collection of gods. Rather, Inca teachers were sent to study their farming and irrigation systems and

*Replica* tumis, *knives that were used in human sacrifice by the Moche people, on sale at the Huaca de la Luna site.*

**BELOW:** murals at the Huaca de la Luna.

*A brightly colored fishing boat at Santa Rosa.*

Chimu goldsmiths were sent to Cusco. It wasn't until the Incas, under Tupac Yupanqui, sabotaged the aqueducts after repeated attempts to invade Chan Chan that the fearless Chimu left the protection of the city – and were conquered.

An entrance ticket to Chan Chan also allows visitors to see the **Huaca del Dragón** – also known as the Huaca Arco Iris (the Rainbow Temple) – with its beautifully restored wall carvings, and the ruins of **Huaca La Esmeralda** nearby. Licensed guides can be hired at the ticket office. Tourists are advised to begin their visit in the morning and avoid going alone; the tourism police at Chan Chan frequently go home in mid-afternoon, and there have been a number of thefts at the site. Visitors should also avoid vendors hawking what they claim is antique pottery. Most pieces are fakes, and genuine items can be confiscated and the holder fined or jailed for trying to take them out of Peru.

Archeology enthusiasts should also visit the **Huaca el Brujo**, a recently discovered site a few hours outside Trujillo in the Chicama valley. Ask at the Tourist Information Office for details.

## Sugar and surf

Before you set off north, another short trip (about 15 km/10 miles) from Trujillo is to the seaside village of **Huanchaco**. Two centuries ago, when Huanchaco residents paid taxes to the Spanish Crown, it was a quiet village of men who fished and women who wove baskets in the sunshine. Today Huanchaco is a popular destination for surfers and beach lovers, although it still retains a village air. Sun-bronzed fishermen head out each morning with their nets tucked into *caballitos de totora*, literally "little horses" woven from *totora* reed. The design of these peapod-shaped boats is not very different from that of the craft used by pre-Inca people, and the *caballitos* contrast startlingly with the brightly colored surfboards that now share the Pacific waves.

Some 40 km (25 miles) north of Trujillo (there are buses) are vestiges of one of the sources of Trujillo's past wealth: sugar. Owing to its gentle climate, the Chicama valley region produces most of Peru's sugar crop, an important product in a country where three spoonfuls go into every cup of coffee and all children seem to be born with a sweet tooth. Land

## Little Reed Horses

Imagine a little army of horses, heads held high, setting out to sea each day. Walk along the beach in Huanchaco in the early morning and you will see just this. Huanchaco's *caballitos de totora* are one-man reed rafts with high prows that resemble the head of a horse. The design of the craft dates back to the Moche civilization that first ruled this coast some 2,000 years ago.

Huanchaco's 40 or so fishermen paddle out to sea each day to set nets for scale fish, and traps for crab and octopus. At midday they surf back in with their catch for the restaurants of Huanchaco and markets of Trujillo. The rafts, made of bundled reeds, remain tough and buoyant for about three months. To build a new *caballito*, cut, dried, and bundled reeds are lashed tightly together, which takes the most experienced less than an hour. Each fisherman has two rafts – one for fishing in the morning and one for the afternoon so that they don't get saturated with water. For a small fee, the friendly fishermen will take you out for a ride.

*Recommended Restaurants on page 179*

reform, begun in the late 1960s, turned most of the great haciendas into cooperatives, but the opulence of the past is still evident. The most impressive are Casa Grande and Hacienda Cartavio, now large-scale agro-industrial projects; the latter is where the sugar is used to make Cartavio rum.

## Magic and Moche finds

The next stop north is the busy port of **Chiclayo ❻** some 200 km (125 miles) up the Panamericana – there are regular bus services as well as frequent flights from Lima and Trujillo. This bustling city is a major commercial hub for northern Peru, and is a lively and friendly spot with few pretensions. This vitality is reflected in the architecture of the city center, in which the modern happily coexists with the colonial in the winding streets.

One unmissable sight within the city is the extensive **Mercado de Brujos** (Witchcraft Market), also known as the Mercado Modelo, one of the most comprehensive in South America. Here is an overwhelming choice of herbal medicines, potions, charms, and San Pedro cacti, from which a hallucinogenic drug is extracted and used by *curanderos* (healers) in traditional shamanic healing rituals.

A short distance away is the coastal resort of **La Pimentel**, with a good sandy beach – an excellent place to try the local specialty of *pescado seco*, a kind of ray-fish known as *la guitarra*, which can often be found hanging out to dry in the sun in Chiclayo's market. Just south of Pimentel is **Santa Rosa**, where beautiful fishing boats can be seen drawn up on the beach.

Chiclayo is, of course, the starting point for visits to two of the continent's most exciting archeological digs. The greatest attention has been lavished on the Moche burial area at **Sipán ❼** (open daily 9am–5pm; entrance fee; guided tours available), about 30 km (18 miles) south of the city. Here, Peru's best documented grave, known as the tomb of El Señor de Sipán *(see pages 180–1)*, was uncovered in the late 1980s, originally by *huaqueros* (grave robbers), before the excavation was

taken over by Dr Walter Alva. The site is well worth visiting, but to see the stunning gold, silver, and ceramic artifacts taken from it (when they're not touring the world's museums) you must visit the **Museo Brüning** (open daily 9am–5pm; entrance fee), which is in Lambayeque, about 17 km (10 miles) from Chiclayo.

From Lambayeque you can go on to the huge site at **Túcume**, with its numerous pyramids. The excavation here was originally directed by Norwegian Thor Heyerdahl *(see page 35)*.

Travel north from Chiclayo through the great coastal desert, sometimes turned green by the heavy rains induced by El Niño. **Piura ❽** is a hot commercial city best known for its folk dance, the *tondero*, a more rustic version of Trujillo's *marinera*, and the black magic still practiced by the descendants of slaves. The *tondero* is a lively barefoot Afro-Peruvian dance accompanied by strong rhythmic music and sashaying dancers in multicolored outfits. But many Peruvian visitors come to see more than the dancers. There are Lima business executives who travel

*Bottled herbs at the Mercado de Brujos.*

**BELOW:** fruit seller at the Mercado de Brujos.

Map on pages 168–9

*Piura is famous for its cuisine, with its sharp flavors and elaborate preparation. The best dishes include* seco de chavelo *(mashed plantains with fried pork),* majado de yucca con chicharrón *(mashed manioc with fried pork),* chifles *(fried plantain), and* natilla *(molasses made from goats' milk and sugar cane).*

here annually to consult the area's *brujos* – witch doctors and folk healers who use herbs and potions to cure patients.

Piura has a proud history, beginning with its foundation by the Spanish in 1532 – three years before Lima – and continuing through the War of the Pacific with Chile (1879–83). That war's most famous Peruvian hero was Admiral Miguel Grau, and his home on Jirón Tacna across from the Centro Cívico has been converted into a museum, the **Museo Naval Miguel Grau** (opening hours vary; free admission). Of interest there is the scale model of the British-built *Huascar*, the largest Peruvian warship in that conflict. Grau was commander of the vessel and used it to keep the invading Chilean forces at bay until he was forced to scuttle his ship in the Battle of Angamos, an event still remembered every year on October 8.

### Hemingway haunt

North of Piura, on the way to the Ecuadorian border, lies **Talara**, a desert oasis and petroleum-producing center. Closer still to the northern border are some of the best and most fashionable beaches in

**BELOW:** fishermen in Punta Sal.

Peru: **Máncora**, **Punta Sal**, and **Playa La Pena**. **Cabo Blanco** (south of Máncora) is a popular spot for marlin fishing, once frequented by Ernest Hemingway, but experts say the marlin have now been carried south by the Humboldt Current to Máncora. Peru's coast has some of the world's most spectacular waves, and Máncora is frequently the site of international surfing competitions.

**Talara** is as unattractive as any oil town, and travelers are recommended to seek accommodations in the above-mentioned beach resorts. Camping is permitted at Cabo Blanco and other nearby beaches. South of Talara are the **Brea Tarpits**, where the Spanish boiled tar to caulk their ships.

### Frontier town

About 140 km (85 miles) north of Talara is **Tumbes** , a frontier town with a military post and immigration offices, although it is about 30 km (18 miles) from the Ecuadorian border. Although there has been an ongoing effort to give this city a facelift, there continues to be a problem with theft – particularly affecting tourists, often occuring near the bus offices or at the colorful outdoor market. A few miles outside the city, at the actual border, known as **Aguas Verdes** on the Peruvian side, travelers are barraged by unscrupulous money-changers, porters, and over-friendly individuals with dubious motives. Police corruption is notorious here, although that is something which affects Peruvians far more than outsiders, and focuses on the widespread cross-border trafficking in contraband items.

Tumbes is also within spitting distance of the few Peruvian beaches that offer white sand and warm water for swimming year-round. **Caleta La Cruz**, which has an attractive fishing fleet, can be reached by taxi, in *colectivos*, or by combis heading north from Máncora, as can **Zorritos**, a larger fishing village with a couple of hotels. **Puerto Pizarro** has intriguing mangrove swamps around the village with some interesting birdlife, and boat tours can be arranged with fishermen in the port. ❑

# RESTAURANTS

## Restaurants

Prices are per person for a two-course meal, excluding wine:
**$** less than US$10
**$$** US$10–20
**$$$** more than US$20

### Chiclayo

**El Huaralino**
Calle Libertad 115, Urb. Santa Victoria
Tel: (047) 270 330
Among Chiclayo's best; serves great Peruvian food and specialties from Chiclayo. **$$**

**Restaurant Típico la Fiesta**
Av. Salaverry 1820 (in 3 de Octubre district)
Excellent local dishes. **$$**

**Romana**
Balta 512
Tel: (074) 223 598
Popular place; good local food. **$**

**Las Tinajas Norteñas**
Av. Elías Aguirre 957
Delicious seafood. **$**

### Huanchaco

**Club Colonial**
Calle Grau 272, Plaza de Armas
Tel: (044) 461 015
This beautiful mansion offers Peruvian and French dishes in colonial surroundings. **$$**

**Restaurant Big Ben**
Av. Larco 836
Tel: (044) 461 378
Another branch of the Trujillo restaurant. Wonderful fresh seafood is served at lunchtime daily. Pick a table overlooking the sea, and enjoy a long, slow lunch to the sound of the waves. **$$**

### Piura

**La Santitos**
Calle Libertad 104
Tel: (073) 332 380
Very popular with locals, this eatery is often full on account of its tasty, simple fare. **$$**

### Trujillo

There is a concentration of cheap, clean restaurants near the market, including several good *chifas* (Chinese restaurants) and a number of vegetarian places on Bolívar.

**El Cuatrero**
Av. Larco 1094
Good, inexpensive meat grills. Known to locals and highly recommended. **$**

**Mar Picante**
Av. America Sur 2199
Tel: (044) 221 544
This restaurant serves wonderful seafood, including excellent ceviche, at amazingly low prices. **$**

**De Marco**
Francisco Pizarro 725
Tel: (044) 234 251
Peruvian and international cuisine. Popular for ice creams. **$**

**El Mochica**
Jr. Bolivar 462
Tel: (044) 224 401
Criollo fare, specializing in fish and seafood. Often full so, it is advisable to book in advance. **$**

**Restaurant Big Ben**
Calle España 1317
Tel: (044) 221 342

Serves delicious seafood and meat dishes. **$$**

**Romano Rincón Criollo**
Estados Unidos 162
Tel: (044) 244 207
Great criollo food accompanied by a lively atmosphere. There is a good value lunch menu, and it is recommended by locals. **$$**

**Il Valentino**
Jr. Orbegosa 224
Tel: (044) 295 339
If you've had your fill of criollo food, try the great pizzas and Italian food at this popular eatery. **$**

**RIGHT:** alfresco dining on the north coast.

# BURIED TREASURES

**Excavations of grave sites in Peru have revealed fascinating evidence of rich and varied cultures that flourished long before the Incas**

The architectural remains of the Inca Empire are so awe-inspiring that it is easy to forget that a number of earlier civilizations flourished in Peru. They left no written records, so much of the information that has been gleaned about them comes from grave sites.

The best-known are at Sipán and Sicán, both in northern Peru. Originally unearthed by grave robbers in 1987, the tomb of the Lord of Sipán, believed to be a ruler of the Moche period (*c.*100–700 AD), yielded unimaginable riches: gold masks, turquoise and lapis lazuli jewelry, copper headdresses, ceramic pots, and domestic implements provided archeologists with vital information about the Moche way of life.

At Sicán, the first site to be excavated using radar, similar riches were discovered, including golden death masks, a copper crown, and a beaded cloak. The Sicán era spanned the 9th and 10th centuries, the period between the Moche and the Chimu. At both sites, there is evidence of what appears to be human sacrifice: at Sicán the bodies of young women were buried with that of their lord, and at Sipán servants or soldiers accompanied their master to the grave. The Sicán site museum is at Ferreñafe, north of Chiclayo.

In the southern desert, at the Paracas Necropolis (*c.*1st century AD), excavations in the 1920s by archeologist J.C. Tello yielded hundreds of mummified bundles, wrapped in intricately embroidered cloth. Examples of these textiles can be seen in the Museo de la Nación in Lima. At the Chauchilla Cemetery, farther south, remains of the Nazca culture (*c.*200–800 AD) were discovered in the early 1900s. Designs on the pottery buried with the dead gave important clues about their daily lives.

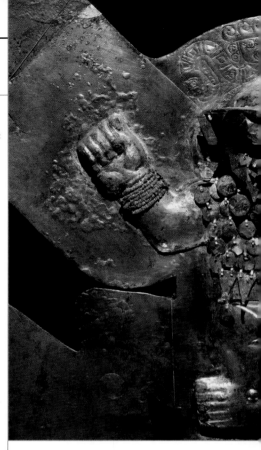

**ABOVE:** a gold representation of a Moche deity found at the tomb of the Lord of Sipán. Like most of the important Sipán finds, this artifact has now been placed in the Museo Brüning in Lambayeque.

**BELOW:** an archeologist painstakingly excavates a skeleton buried with copper artifacts at the Sipán site.

**ABOVE**: a golden mask from the Tomb of the Lord of Sipán, its opulence denoting the status and importance of the wearer during his earthly life.

## DISTURBING THE DEAD

The smuggling of antiquities is a multi-million-dollar international trade, so it's little wonder that ancient grave sites have attracted looters. Around the Cemetery of Chauchilla, near Nazca, the desert is strewn with bones and skulls unearthed by *huaqueros* (grave robbers), stripped of valuables, and left to bleach in the sun. Priceless treasures have been lifted from burial sites all over the country and sold to collectors.

It was the *huaqueros'* discovery of the Sipán tomb in the late 1980s that provoked a clamp-down. Initiated by Dr Walter Alva, curator of the Museo Brüning in Lambayeque, a government-backed program now targets looters, rewards informers, and uses education campaigns in an attempt to end the lucrative trade. At a local level, it is having a measure of success. Aerial surveillance is vital to the program due to the large number of sites. Archeologists board air-force flights over the Lambayeque Valley to chart mounds that may conceal ancient complexes and sites where human destruction is obvious.

**ABOVE:** the skeleton of the Lord of Sipán was adorned with gold ornaments, including pieces to cover the eyes, ears, and face. On his feet were a pair of copper slippers that would have been used for ceremonial occasions. The bodies of servants and soldiers were buried in the tomb, along with jewelry, utensils, and ceramic pots to make him comfortable in the afterlife.

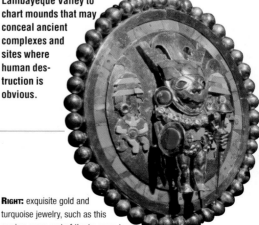

**RIGHT:** exquisite gold and turquoise jewelry, such as this earring, were part of the treasure trove at the Sipán site.

*Recommended Restaurants on page 191*

# NORTHERN SIERRA

Journeys in the highlands are long and the roads
are poor, but the rewards are friendly towns,
breathtaking scenery, and some spectacular ruins

Lima

**A**cross the dusty desert into the Andean highlands lies **Cajamarca ⑩**. Now dotted with cattle herds and dairy farms, where Peru's best cheese is made, this was one of the largest cities in the Inca empire and marks the site where the Inca people and the Spaniards had their first showdown. According to Spanish chronicles, it was in Cajamarca that the Inca Atahualpa was kidnapped and later executed.

Pizarro had sent envoys to the Inca, camped in the valley with his huge army, telling him that "he loved him dearly," and wished to meet him in Cajamarca. But Atahualpa walked into an ambush: in the Plaza de Armas the heavily armed Spaniards massacred thousands of Inca subjects who were futilely trying to protect their leader. Despite the Spaniards' numerical disadvantage, their audacity in kidnapping the Inca threw an already divided kingdom into confusion.

A demand went out across the Inca empire to assemble an outrageous ransom for Atahualpa's release. Leading llamas laden down by riches, groups of people from as far away as Cusco began the journey to Cajamarca, filling the "Ransom Room" with some of the kingdom's most valuable treasures – which the Spanish promptly melted down into bullion. The Ransom Room is still there; a red line on one wall shows where the tall and powerful Atahualpa allegedly drew a mark, agreeing to have his subjects fill the room to that line twice with silver and once with gold.

But once the majority of the ransom had been collected, the conquistadors, afraid that the Inca would serve as a focal point for rebellion as long as he remained alive, had him garroted after he had been baptized with Pizarro's own name – Francisco.

## Coming to Cajamarca

Cajamarca can be reached by daily flights from Lima, by bus from Trujillo, which takes about nine hours, or Chiclayo (about seven hours), or on a better, faster road that turns off the

**Main attractions**
IGLESIA SAN FRANCISCO
EL CUARTO DEL RESCATE
COMPLEJO BELÉN
CERRO APOLONIA
BAÑOS DEL INCA
VENTANILLAS DE OTUZCO
KUÉLAP RUINS

**LEFT:** the view from Cerro Apolonia.
**BELOW:** Cajamarca's Plaza de Armas.

every evening by locals stopping for a chat with friends, and all day long by birds dipping down for a drink.

The **Catedral** (Jirón Cruz de la Piedra; open daily 8am–11am and 6–9pm), founded in 1776, is the most noteworthy building on the plaza. Its carved wooden altars are covered in gold leaf, and its facade of intricately carved volcanic rock is impressive.

On the opposite side of the plaza is the **Iglesia San Francisco** (Church of San Francisco; open Mon–Fri 9–12pm and 4–6pm), older and more ornate than the Cathedral, and home to the **Museo de Arte Religioso** (Museum of Religious Art; open Mon–Fri 2–5pm; entrance fee), which is filled with colonial-era paintings and statues, often portraying violent and bloody subjects. A guided tour of the museum, which is a veritable storehouse of silver candelabras, gold altar vessels, jeweled vestments, and portraits of saints, includes entrance to the church's eerie catacombs – precursor to the present city cemetery.

Situated next door to the Cathedral stands the Hotel Sierra Galana, a better-than-average lodging house with rooms

Panamericana near Pacasmayo (about five hours).

The hub of this slow-paced city of some 120,000 inhabitants, built on the banks of the Río San Lucas, is the **Plaza de Armas**, the spot where Atahualpa was executed. It is still sometimes said that the pink grain on a stone slab, where the Inca was allegedly killed, is the indelible mark of his blood. The massive Inca palaces that stood here are gone, and the plaza is now ringed by colonial buildings, the Cathedral, and the lovely San Francisco church.

The center of the square is graced by an imposing stone fountain, frequented

*Recommended Restaurants on page 191*

furnished with heavy wooden antiques. There are a number of reasonable places to stay in Cajamarca, located in and around the Plaza de Armas, and a handful of inexpensive restaurants. One of them is the family-run Restaurante Salas, described by one *cajamarquino* (the name by which the city's citizens are known) as the "city's nerve center." Here locals catch up on the news and gossip while downing the city's best, and most economical, home cooking: anything from crisp salads and thick *chupe verde* (potato and vegetable soup) to hearty beef ribs and spicy *cuy* (guinea pig) stew. No meal is complete without *panqueque con manjar blanco*, a sweet, rich dessert consisting of a thick crêpe bathed in a condensed milk sauce. Hung on the restaurant's walls are paintings by local artist Andrés Zevallos, one of the founding fathers of Cajamarca's longstanding community of poets, writers, painters, and musicians. Most notable of these was Mario Urteaga, the only Peruvian artist to have his work in the permanent collection at New York's Metropolitan Museum of Art, and a person so much loved in his hometown that the procession at his funeral in 1957 lasted into the night. Urteaga's oils depict *campesinos* (subsistence farmers), simple yet human, and the Cajamarca countryside was his studio. Today, local photographer Victor Campos Río captures the beauty of the country and its people in photographs and documentary films.

## A king's ransom

A few blocks from the main plaza, on Avenida Amalia Puga, is **El Cuarto del Rescate** (The Ransom Room; open Mon–Sat 9am–1pm and 3–6pm, Sun 9am–1pm; entrance fee, which also gives admission to the Complejo Belén and the Ethnographic Museum, *see page 186*). This is the sole surviving Inca structure in the city, and there is some debate about whether it was where Atahualpa was imprisoned, or where the treasure collected from across the empire was stored. As *rescate* means both "ransom"

and "rescue" in Spanish, it could be either; whichever it was, it forges a very real link with a past that sometimes seems almost mythical.

Also close to the plaza, on Apurímac, is the **Teatro Municipal**, now known as the **Teatro Cajamarca**, rescued by this culture-loving city after being used first as a movie theater and then as a storehouse for industrial cleaners. Built by a wealthy German merchant, the theater has an impressive stamped metal ceiling, and its seating almost exactly duplicates that in the original plans. Ticket prices are kept low to entice students and less affluent *cajamarquinos*, but unfortunately performances are not staged on a regular basis.

## The Complejo Belén

Heading east along Junín from the theater you will come to the **Complejo Belén** (open Mon–Sat 9am–1pm and 3–6pm), housing the Institute of Culture, Cajamarca's most picturesque chapel, a museum, and an art gallery. The 17th-century Belén church is undoubtedly the city's loveliest, with elaborately carved stone and woodwork

*One thing is conspicuously absent on Cajamarca's cathedral – its belfries. They were deliberately left unfinished because the tax that Spain imposed on churches only became payable when a building was completed.*

**BELOW:** candle sellers outside Cajamarca Cathedral.

**BELOW:** the
Complejo Belén.

and brightly colored statues and side altars. The small white carved dove suspended over the pulpit represents the Holy Spirit and allegedly gives those who stand under it the power of eloquence. The chapel's cupola and altar depict the three levels of life: on the ground level are the common people, in an intermediary area the saints and priests, and on the top level – heaven – God and the Virgin Mary, represented by the sky-blue dome of the cupola. Many visitors are fooled by the brilliantly painted details on the upper walls and ceiling of the church; these saints and cherubs are not made of painted wood or plaster, but are intricately carved stone. More carving is found on the massive wooden doors in the church, most of them solid pieces of Nicaraguan cedar.

Connected to the church is the **Pinacoteca**, a gallery of local artists' work in what was once the kitchen of a hospital for men. Off the Pinacoteca is the former hospital ward, a room with alcoves along its side walls. The alcoves were the patients' "bedrooms," and the images of saints originally painted above them cor-

responded to their illnesses. The sickest were bedded closest to the altar, conveniently located near the door to the cemetery. An example of an alcove with blankets and its painted saint can be seen across the street at the **Museo Etnográfico y de Arqueología** (Ethnographic and Archeological Museum; open Mon–Fri 8.30am–2.30pm), which once a maternity hospital. The only difference between the two hospitals was that from the tops of the women's alcoves dangled long scarves, which the patients pulled to help them when giving birth.

The museum has an interesting collection of ceramics from indigenous cultures that dominated this region of Peru, various samples of local handicrafts, and costumes used during the annual carnival celebrations – the most raucous in the country. Across the street at the **Instituto Cultural**, Spanish-language books and the area's best postcards are on sale. The Institute has details of ongoing archeological digs that can be visited from October to May, before the highland's rainy season begins. Excavations include the

Huacaloma and Kuntur Wasi digs sponsored by the University of Tokyo.

## Cajamarca by night

There's not a lot to do in Cajamarca after sunset. The town rolls up its sidewalks early, as befits a farming community where work begins at sunrise. But nocturnal souls can listen, and dance, to boisterous local music at the Emperador, or join the camaraderie at the Sitio Bar connected to the Hostal Cajamarca behind the Complejo Belén. Here local people meet to sing, drink, and play their music, ranging from *boleros* to the *huaynos* of the Andean highlands; however, the food isn't always as good as the music. There is also live jazz music at the Peña Usha Usha, at Amalia Puga 142.

## Scaling the heights

For the physically fit, the best way to delight in Cajamarca's charms is from above. That means climbing steep **Cerro Apolonia** (open daily 9am–1pm and 3–5pm; entrance fee). Stone steps take climbers as far as a little chapel – a miniature version of Nôtre-Dame Cathedral, about halfway up the hillside – and

the rest of the journey is on a curvy road bordered by cacti, flowers, and benches for the fatigued. Near the top is the **Silla del Inca** (the Inca's Chair), a rock cut into the shape of a throne where, it is said, the Inca Atahualpa sat and looked out over his kingdom. A bronze statue of the Inca, and parking for those who arrive by taxi or car, top the hill.

The view is of green, rain-fed fields, red-tiled roofs, and whitewashed houses. At night, the Cajamarca skies – which in daytime may switch in minutes from brilliant blue to stormy gray – are usually clear and star-studded. Early risers are in for a special treat: sunrises in these highlands are beautiful, and the show is a long one. It can take the sun up to 45 minutes to switch from a silhouetting blue-black to a brilliant red-orange before lightening to a hazy yellow.

An equally spectacular view of the city can be found at Hacienda San Vicente (Jirón Revolución; tel: 076-822 466), the most intriguing hotel in town. A charming country inn perched on a steep rocky hill at the edge of Cajamarca, this lodge was constructed using Inca techniques, with a few modern

**TIP**

If you enjoy adventurous travel, try to get to the Parque Nacional Cordillera Azul, an isolated park which protects mega-diverse cloud forest on the border of San Martín and Loreto provinces. The area is home to the Cacataibo-Camano people and an amazing variety of wildlife. Talk to agencies in Tarapoto or Moyobamba about organizing a trip.

**BELOW:** street vendors in Cajamarca.

# Huallaga, Valley of Coca

**The battle against the cultivation of coca for cocaine has made the fertile Huallaga valley something of a no man's land, though the ubiquitous coca leaf is innocent enough.**

I n *la ceja de la selva* (the eyebrow of the jungle), where the mountain flanks meet the Amazon basin, lies the broad tropical valley of the Río Huallaga. Maize and rice are grown on a large scale in the fertile valley, but it is known for another product – coca.

In the Andean highlands of both Peru and Bolivia, coca has been a part of the traditional culture for more than 4,000 years. The leaves are for sale in any mountain market. Ask at a café for *mate de coca* and you will get a cup of coca-leaf tea, a drink that is the best prevention and treatment of the symptoms of *soroche* – altitude sickness.

Coca gives energy, and dulls the senses against cold, hunger, and exhaustion. The biggest consumers have always been miners, who use up to half a kilo a day each, but it is used at many other times. Before giving birth, a woman chews the leaves to hasten labor and ease the pain. When a young man wants to marry a girl, he offers coca to her father. And when somebody dies, *mate de coca* is drunk at the wake and a small pile of leaves placed in the coffin.

Coca was first cultivated in the Andes around 2000 BC. Centuries later the Incas turned its production into a monopoly, as a means of controlling subject populations. Its use was restricted to royalty, priests, doctors, and the message runners, known to travel vast distances on the energy gained from chewing the leaves. The Incas had relaxed their monopoly by the time the Spanish arrived, but the Catholic Church tried to ban the leaf, denouncing it as "the delusion of the devil." However, it changed its tune, and established a monopoly of its own, when it found that the Indians needed the leaf to survive the brutal conditions in the mines and plantations.

Back in Europe and the United States, coca was almost unheard of until the mid-1800s, when a Parisian chemist, Angelo Mariani, marketed a wine made from the leaf that became immensely popular. This Vin Mariani inspired American soft-drink companies to produce other coca-based drinks, such as Coca-Cola. At the same time, cocaine was being developed, and was quickly taken up by such luminaries as Sigmund Freud, who called it a "magical substance."

In the 1970s, the drug became more popular, particularly in the United States. Much of the crop grown in the Andes is crushed by foot in chemicals, turned into a gummy paste and flown to Colombia. After being refined into powder, the cocaine is then smuggled into North American and European cities.

Cocaine has brought violence to the Huallaga valley, in the shape of a complex conflict between the Peruvian drug squad – backed by US Drug Enforcement agents – and Colombian cocaine traffickers, left-wing guerrillas, and the coca farmers themselves. More than 40 light aircraft used by drug-traffickers to transport the paste to Colombia have been shot down over Peruvian airspace in an ongoing anti-drug offensive.

Although the Huallaga valley is an area of great natural beauty, and around the fringes there are places, such as Tingo María, that can be visited safely, only the most foolhardy tourist will venture into the heart of the valley. ❑

**LEFT:** brewing *mate de coca* (coca-leaf tea).

twists. The walls are made of packed earth painted with ocher and vegetable dyes. Skylights give illumination, fireplaces heat common areas after nightfall, and guest rooms are decorated with local handicrafts. San Vicente was built on the site where a colonial estate house once stood; its original chapel remains next door, and on San Vicente's day local farmers still take up their musical instruments and bouquets of flowers and parade to the tiny church.

## Inca bathing place

If you look out from the Cerro Apolonia by day, you may see a white mist hovering over the edge of the city. This is the steam rising from the **Baños del Inca**, (open daily 6am–6.30pm), reputedly the Incas' favorite bathing spot. A sign over a huge stone tub at the bubbling mineral springs claims that it was here that Atahualpa bathed with his family. The springs are so hot at their source that local people use them to boil eggs. Whether or not they are curative, as the locals believe, they merit a visit – you can get a bus or a *colectivo* (a taxi which takes a number of different people) from the center of town. The city has channeled the water from the springs into a lukewarm Olympic-sized outdoor pool, and built rustic cabañas where families or groups of friends can splash privately, and modern "tourist baths" where one or two people can soak in tiled hot tubs. There is a minimal entrance fee for the use of these facilities.

At the springs, several tourist hostels have sprung up, all of them with bathtubs or swimming pools fed by the springs. The best-known and most impressive, despite its rustic appearance, is the Laguna Seca (Calle Manco Cápac 1098; tel: 07-894 600, reservations in Lima; tel: 01-212 2037), a converted hacienda (farm estate), which has a pool, a pungent sauna where eucalyptus is steamed on hot coals, a weight-lifting room, and – something you don't find every day – a small bullfighting ring and a cockfighting arena, as well as "Baños del Inca" water running into the deep bathtubs of every room.

## Ceramic traditions

Cajamarca and its environs are good places for buying ceramics. The Com-

*The hot springs outside Cajamarca were the scene of the first meeting between Atahualpa and the Spanish conquistadors. Following custom the Inca ruler offered the "bearded foreigners" chicha served in gold cups, but they poured it away in disgust.*

**BELOW:** the Baños del Inca.

*Traveling anywhere even slightly off the beaten track in Peru is often done by pick-up truck. Even those who at first find it an odd form of public transport soon come to accept it as the norm. Be prepared for plenty of dust and bumps, and try to book a seat inside the cab if you can.*

plejo Belén artisan shop and others near the Plaza de Armas are filled with pottery, as well as good-quality knitted sweaters, baskets, leather goods, and the gilt-framed mirrors popular in this northern region. But the most fascinating – and least expensive – spot to buy ceramics is a few kilometers to the south of the city at the village of **Aylambo**, where there is a series of ecologically balanced workshops. Sewage at the workshops is processed into natural gas, which is used to generate heat and light, and, rather than buying expensive fuel and imported heat-resistant bricks, the students who learn their skills at the workshops collect kindling from the hillside and make their own heat-tolerating kiln tiles – in much the same way as their ancestors did.

Products here range from plates bearing traditional Indian motifs to teapots with modern glazes – designed and concocted by the students – and the proceeds from pottery sales go to the people who work in the studios. Aylambo artisans, who range in age from children to the elderly, are not charged a fee to learn the crafts, but economic necessity would force them to leave the workshop and find paid jobs if study stipends were not available. The long-term goal of the project is to inspire a series of environmentally sound workshops providing jobs, reclaiming ancient pottery designs, preventing further deforestation of the hills, and keeping *cajamarquinos* living in the countryside.

## Beyond the city

There are many possible excursions outside Cajamarca, all of which are best organized through a travel agency which can arrange transportation to the isolated area; there are several agencies in Cajamarca that provide these services. From here it is possible to visit the puzzling **Ventanillas de Otuzco** (about 8 km/5 miles from town), the cliffside "windows" that served as ancient Indian burial grounds. Anthropologists and archeologists still have not unraveled the mystery of how the pre-Inca people were able to open the burial holes on the sides of sheer cliffs, but they have counted the openings to get an idea of the population – and importance – of the area before the conquistadors' arrival.

Equally astonishing is the site of **Cumbemayo**, about 24 km (15 miles) from Cajamarca, a valley cut by an Inca irrigation ditch of carved rock. The sophistication and precision of the ditch's angles – hewn by stone tools – leave modern-day hydraulic engineers marveling. Sharp turns in the ditch prevent the water from rushing too fast, as do imperceptible inclines. In the same valley are Los Frailones (The Friars), huge rocks that have eroded into the shape of hooded monks – sparking a number of local legends – as well as some primitive petroglyphs and caves once used as places of worship.

Those who start their countryside ramblings early may have time to reach the dairy farm called **Hacienda La Colpa** before cow-calling time. Every day, just before 2pm, the cows at this cooperative are called by name – to the delight of the crowd that gathers to watch. The animals respond by sauntering up to the milking

## The Kuélap Ruins

The ruins of Kuélap rival Machu Picchu in their magnificence. This extensive citadel was the principal administrative center of the Chachapoyas civilization (AD 200–1475), and its jungle-covered ruins were rediscovered in 1843. The center is thought to have been a sanctuary for a powerful elite who administered agricultural production and religious practices.

This enormous complex extends on a north–south orientated platform for more than 600 meters (1,900 ft), with stone walls up to 19 meters (62 ft) high. Despite its grand dimensions, the city only has three narrow entrances, which served to control entry to the site and strengthen its defenses. Inside the complex are 335 circular buildings, some near complete, adorned with geometrical friezes. There's also an ingenious system for channeling rainwater. A guide can be arranged in Chachapoyas, which is two hours from the site by road, and you're unlikely to have to share the ruins with any other visitors.

areas bearing their names. Colpa is an example of the many cooperative dairies outside Cajamarca, famous for its butter, cheese, and *manjar blanco* – a milky dessert. A hostel offers travelers a pastoral spot to spend the night, although most people, after admiring the nearby pretty village of Llacanora, head back to Cajamarca.

## Toward the Amazon

There is a rough but scenic route from Cajamarca, via the small city of Celendín, to **Chachapoyas** ⓫, heart of the pre-Inca culture of the same name. Little is known about the Chachapoyas period, which was roughly contemporary with the Chimu (*c.*1000–1400), but its people were certainly good at building cities and, judging by their fortifications, must have felt themselves under threat. There are buses to Celendín (about 120 km/75 miles from Cajamarca) on a slow road, but from there on the usual method of transport is by truck. If your time is limited, or you visit during the rainy season when the road gets washed away, it's advisable to access Chachapoyas from Chiclayo. This road is in much better condition, and there are more buses. There are also flights from Lima to Chachapoyas.

Chachapoyas alone, although pleasant, would not be worth the long journey, but the spectacular surrounding area, the sense of visiting a spot which still sees few tourists, and the opportunity to visit the area's many hilltop ruins make it a trip worth taking.

The best of the sites is **Kuélap** (*see opposite*), a great pre-Inca walled city perched high above the Río Utcubamba. The location and the ruins are nothing short of spectacular, but they receive less than 500 visitors a year. Discovering Kuélap is a real off-the-beaten-track adventure that's worth the journey there. Minibuses leave in the morning for the village of **Tingo**, from where a road goes to within 15 minutes' walk of the ruins. Discoveries are still being made in this area. In 1997, 219 mummies were uncovered in a cliff tomb up by a lake near Leimebamba (near Celendín), where they are now housed. Vilaya Tours (tel: 044-777 506) offer visits to these areas, or ask a local guide to accompany you. ❑

*Take a supply of ball point pens with you to give to village children. They need them for school and may even prefer them to money.*

---

### Restaurants

#### Cajamarca

**El Batán**
Del Batan 369
Tel: (076) 366 025
Good local and international food. There's an art gallery on the first floor and live music at weekends. **$$**

**El Cajamarques**
Amazonas 770
Tel: (076) 362 128
Good food in colonial setting; the most elegant restaurant in town. **$$**

**Carpa Bruja**
Jr. Amalia Puga 519
Tel: (076) 342 884

The "Witches' Tent" conjures up tasty international dishes with lots of salad and vegetables. Perfect for vegetarians. **$$**

**Los Faroles**
In Hostal Cajamarca,
Jr. Dos de Mayo 311
Live music in the evenings, local food. **$$**

**Don Paco**
Jr. Amalia Puga 726
Tel: (076) 362 655
Great Peruvian dishes and breakfasts until late in the day. **$**

**Querubino**
Jr. Amalia Puga 589
Tel: (076) 340 900

A hip hangout with a diverse menu and modern art on the walls. Often has a live band. **$$**

**Restaurante Salas**
Jr. Amalia Puga 726
Tel: (076) 362 876
Popular with locals; inexpensive regional dishes. **$**

#### Chachapoyas

**El Chacha**
Plaza de Armas, Grau 545
Tel: (041) 477 107
Serves good Peruvian dishes in big portions. **$**

**El Tejado**
Plaza de Armas, Grau 534
Tel: (076) 777 654

If you're hungry, El Tejado serves large set meals. **$**

**La Tushpa**
Ortiz Arrieta 753
Tel: (041) 803 634
The steaks here are especially good – and, unusually for Peru, can be ordered rare. **$$**

**Yana Yaku**
Ortiz Arrieta 532,
Plaza de Armas
Pleasant café overlooking the plaza. **$**

● ● ● ● ● ● ● ● ● ● ● ● ● ●
*Prices are per person for two courses, excluding wine.*
**$** = *less than US$10*
**$$** = *US$10–US$20*
**$$$** = *more than US$20*

*Recommended Restaurants and Cafés on page 203*

# CALLEJÓN DE HUAYLAS

Spectacular scenery and the challenge
of climbing Huascarán, Peru's highest mountain,
are among the attractions of this remote area

Lima

**S**tretching for 160 km (255 miles) and ranging in altitude from a mere 1,800 meters (5,900 ft) to 4,080 meters (13,380 ft), the valley known as the **Callejón de Huaylas** rates as one of the finest areas in all of South America for its superb mountain vistas and a wealth of opportunities for outdoor pursuits. Many dedicated enthusiasts arrive prepared for sports ranging from trekking and climbing to snowboarding, paraskiing, and skiing, while others are content to spend their days relaxing in a spectacular mountain setting and exploring the villages that sprawl along the hillsides.

The Callejón de Huaylas is bordered on the east by the **Cordillera Blanca** (White Mountains) – a mountain range with the greatest number of 6,000-meter (20,000-ft) peaks outside the Himalayas – and on the west by the lower range known as the Cordillera Negra (Black Mountains) for their sparseness of vegetation and complete lack of snow. To the north, the valley terminates with the Cañón del Pato, a narrow gorge of a canyon with sheer rock walls, steep precipices, and a dirt road winding its way through numerous crudely constructed tunnels down toward the coast. There are daily bus services from Chimbote to Huaraz – go by day for the exciting views. The hair-raising narrow road has been widened, and is now known as the Carretera de Huallanca, which is good news for those approaching Huaraz from the north. The 40-km (25-mile) wide Callejón de Huaylas is renowned

not only for its breathtaking scenery but also for Inca and pre-Inca history, unusual flora and fauna, lively markets, and traditional villages.

## Disaster area

The Callejón de Huaylas is also well known for a history of natural disasters. Earthquakes and alluvions – the name given to floods of water combined with avalanches and landslides – have caused considerable damage over the past 300 recorded years. The capital city of Huaraz was severely damaged

**Main attractions**
THE CORDILLERA BLANCA
HUARAZ
PARQUE NACIONAL HUASCARÁN
CORDILLERA HUAYHUASH
CHAVÍN DE HUANTAR

**LEFT:** Cordillera Blanca.
**BELOW:** watching the world go by.

by an alluvion in 1941 when an avalanche caused Laguna Calcacocha to overflow. Much of the central district was destroyed, and nearly 5,000 lives were lost. The most tragic disaster occurred in 1970, when an earthquake measuring 7.7 on the Richter scale devastated the entire region and was responsible for more than 80,000 deaths.

More than 30,000 people died in Huaraz, and over 80 percent of the city was flattened, but hardest hit was the village of Yungay. The entire town and most of its inhabitants completely disappeared under a massive avalanche of rock and snow when part of the Huascarán massif broke loose and plunged down the valley.

*Flowers on the mountain slopes.*

In the aftermath of these catastrophes many of the towns and villages have been almost completely rebuilt, mainly with uninspiring concrete structures. Understandably, the need to rehouse people was given priority, and little thought was given to preserving an archi-

**BELOW:** fish stall in Huaraz market.

tectural heritage. The colonial charm encountered in other highland areas has been all but lost. Sadly, these natural disasters also took a heavy toll on the archeology of the region. Notably lacking are many ancient remains, primarily from the Inca empire, which did not survive the calamities.

## Mountain retreat

The center of most commercial activity and the common destination for visitors to the Callejón de Huaylas is the city of **Huaraz** ⑫. There is an airport just outside the town, but flights from Lima are very unreliable, so most people get here by bus, from either Lima or Chimbote – both journeys take about eight hours on a paved road. There are frequent services, and the more expensive buses are quite comfortable. As the capital of the department of Ancash, and with a population of more than 80,000 inhabitants, Huaraz is well equipped to support the demands of tourism and all necessities are readily available. Scores of low-cost hostels offer accommodations of varying kinds, some very basic, others very comfortable, and there are a few higher-priced hotels for those who would like a bit more comfort during their mountain retreat.

Before departing for remote regions, or after a long trek in the mountains, you'll find plenty of activity in the bustling town of Huaraz. Along the main street of Luzuriaga, vendors sell a wide selection of woolen goods, pan flutes, and ceramic replicas of the Chavín temple. Store-front tour companies set out brightly colored billboards promoting day trips to popular tourist sites and advertise an assortment of climbing and trekking gear for hire. Other traditionally dressed highlanders sell regional food specialties from wooden carts. Andean cheeses, rich honey, and *manjar blanco* (a sweet, milky concoction used as a dessert or filling) are a few tasty edibles that are worth trying. A wide range of restaurants caters to international tastes: pizzerias, Chinese food, and hamburgers are found alongside more typical dishes such as *lomo saltado* (strips of beef

*Recommended Restaurants and Cafés on page 203*

with potatoes), *pollos a la brasa* (griddled chicken), and *cuy* (roasted guinea pig).

Worth a visit is the **Museo Arqueológico** (Avenida Luzuriaga 762; open Mon–Sat 8.15am–6.30pm, Sun 8.15am–5pm; entrance fee), off the **Plaza de Armas**. It has an interesting collection and is considered noteworthy for its display of stone monoliths from the Recuay culture, which date from 400 BC to AD 600. Also on display are mummies, ceramics, and household utensils dating from the same period.

Huaraz nightlife, too, has plenty to offer. There are several cinemas showing recent US films in English with Spanish subtitles, although the sound system frequently leaves something to be desired. *Peñas*, or folklore nightclubs, entertain with traditional Andean musical groups in the early evening, and switch to disco later on for serious high-altitude dancing. Tambo Taverna and Amadeus Taberna are the most popular and are packed to capacity on weekends and during high season.

The outlying area of Huaraz offers numerous opportunities for day excursions. Footpaths lead to a number of small villages and agricultural areas within walking distance of the city center. Rataquenua, Unchus, Marían, and Pitec are just a few of the pueblos that can be visited in a few hours.

About an hour by local bus south of Huaraz lies the small town of Catac, often visited by those keen to see the giant *Puya Raimondi*. This unusual plant is often referred to as a cactus, but is actually the largest member of the bromeliad family. It is a rare species, considered to be one of the oldest in the world, and is found in only a few isolated areas of the Andes. At its base, the *Puya Raimondi* forms a huge rosette of long, spiked, waxy leaves – often reaching a diameter of 2 meters (6 ft). As it begins to flower, a process that takes its entire lifespan which is estimated to approach 100 years, it sends up a phallic spike that can reach a height of 12 meters (39 ft).

As the final flowering begins, usually in the month of May, the spike is covered in flowers – as many as 20,000 blooms on a single plant. During this season, if you are incredibly lucky, groups of *Puya Raimondi* may bloom together, creating an unbelievable picture set

**TIP**

If you're looking for somewhere to go out in Huaraz, try the **Tambo Taverna** at José de la Mar 776, or the **Montrek Disco**, on the corner of Sucre and Bolívar, which is in a converted cinema.

**BELOW:** taking a break in Huaraz.

**TIP**

Be careful visiting the Mirador or along the Pitec Trail, as there have been reports of muggings in these areas in recent years. It's best to go in a group or with a reliable local.

against the backdrop of the snowy peaks of the Cordillera Blanca.

## Trekking

The Huaraz area is a trekker's paradise. Just above the city is **El Mirador**, a scenic lookout marked by a huge white cross. The route heads uphill east along city streets, which eventually turn into a footpath beside an irrigation canal lined with eucalyptus trees. Fields of wheat ripening in the sun add a serene, pastoral feel. At the top, the highest mountain in Peru, **Huascarán** (6,768 meters/22,200 ft; *see opposite*), dominates the northern horizon; the lower Vallunaraju (5,680 meters/18,600 ft) peeks out over the foothills to the east, and the city of Huaraz sprawls below.

Another popular choice is the **Pitec Trail to Laguna Churup**. There is no public transportation to this small village 10 km (6 miles) from the center of Huaraz, but often a taxi driver or someone driving a pick-up truck can be found at *el puente* (the bridge) at Huaraz who will navigate the rough road to Pitec. Walking is an option – it takes around two hours at a slowish pace – but it's nicer to be fresh at the trailhead and then walk back down to Huaraz afterwards.

The trail begins at the parking lot before the village of Pitec is reached. A well-worn footpath heads north up a ridgeline, and the Churup massif rises just above 5,495 meters (18,000 ft) in the distance. At the base of this mountain is the destination of the hike, Laguna Churup, fed by glacial melt-off and surrounded by huge boulders. A picnic lunch and a midday siesta in the warm sun reward the effort of getting here. A leisurely hike back to Huaraz follows a cobbled road through *campesino* (subsistence farmer) homesteads.

## Ancient remains

About 8 km (5 miles) north of Huaraz, and easily reached on foot, is the small pre-Inca ruin of **Willkawain** (open daily 8am–5pm; entrance fee). Little is known about this three-storied structure which stands in the middle of an agricultural valley, but, because of the typical masonry style, it is thought to date from the expansionist period of the Wari-Tiahuanaco culture (200–700). The windowless inner chambers can be explored with a flashlight, or with candles proffered by any one of the hordes of schoolboys who haunt the site and offer their services as guides, for a small fee. Most of the rooms within the construction are inaccessible from the debris of centuries, but a few of them have been opened up to reveal a sophisticated ventilation system and skillful stone craftsmanship. Willkawain is a good walk for acclimatization when you first arrive in Huaraz.

Longer excursions to the surrounding country are as simple to arrange as locating the proper rural bus to take you there. A major road stretches the length of the Callejón de Huaylas, running alongside the Río Santa, and local transportation is readily available to a variety of villages situated along the route. It is also very easy to negotiate a minibus tour with one of various agencies in the center of town.

The village of **Monterrey**, just 5 km (3 miles) outside Huaraz, is worth a visit

**RIGHT:** the giant bromeliad *Puya Raimondi.*

*Recommended Restaurants and Cafés on page 203*

for its *baños termales* (hot springs). Two swimming pools of warm water, and private baths of the steaming variety, are extremely inviting, especially after a rigorous trek in the mountains. About 35 km (22 miles) farther up the valley is **Chancos**, which claims to have its own Fountain of Youth – more thermal baths with natural saunas and pools of flowing hot water.

Buses frequently leave Huaraz, loaded with an assortment of *campesinos*, their chickens, *cuyes* (guinea pigs), and children, heading for the small village of **Yungay** ⑬, which lies north down the valley. This is the village described earlier in this chapter that was completely destroyed by the 1970 earthquake. During the most recent rebuilding of Yungay, the village site was shifted a few kilometers north of its original location in the hope that it would now be out of the way of any future natural disasters. All that remains of the abandoned Yungay, now known as Campo Santo, is a solitary monument dedicated to those whose lives were lost, and a few battered palm trees that once lined the charming Plaza de Armas.

## Llanganuco to Santa Cruz

Yungay is the turn-off point for the popular two-hour ride up to the **Lagunas de Llanganuco**. *Camionetas*, small pick-up trucks, wait in the plaza to transport hikers and sightseers up the valley to the dazzling, glacier-fed lakes. It is also one of the starting points for the **Llanganuco to Santa Cruz Loop**. One of the most frequently hiked trails in the region, this five-day route passes under a dozen peaks over 5,800 meters (19,000 ft), and panoramic views abound.

**Caraz** ⑭ is the end point of this loop, a pretty town that was fortunate enough to survive several recent earthquakes with relatively little damage. Fields of flowers line the road as you approach, and at the other side of town groves of orange trees sit beneath snowy mountain peaks. There are several small hotels and a few basic restaurants around the Plaza de Armas.

If you choose to start, rather than finish, your trek here, you can get a bus from Huaraz, which is only about 65 km (40 miles) away. From Caraz you can take gentle walks in the nearby hills, or visit the stunning turquoise-blue **Lago**

> **TIP**
>
> Be well prepared for your trek. In recent years Huaraz has become geared up to the influx of outward-bound visitors and is able to cater for most needs. The Casa de Guías at Plaza Ginebra 28 (tel: 043-421 811) can supply the names of recommended mountain guides, and a lot of other information.

**BELOW:**
Huascarán's lofty summit, accessible for the very fit.

## Climbing Peru's Highest Mountain

Huascarán is Peru's highest mountain and presents the ultimate challenge for many mountain-mad visitors to Peru. It has two summits: the south one, at 6,768 meters (22,200 ft), is 113 (meters) 370 ft higher than its more frequently climbed northern sister.

The climb is not one of Peru's most technical, but it does require a high level of fitness and some high-altitude mountaineering experience.

The ascent begins at the village of Musho, from where donkeys and *arrieros* (muleteers) are hired to transport climbers' gear to the Huascarán base camp above the tree line. The trail then continues up a steep ridge to the moraine camp. From here climbers progress across the glacier to Camp One, at 5,200 meters (17,000 ft). Wide crevasses, icy cracks, and massive pillars of

tumbled ice are constant reminders that glaciers are anything but static piles of snow.

Next comes the climb to La Garganta (The Throat) at 5,790 meters (19,000 ft), a technical test with a 100-meter (300-ft), 70-degree ice wall. After a final cold night at La Garganta Camp, comes the summit route, a series of zigzag traverses across the saddle between the two peaks of Huascarán. Breathing is so labored that several breaths are needed for each step. Finally, Peru's highest summit is in sight, with the lofty peaks of the Andes spread out all around. For the personal challenge and the magnificent scenery, the climb is unforgettable.

For advice on hiring a certified guide, contact the Casa de Guías in Huaraz *(see above)*.

Don't forget the usual
health precautions when
trekking or climbing:
altitude sickness can
be a problem if you are
not acclimatized; guard
against hypothermia
by bringing the right
clothes and being aware
of early symptoms
*(see page 122).*

**BELOW:**
transporting
potatoes near
Cashapampa.

**Parón**, some 30 km (18 miles) up a rugged, winding road. It's a magnificent all-day hike, or a relatively inexpensive trip by taxi.

## Reserve in the Sierra

Much of the Cordillera Blanca above 4,000 meters (13,000 ft) and the area around Huascarán mountain fall within the confines of **Parque Nacional Huascarán**. The park is easily visited from Huaraz, and its office, where you can get information before your visit, is located there. Established in 1972, the park marked Peru as a frontrunner in Latin America in the area of conservation. Huascarán National Park was formed to protect the indigenous wildlife, archeological sites, geology, and natural beauty of an area threatened by mining and other commercial interests. An entrance fee is charged to help offset the cost of providing park guardians and preserving trails.

Of the more interesting wildlife that you can possibly see, with a little patience and a bit of luck, is the vizcacha, a small, rabbit-like animal with characteristics similar to the North American marmot; the vicuña, a cameloid cousin to the llama; and the stealthy puma.

## Valley life

Throughout the Callejón de Huaylas, a lifestyle dating back centuries continues to thrive. The traditional dress of the villagers has not changed radically in many years. The women, especially, hold on to their heritage, wearing layers of colorful woolen skirts and embroidered blouses which developed during colonial times. In addition, each wears a hat whose style may vary significantly from village to village. The custom of hat-wearing can also be used to indicate marital status, as in the village of Carhuaz. There, a woman wearing a black band round her fedora is a widow, while a rose-colored band is worn by single women, and a white one shows that the wearer is married.

Agriculture, the mainstay of the valley, has also seen little change over the centuries in either methods or crop variety. Double-yoked oxen still drag crude wooden plows through the black, fertile soil. Honey-colored wheat can be seen ripening throughout the valley, and maturing fields of quinoa, a high-altitude

*Recommended Restaurants and Cafés on page 203*

grain rich in protein, are easily recognized by the rich colors of burned orange, fiery red, and deep purple that blaze along the hillsides.

Corn – the sacred crop of the Incas and one of the earliest foods, which took man from hunter-gatherer to farmer – is grown in abundance, and is the staple of life along with the ever-present potato. From it, a thick, slightly fermented corn beer called *chicha* is made. *Chicha* is drunk in great quantities in the highlands, especially during festivals. It was originally the royal drink, considered suitable only for consumption by the ruling Inca and his courtiers.

Festivals play a large part in the lifestyle of the indigenous people who inhabit the Callejón de Huaylas. They provide a way to break out of the monotony of day-to-day existence and reaffirm the traditions that give continuity to life in the Andes. Since the Spanish conquest, festivals have assumed a religious veneer and coincide with Catholic feast days, but underneath still lies a strong thread of meaning left behind by ancient cultures. The Catholic Church, which has always been good at assimilating pre-existing customs, is well aware of this, but has wisely decided to turn a blind eye.

Every month of the year sees a celebration, or several, in full swing. Some are particular to one village, while others are observed throughout the whole area. The major festivals of San Juan (St John on June 24) and San Pedro and San Pablo (St Peter and St Paul on June 29), celebrated all over the region as in many other parts of the continent, are particularly lively, especially since they fall at the same time as the national day that has been set aside to honor the *campesino* and the ancient Andean celebration of the winter solstice.

On the eve of San Juan, fires are lit throughout the valley, burning the chaff from the harvest and the wild *ichu* grass on the hillsides, and having absolutely nothing to do with John the Baptist. From a high mountain camp, the fires look like starlight brought to earth, and the next day the valley is thick with smoke.

*Semana Santa*, or Easter, is another widely celebrated festival. Many villages have their own special traditions, but the celebrations are always colorful and abundant. Processions of finely adorned religious figures carried on litters, scenes of the Resurrection sculpted in flower petals on the ground, and folkloric bands playing music throughout the village are common events during the festivities of Holy Week.

## Chavín de Huantar

Many visitors to the Callejón de Huaylas come not only for the majestic mountains and typical highland life but also to see one of the oldest archeological sites designed by one of the most influential cultures in the Americas. At the temple complex of **Chavín de Huantar ⑮** (open daily 8am–5pm; entrance fee) lie the remains of one of the most important pre-Inca cultures. Dating from around 800 to 300 BC, the Chavín culture was typified by a highly developed artistic style and a cult whose influence lasted longer than that of the Roman empire, and was so widespread that archeologists have termed this formation period "the

*In Carhuaz, the color of the band on a woman's hat denotes her marital status. A rose-colored band means that she is single, while married women wear a white band.*

**BELOW:** market stall in Carhuaz.

# Cordillera Huayhuash

**Once a place where few outsiders dared to tread, the Cordillera Huayhuash is now considered one of the most beautiful trekking areas in Peru.**

The high peaks of the Cordillera Huayhuash have long held the fascination of climbers. Joe Simpson's epic retreat from Siula Grande, recounted in the book and film *Touching the Void*, first brought the Huayhuash to international fame. In recent years, while other trails have become overpopulated, this remote region has gained a reputation as the most challenging, and beautiful, trekking destination in Peru.

Until a few years ago, this isolated range to the south of the Callejón de Huaylas was the haunt of bandits, and home to just a handful of rugged mountain men. Sendero Luminoso guerillas used the area as a base in the 1980s and early 1990s, so until the late 1990s the Huayhuash remained largely undiscovered by Peruvians and foreigners alike, keeping it mysterious and unspoiled: a real zone for adventure.

Though there are several routes through the Huayhuash that allow walkers to see parts of it, the best way to visit this magnificent range is to do the full Circuito del Huayhuash, a 12- to 14- day trek of some 170 km (102 miles). This route passes over a series of high passes (all well above 4,000 meters/13,300 ft), overlooked by awe-inspiring, glacier-shrouded peaks. Trekkers rarely descend below 3,000 meters (9,900 ft), making this a taxing high-altitude trek which demands good levels of fitness.

The spine of the Huayhuash is made up of over 20 individual mountains, six of them at over 6,000 meters (19,800 ft); Yerupaja, at 6,617 meters (21,836 ft), is the second-highest peak in Peru. Slopes of rock and ice extend down into wide grassy valleys with azure-hued glacial lakes. From the mountain paths, the stone-walled, grass-roofed huts of the people who graze their animals here are just visible.

From April to early June the landcape is green and dotted with wild flowers; by July, it has dried to a yellowish hue for the coldest and driest part of the year, when there are nightly freezes and skies as clear as glass. This is the best time for trekking, as daytime temperatures are warm. By September the rains begin, and bitter snowdrifts come to the highest passes and valleys.

Though it was declared a "reserved zone" in 2002, the Huayhuash is not a national park; there is controversial mining on its borders, and even in its remotest spots, this is still a human landscape. Walkers begin and end their treks in the villages of Llamac or Pacllon, and the small village of Huayllapa is visited on most itineraries. People here are extremely poor, though they welcome and benefit from tourism by accompanying walkers as guides and *arrieros* (muleteers), as well as collecting nominal fees at campsites.

Many agencies in Huaraz offer trekking in the Cordillera Huayhuash. Not all have received rave reviews for their services, so check the terms of any contract carefully before you decide on a trek. The Huayhuash is a delicate environment, so try to gauge whether the services you hire will be environmentally responsible and ethical, using *arrieros* from the local area, for example. One highly regarded operation that offers trekking in the Huayhuash is The Moving Mountains Project (www.movingmountainsproject.com). This not-for-profit organization uses local guides and *arrieros*, and all proceeds from its guided walks are returned to Huayhuash communities. ❑

**LEFT:** trekking in the Cordillera Huayhuash.

Chavín Horizon." Recently some archeologists have come to believe that this culture culminated at Chavín, rather than originating there, but as yet there is no firm evidence either way. The Huaylas culture, which once occupied this valley, was briefly dominated by this more sophisticated civilization.

Archeologists have been able to learn very little about the culture because it left no written records, so much of what is suggested is based on pure supposition. But it is widely accepted that, at the time the Chavín culture was emerging, mankind was moving from a hunter-gatherer way of life to a society based on agriculture, which gave people new-found leisure time to devote to cultural pursuits. The theories that have been put forward about this mysterious culture are mostly based on the study of this 7-hectare (17-acre) site containing a temple, plazas, and a multitude of stone carvings and drawings.

The temple is thought to have been a major ceremonial center, and felines, principally the jaguar, were the most important deities of the cult. It is also believed that the Chavín people were not warlike: their influence on the architecture and sculpture of the northern coast and central highlands appears to have been spread by peaceful means.

## Visiting the temple

The site is actually located across the mountains in the next valley to the east, near the village of Chavín, but is most accessible from Huaraz. There are regular buses, and the journey takes about three hours. Tours of the site can also be arranged in Huaraz, where there are several agencies. If you go under your own steam you will find guides to show you around, but they may not speak much, if any, English.

What first strikes most visitors upon their arrival at Chavín de Huantar is the quality of the stonework found in the temple walls and the plaza stairways. The drystone masonry construction reflects a sophistication not expected from a culture that flourished more than

3,000 years ago. Added to this are huge stone slabs with highly stylized carvings of jaguars, eagles, and anacondas; the designs are intricate and fluid.

The temple sits above a large, sunken plaza where it is believed pilgrims came to worship during certain seasons. On one side sits a large granite slab with seven hewn-out indentations that must have served as an altar stone for group rituals. Two 3-meter (10-ft) high stone portals overlook the plaza and represent the entry way into the interior of the temple. Finely etched bird-like figures, one male and one female, face each other across a stairway, symbolically divided into two halves – one painted black and the other white.

Niches set around the outside of the temple walls originally held protruding sculpted stone heads, human in shape but with the snarling grin of a jaguar. Some theories suggest that the eyes were originally inset with crystals, which would reflect the light of the moon and ward off evildoers. Only one of these so-called keystones remains in place; a few have been stolen over the years, and the rest are safely stored within the temple.

*The first Spaniards were considered liberators of sorts, and the daughter of Kuntar Guacho, the lord of Huaylas, was given as mistress to the conquistador Francisco Pizarro himself.*

**BELOW:** llama trail.

**TIP**

Llamatrek is an initiative started by villagers in the valleys around Huaraz, as a way of attracting tourists while maintaining the traditional use of llamas as cargo animals. You can trek the relatively untraveled route from Olleros to the ruins of Chavín de Huantar, with the llamas and their owners, who will share their culture with you along the way. Llamatreks can be booked through AndesTrek (*see Travel Tips, page 341, for details*).

**BELOW:** a carved head at Chavín de Huantar.

The interior of the temple is a subterranean labyrinth of passages and galleries set on at least three levels which are connected by a series of ramps and stairs. Though there are no windows, a highly engineered ventilation system allows the continuous flow of fresh air throughout – another marvel produced by an ancient civilization. Some of the rooms contain the remains of the sculpted heads and intricately carved slabs that portray a variety of Amazonian and highland animals.

## Granite god

At the heart of the underground complex two narrow passageways cross, and at their junction stands the crowning glory of the Chavín religion – the Lanzón de Chavín. This 4-meter (13-ft) high granite monolith is thought to be the principal god-image worshiped by this cult. Its Spanish name comes from the lance or dagger-like shape of the monolith, which appears to be stuck in the ground. A mythological image emerges from the elaborate stone carving, and its demeanor is in keeping with most of the terrifying god-images created by the Chavín people.

The large head of the monolith is square and human-like, yet definite feline characteristics are noted in the grinning mouth, which has a long fang protruding from each corner. The nose has two big holes for nostrils, and an arm and a leg are visible on each side. Round earrings dangle from the creature's ears, and long flowing hair is made up of intricately carved serpents. Carved into the top of the head are thin, grooved channels, and some speculate that animals, or even humans, may have been sacrificed to this god.

Above the god-image there was once an opening in the ceiling, now closed to preserve the figure from exposure to the elements. Here, many believe, a sacrificial rock may have been positioned and, as animals or people were slaughtered, the blood would flow through the opening in the ceiling and run down through the channel in the figure. However, some other archeologists disclaim the sacrificial theory and suggest instead that the Lanzón was merely the dominant figure for worship.

Two other monoliths are considered important in the Chavín cult, but both are now housed in the Museo de la Nación in Lima (*see page 159*). The 1.8-meter (6-ft) stone called the *Stela Raimondi* is named after the archeologist Antonio Raimondi (who also gave his name to the *Puya Raimondi* cactus described on *page 195*); he moved the stela to the Museum of Anthropology and Archeology in Lima at the end of the 19th century after it had been used as a table by a *campesino* who had discovered it in 1840. It depicts a monstrous feline anthropomorphic god, with widespread arms, claw-like feet, and a tangle of serpents representing its hair.

The second major piece is the Tello obelisk, which was discovered by archeologist Julio C. Tello. This towering, intricately carved piece also depicts feline images, as well as a caiman – a creature not normally associated with highland culture. The significance of this, as of much that we see at the temple, is a mystery, but the experience of a visit is unforgettable. ❑

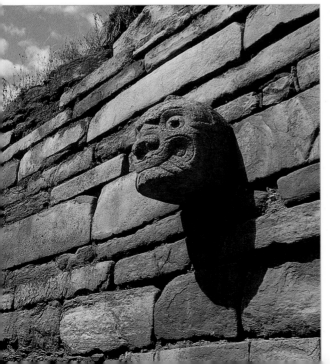

# RESTAURANTS AND CAFÉS

## Restaurants

Prices are per person for a two-course meal, excluding wine:
**$** less than US$10
**$$** US$10–20
**$$$** more than US$20

### Huaraz

### Alpes Andes
Casa de Guías,
Plaza Ginebra 28G
Tel: (043) 421 811
Good for breakfast.
Cozy in the evening. **$**

### Amma
Parque Ginebra (next to the Casa de Guías)
Tel: (01) 9711 7079
This cozy place has a wood oven and grill in which it cooks all its mouthwatering meats. It does a fantastic teriyaki spatchcocked chicken and serves fine margaritas. **$$**

### Bistro de Los Andes
Jr. Julián de Morales 823
Tel: (043) 429 556
Known for good Peruvian food with a French influence. Thoughtful decor makes this one of the prettier places to eat in Huaraz. **$$**

### La Brasa Roja
Av. Luzuriaga 919
Tel: (043) 427 738
Pasta, pizza, and chicken from the grill, plus great hamburgers and good vegetarian options. Great value. This place is popular with locals and deservedly so. **$**

### Café Andino
Jr. Lúcar y Torre 530
Tel: (043) 421 203
A relaxing place for coffee and cake. US-run, with a book exchange. **$**

### Chalet Suisse
Pedro Cochachín 357
Tel: (043) 721 949
This chalet-style restaurant in the Hotel Club Andino is one of the best in Huaraz and is well know for its Swiss cheese fondue. It caters to non-house guests too, but reservation is essential. **$$$**

### Encuentro
Av. Luzuriaga 6ta cuadra (Parque del Periodista)
Tel: (043) 427 971
Though there are three Encuentros in Huaraz, this is the best for its tranquil location on the square known as Parque del Periodista. They do a lot more than pastas and coffee and are just the spot for a light meal. **$**

### El Horno
Av. Luzuriaga 6ta cuadra (Parque del Periodista)
Tel: (043) 424 617
BBQ meats, salads, pasta, and vegetarian dishes. They do an excellent lasagne, and pizzas are baked in their wood oven. **$$**

### Monte Rosa
Jr. José de la Mar 661
Tel: (043) 421 447
This restaurant serves great Argentine beef, bountiful salads, and good pizzas and pastas. They even do a mean Swiss cheese fondue. **$$**

### Pizzeria Bruno
Luzuriaga 834
Tel: (043) 425 689
French owner Bruno creates authentic Italian pizzas. **$**

### Siam de los Andes
Gamarra esq. Juan de Morales
Tel: (043) 509 173
Authentic Thai cuisine, including delicious stir-fries and curries. **$$**

### Las Tulpas y Chimichurri
Jr. Julián de Morales 759
This place serves Peruvian classics like *cuy* (guinea pig) and ceviche, as well as international and vegetarian fare and good desserts. There's an attractive shady garden out front. **$**

**RIGHT:** chicken wings on a bed of quinoa.

*Recommended Restaurants on page 213*

# CENTRAL SIERRA

Isolated for years by geography and then terrorism, Ayacucho and the other towns of the Central Sierra are places to enjoy traditional Peru and some spectacular scenery

Lima

H istorically, **Ayacucho** and the central highlands have been the link between Lima (and other coastal towns) and Cusco, with the vast eastern jungle region beyond it. It is also here that much of Peru's mineral wealth is to be found, which brought both riches and hardship to the area. In the 1980s, terrorism and emergency military rule made the highland provinces unsafe and unwelcoming, but with the return of peace and the building of a breathtaking highway from Lima, the area is once again welcoming travelers who enjoy its traditional way of life, handicrafts, and often spectacular mountain scenery.

These mountains in Central Peru contain caves where, as at Pikimachay, traces have been found of the first inhabitants dating back to over 15,000 years ago. Ayacucho was also important during the Wari (or Huari) culture, which dominated the region for several hundred years before falling to the Inca in the 14th century. The Incas themselves used it as a communications center, as its river valley was on the main route up to what is now Ecuador, and south into Chile. Mining in the area continues, as it has done for centuries, with the giant Cerro de Pasco mine still being one of the world's most important producers of copper. To the north are the imposing peaks of the Cordillera Occidental, and the mysterious rock formations at Marcahuasi, which attract many visitors.

Much of this area was off-limits for travelers in the 1980s and 1990s, because Ayacucho was the center of activities for Abimael Guzmán and his Sendero Luminoso (Shining Path) guerrilla group. More than half of the 69,000 people killed by the rebel group and in the armed forces' counter-insurgency campaigns came from these provinces, the vast majority of them were innocent peasants. This violent period provoked a massive migration to Lima and other coastal cities, and created a climate of fear and suspicion.

**Main attractions**
AYACUCHO CATHEDRAL
SANTA ANA
VILCASHUAMÁN
HUANCAVELICA
LIMA–HUANCAYO PASSENGER TRAIN
CAPILLA DE LA MERCED, HUANCAYO
RESERVA NACIONAL DE JUNÍN

**LEFT:** statue of José Antonio Sucre in Ayacucho.
**BELOW:** Ayacucho's colonial entrance.

*Street art using flower petals during Ayacucho's Easter celebrations.*

In recent years however, with the capture of Guzmán and the virtual disappearance of Shining Path, many people have returned and taken up their traditional pursuits again. The best times to visit are during Easter Week, which is given up entirely to processions and fiestas, or the week at the end of April, when Ayacucho's patron saint is remembered with more riotous celebrations. Another festival well worth attending is the Fiesta de las Cruces in May, when the famous scissor dance is performed in which a pair of men wielding huge tailors' scissors try to cut each other's trousers.

## Churches and mansions

Ayacucho was founded by Francisco Pizarro in 1540 as an important communications link between Lima and Cusco. The city was at first called Huamanga, after the local stone similar to alabaster, and is still often, somewhat confusingly, called this by locals. The name was changed in 1824, after Republican forces finally freed Peru of Spanish troops at the nearby battle on the plain of Ayacucho. The impressive archway known as the **Arco de San Francisco de Asis**, or Arco de Triunfo, on the Jirón 28 de Julio in the city center was built in 1924 to commemorate the victory.

Ayacucho's reputation as a city with "a church on every street corner" may be exaggerated, but it does have 33 churches, most of them still in regular use. Perhaps the most impressive is the **Catedral Ⓐ** (open daily 10–11am and 5.30–7pm) on the Plaza Mayor de Huamanga (previously Plaza Sucre). Built in 1612, it has superb gilt altars, a silver tabernacle, and a beautifully carved pulpit. It also contains Stations of the Cross paintings brought from Rome. During the famous *Semana Santa* celebrations during Easter Week, this is one of the most visited churches in all Peru. The procession of its statues round the city by different *cofradías* or brotherhoods rivals that of Seville in Spain. The faithful start the week on Palm Sunday with a candlelight procession when a precious

Ayacucho

statue of Christ from the Cathedral is carried on the back of a white donkey. Each day after this there are more processions, with each statue from the church being revered by its own group of worshipers. At dawn on Easter Sunday, all the bells of the city celebrate Christ's resurrection, the doors of the Cathedral are flung open, and 250 men carry the statue of Christ around the square.

Another outstanding church, the Jesuit **Templo de la Compañía** ❸ (open Mon–Sat 9am–noon, Sun 11am–1pm), built in 1605, boasts an unusual carved facade of orange-red stone and has a lovely gilded altar. The interior also has richly carved wood and 17th-century religious paintings.

A few blocks away up Jirón 9 de Diciembre stands the **Templo de Santo Domingo** ❻ (Mass daily 7am and 6pm). It has an altar richly decorated with gold leaf, but it is this church's role in history that is most significant: bells in its small towers rang out the first peals of Peru's independence following the decisive Battle of Ayacucho. Round the corner on Jirón Callao, the finest carved pulpit of all Ayacucho's churches is to be found in the **Iglesia de San Francisco de Paula** ❹ (Mass daily 7am, Sun 9am).

Although Spanish colonial architecture is the pride of Ayacucho, this was an important area for many civilizations prior to the arrival of the Spaniards. Five hundred years before the Incas, the Wari empire dominated these highlands, and traces of that and other influences are to be found at the **Museo Hipólito Unanue** ❺ (open Mon–Fri 9am–5pm, Sat until 1pm; entrance fee), part of the **Instituto Nacional de Cultura** on Avenida Independencia. The museum's collection ranges from 1500 BC stone carvings to Wari ceremonial bowls, Chancay textiles, and stone and ceramic Inca pieces.

Ayacucho has several other museums that are worth visiting. **The Museo Joaquín López Antay** in the colonial Casona Chacón (now a bank) on the Plaza de Armas has a good collection of local art, popular objects, and photographs of the city and its surroundings (open Mon–Sat 9.15am–1pm and 3–6.30pm). The nearby **Casona Jauregui** is another exquisitely proportioned

*Ayacucho is sometimes known as "La Ciudad de las Iglesias" on account of the large number of churches within the town.*

**BELOW:** Easter processions in Ayacucho.

17th-century mansion which holds temporary exhibitions.

The **Museo Mariscal Cáceres**  (open Mon–Fri 9am–3pm, Sat until 1pm), housed in the elegant 17th-century **Casona Vivanco** on Jirón 28 de Julio, has a fine display of colonial paintings and furnishings. It is named after Andrés Cáceres, a young man from Ayacucho whose rapid military ascent stemmed from his successful organization of *campesinos* (subsistence farmers) to resist the Chilean invaders during Peru's otherwise disastrous performance in the War of the Pacific in the 1880s. Cáceres was rewarded by being made president of Peru in 1886. The *casona* is one of the best-preserved of the colonial mansions which are the hallmark of Ayacucho (open Mon–Sat 9am–12.30pm and 2–5pm).

Another splendid mansion is the **Casona Boza y Solis** , the seat of the provincial prefecture. Built in 1740, it has a two-story interior courtyard and a wide staircase lined with beautiful imported colored tiles. It also contains the cell where the local heroine of independence, María Prado de Bellido, was held until she was executed by a Spanish firing squad in 1822 (open Mon–Fri 8am–6pm).

## Arts and Crafts

Ayacucho is a center for many traditional handicrafts. A good place to see artisans at work and to purchase their wares is the **Santa Ana**  neighborhood behind the Alameda Bolognesi. Many of the houses here still contain family workshops, where several generations make rugs, tapestries, and carpets. Filigree and silver work as well as *retablos* (painted altars) of all shapes and sizes can be bought in Santa Ana and other parts of the city. Another specialty of the city are the etched *mates burilados* (gourds). These often show surprisingly complicated scenes of everyday life or from the Bible, etched onto dried gourds of every dimension. The local huamanga alabaster is also still worked with great skill into biblical scenes, cribs for Christmas and other, more modern fantasies.

Shopping is also a lively experience at the city's sprawling market, a block south of Avenida San Martín. Here, stalls offer everything from handicrafts and hand-

**SHOP**

Artisans in Cochas Chico continue an ancient tradition of engraving pumpkin gourds with rural scenes. A good place to buy these beautifully crafted objects is the Sunday market in Huancayo.

**BELOW:** memorial commemorating the Battle of Ayacucho.

LA NACION
A LOS VENCEDORES DE AYACUCHO

Recommended Restaurants on page 213

knitted sweaters, to rubber boots and hot peppers and other medicinal herbs. Delicious fresh-made bread, with cinnamon and aniseed, is sold from cloth-covered baskets, as are herbal drinks known as *emolientes*. You can safely try the bread, but it is perhaps advisable to leave the drinks to the locals: the glasses are not usually properly washed.

But the local drink of *ponche* is well worth a try. This is a milk-based punch flavored with peanut, sesame, clove, cinnamon, walnuts, and sugar, and spiked with *pisco*. You could accompany this with one of the hearty local dishes such as *puca picante*, a stew made of pieces of pork, potatoes, and toasted peanuts, served with rice and parsley.

## Battle site

In the rolling hills 37 km (22 miles) northeast of the city is the village of **Quinua**. It was on the plain 1 km (⅔ mile) outside the village that the decisive battle of Ayacucho was fought against the Spanish troops on 9 December 1824. Although outnumbered almost two to one, the Venezuelan general Antonio José de Sucre emerged victorious from the battle, which was the last fought by the Spaniards in Latin America. (Some local guides will even tell you that no battle as such was fought, since the Spanish commander Virrey de la Serna decided to avoid bloodshed and withdrew.) The place of the encounter is marked by a hideous 1970s obelisk some 44 metres (144 ft) high, built with Venezuelan oil wealth. Its one redeeming feature is the spectacular scenery to be seen from its viewing platform. The broad plain is a popular place for weekend picnics, and each December the victory is celebrated by an eight-day extravaganza. Dancing and craft exhibitions are central to the celebrations, with the scissor dance *(see page 206)* once again to the fore.

The village of Quinua itself is a center for handicrafts, and has been so successful that as many as 7,000 people now live there, most of them producing crafts of one kind or another. Almost all the red-tiled roofs are topped with good-luck symbols: small ceramic churches or pairs of bulls, made originally for festivals coinciding with the branding of cattle. These pieces are also on sale in the village's

*Óscar Durand, the last leader of the guerrilla group Sendero Luminoso, was captured near Huancayo in 1999. This marked the end of the group's activities, which had brought death and misery to many.*

**BELOW:** bartering in Huamanga market.

**BELOW:** the abandoned church at Santa Barbara.

many stores, together with handmade guitars and sculptures in huamanga stone.

Several tour companies in Ayacucho organize day trips that include Quinua and the battlefield, and also a visit to **Vilcashuamán**, once an important administrative center for the Inca empire, and interesting above all for the Spanish constructions built directly on top of Inca architecture. The village is most famous for its *usnu* or ceremonial Inca pyramid, which has been preserved almost intact. Inca remains are also to be found at **Intihuatana** (a 30-minute walk from the highway). Next to a lagoon thought to have been artificially constructed by the Incas, there are the remains of a palace, a tower, a Temple of the Sun, a sacrificial stone, and a boulder carved with 17 angles.

Another stopover is at the Huari (Wari) ruins about 20 km (12 miles) outside Ayacucho on the way to Quinua. These extensive ruins, in a landscape full of tuna cactuses, are thought to be the remains of the Wari culture which flourished here between the 6th and 11th centuries. Archeologists have estimated that up to 50,000 people lived in this settlement, occupying as many as 15 different "neighborhoods." There is a small museum on site, but most of the finds have been taken to the archeological museum in Ayacucho for safekeeping.

As well as the tuna cactuses, you may also find in these high valleys the *Puya Raimondi*, a strange-looking plant that lives to be 100 years old but dramatically flowers in great profusion only after 80 years of growth. The rivers that cut the valleys around Ayacucho also offer good fishing for trout and other native species. No permit is necessary, but there are seasons for different fish – best to ask a local expert.

## North from Ayacucho

Ayacucho's nearest northern neighbors – although it takes several hours to reach them – are the towns of **Huancavelica** and Huancayo. Huancavelica has a lengthy past as one of Peru's main mining towns. Silver was discovered here soon after the Spanish conquest, and through the 17th and 18th centuries it was a great creator of wealth, although many of the indigenous people who worked in the mines suffered from mer-

## The Train to the Skies

The train journey from Lima to Huancayo is one of the most spectacular in the world. The line rises 346 km (215 miles) from sea level to a height of 4,800 meters (16,000 ft) at the Ticlio pass, and is one of the highest in the world. There are 26 stations, 58 bridges, and 69 tunnels through the Andes. Construction of the railway started in the late 1800s by the US engineer Henry Meiggs, and took over 40 years to complete. It is an engineering wonder – but to pay for it, the Peruvian government of the day almost went bankrupt. It was used for transporting copper and zinc from mines in the Andes and farm produce from the valleys.

The train makes the 12-hour journey from Lima and the shorter return trip approximately twice a month during the dry season (April through October), so it is vital to book in advance. Reservations can be made by phone at (51) 01-226 6363 or online at the excellent Ferrocarrilcentral website (www.ferrocarrilcentral.com.pe). There is also up-to-date information at www.incasdelperu.org.

cury poisoning and died very young. The mines at **Santa Barbara**, some 5 km (3 miles) outside the city, can be visited. As in Ayacucho, some of this mining wealth was spent on the city's churches. The **Catedral** in the Plaza de Armas in the center of Huancavelica has a fine gilded altar and some baroque paintings. Nearby, **San Francisco** shows how Spanish colonial architecture became far more baroque in the 18th century, while the church and convent of **Santo Domingo** includes paintings shipped especially from Rome.

More interesting is the bustling city of **Huancayo** ⓱, situated some 400 km (250 miles) northwest of Ayacucho. The city's name means "place of stones," and from the remaining monuments it is easy to see why. Its main attractions are the **Capilla de la Merced** (open Mon–Sun 9am–noon, 3–6.30pm), the colonial church where the Peruvian constitution was signed in 1839. The people of Huancayo are also very proud that it was in their city that slavery was abolished in Peru in 1854, and the statue in the main plaza honors Mariscal Ramón Castilla, who pushed the measure through.

There is also an interesting regional museum in the **Museo del Colegio Salesiano** in the El Tambo district, while the Cerrito de la Libertad is a hill overlooking the city with panoramic views. A short walk farther on are the remarkable eroded stone towers known as the **Torre Torre**, which also give views over the town.

Huancayo is known throughout Peru for its boisterous festivals. The most famous – as in Ayacucho – is the Fiesta de las Cruces, which is held every May. There is also a Sunday market which brings in artisans from all the surrounding area, and is a good source of bargains.

Huancayo is also the starting point for journeys to the Mantaro valley, which has several places well worth a visit. About 8 km (5 miles) from Huancayo is the village of **Cochas Chico**, where some of the best local handicrafts can be bargained for. There is also the Convento de Santo

Ocopa, founded some 250 years ago as a training place for missionaries who were setting off to evangelize in the vast Amazon regions of Peru. In the convent there is a precious library, with texts dating back to the 15th century. Further north, the **Santuario Warivilca** is a fortified ruin from the days of the Wari empire.

The mountains here form the Cordillera Huaytapallana, which is 17 km (11 miles) long and has five peaks over 5,000 meters (16,400 ft) high, with many important glaciers. The highest of the peaks is the Nevado Lasuntaysuyo, which is always covered in snow.

Some 40 km (25 miles) from Huancayo is the small town of **Jauja**, famous above all for being the capital of Spanish Peru before Lima was founded, and for the expression *país de Jauja*, referring to a never-never land of milk and honey. Its narrow streets and blue-painted houses seem to reflect hundreds of years of unhurried existence. Boats can be rented

*The Cerrito de la Libertad which overlooks Huancayo.*

**BELOW:** traditional highland weaving techniques.

Papa a la huancaína, *a specialty of Huancayo.*

**BELOW:** the Laguna de Paca in the Río Mantaro valley.

by the hour to take you to the nearby Laguna de Paca.

Some 170 km (105 miles) north of Huancayo is a favorite destination for keen birdwatchers: the **Reserva Nacional de Junín**. The lakes here abound with aquatic birds and the large Andean species.

The northernmost town of any importance in the central highlands is **Huánuco**. Previously part of the Wari (or Huari) and then the Inca culture, the modern city was founded by Gómez de Alvarado in 1539. It has always been the market center for a mainly agricultural and wooded region, and maintains much of its slow charm today. The central square or Plaza de Armas has a 19th-century sculpture by an Italian designer but, unlike many other Peruvian cities, its Cathedral is modern, dating from 1966. Two older churches though, are the **Iglesia San Cristóbal**, the first built by the Spaniards, which is adorned with fine wood carvings, and the **Iglesia de San Francisco**, first constructed in 1560 but remodeled in the 18th century in neoclassical style (open daily 6–9am and 5–8pm).

This sleepy town comes to life during carnival week, celebrated here in August. In January, it is host to the *danza de los negritos*, when dancers wear black masks to represent the black slaves imported to work in the silver mines, most of whom died out.

Five km (3 miles) outside Huánuco stands **Kotosh** and its famous **Templo de las Manos Cruzadas**. As the name suggests, this temple, which is believed to be several thousand years old, has carvings of crossed hands on the walls. According to some archeologists, this is a sign that the ancient people who lived here had a dual vision of the universe.

Also close to Huánuco are the amazing, colossal rock formations of **Marcahuasi**. These are a magnet for rock climbers, but have also bred several strange theories that they represent huge human profiles sculpted by a people who inhabited the earth before mankind. The copper-rich stones are reported to have protective properties, and are said to shield visitors from negative energy. A large flat plain in the middle of the formations is the scene each year (July 28–30) of a local festival bringing together music and dance groups from all the surrounding villages. ❑

# RESTAURANTS

## Restaurants

Prices are per person for a two-course meal, excluding wine:
**$** less than US$10
**$$** US$10–20
**$$$** more than US$20

### Ayacucho

#### Los Alamos
Jr. Cusco 215
Tel: (066) 312 782
Local chicken and meat dishes a specialty. A quiet haven set around a pretty courtyard. **$**

#### Chifa El Dorado
Jr. Cusco 144
Tel: (066) 811 318
If you're hankering after some crunchy Chinese vegetables with a dash of soy, this is the place. All the good Chinese standards are on the menu. **$**

#### Cuatro Leños
Calle M. Cáceres 1038
Tel: (066) 970 6197
Specializes in meaty grills. The beef heart *anticuchos* are memorable, and of course they do a good BBQ chicken. **$**

#### El Monasterio
Jr. 28 de Julio 178
(Centro Cultural)
Tel: (066) 813 905
This *pollería* serves flavorful chicken and fries, as well as good *lomo saltado*, pastas, and salads. The huge portions are incredibly cheap. **$**

#### Restaurant La Casona
Jr. Bellido 463
Tel: (066) 312 733
Pork dishes and highland food. Often has excellent live music on weekends. **$**

#### Restaurant La Tradición
Calle San Martín 406
Tel: (066) 312 595
International and Peruvian food and a friendly atmosphere. **$$**

#### Urpicha
Jr. Londres 272
Tel: (066) 813 905
This lovely restaurant is in the gorgeous setting of a colonial house decorated with Peruvian art. There's good *ají de gallina* and a scrumptious pork roast *adobo asado*. Wash it all down with *chicha morada* and while away the afternoon. **$**

### Huancayo

#### La Cabaña
Av. Giraldez 652
Tel: (064) 223 303
Huancayo's top dinner spot is open every day from 5pm. It is known for the excellent *antichuchos*, as well as great pizzas, good drinks, and the cozy, candlelit atmosphere. Live music on Thursday, Friday, and Saturday nights. **$$**

#### La Estancia
Av. Mariscal Castilla 2815, El Tambo
Tel: (064) 361 019
Traditional Andean *pachamanca* cooked with hot rocks in a hole in the ground for lunch every day. Tender meats, dumplings, and potatoes and Andean herbs, all wrapped in leaves – a delicious Andean feast. **$$**

#### Huancahuasi
Av. Mariscal Castilla 2222, El Tambo
Tel: (066) 244 826
Without doubt the best restaurant in Huancayo, and often packed with Peruvian tourists. On weekends they do a fine *pachamanca* – meat, potatoes, and vegetables cooked with hot rocks in an earth oven. **$$**

### Huánuco

#### Pizzeria Don Pancho
Av. Prado 465
Tel: (066) 516 906
Good crispy pizzas and a wide variety of pasta dishes. Open until late. **$**

**RIGHT:** *humitas de choclo*, delicious parcels of corn mixed with cheese, onion, and garlic.

*Recommended Restaurants and Cafés on page 227*

# THE NORTHERN AMAZON

Travel by river boat through the Amazon region
and discover the huge diversity of flora
and fauna – but don't expect to keep to
a schedule, for time means little here

Lima

**V**iewed from the air, Peru's Amazon looks like an endless sea of lumpy green sponges, stretching in all directions to the horizon. It is this thick umbrella of trees – the jungle's equivalent of an enormous housing project – that creates the millions of homes below in which animals and specialized plants live. If you were able to enter the upper canopy slowly from the top you would soon discover that the first layer is virtually a desert. The crowns of the trees are exposed both to the fierce tropical sun and to winds that frequently snap and topple the tallest of them. To reduce evaporation, the leaves at this level are quite small. Many of the epiphytes – plants that live on top of other plants – actually take the form of cacti, to reduce their loss of water.

As you descended through the upper canopy, however, you would immediately begin to enter a different world of reduced light. Protected from direct sun and wind, the leaves are thus larger in size than those above, and the fierce struggle for light has begun. Traveling farther down toward the jungle floor, you would see that leafy plants are much less abundant. Although explorers traveling by river often reported thick and impenetrable jungle, under the canopy away from the rivers it is possible to move about quite easily, as most branches and leaves are well off the forest floor.

The air here is calm even in strong storms, and at times completely still.

The sound of insects is overpowering, as millions of unseen little creatures call to one another. At the bottom-most level the leaves are very large; less than 5 percent of the sun's light actually reaches the jungle's floor.

## Biodiversity

It is this enormous variation of light, wind, and temperature that, together with the thousands of different species of plants, affords millions of different homes for animal and plant species. Whole communities of insects, birds, and

**Main attractions**

PILPINTUWASI BUTTERFLY FARM
IQUITOS
TRAVELING BY RIVER BOAT
STAYING IN AN ECO-LODGE
RESERVA NACIONAL PACAYA-
SAMIRIA
PUERTO CALLAO

**PRECEDING PAGES:**
Peruvian Amazon.
**LEFT:** Brazil nut
tree. **BELOW:** poison
arrow dart frog.

*In 1743 the French scientist Charles-Marie de la Condamine used rubber latex to waterproof his instruments, and was the first European to introduce the substance to the Old World.*

other animals are specialized and adapted to different levels of the rainforest, so it is not surprising that it contains the highest species diversity in the world.

Parque Nacional Manu *(see pages 228–33)* in southeastern Peru, for example, covering an area roughly half the size of Switzerland, houses over 800 bird species (approximately the same number as is found in the whole of North America), 20 percent of all the plant species found in South America, and more than 1,200 species of butterfly (Europe has just 400). A recent study by the Smithsonian Institution of the insects in Manu's upper canopy has increased the total number of the world's estimated animal species by 30 million.

## Push toward conservation

Jungles have existed for hundreds of millions of years, but it is only within the past 100 years that they have been on the decline. The trend is in direct relation to the population of human beings. In the course of the past century humans have destroyed half of the world's rainforests. At the present rate of destruction, most experts agree, the majority of the remaining rainforests will have disappeared within the next 20 years.

Tampering with the jungles is not a modern phenomenon, of course. Europeans have long viewed the Amazon as a storehouse of raw materials. The 16th- and 17th-century search for gold was replaced by quests for other valuable commodities native to the Amazon jungle and found nowhere else in the world: quinine (which allowed British troops to conquer India without succumbing to malaria), cocoa (the basis of the world's chocolate industry), mahogany, vanilla, and others. No product made a bigger impact, however, than that which naturally exudes from three species of Amazonian tree: the sticky white latex called rubber.

## The rubber boom

The commodity had been known about for a very long time – Columbus reported tribes using strange "elastic" balls in their games – but its commercial use was limited due, to the fact that natural rubber grew soft and sticky in hot weather and brittle and hard in cold. In 1844, however, Charles Goodyear invented the process of vulcanization, which allowed

**BELOW:** red howler monkey.

*Recommended Restaurants and Cafés on page 227*

rubber to stay tough and firm at all temperatures. This revolutionized the rubber industry. With John Boyd Dunlop's later invention of the pneumatic tire, suddenly an enormous demand was created, which only the Amazon could satisfy.

The ensuing rubber boom was short-lived – it lasted from around 1880 to 1912 – but it transformed the Amazon's economy. Rubber trees in the most remote regions were soon being tapped, the latex gathered in cups, then coagulated into large balls that were cured over a fire. The tappers themselves were bankrolled by entrepreneurs who amassed enormous wealth and lived in luxury in newly burgeoning jungle cities such as Manaus in Brazil and Iquitos in Peru.

In the midst of the boom, however, an English adventurer named Henry Wickham quietly collected 70,000 rubber seeds and smuggled them out of the Amazon. First planted in Kew Gardens in England, and then transplanted to tropical Asia where they were safe from indigenous diseases, the seeds flourished. By 1912 the Amazon rubber boom was at an end.

In the latter half of the 20th century the largest destructive force on the Peru-vian Amazon was the unmanaged influx of peasants from the Andes and the coast. Since the 1960s, successive governments, both military and civilian, have viewed the eastern Andean slopes and the Amazon basin as regions of unexploited natural resources, believing that their development would provide a politically painless solution to several urgent problems: land hunger in the Andes, the migration of masses of the rural poor to coastal cities, and the need to populate border regions in order to defend national sovereignty.

As a result the Belaúnde government financed the construction of a "marginal highway," a road paralleling the Andes to the east, which, it was hoped, would help open up the area to colonization and industry. But the idea of settling the Amazon ignored reality: less than 5 percent of the Peruvian Amazon's soil is suitable for agriculture, and much of the region supports populations of indigenous peoples and settlers that are already large in relation to the exploitable resources.

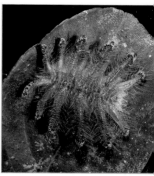

*The monkey slug caterpillar mimics the tarantula spider.*

**BELOW:** a caiman lying in wait.

*A scale breasted woodpecker feeding on fruit.*

**BELOW:** a giant anteater combing the forest floor.

Peruvian Amazon have been deforested; 300,000 hectares (741,300 acres) are deforested every year.

An additional impact on Peru's rainforest was the illegal cocaine industry, mostly concentrated in the north-central jungle's Huallaga valley *(see page 188)*. Hundreds of thousands of hectares of virgin rainforest were destroyed in order to grow illegal plantations of coca shrubs – all to support the drug habits of North Americans and Europeans. The US government pressurized Peru to use a major defoliant – Spike – on coca plantations, but protests by local and international conservationists about the effect such a chemical could have on the surrounding jungle prevented its use. In recent years, however, many hectares of coca-leaf plantations have been turned over to legal cash crops such as cocoa, coffee, or corn, and a government program has been initiated to help farmers find markets for their new crops.

As a consequence, agriculture that began on a few relatively fertile terraces in the eastern Andes has now spread to land ill-suited to continuous exploitation. With inadequate knowledge of better practices, many farmers work the land too long, allowing no time for it to renew itself. Once the soil has been drained of nutrients, poor farmers, unable to buy fertilizer, have no alternative but to move on, carving yet another plot from the forest.

The result has been extensive deforestation of Peru's cloud forest, where an estimated 50 percent of all neotropical plant species are found. Thus far over 70,000 sq km (27,000 sq miles) of the

## System of protection

In spite of increasing rainforest destruction, however, a number of encouraging developments have taken place.

*Recommended Restaurants and Cafés on page 227*

Peru currently has roughly 5 percent of its territory protected by a system of around 50 national parks, reserves, sanctuaries, and other designated areas, a process that has thrived since it was begun in the 1960s. During the past few decades considerable ecological awareness has developed and, as a consequence, there has been a proliferation of conservation organizations. In 1990 a giant 1.5 million-hectare (3.75 million-acre) "reserved zone" was declared in the Madre de Dios region – Peru's southernmost department, which contains some of the richest rainforest found anywhere in the world. This area – including almost the entire watershed of the Río Tambopata – is currently at the forefront of tropical rainforest conservation.

## Eco-tourism develops

The idea is to convert the zone not into a park but rather an "extractive reserve," which means an area of rainforest where renewable yearly harvests of Brazil nuts, rubber, and other rainforest products will create more revenue, in the long run, than the permanent destruction caused by unmanaged farming, logging, and cattle-ranching. The scheme was pioneered by the Brazilian rubber tapper Chico Méndez (who was murdered in 1988 by Brazilian cattle-ranchers, and whose story has been made into a film by David Puttnam), but it remains to be seen how such ideas fare.

The practice of so-called eco-tourism has also developed over the past three decades. This new "green" tourism is based on the belief that the rich natural rainforest can not only be preserved, by using it as an extractive reserve, but can also attract tourist dollars. If the eco-tourism industry is managed responsibly, the income it generates, pumped into local economies and national-park infrastructures, may well prove to be one of the few counter-destructive economic forces currently available for preserving the jungle.

## The northern jungle

Some 3,200 km (1,990 miles) upriver from the Amazon's mouth lies the jungle-locked city of **Iquitos** ⓲. The capital of the department of Loreto, it has a population of 500,000, and is linked to the exterior world only by air and river

*60 percent of Peru lies within the Amazon basin, but this region is home to only 12 percent of the population.*

**LEFT:** a local man in his dugout canoe.

## Ayahuasca: the Sacred Vine

Ayahuasca *(Banisteriopsis caapi)* is a rainforest vine with hallucinogenic properties that is used to promote knowledge and healing under the guidance of a shaman. The vine has been used for centuries by Amazon tribes as part of traditional celebrations and initiations. It has also been used to make predictions, in decision-making, and to aid the resolution of interfamilial and inter-tribal conflicts. Today, it is principally used as a key to self-knowledge and expanded consciousness.

Extract of the vine is prepared as a bitter-tasting drink which is administered by the shaman. After some time, this promotes vomiting – part of the cleansing process – and then a state in which visions are experienced, leading to a mental state of clarity, certainty, and self-awareness.

Courses in Ayahuasca are used in some Amazon clinics to treat alcoholism and drug addiction, and, in recent years, drinking Ayahuasca has become a popular activity for tourists. Some shamans conduct Ayahuasca ceremonies for groups, but if you are attracted by the idea, do your research carefully. While at its best, Ayahuasca is said to be profoundly enlightening, a bad experience could be very frightening.

boats. At one time the clearing-house for the millions of tons of rubber shipped to Europe, Iquitos still displays the vestiges of its former status as one of the most important rubber capitals in the world. Houses both near the main plaza and the river are still faced with *azulejos* (glazed tiles), which at the height of the rubber boom were originally shipped from Italy and Portugal along with other luxury goods such as early 20th-century ironwork from England, glass chandeliers, caviar, and fine wines.

On the **Plaza de Armas** stands the Casa de Fierro, or Iron House, which was designed by Gustave Eiffel for the Paris Exhibition in 1898 and now houses a good restaurant upstairs called the Amazon Café. It is said to be the first prefabricated house in the Americas and was transported unassembled from Paris by a local rubber baron. It is entirely constructed of iron trusses and bolted iron sheets. This sounds more impressive than it looks, and it is more interesting as a symbol of the town's short-lived affluence than as a piece of architecture.

Also on the plaza is the house of Carlos Fitzcarrald, the Peruvian rubber baron who dragged a steamship over the pass that bears his name, thus opening up the department of Madre de Dios. The German director Werner Herzog shot part of his film *Fitzcarraldo* here, and several of the refurbished steamships that he used are still in port. Hundreds of *iquiteños* were used as extras in the movie, which created a brief mini-boom of its own.

Iquitos today is a colorful, friendly city that seems to have a monopoly not on rubber but on three-wheeled taxis (charging approximately 50 cents a ride); motor scooters, with the consequent din as they are continually revved up; Amazon views; and a very special atmosphere. It is located some 80 km (50 miles) downriver from where the **Marañón** and **Ucayali** rivers join to create the River Amazon.

The local dish is *paiche a la loretana*, a fillet of a huge primitive fish, served with fried manioc and vegetables. Exotic fruit juices are sold on the street corners, as are ice creams that are flavored with mango, papaya, *granadilla* (passion fruit), guanabana, and many other fruits.

You can take a taxi or simply walk

**RIGHT:** banana cargo.

## Pilpintuwasi Butterfly Farm

If you are spending a few days in Iquitos, it is worth taking a day trip to **Pilpintuwasi Butterfly Farm** just outside the city at Padre Cocha. On the banks of the Nanay River is a huge walk-through butterfly enclosure, with exhibits that explain the fascinating lifecycle of the butterfly. It is a delight to walk around surrounded by drifts of the colorful creatures. Located on the same site is the **Amazon Animal Orphanage**, a refuge for injured or previously caged animals. There is a magnificent jaguar and a giant anteater, as well as monkeys, tapirs, parrots, sloths, and a number of other denizens of the jungle, all rescued from unhappy captivity or recuperating from maltreatment.

The Butterfly Farm and the Animal Orphanage are a 20-minute boat ride from the Bella Vista sector in Iquitos (ask for Pilpintuwasi). In the dry season, there is a 15-minute walk from where the boat leaves you, in the wet, you are brought right to the front gate. Tel: (063) 232 665; open Tue–Sun 9am–4pm; entrance fee. For more information see www.amazonanimalorphanage.org.

down from the main plaza to the picturesque waterfront district of **Belén**, to the southeast of the town, where the houses float on rafts in the water. A Venetian-style labyrinth of canals, canoes, and stores, Belén is the center for an incredible variety of Amazon products: exotic fruits, fish, turtles, edible frogs, herbal medicines, and waterfowl. Plowing the waterways are a plethora of small canoe-taxis paddled by *iquiteños*, some as young as five years old. A canoe tour of one of the most unusual waterfronts in the world costs just a few dollars.

Some 15 km (9 miles) south of the city is the beautiful **Lago Quistacocha**, set in lush tropical jungle, which can be reached by bus. There is a small zoo, the Parque Zoológico de Quistacocha (closed Monday; entrance fee), where jaguars, ocelots, parrots, and anacondas can be seen, as well as the giant paiche fish – the one that features in the local dish – which are bred here in hatcheries.

## Jungle lodges

Iquitos has long been a center for excursions into the surrounding jungle. It should be remembered, however, that because there are a lot of people in this area, and the Amazon here is a main waterway, you must travel well beyond a 60-km (37-mile) radius of the city to see wildlife such as caiman, monkeys, macaws, or pink dolphins – in fact, the last are found only on remote tributaries of the upper Amazon and Orinoco rivers.

A good way to become acquainted quickly with the jungle is to visit one of a number of lodges that have been set up on nearby rivers. Although many of the two- or three-day lodge tours can be booked through a travel agent in Lima, they are much cheaper if arranged in Iquitos. Avoid the numerous individuals in the airport and the city who are keen to set up a "jungle lodge tour" on behalf of foreign visitors. Since these men are paid on a commission basis, you can buy the same package deal more cheaply by simply walking into a lodge's downtown office, most of which are clustered around Jirón Putumayo near the Plaza de Armas. *(See Travel Tips, pages 330–1, for details of Amazon lodges.)*

**Explorama Lodges** is one of the

**EAT**

A typical *iquiteño* specialty is *juanes*: rice, chicken, olive, and hard boiled egg, all wrapped in the leaf of a *bijao* plant. Served with a spicy *ají* condiment, they are delicious.

**BELOW:** Casa de Fierro, Iquitos.

# The Amazon by River Boat

**In Peru's Amazon regions, rivers are highways and river boat is the only way to get around and to experience the slow-paced life of the Amazon.**

River boats vary from *pequepeques* (small dugouts with outboard motors) to *lanchas* (larger cargo and passenger boats) and luxurious tourist boats with air conditioning and cocktails at sunset. Boats ply the tributaries of the Ucayali, Huallaga, Marañón, and Amazon rivers, and any number of lesser waterways in between.

To truly experience river life, buy yourself a hammock in Iquitos (for about US$10) and a ticket on a *lancha*. Locals travel on these boats, along with bags of bananas and mangoes, sacks of corn, cattle, pigs, chickens, dogs, and pet monkeys. You can string up your hammock in the middle of the friendly melee, opt for a private upper deck, or even pay for a cabin with a proper bed. The latter options offer more space and quiet and provide you with somewhere secure to leave your belongings. If you can speak a bit of Spanish, hanging out with the locals can be a rewarding experience. As the boat churns its way along, you'll

share snacks and jokes, and cement friendships.

Meals are served three times a day, and the quality of the food depends on the boat and on which deck you choose. On the better boats, the upper-deck fare is good – meat and rice or river fish bought from settlements along the way. It is

also worth sampling the wonderful array of tropical fruits sold by villagers en route. Depending on the amount of cargo to load and unload at different ports, there may be time to get off and explore.

Nights on the river are magical: hammocks sway gently as you drift through the jungle underneath a star-studded sky. Get up early and you'll be treated to an Amazon sunrise as the boat floats through the early morning mist. During the day, keep your eyes peeled for pink dolphins which sometimes play around the boats as they dock. Traveling by river boat is all about the journey – it's a time to stop and observe and become part of life here and, best of all, you might even be the only tourist on the boat.

Tickets can be bought from travel agencies in Iquitos, although it is best to buy them at the dock as this gives you a chance to see the boat you'll be traveling on. There are daily departures to Pucallpa, a journey of four to seven days (depending on water levels and cargo loading and unloading times), for which the Henry boats are recommended. The three to four-day journey to Yurimaguas is best made on the Eduardo boats, of which Eduardo III is the most highly recommended. Tickets for this service must be reserved in person at the company's offices on the docks. Traveling to Manaus in Brazil takes around 10 days and requires a boat change at Tabatinga on the border.

Boats leave from Puerto Masusa on Avenida La Marina, but don't expect them to stick to any schedule. To ply these routes in five-star style, contact Amazon Tours and Cruises *(see Travel Tips, page 343)*, or Amazon Cruises toll-free in the US: 1-800 747 0567; www.amazoncruise.net. ❏

**LEFT AND ABOVE:** the Eduardo III river boat.

*Recommended Restaurants and Cafés on page 227*

largest companies, with five different lodges, all of them well run and efficient. One of the advantages of booking into one of the Explorama lodges is that they also provide access to the canopy walkway at the Amazon Conservatory of Tropical Studies (ACTS). First opened in 1992, it is now around 500 meters (1,640 ft) in length, and reaching a height of up to 35 meters (115 ft) it offers breathtaking views for birdwatching from a unique perspective. One of the most beautiful sights is that of mixed flocks of birds feeding in the early morning and late afternoon. Sloths, marmosets, and monkeys can also be spotted.

Other lodges in the area offer river trips to the beautiful Río Yarapa, where river dolphins can be seen, and interesting shamanic tours for the more esoterically minded travelers.

## Slow boats

A commercial river boat *(see opposite)* traveling either upriver toward Pucallpa or downriver toward Brazil is a great way to experience the Amazon. Although not much will be seen in the way of wildlife along the way (boats traveling upstream hug the banks, those in the opposite direction travel down the center of the river), the traveler will still see how people live along the Amazon and also enjoy beautiful sunsets and magnificent scenery.

Be warned that life along the Amazon is slow and leisurely – you should never travel by river boat if you are in a hurry or have an inflexible schedule. Boats often break down, linger sometimes for days in port, and are generally unpredictable.

Another way to see the Amazon, and one highly recommended for those who have a little more time and want to get off the beaten path, is to hire a small boat and guide of your own. In every Amazon port there are boat-owners who are willing to rent you their services at only a fraction of the cost paid at a typical jungle lodge. If you make up a small group, it is even more economical. As with the commercial river boats, the best way to locate a small boat and guide in Iquitos is simply to ask about on the wharves. With a boat, the entire Amazon suddenly opens up for your exploration.

Only 100 km (62 miles) from Iquitos,

**TIP**

You can do your bit for conservation by refusing to buy anything made from animal products. If local people see that tourists would rather look at the live creatures than buy articles made of shell or feather, the trade will become much less attractive.

**BELOW:** young *iquiteños.*

**EAT**

The paiche fish grows to a length of 2 meters (6 ft) and can weigh more than 80 kilos (176 lbs). This delicious fish is eaten throughout the Amazon region.

for example, is the biggest national park in Peru, the 2 million-hectare (5 million-acre) **Reserva Nacional Pacaya-Samiria**, a wildlife-packed lowland jungle area that can only be reached by hiring a boat and a guide, in either Iquitos or the village of Lagunas, and staging your own expedition.

## The central jungle

Seven days' travel upriver from Iquitos on the Río Ucayali is **Pucallpa** ⑲, a rapidly growing city of 200,000 that can be reached from Lima by air – there are several flights daily – or on a 24-hour bus journey.

Most people arriving in the city prefer to stay at Puerto Callao on the nearby **Lago Yarinacocha**, a 20-minute bus journey from the city, which is the main tourist attraction of the area. Based here are the **Hospital Albert Schweitzer**, which serves provides medical care for the local Indian population, and the **Summer Institute of Linguistics**, a non-denominational missionary organization studying many of Peru's indigenous jungle languages with the intention of concocting an alphabet so that the

Bible can be translated into these hitherto unwritten languages. The latter organization, which can be visited by appointment only, has attracted a great deal of criticism from those who believe that through its influence indigenous peoples are in danger of losing their own culture and tribal identity.

In **Puerto Callao** you can visit the fascinating artisanal cooperative **Maroti Shobo**, where high-quality ceramics and weavings made by the Shipibo people from the surrounding villages are displayed and sold, and are sent to museums all over the world.

The Shipibo people have inhabited the area for at least the past 1,000 years, and trips can be arranged to some of their villages. There are a couple of lodges on the lake, and more wildlife than you might expect, considering the nearby population. The lodges will also organize jungle excursions, and private excursions by motor canoe into the surrounding jungle and canals are easy to arrange from Puerto Callao. While traveling on the canals, you may see numerous piranhas, caiman, and the occasional monkey. ❑

**BELOW:** giant waterlillies.

# RESTAURANTS AND CAFÉS

## Restaurants

Prices are per person for a two-course meal, excluding wine:
**$** less than US$10
**$$** US$10–20
**$$$** more than US$20

### Iquitos

#### Al Frío y Al Fuego

Restaurant departure point: Av. La Marina
Reservations: Jr. Pevas 252
Tel: (065) 224 862
Surely one of world's most romantic places to eat. This restaurant is a breezy, floating palm-roofed pavilion in the middle of the Río Itaya. You are ferried there by lamplit boat and offered a menu cooked by Iquitos' only Cordon Bleu chef, Cesar Moran. Try the *patarashca*, a river fish called *doncella* cooked in a palm leaf with fried or steamed yucca. **$$$**

#### Amazon Café

Jr. Putumayo 182
Tel: (065) 225 722
Exotic *iquiteño* dishes and plenty of fish make this a good choice. Try the excellent *ceviche de paiche*. **$$**

#### Antica Pizerria

Jr. Napo 159
Tel: (065) 241 988
This roomy restaurant is popular with tourists for its wood-oven pizzas, meat from the grill, pasta dishes, and good salads. They also serve decent breakfasts. Try the Loretano Breakfast: it's a whopper. **$$**

#### Blanquita

Calle Bolognesi 1181
Tel: (065) 267 015
This is the place to eat for Iquitos locals in the know. Run by a group of ladies, it's a classic *iquiteña* mother's kitchen cooking. Try the *juanes (see page 223)*, *humitas* (corn dumplings steamed in a corn leaf), empanadas, fish cooked in jungle leaves, BBQ chicken and *anticuchos* (kebabs). **$**

#### Chifa Long Fung

Jr. San Martín 454
Tel: (065) 233 649
Iquitos's most celebrated Chinese restaurant, this huge place is often full and you may have to queue for a seat, but the food is certainly worth it. **$**

#### Huasai

Calle Fitzcarrald 131
Tel: (065) 242 222
Very popular with locals, this unpretentious eatery serves *juanes (see page 223)*,

Iquitos chorizo with fried plantains, and jungle-style fish. **$**

#### El Mesón

Malecón Maldonado 153
Tel: (094) 231 857
Right on the Iquitos riverfront, this popular place serves all the Iquitos specialties. You can take a table on the pedestrian boulevard outside and eat your meal only a stone's throw from the Amazon. **$**

#### Nikoro

Calle Pevas 100
Right at the end of Calle Pevas overlooking the water, this

bohemian place is a wonderful hangout from breakfast until late at night. It's open-sided with a palm roof and pot plants, and has a simple menu for breakfast and lunch. In the evening it's an atmospheric bar. **$**

#### Restaurante Fitzcarraldo

Jr. Napo 100–116
Tel: (065) 236 536
This breezy spot is right on the waterfront: you can drink your cold jungle juice and watch the Amazon slide by. They do a great ceviche served with fried banana and yucca. **$**

**RIGHT:** ingredients for a fish stew.

# MANU TO MALDONADO

One of the truly pristine areas of the tropics,
this southern corner of Peru is a birdwatcher's
paradise. It can be reached from the
gold-boom town of Maldonado

Lima

The traditional hopping-off point for Peru's little-explored southern jungle is the city of Cusco *(see map on pages 238–9)*, where a variety of tours is available, along with a wealth of information on some of the national parks in the southern region, but the area has been included in this section of the book to offer continuity to readers who are interested in all aspects of travel in the Peruvian Amazon.

The adventurous traveler can go from Cusco by rail and truck to **Quillabamba** and **Kiteni** and from there hire a boat through the **Pongo de Manique**, a narrow gorge surrounded by lush jungle and waterfalls on the upper **Río Urubamba**, a journey described in Peter Matthiesson's 1962 classic, *Cloud Forest*. It must be emphasized that transport is infrequent in this area, and you should be extremely flexible. There is a government air service that operates from the mission town of **Sepahua** (lower down on the Urubamba) to Pucallpa and then to Lima, but the flights are extremely unreliable. If you are highly adventurous and self-sufficient – only very basic food is available – you may find a boat to take you all the way to Pucallpa.

## Parque Nacional Manu

Also accessible from Cusco is what has been called the most bio-diverse rainforest park in the world, located in Peru's southernmost jungle department of **Madre de Dios**. At 1.8 million hectares (4½ million acres), the **Parque Nacional**

**Manu ⓴**, one of the few truly pristine regions of the tropics, is perhaps the best area in the Amazon rainforest for watching wildlife. In many other jungle areas, because of the proximity of humans, you may be lucky to see anything other than birds, insects, or an occasional large animal, but in Manu you will see so many monkeys (there are 13 different species) that you may grow tired of them. Besides an abundance of turtles, you'll have a great opportunity to see giant otters, peccaries, capybaras, tapirs, and even the occasional jaguar.

**Main attractions**

PARQUE NACIONAL MANU
MANU LODGE
RESERVA NACIONAL TAMBOPATA
COLPA DE GUACAMAYOS
PUERTO MALDONADO

**LEFT:** red, green, and scarlet macaws.
**BELOW:** traveling by river boat.

# Jungle Lodges

**Whether it's to the Northern Amazon from Iquitos or the southern rainforest from Puerto Maldonado, a visit to a lodge is an unforgettable experience.**

Jungle lodges vary from basic to five-star, and accommodations are in the form of hammocks or individual cabins with comfortable beds. Food is generally simple, but includes plenty of river fish prepared in imaginative ways. However, it's what can be seen around the lodges that most visitors come for. Sightings of colorful macaws and chattering monkeys are almost guaranteed, and if you're lucky, you might see a caiman or pink river dolphin. Rainforest walks reveal rubber trees and Tarzan-style vines, while on the ground there are busy termites and frogs perfectly camouflaged as leaves. High up in the canopy you might glimpse a three-toed sloth or tiny lion-faced monkeys small enough to fit in your hand.

In some areas, there are opportunities for fishing for piranhas or peacock bass and spots where it's safe to swim. Where there are isolated jungle villages you may have a chance to meet the locals, and perhaps even trade for handicrafts.

Bookings can be arranged in Lima before you start your trip, or in Cusco or Iquitos. There are various tour companies, some of which run their own lodges. In Iquitos, **Explorama Tours**, one of the largest and most reliable companies, has three lodges, all well-run and efficient: Ceiba Tops Luxury Lodge, 40 km (25 miles) from Iquitos, has comfortable bungalows, hot water, good food, and attractive jungle walks. Explorama Lodge, 60 km (40 miles) from Iquitos at Yanamono, is a little more basic: there's no hot water or electricity, but it's perfectly adequate and runs good jungle hikes. The third lodge is the ExplorNapo, 140 km (90 miles) from Iquitos on the Río Napo, the most rustic of all, but facilities are good and you get a chance to explore primary forest, plus access to the canopy walkway at the Amazon Center for Environmental Education and Research. **Amazon Tours and Cruises** in Iquitos runs a lodge on the Río Momón and organizes river cruises and more adventurous expeditions.

There are numerous lodges in the southern jungle, including three in the Cultural Zone of Parque Nacional Manu, for which you don't need a permit. These are the Manu Cloud Forest Lodge, near the Río Unin; the Amazon Lodge at Río Alto Madre de Dios; and the Albergue Pantiacolla Lodge. The only accommodation in the Manu Reserve Zone is the comfortable Manu Lodge. Overlooking a rainforest lagoon, it has both an expanding trail system and experienced (English-speaking) guides to help you spot the rarer bird species.

There are two very good agencies which will organize trips to the Manu lodges: the first is **Manu Nature Tours** in Cusco, which also runs all-inclusive tours to Colpa Lodge, on the Río Tambopata, where macaws can be watched close up. The other is **Manu Expeditions** in Lima, run by English ornithologist Barry Walker. He specializes in camping trips with knowledgeable guides, but will also organize customized trips to most of the above lodges.

The best-known lodge in the Reserva Nacional Tambopata Candamo is Explorers' Inn, 60 km (38 miles) from Maldonado. Newer lodges in Tambopata include the no-frills Tambopata Research Center and the Ese'ejas community-run Posada Amazonas *(see page 232)*. Reserva Amazónica and Libertador Tambopata Lodge both offer good service and reasonably priced packages. For details of tour operators and hotels listed here, *see Accommodations, pages 330–1, and Activities, page 343.* ❑

**LEFT:** Yarapa River Lodge.

*Recommended Restaurants on page 233*

Manu is also an unparalleled place for birdwatching. Founded in 1973, the park was declared a Biosphere Reserve in 1977, and a Unesco World Natural Heritage Site ten years later. It harbors over 1,000 species of bird – 300 more species than are found in the United States and Canada combined. The world record for the number of species seen and heard in one day was set in Manu in 1982, when 331 species were recorded in just a few square miles of forest.

Located right in the Reserve Zone is **Manu Lodge** *(see Travel Tips, page 331)*, which overlooks a tranquil rainforest lagoon; its expanding trail system provides access to seasonally flooded forest, high-ground forest, and patches of bamboo. There are also experienced guides to help visitors find shy bird species. Large, rare game-birds such as razor-billed curassows and piping-guans have been hunted out of most areas, but are easy to see at Manu Lodge. Also seen are macaws, pale-winged trumpeters, the tall jabirú storks, roseate spoonbills, and five species of large eagle, including the majestic harpy eagle. New species are continually being discovered. The rare rufous-fronted ant-thrush, for example, was previously known from only one location but has now also been found at Manu Lodge.

By far the easiest way to visit Manu is with one of the local tour operators such as **Manu Nature Tours** or **Manu Expeditions** *(see Travel Tips, page 331)*, since all preparations for the trip must be made in advance and permits are required for entry into the reserve (although you don't need a permit for the Cultural Zone). The tour operator arranges all permits, transport, equipment, gasoline, and food supplies for the trip. It can take up to two days to reach this isolated area by traveling overland from Cusco, down through the cloud forest and later transferring to a boat – an unforgettable experience. There is also the option of chartering a small plane, which can fly to the junction of the Madre de Dios and Manu rivers. This is much more expensive, but a good idea if your time is limited. Prices depend on the number of passengers.

## Reserva Nacional Tambopata

There are yet more chances to see birds in Peru's second-largest reserve: the **Reserva Nacional Tambopata**. Created

**EAT**

The harvesting of wild Brazil nuts is a major economy of the jungle and does not destroy its ecosystem. Fresh Brazil nuts are richer in flavor than processed ones as they still contain many of their natural oils. Large bags of ready-shelled nuts can be bought very cheaply, either plain or with a sugar coating.

**BELOW:** wildlife-watching at an oxbow lake.

**TIP**

If you are on a low budget and can't afford the packages offered by the lodges, try staying with a local family. Arrangements can be made with contacts at Puerto Maldonado airport.

by the Peruvian government in 1989, this 1.5 million-hectare (3.8 million-acre) zone has been set up both as an extractive reserve (for rubber, Brazil nuts, and other products) and for eco-tourism. The reserve encompasses the entire watershed of the **Río Tambopata**, one of the most beautiful and least disturbed areas in Peru.

The river begins high in the Andean department of Puno; several tour companies lead kayak expeditions down the Tambopata, which offers a spectacular transition from the Andes to the low jungle. The reserve protects the largest macaw lick in South America, the **Colpa de Guacamayos**. Here birdwatchers can view one of the world's phenomenal avian spectacles, as hundreds of red, blue, and green parrots and macaws gather at the lick daily. Squawking raucously, they wheel through the air before landing together on the river bank to eat clay. This breathtaking display can only be seen where there is undisturbed rainforest with healthy populations of wild macaws, as in southeast Peru.

Trails around the macaw lick offer birding in both floodplain and high-

ground forest. Orinoco geese and large horned screamers can also be seen along clear streams near the Andean foothills. Comfortable accommodation is provided at the macaw lick by **Tambopata Research Center Lodge**, run by Rainforest Expeditions. The only lodge in the uninhabited area of the reserve, it is about six hours from Puerto Maldonado in a speedboat, but twice that in one of the river boats known locally as *pequepeques*. Rainforest Expeditions, in conjunction with the Ese'ejas community, also runs Posada Amazonas, near Lago Chinbadas, where giant river otters and harpy eagles can be seen, and where mammals such as peccaries, tapirs, and a rodent known as a pacarana congregate at a nocturnal salt lick.

Also in the Tambopata Reserve is the **Explorers' Inn** lodge, around which some 500 bird species can be seen. These include quetzals, manakins, and many antbirds. The lodge trails also provide good access to patches of bamboo popular with bird specialties like the Peruvian recurve-bill, the white-cheeked tobey-flycatcher, and Goeldi's antbird.

The forests of southeast Peru offer the

**BELOW:** sunset on the River Manu.

finest birdwatching experience. However, identifying all the different species, and finding elusive birds in the forest undergrowth, can prove overwhelming for an ornithologist inexperienced in tropical forests, which is why an expert guide is invaluable.

Birdwatching tours also help to support local families, who will conserve rainforest birds as if their livelihoods depend on it. Local people won't hunt macaws for trade or feathers if they can make more money by taking visitors to see them. By choosing such tours, visitors can make a positive conservation impact. However, the birds can't survive without the pristine rainforests in which they live, and conservation organizations and indigenous peoples are joining the battle to preserve them.

## Boom town of the south

From Cusco you can reach **Puerto Maldonado ㉑**, the capital of the Peruvian department of Madre de Dios, either by air or along the 500-km (310-mile) road, a trip that takes two and a half days; it's a bit uncomfortable, but worth it for the scenery. Long cut off from the rest of the world both by rapids on the **Río Madeira** and by the Andes, Puerto Maldonado, a thriving rubber town at the turn of the 20th century, lapsed into anonymity again until the discovery of gold in the 1970s and the building of an airport in the early 1980s turned the city into a gold-rush boom town.

Set on a bluff overlooking the Madre de Dios and Tambopata rivers, Puerto Maldonado has a pleasant **Plaza de Armas**, and numerous hotels for miners on brief trips to town, but not much to see or do. In 1897 the rubber baron Carlos Fitzcarrald traveled through here after having dragged his steamship, with the help of hundreds of Indians, over what is now known as the Fitzcarraldo pass and down the Manu and Madre de Dios rivers on his way to Iquitos via Brazil *(see page 222)*. You can make an excursion, about half an hour from the city, to the site where locals will tell you Fitzcarrald's steamship is located,

beached a little way inland. Actually, this isn't his boat at all; it is the remains of a German hospital ship which once plied the Madre de Dios.

Buy a bag or two of Brazil nuts while you are here. These rich, abundant, and inexpensive nuts will help encourage the preservation of Madre de Dios's rainforest, where around 30 percent of the population is employed in nut extraction.

Only an hour south of Puerto Maldonado is **Lago Sandoval**, a beautiful jungle lake that can be reached by boat from Puerto Maldonado's port. Three hours farther downriver, and well worth an overnight fishing expedition, is **Lago Valencia**, which is quite remote and relatively free of tourists. A several-day expedition can be mounted to the 100,000-hectare (250,000-acre) **Reserva Nacional Pampas de Río Heath**, a wild area of plains and swamps located on the Río Heath bordering Bolivia. ❏

*Mealy, blue-headed parrots at the Blanquillo clay lick.*

### Restaurants

#### Puerto Maldonado

**El Califa**
Av. Piura 266
Tel: (082) 571 119
This restaurant does all the jungle specialties like *platano frito*, yucca, *ensalada de chonta* (palm-heart salad), and tasty BBQ meats. **$**

**Carne Brava**
Av. Fitzcarald 539
Tel: (082) 575 366
As the name suggests, there's little for vegetarians here, but they do excellent grilled meats and fine steaks. **$**

**Pollería Astoria**
Av. León Velarde 701
Tel: (082) 571 422
A decent *pollería* where you can get good chicken and chips on a budget. They'll include a salad if you ask. **$**

**El Tigre**
Av. Tacna 456
Tel: (082) 572 286
This simple place makes good ceviche at lunchtime and is popular with locals. **$**

**Wasai**
Jr. Billinghurst s/n (first block)
Tel: (082) 572 290
A local favorite which does all the Peruvian standards well. **$**

• • • • • • • • • • • • • • • •
Prices are per person for two courses, excluding wine. **$** = less than US$10;
**$$** = US$10–US$20; **$$$** = more than US$20

# BIRDS OF THE AMAZON

**For the keen amateur ornithologist, seeking out some of Peru's exotic birds may turn out to be the experience of a lifetime**

Nowhere in the world is there such a plethora of birdlife as in the Amazon rainforest. The Parque Nacional Manu alone is home to over 1,000 different species. Their names are often as exotic as their appearance: from golden-headed quetzals to yellow-rumped caciques, roseate spoonbills to pale-winged trumpeters, they represent a birdwatcher's dream. Who wouldn't think their trip worthwhile if they spotted a paradise tanager, known as the *siete colores* because of its seven-colored plumage? Or a jabirú stork, one of the largest flying birds in the Americas, up to 1.4 meters (4½ ft) in length?

Many species fly in mixed flocks: insectivorous birds, such as woodcreepers and antbirds, will flock together, sometimes as many as 100 of them traveling in a great cloud. This makes individuals difficult to distinguish on first sighting, but they tend to stick to the same feeding areas so, if you identify their territory, you will have a great opportunity to spot a variety of species together.

The same applies to the mixed flocks of fruit-eaters, which include tanagers, fruitcrows, and parrots. Once you identify a food source you have an excellent chance of seeing a large number of birds. Not that rainforest birds are always easy for the uninitiated to spot, which is why an experienced guide is invaluable, and one usually accompanies visitors on organized tours.

The oxbow lakes of the Amazon are the habitat of herons, hoatzins, egrets, and wattled jacanas, species not difficult to spot as they forage for food on the shores. Raptors, flying high above the canopy, can present more of a problem, but the harpy eagle and the crested eagle, among other majestic creatures, can be spotted from vantage points at clearings or on riverbanks.

**ABOVE:** hoatzins can manage only short, clumsy flights. They form mating groups, and share the rearing of their offspring. The young have clawed wing bends, to help them clamber about in trees.

**BELOW:** yellow-ridged toucans are gregarious birds and usually fly in pairs. Their bills may be one-third of the total length.

**LEFT:** rufescent tiger herons are frequently spotted in and around the lakes and streams of Parque Nacional Manu. They can also be spotted flying over clearings.

## STAMPING OUT THE BIRD TRADE

One of the most spectacular sights in the Peruvian Amazon is that of macaws gathered at the huge salt licks in the Reserva Nacional Tambopata. But some people still regard exotic birds as interesting pets, and the macaws and parrots that inhabit the same part of the rainforest can be trapped, exported, and sold on the international market. Although the Convention on Trade in Endangered Species (CITES), signed in Washington DC in 1972, protects the species that are most under threat, it is not strictly adhered to, and doesn't affect birds whose numbers are high. The influx of tourists has helped to create an alternative source of revenue, making the trade less economically attractive to local trappers.

**BELOW:** the wattled jacana is an unusual species in that the female takes more than one mate, lays several clutches of eggs, and leaves the males to rear the young.

**RIGHT:** blue-headed parrots have powerful beaks which they use for cracking nuts open. They are sociable birds, often seen in groups.

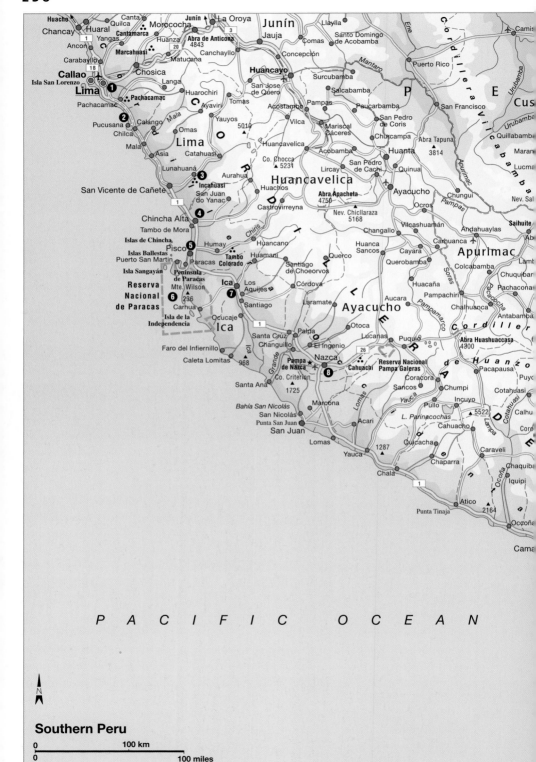

Southern Peru

0    100 km

0    100 miles

Parque Nacional Fitzcarrald

P E R U

Madre de Dios

San Silvestre
San Miguelito
Santuario Nacional Manuripi

Firmeza
Manuripe
Barcelona
Mavila
Lucerna

Heath

Madre de Dios

Bolivar

Chive

Las Piedras
Puerto Heath

Madre de Dios
Inambari
Las Hormigas
Filadelfia
Puerto Maldonado

Co. Atalaya
4382

Manu

Pilcopata

Puerto San Carlos
Puerto Leguia

Reserva Nacional Pampas de Río Heath

Santiago de Pacaguaras

Picchu  Lares
Urubamba
Anta chaca
Calca
Pisac
**15**  Cusco
Ccatca
Urcos
Ocongate

Quince Mil

Guarayos

Ixiamas
Tequeje

Paucartambo

Sanire

Marcapata

Lanlacuni Bajo

Puno

1168

Unduma

Yaurisque
4506  Paruro
Cotabambas
Acomayo
Pomacanchi
progreso
Cusipata
Combapata

Macusani

Coasa
Limbani
Patambuco
Sandra

Nev. Allincapac
5784
Ayabata
Pacchari
Belem
San Rafael

Tumupasa

Quinota
Yanaocac
Sicuani

Abra La Raya
4312

Crucero

Carabaya

Sina
Piuna
Pata
2157
Santa Cruz
San Buenaventura

Vellile
Quehue
El Descanso
Yauri
Hector Tejada
Llalli

Nuñoa
San Anton
Santa Rosa

Rosario

Nev. de Sumpani
5159
Azangaro

Asillo
Putina
Arapa
L. de Arapa
Taraco

Nudo de Apolobamba

Pelechuco
Apolo

B O L I V I A

5005
Suyokotambo
Orcopampa

Ayaviri

Pucara
Vilavila

Putina
Huancane

Reserva Fauna Ulla Ulla

Juán José Perez
Mocomoco
Mapiri

Guanay
Suapi

Lampa
5640
Nev. Mina Punta

**27**
Juliaca

Rosaspata
Moho
Puerto Acosta

Camata
Consara

Tipuani
Caranavi

Trinidad

Chivay
Madrigal
Achoma

Deustua
Santa Lucia

**14**
Cañon del Colca
5601
Sibayo
Colca

L. Lagunillas

Tiquillaca

**28**
Silustani
Coata

Puno

Parque Nacional Titicaca
Capachica
Isla Taquile
**29**  **30**
Islas de los Uros

Puerto Carabuco

Lago Titicaca

Qulabaya

Sorata
6428
Nev. Ancohuma

Coroico
3

Imata
Arequipa
Reserva Nacional Salinas y Aguada Blanca

Abra Toroya
4690
Ichuña

Chucuito
San Antonio de Esquilache

Isla del Sol
Ilave

Copacabana
Isla de la Luna
San Pablo
Achacachi
Huarina
Nev. Huayna Potosi
6088

Lluta
Vn. Chachani
6079
Vn. Misti
Tarucani

Nev. Jatucaci
5356

Juli
Pomata
Yunguyo
Tiquina

Huarína

Irupana

Arequipa  **13**
Vitor
Yura

Vn. Pichupichu
5669
L. Jucumarini

Abra Chocajinani
4450
Sorapa
32
Nev. Cercacerca
5428

Lago de Huainamarca
Golfo de Taraco
Tiahuanaco
Guaqui
Laja

La Paz
Nev. del Illimani
6882

Tabaya
Polobaya Grande
Puquina
Omate

Matalaque
Coralaque

Abra Gallatini
4400

Desaguadero
Huacullani

Guaqui
Viacha

Haunamarca
1707
30
Matarani
Cachendo

Moquegua
3393
Suches
5810

Mazo Cruz

Caramarca

Serranía de Sicasica
Aracu
5870
Luribay

Mollendo
Mejia
Punta de Bombon
Moquegua
**11**
Torata
Tacalaya
5810
Taruca

Santiago de Machaca
Achiri
Corocoro

Calacoto
Umara

Patacamaya
1

Santuario Nacional Lagunas de Mejia
Yerba Buena
Fundición
Hospicio
L. Aricota
Candarave
Inoca

Co. Cirque
5088
General Camacho

Ulloma

Puerto Japones
San Pedro de Curahuara

Desaguadero

Ilo
34
1775
Camaria
Tacna

Curibaya
Tarata

Mauri

Estique
Charaña

Totora

San Pedro de Curahuara

Toledo

Punta Coles
Las Yaras
Ite
Sama

Pachia
**12**
Tacna

Visvir
Cosapilla

Okoruro

Curahuara de Carangas
Oosapa

Corque

Boca del Rio
36
1
Hospicio
Putre

Parque Nacional Lauca
Nev. de Putre
5815
Caquena
Sajama

Nev. de Sajama
6520

Turco

Arica

Col. P. Negro
5540

Belen
Vn. Guallatiri
6060
Chungara
Timalchara

Macoya
Jaruma

Sacabaya
Sajama

C H I L E

Caleta Vitor
Iquique
Chilcaya

Huachacalla

*Recommended Restaurants on page 255*

# THE SOUTH COAST

The cryptic Nazca lines attract many people to the southern coast. For others, wildlife, sandsurfing, and Afro-Peruvian music have an appeal that isn't at all mysterious

Lima

**P**eru's southern desert coast, although inhospitable at first glance, is a historical and geographical encyclopedia of a handful of highly developed pre-Inca cultures known for their masterful pottery, fine weaving, medical advances, and for the enormous and mysterious drawings they left on the desert plain at Nazca.

The south coast is also where ancient indigenous peoples proved once again that they could at least adapt to the harsh physical reality of their environment even if they could not tame it. This time it was not the imposing Andean mountain chain that separated the different tribes, made agriculture difficult, and left the people subject to the subtle changes in climate. Rather it was the parched and desolate desert, often compared to the deserts of North Africa, that proved to be the obstacle.

## South of Lima

Starting your southward journey from **Lima ❶**, the first place of any interest you will come to is **Pachacamac**, some 32 km (20 miles) south of the capital and normally visited on a day trip from the city. Although the more recent Inca culture has overshadowed much of the earlier development of this site, the artisan work left by the pre-Inca civilizations proves that they were more sophisticated in terms of both ceramics and textiles. The ruins of the original settlement occupy a vast site on a low sand-hill overlooking the ocean. There is also a

reconstruction of the Inca Templo de las Vírgenes (House of the Chosen Women), also known as *mamaconas*.

Heading south for another 35 km (22 miles) you will come to **Pucusana ❷**. This coastal resort town, very popular with *limeños*, is also a charming fishing village with panoramic views from its cliffs and good seafood in several of its restaurants. During the Peruvian summer, from January to April, the beaches at Pucusana, La Isla, Las Ninfas, and Naplo can get crowded on weekends. If you want peace and quiet, go on a weekday,

**Main attractions**
PACHACAMAC
RESERVA NACIONAL DE PARACAS
ISLAS BALLESTAS
ICA BODEGAS
LAGUNA DE HUACACHINA
NAZCA LINES
CHAUCHILLA CEMETERY

**PRECEDING PAGES:** southern Peru's coastal highway. **LEFT:** the mysterious Nazca lines. **BELOW:** visiting the Ballestas Islands.

**TIP**

If you want to try river-running on the Río Cañete you must organize it in advance in Lima. The trips are suitable for novices.

**BELOW:** the pre-Inca pyramid at Pachacamac.

when Pucusana reverts to being a fishing town and vacationers are fewer. Also, local fishermen ferry passengers around the island in the bay, and to other beaches, so you may be able to negotiate a ride to one of the more isolated stretches of sand, such as Naplo, first arranging to be picked up later in the day.

You may want to take a trip past the **Boquerón del Diablo**, literally the Devil's Big Mouth, which is a tunnel carved in the rock. If you decide to tempt fate by entering the tunnel either on foot or in a boat, do not be surprised if the astonishing din, described as "the groans of a thousand devils," makes you wonder if you will ever come out alive.

Some 75 km (47 miles) down the coast is Cañete, from where a road goes inland to **Lunahuaná ❸**, a pretty village that has begun to attract *limeños* and foreign visitors. The village is set in a wine-growing valley; there are a couple of wineries that can be visited, and a wine festival – the *Fiesta de la Vendimia* – in March. The Incawasi ruins lie just outside the village, and river-rafting trips on the Río Cañete during the rainy season have become popular.

Back on the coast, about 55 km (34 miles) south of Cañete, lies **Chincha Alta ❹**, a city known for wine, fine-quality cotton, excellent athletes, and ferocious fighting cocks. Its name may be derived from *chinchay* – the Yauyo people's word for feline – although when the Spanish named it in 1571 it was more pompously called Pueblo Alto de Santo Domingo. Grapes and cotton flourish here, thanks to an elaborate system of irrigation and the re-routing of the Cochas River.

The city's fairly modern coliseum pays tribute to the long sporting tradition here. Chincha has turned out a number of the country's sports stars, principally in the fields of soccer (football) and boxing. The great Peruvian boxer Mauro Mina came from Chincha, and defeated a number of North Americans, including Floyd Patterson, before a detached retina prevented him from going for the world light heavyweight title. Another distinguished Chincha athlete, Fernando Acevedo, was a Pan-American running champion in 100- and 200-meter events. His nickname was "The Harpoon of Chincha."

This town, and nearby El Carmen, are home to much of Peru's black population,

*Recommended Restaurants on page 255*

descendants of slaves brought here to work on coastal plantations. As such, it is the center for Afro-Peruvian dances, including the energetic and amusing *El Alcatraz*, in which a gyrating male dancer with a lighted candle in his hand attempts to ignite the cloth tail hanging from his partner's brightly colored skirt. Many of these dances are accompanied by rhythms supplied by the *cajón*, which is simply a hollow box pounded by open-palmed drummers to produce a rever-berating rhythm. The *Fiesta Negra* in February and *Fiestas Patrias* in late July are the best and most atmospheric times to see and hear Afro-Peruvian music.

Close to Chincha is the **Hacienda San José** (open Mon–Sat 9am–3pm; entrance fee), a large country estate built in 1688. The estate was a rich sugar- and cotton- growing operation, and at its height owned 1,000 slaves. A fascinating but sinister feature of the hacienda is the labyrinth of catacombs under the house, which were once used for storing and punishing slaves. Tunnels are said to lead all the way to the port of Pisco, where slave ships unloaded their human cargo.

Today, the hacienda is surrounded by colonnaded courtyards and cool terracotta floors, and is set in green gardens full of trees. Before the 2007 earthquake Hacienda San José was a tranquil country hotel. Although the restaurant is open for lunch, the building will need much reconstruction before it its operational as a hotel once again. Visitors are welcome, however, and can be shown around by the one of the descendants of the slaves.

## Pisco

Continuing south on the Panamericana you come to **Pisco 5**, a port city that gave its name to the clear white-grape alcohol that is Peru's national drink, and is used to make the cocktail called a *pisco sour (see page 247)*. The invention of *pisco* is believed to have been a mistake made by the Spaniards when they were introducing grapes and wine production into the dry coastal area of the New World. But it seems that once they tried this smooth yet potent version of brandy they decided it had merit of its own – and many Peruvians have gone on thinking so ever since.

The city of Pisco (pop. 90,000) joined the bandwagon when revolutionary fever

*Paracas Bay, south of Pisco, is a popular birdwatching and fishing destination.*

**BELOW:** getting ready for the annual Fiesta Negra.

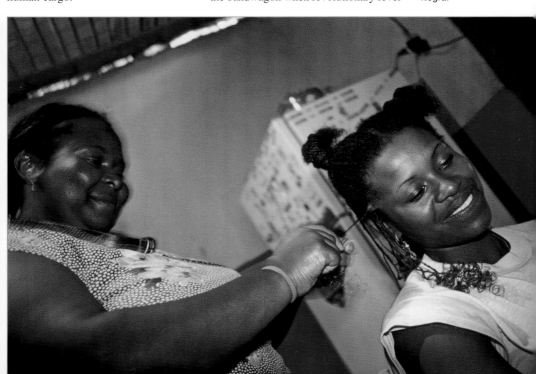

*The Humboldt penguin is one of the few species that lives far from the cold Austral southern zone. There are about 1,500 of them in and around Paracas.*

overtook the continent in the early 1800s. In Pisco's **Plaza de Armas** is a statue to General José de San Martín, the hero of the War of Independence against the Spanish. Originally, Pisco stood on another spot not far away, but an earthquake in 1687, and subsequent pirate attacks, badly damaged many of the structures in the city, prompting the viceroy, Count de la Monclova, to order it to be moved to a safer spot. Construction of the opulent baroque **Catedral** started shortly afterwards, and was only completed in 1723. This was all but destroyed in August 2007 when the city was rocked by a devastating earthquake which laid waste to much of the city center and killed hundreds of people *(see below)*.

Post-earthquake, several hotels are still operating as normal, and Pisco continues to be a good base for visits to the Paracas Peninsula National Reserve and the Islas Ballestas. The offices of all the city's tour agencies were centered around the Plaza de Armas and were consequently destroyed in the earthquake. Tours are still operating, however, and your hotel will be able to put you in touch with guides. *Pisqueños* are a

**BELOW:** a church near Pisco, damaged by the 2007 earthquake.

strong, proud people who have vowed to rebuild their city and, in general, would rather that tourists continue to visit than stay away.

Pisco's small military airport serves as the emergency landing strip when heavy fog prevents planes from descending in Lima; passengers are then bussed to the capital or have to wait until the weather clears before completing their journey. In the 1960s and 1970s aerial research into the whales that visit this coast was based here.

Then, in late 1988, Peruvian scientists, in conjunction with experts from the Natural History Museum at the Smithsonian Institution in the United States, announced the appearance of a new whale species. One of these mammals, named the Mesoplodon Peruvianus, was inadvertently picked up by fishermen working the waters between Pucusana and Pisco. The 4 meter- (13 ft-) long sea mammal is one of the smallest members of the whale family.

### Peru's Galápagos

Some 15 km (9 miles) down the coast lie the bay and peninsula of Paracas which,

## The Pisco Earthquake

On August 15, 2007, southern Peru was struck by one of the strongest earthquakes in the country's history. Measuring 7.8 on the Richter scale, the epicenter was very close to the city of Pisco and nearby Ica and Chincha also suffered extensive damage. The earthquake was even felt in Lima, 260 km (156 miles) away.

In Pisco, the damage was most

severe around the Plaza de Armas, where many beautiful colonial churches and buildings were brought down or damaged beyond repair. Many people had fled for protection into the 300-year-old cathedral, the roof of which subsequently collapsed, killing 150. When the shaking stopped the city's streets were filled with rubble and the roads had become impassable. Strong aftershocks continued through the night – one of the coldest on record.

Only when dawn came could the damage be assessed: Pisco had been close to devastated. Over 500 people had been killed and 80 percent of the city's homes were destroyed. Pisco's small hospital was overwhelmed with casualties and electricity and water were cut off for days.

While donations of tents and prefabricated houses came in from as far away as Turkey, the Peruvian government was criticized for doing little, and local people have since complained that they have seen none of millions of dollars in foreign donations intended for the earthquake victims. Despite the devastation, the people of Pisco are keen for tourists to keep coming, and whilst there's little money for rebuilding, there's certainly the will. *Pisco se va a levantar*, say its citizens. "Pisco will rise again."

together with the Islas Ballestas, comprise the **Reserva Nacional de Paracas ❻**. The area, named after the Paracas winds – blustery sandstorms that sweep the coast – has a wide variety of sea mammals and exotic birds, among them the red and white flamingos that allegedly inspired General San Martín to design the red and white independence flag for the newly liberated country. A monument marks the spot where San Martín set foot in Peru on September 8, 1820, after liberating Argentina. (A law passed by the National Congress has made September 9 a provincial holiday.)

Not long after San Martín's arrival, a shipload of British troops under the command of Lord Cochrane dropped anchor in the same bay and headed to shore to help him plan his strategy against the Spanish. The British motivation was not to liberate a struggling people from their colonial masters, but to break Spain's monopoly on trade in the region.

The beach here is lovely, although craggy for swimming, and the waters contain jellyfish – some of them enormous and with a very unpleasant sting. There are a number of good jellyfish-free beaches around the isthmus: La Mina, Mendieta, La Catedral, and Atenas, the latter very popular for windsurfing. The famous **Candelabro**, a candelabra-shaped drawing scratched onto the highest point of a cliffside overlooking the bay, can be seen from the beach, although it is best viewed from a boat. Some scientists link the drawing to the Southern Cross constellation; others say it is actually a stylized drawing of a cactus – a symbol of power from the Chavín culture, which flourished farther north but whose influence has been found at great distances from its seat of power. The magic associated with the cactus is related to both its hallucinogenic powers and its use by high priests in ancient indigenous cultures.

## Trips to the Islas Ballestas

A visit to the **Islas Ballestas** is highly recommended, and should be organized in Pisco as you usually have to go with a tour group. Ask your hotel to arrange this. Most of the trips start off quite early in the morning. For reasons of conservation visitors are not allowed to land on the island, but boats will take you close enough for a good view of the wildlife. Here sea lions, seals, penguins, guano-producing birds, and turtles rarely found at this latitude converge before photo-taking tourists. Dozens of bird species thrive here, among them albatrosses, pelicans, boobies, cormorants, and seagulls. Most Islas Ballestas tours also take in **Punta Pejerrey**, nearly at the northernmost point of the isthmus and the best spot for seeing the Candelabro. During the 19th century, this region was important for its guano – mineral-rich bird-droppings used as fertilizer in Europe – and guano collection still continues today, though on a smaller scale.

On the exact opposite side of the isthmus is **Punta Arquillo** and the *Mirador de Los Lobos*, or sea lion lookout point. This rough and rocky place can be reached by an hour's trek on foot, but take care, because the sun is very strong. It is far better to go by car, and if you are with a tour group transport may be provided.

*The Islas Ballestas are home to a variety of marine life, including sea lions. Boat tours to the islands can be arranged in Pisco.*

**BELOW:** Peruvian boobies and Humboldt penguins on the Islas Ballestas.

Looking down on the sea lion refuge you will find yourself almost face to face with a congregation of noisy sea mammals.

On lucky days, a look skyward is rewarded by the sight of a pair of condors soaring above. These majestic birds sweep down on sea lion carcasses, looking particularly for the seal's afterbirth during the breeding season, then use the intense coastal winds to wing themselves up to the high altitudes they normally frequent. So well known was the birds' presence at Paracas that, when the nature reserve was being named, one scientist pushed for the name Parque Nacional de los Cóndores (Condor National Park), but was unsuccessful.

Extensive exploration of the peninsula is best done with the help of a guide, as paths are not clearly marked and it is easy to become lost. In June and August, Paracas is foggy – a reaction to the heat and extremely sparse precipitation combined with the water-laden ocean winds that caress the coast. A meteorological office here recorded only 36.7 mm (1½ inches) of precipitation during a 20-year period, although the effects of the particularly harsh 1998 El Niño brought heavy rain to the area, and turned the desert green for a while.

## Desert burial grounds

Paracas is the name not only of the area but also of the ancient Indian civilization founded here over 3,000 years ago, a pre-Columbian (and pre-Inca) culture that was uncovered in 1925 when Peruvian archeologist Julio C. Tello found burial sites under the dunes. The sand and the extreme dryness of the desert protected the finely woven textiles around and inside the funeral bundles, which were buried when the Paracas culture thrived from 1300 BC to AD 200. The best examples of textiles and funeral bundles, and information about how the burial pits were arranged, can be found in several museums in Lima. Recommended are the Museo de la Nación, the Museo Nacional de Arqueología, Antropología y Historia in Pueblo Libre *(see page 159)*, and the private Museo Amano collection of textiles in Miraflores. The Museo Regional in Ica *(see page 249)* also has an interesting collection of pre-Columbian artifacts. The **Museo Julio C. Tello** (opening times vary – check with tour agencies; entrance fee), near the necropolis on the isthmus joining the Paracas peninsula to the mainland, has exhibits of artifacts discovered during the archeological dig, and although much of the collection was lost in a robbery, it is well worth a visit.

The discovery of hundreds of so-called "funeral fards" – or burial cocoons – gave anthropologists and archeologists yet another small insight into this civilization. The fine weavings in both cotton and wool, with intricate and highly detailed embroidered designs, still astound modern-day textile experts, particularly those who are interested in how the Indians were able to develop permanent dyes with such brilliant tones.

The elaborately wrapped funeral bundles show that the Paracas culture performed skull trepanation, crude "brain surgery" designed to treat fractures and tumors, common injuries among a people whose battles were fought using

*Traditional paddles and oak barrels at the Tabernero winery near Chincha.*

**BELOW:** harvesting grapes at a *bodega* near Ica.

TA C

Recommended Restaurants on page 255

stone-headed clubs and slingshots. The Paracas also practiced the intentional deformation or molding of infants' skulls for esthetic reasons. The results, akin to a conehead shape, were not only considered attractive but also clearly identified an individual's clan, since the molding differed significantly from tribe to tribe.

Heading some 48 km (30 miles) inland from Pisco you will come to remains dating from another culture: the Inca **Tambo Colorado**. This adobe settlement, called *colorado* (colored) because of the red paint on many of the walls, is among the best Inca ruins on Peru's southern coast. Among the buildings still standing at this complex is one that is believed to have been a temple.

## Treading the grapes

About 80 km (50 miles) farther south along the coast is **Ica ❼**, a bustling oasis amid one of the continent's driest deserts, and Peru's richest wine-growing region. Ica was hit quite badly by the El Niño flooding in 1998, but thanks to rapid clean-up and reconstruction work life got back to normal fairly fast. Ica suffered

again in the 2007 earthquake *(see page 244)*, and many buildings were damaged beyond repair. Rebuilding is underway, but it may be some years before the town returns to normal.

Local vineyards and wineries can be explored all year round, but there is most to see during the grape harvest, from February to early April. The **Bodega El Carmelo** *pisco* distillery, which is open to the public, has an ancient grape press made from a tree trunk. Tours (in Spanish) can be taken at the **Vista Alegre** wine and *pisco* distillery in Ica, where there is a good shop. Peruvian wines tend to be very sweet, although the best ones, Ocucaje and Tacama, and Tabernero, are finer and drier. It is difficult to arrange to visit these vineyards, which are some distance from town, but the wines can be bought all over the country.

Every March, the city goes all out with its annual wine festival, featuring grape-treading beauty queens and a flow of homemade wine that the locals swear is better than anything available for sale. The week-long event, called the *Fiesta Internacional de la Vendimia*, is punctu-

*A feature of the Fiesta de la Vendimia is the* yunza *dance. Hatchet-carrying men and skirt-flouncing women dance around a tree, drinking the season's new wine and stopping at intervals to take swings at the unlucky tree. The dance continues until the tree falls; the couple responsible for the felling are promised a year of good luck.*

**LEFT:** the Inca ruins of Tambo Colorado.

## Pisco Sour Recipe

**Serves 6**

**INGREDIENTS**
2 egg whites
1 measure sugar
3 measures *pisco*
1 measure lemon juice
½ glass of ice cubes
Angostura bitters

**1** Combine the egg whites and sugar in a blender to a foamy consistency.

**2** Add the *pisco*, then the lemon juice and ice cubes.

**3** To serve, divide half of the mixture evenly between 6 chilled glasses, then pour out the remaing liquid, so that each one has foam on top.

**4** Add a few drops of Angostura bitters to each glass and enjoy while chilled. ¡Salud!

*Townspeople in Ica were amazed when the statue of the Señor de Luren survived the 2007 earthquake, despite the near destruction of the church in which it was housed.*

ated by sports contests, cock fights, music, drinking, religious ceremonies, dancing, and general merrymaking.

Although the festival is the best time to experience the area's wine heritage, hotels fill up fast at fiesta time, and the rates rise steeply as well. The same problem arises during the week-long celebration of the town's foundation in mid-June, and at the festival of *El Señor de Luren*, on Maundy Thursday, when an image of the crucified Christ is paraded around the city in all-night processions. A second procession in honor of the city's patron saint takes place on the third Monday in October.

The statue is believed to have arrived in Ica more than four centuries ago, carried to shore on a wave, then transported to the town. Records from the San Francisco monastery in Lima show that the image was purchased by a friar in 1570. A treacherous storm at sea, and the fear that the ship in which the statue was being transported would sink, apparently prompted the ship's captain to toss much of the cargo – including the wooden box containing the statue – overboard. Religious Ica residents took the icon's intact arrival as a miracle.

## Disasters and revolutions

Although Ica was founded by the Spanish in 1536, European attempts to control the city were constantly fraught with problems. The city residents resisted the Spanish presence, and Ica was never granted a coat-of-arms, owing to its repudiation of attempts to make it a colonial center. Local residents remain proud of that rebellious image. The town has also suffered natural disasters: strong earth tremors caused damage in 1568 and 1571, and a devastating earthquake in 1664 completely leveled it, leaving 500 people dead – a phenomenal toll in those days.

Almost 300 years later, in 1963, floods seriously damaged much of the town, which explains why most of its colonial buildings have been replaced by more modern structures. Still, the city center retains its square-block layout, based on a chessboard design.

Churches worth visiting are **La Merced**, just off the Plaza de Armas, with its delicately carved wooden altars, and **San Francisco** (on the corner of Municipalidad and San Martín) with some admirable stained-glass windows. There are plans to rebuild it in the com-

**BELOW:** Laguna de Huacachina.

Recommended Restaurants on page 255

ing years. Competing with the Christian importance of Ica is the city's widespread reputation for witchcraft, for which it is well known across the country.

One of the city's most famous sons was José de la Torre Ugarte, author of Peru's national anthem. He was born in Ica in 1786 and served as a local judge until he joined the revolutionary troops under General San Martín. After Peru's independence, he turned to politics, but found it an even more dangerous line of work than being a freedom fighter: in a power struggle between factions in the congress, he was condemned to death. When spared by the colonel commissioned to execute him, Torre Ugarte returned to a career in law.

The first civilian president of Peru was also from Ica, although Domingo Elass's tenure in office was short-lived owing to political upheaval in the newly independent country. His attempt in 1854 to start a revolution of his own failed, although he was initially able to take control of Arequipa before fleeing to exile in Chile.

## Ica's regional museum

Today, just a 20-minute walk or a short bus ride from Ica's center, this region's role in the revolution is traced in a room at the **Museo Regional** (Av. Ayabaca block 8; open Mon–Fri 8am–7pm, Sat and Sun 9am–6pm; entrance fee), one of Peru's most interesting small regional museums. But even more interesting are exhibits of mummies, ceramics, and skulls from the Paracas, Nazca, and Inca cultures. On display are a number of *quipus* (also spelled *kipus*), the mysterious knotted strings believed to have been used to keep calculations, records, and historical notes for the Incas, who had no system of writing.

Since only selected members of the Inca civilization were permitted to "read" the *quipus*, the meaning of these knotted strings has been lost in intervening centuries, although some experts maintain that they were a sophisticated accounting system in which colored strings represented commodities and knots showed quantities. It is thought that the *quipus*

may have been crucial in keeping food inventories in the Inca empire.

The regional museum also has an excellent collection of Paracas textiles and feather weavings. Most visitors find their curiosity piqued by the rehydrated mummy hand on exhibition – a must for those who think they have seen everything. Placed in a saline solution after being buried for centuries on the desert coast, this hand was part of an experiment by scientists who hoped that rehydration would provide medical information about the deceased individual.

On the **Plaza de Armas** is the **Museo Cabrera** (Bolívar 178; open Mon–Fri 9.30am–1pm and 4–7pm; entrance fee), intriguing for the number (over 10,000) and variety of stones it contains.

## Dunes and lagoons

Outside Ica is **Las Dunas**, a full-scale resort and the most luxurious hotel complex of the area. With a restaurant, pool, sand-surfing, and horses to hire, this hotel regularly attracts diplomats and was featured in the US television series *Lifestyles of the Rich and Famous*. It is said that some foreign diplomats make an-

*Pre-Columbian wooden idol in the Museo Regional, Ica.*

**BELOW:** red and white flamingoes in the Paracas national reserve.

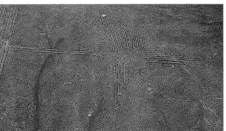

*El Colibrí (The Hummingbird) is about 70 meters (230 ft) long. The last line on its beak points towards the sunrise on the summer solstice.*

**BELOW:** a memorial to Maria Reiche.

nual pilgrimages to Ica, staying at Las Dunas and consulting with *curanderos* (healers) and occult practitioners, but this may be a local myth.

Las Dunas was in the forefront of the sand-surfing frenzy that recently overtook this dune-covered coastal area. Principally attracting European sports fans, especially from Italy and France, the hotel has sponsored competitive sandsurfing events on Cerro Blanco – a massive dune some 14 km (8 miles) north of the town of Nazca, purportedly the world's biggest sand dune.

Also on the outskirts of Ica is **Laguna de Huacachina**, a green lagoon of sulfur waters that Peruvians claim has medicinal value. Since Angela Perotti, an Italian living in Ica, began espousing the curative properties of the waters in the 1930s, this spot has become a favorite pilgrimage center for people suffering from rheumatism and skin problems. This peaceful setting just 5 km (3 miles) outside Ica, also draws those just looking for sun, solitude, and sand-surfing beside the palm trees and dunes that ring the lagoon.

## The Nazca lines

Thanks to irrigation, cotton fields and ribbons of orange trees mark the landscape on the voyage farther south along the coast to **Nazca ❽**, the home of the mysterious lined drawings that have prompted theories ranging from the fanciful to the scientific.

Sixty years ago Nazca was like any other small Peruvian town with no special claim to fame, except that it was necessary to cross one of the world's driest deserts to reach it from Lima. But it is that desert – a sketch-pad for ancient Indians – that has since drawn thousands to this sun-bleached colonial town of 30,000 and made the *pampa*, or plain, north of the city one of the greatest scientific mysteries in the New World.

The Nazca lines are a series of drawings of animals, geometrical figures, and birds ranging up to 300 meters (1,000 ft) in size, scratched onto the arid crust of the desert and preserved for about 2,000 years (it is estimated) owing to a complete lack of rain and winds that cleaned – but did not erase – the surface of the *pampa*. The drawings were made by removing surface stones and piling them beside the lighter soil that was revealed beneath.

It wasn't until 1939 that Paul Kosok, a North American scientist flying over the dry coast in a small plane, noticed the lines, then believed to be part of a pre-Inca irrigation system. A specialist in irrigation, he quickly concluded that this had nothing to do with water systems. By chance, the day of the flight coincided with the summer solstice and, making a second pass over the area, Kosok discovered that the lines of the sunset ran tandem to the direction of one of the bird drawings. He immediately dubbed the Nazca *pampa* "the biggest astronomy book in the world."

It was not Kosok, but a young German mathematician who became the expert on the lines and put the backwater on the

*Recommended Restaurants on page 255*

map. Maria Reiche was 35 years old when she met Kosok, serving as his translator at a seminar on the lines. After giving his speech the scientist encouraged her to study the *pampa*, and she dedicated the next half-century to the task.

Reiche concluded that the sketches corresponded to the constellations, and thought they were part of an astronomical calendar made by the people of the Nazca culture, and designed to send messages to the gods. She speculated that her favorite drawing, the monkey, was the ancient symbol for the Big Dipper, the constellation that was linked to rain. When rain was overdue – a common thing in this plain – the Nazca people sketched the monkey to remind the gods that the earth was parched.

There are, of course, many people who do not accept Reiche's theories, denying that the ancient people would have drawn something that they themselves could not see. Because the drawings can only be seen from the air, the International Explorers' Club set out in 1975 to prove a theory that the Nazca people had used balloons. The Explorers' Club made a cloth-and-reed hot-air balloon, the *Con-dor I*, and flew it for 60 seconds, reaching an altitude of 100 meters (330 ft). But the flight, 14 minutes shorter than planned, hardly resolved the issue. It simply added another, rather wacky, theory to the many that surround the Nazca lines.

## Writing from the planets?

One well-known theory about the lines came in 1968 when Erich von Daniken published his book *Chariots of the Gods*, in which he argued that the *pampa* was part of an extraterrestrial landing strip – an idea that Reiche discarded impatiently and which has been given little credence by scientists. The book drew thousands of visitors to the lines, but the newcomers set out across the *pampa* in search of the drawings on motorcycles, four-wheel drive vehicles, and even horses – leaving ineradicable marks of their visits. Now it is illegal to walk or drive on the *pampa*, and Reiche used the profits from sales of her book, *Mystery on the Desert*, to pay guards to patrol the plain.

Other theorists say that the lines marked tracks for running competitions; that they were enlarged designs used in weaving and textiles; or that they are

*The recent increase in the number of people believing in aliens and extraterrestrial life has made Erich von Daniken's theories popular again – but not with scientists and rationalists.*

**BELOW:** *Los Manos* (The Hands) can be seen from a viewing platform north of Nazca.

**TIP**

Flights over the Nazca lines can be organized with tour agencies in Lima and Nazca *(see Travel Tips pages 341–2)*, or direct with the airlines at Nazca airport. It can be a bumpy ride, so it's best not to eat a large meal beforehand.

**BELOW:** the Panamericana in southern Peru.

actually an enormous map of the Tiahuanaco civilization that once flourished near Lake Titicaca. But the idea that the drawings were some kind of message to the gods, appealing to them to send rain, is one that has recently been given backing by new scientific research, and in this barren landscape it is certainly a believable theory. Another idea that has gained a good many sensible adherents is that the lines were walkways linking sacred sites, and were kept clear for many years by the frequent passage of footsteps.

Maria Reiche used to live at the Nazca Lines Hotel (then called the Hotel Turistas), where she gave an hour-long talk on the lines every evening, until increasing age and infirmity made it impossible. Her last trip to the *pampa* was with Phyllis Pitluga, a US astronomer, whose initial computer-based research on the Nazca lines appeared to support their link to the constellations. Other researchers have pointed to the vividly painted Nazca pottery, with its clock-shaped pieces and elaborate solar calendars, as further evidence of close links with the movement of the heavenly

bodies. Reiche died in June 1998. Children waving German and Peruvian flags joined the crowds that lined the streets on the day of her funeral.

## Viewing the lines

Some 20 km (12 miles) north of Nazca, just off the Panamericana, there is a *mirador* (observation tower), although the only lines that can be seen clearly from here are the *arbol* (tree) and the *manos* (hands). The best way to capture the impact of the lines is to fly over them in small propeller planes. Aero Cóndor offers flights from Lima, Ica, and the small airport in Nazca. Lunch and a stop in the archeological museum in downtown Nazca are included in the day-long Lima package, but it is the most expensive of those on offer. The Nazca flight, the cheapest of the options, takes about 30 minutes, and the best time to go is mid-morning. Earlier in the day there is sometimes a haze over the *pampa*; later on, the winds that buffet the plane leave observers more concerned about their stomachs than about the spectacle spread out beneath them.

Unless visitors take the Aero Cóndor flight from Lima, the only way to reach

*Recommended Restaurants on page 255*

Nazca is by bus. The trip can take six to seven hours from the capital, along the Panamericana, but it's quite an impressive trip through the vast coastal desert. If you are approaching Nazca from the other direction, there are also regular buses from Arequipa and Cusco. There have been numerous discussions about building an international airport at Nazca, but the project has never gone farther than the drawing board.

## Red dot in the desert sky

Occasionally, Nazca is deluged with astronomers who find the desert plain an optimal spot for viewing some rare cosmic happenings. On September 23, 1989, the fall equinox, scientists went to Nazca to view Mars – which appeared as a red light in the desert sky for a 12-hour period. This unusual phenomenon only presents itself every 15 or 20 years.

Although the perplexing Nazca lines are what draw tourists to this area, they are by no means the only thing to see. Some 30 km (18 miles) from Nazca is the fascinating **Cementerio de Chauchilla** (Chauchilla Cemetery), where sun-whitened bones and skulls, pottery shards, and mummies litter the plain, although some have recently been reburied. The cemetery otherwise remains as it was, in part to avoid further desecration of the area (most of the mummies were unearthed during tomb looting) and in part because there is not sufficient money available to fund proper storage or exhibition of the mummies and grave artifacts. Grave robbers, or *huaqueros*, are a major nuisance at all the archeological sites in Peru, despite a major crackdown by the authorities *(see page 181)*.

Local tours to the cemetery usually also stop at the **Paredones Ruins** in the grounds of the Hacienda Cantalloc beside the **Cantalloc Aqueducts**, an immense and complicated system built by the Incas and still supplying water to irrigate fields nearby, where cotton is grown.

## Following the Panamericana

The Panamericana continues down the coast from Nazca to **Camaná** ❾ (about 220 km/135 miles), which has some good beaches and is a popular summer resort for Arequipa residents as well as being the hometown of Peru's chess grand master, Julio Granda Zuñiga. Buses from the town center head to La Punta (about 5 km/3 miles) and the fine, although undeveloped, beach area. Camaná was, in colonial times, the unloading point for cargo headed to Arequipa and then on to the silver mines in Potosí in Bolivia.

From Camaña the highway goes inland, and after about 130 km (80 miles) it divides, going farther inland to Arequipa, toward Moquegua and Tacna and the Chilean border, or back to the coast to **Mollendo** ❿. Mollendo and its sister resort, Mejía, 15 km (10 miles) farther south, are popular with upper-class *arequipeños*. Mollendo was a principal port before being replaced by **Matarani**, 14 km (8 miles) to the northwest. Now its attractions are three sandy beaches and its closeness to the **Santuario Nacional Lagunas de Mejía**, a nature reserve that is home to a variety of coastal birds and a stopping place for many migratory species. You can get a bus from the town to the reserve and to the agricultural

*Researchers at the Maria Reiche Center in Nazca have voiced concerns about the risk posed from potential increases in rainfall due to global climate change.*

**BELOW:** mummies in Chauchilla Cemetery.

*The bronze fountain in Tacna's Plaza de Armas is the work of Gustave Eiffel, who designed the Eiffel Tower in Paris, France. He also designed Tacna's cathedral, with its onyx high altar and interesting stained-glass windows.*

**BELOW:** the intriguing sand drawing known as the Candelabro.

lands of the Río Tambo valley, where an ambitious irrigation project means that rice and sugar can be grown. Mejía used to be a fishing village, and a few old fishermen's cottages still remain. There are no hotels, but *arequipeños* spend part of the summer in their holiday homes here.

The road from the valley rejoins the Panamericana, which continues south to **Moquegua** ⑪, a parched and dusty town on the banks of the Río Moquegua, at the spot where the Peruvian coastal desert reaches its driest point. Buildings here – even the Cathedral – are roofed with sugar-cane stalks daubed with mud. Its streets are cobblestones, and its residents' topiary skills are evident on the **Plaza de Armas**, where most of the bushes are trimmed into the form of llamas. Wine and avocados are shipped out of this city, and both are worth sampling.

### Border town

Peru's southernmost coastal city is **Tacna** ⑫, separated from Chile only by a mined stretch of desert that marks the border between the two nations. The Atacama Desert region from Tacna as far as Antofagasta once belonged to Peru and

Bolivia, but the nitrate-rich territory was lost to Chile in 1880 during the War of the Pacific. The treaty of Ancón returned the land to Peru in 1929, and in the 1980s it was one of the main spots in the country for contraband activity. Government-subsidized milk and medicines were smuggled into Chile, while less expensive clothing and imported cosmetics were brought back into Peru.

Unlike other border cities on the continent, Tacna is fairly well developed and has some of Peru's best schools and medical facilities – perhaps owing to its importance as a military base. The downtown area has been refurbished, and its main boulevard is cut by an attractive flower-and-tree-studded promenade. A pedestrian mall passes by the shops, and here ice cream, or cold drinks such as *horchata*, the popular icy cinnamon-laced soy-milk beverage, help offset the intense heat during the Tacna summer. The tree-shaded **Plaza de Armas** is a welcome relief from the unrelenting sun. The centerpiece of the plaza is the huge arch that was built as a monument to the heroes of the War of the Pacific.

The **Museo Ferroviario** (Railway Museum; open Mon–Fri 9am–5.30pm; entrance fee) at the railway station has train engines from the turn of the 20th century when the British began constructing the complicated and, in some cases, rather reckless railway system in Peru. There is also a collection of railway-themed stamps.

### Where tourists are targets

If you are in Tacna at all, it will be because you are on your way to or from Chile, and as Latin American border towns go, it's a very pleasant one. Even so, visitors should be on the alert in the train and bus station areas, and in the evening should avoid entirely the street where the bus companies are. Pickpockets and thieves work these areas, and tourists are an easy target. It would be a shame to leave Peru on a bad note. You can cross the border from Tacna to Arica by bus, train, or taxi, although the train service is slow and notoriously unreliable. ❑

# RESTAURANTS

## Restaurants

Prices are per person for a two-course meal, excluding wine:
**$** less than US$10
**$$** US$10–20
**$$$** more than US$20

## Ica

### Bodega El Catador

Fondo Tres Esquinas 102, Urb. Subtanjalla
Tel: (056) 403 295
A short taxi ride from town, Bodega El Catador offers winery tours and wine and pisco tasting. The restaurant offers good Peruvian fare, and there's sometimes dancing. **$$**

### Caramba Restaurant

Prolongación Ayabaca 862
Tel: (056) 223 236
This place has a cozy atmosphere and serves great Peruvian food, including plenty of fish, seafood, and meats. Try the jelly desserts. **$**

### La Cueva

Domingo Elias 286, Urb. Luren
Tel: (056) 224 975
Good mixed cuisine. **$$**

### El Otro Peñoncito

Calle Bolívar 255
Tel: (056) 233 921
An old Ica stalwart serving good Peruvian fare and good international options. **$$**

### Restaurant Venezia

Jr. Lima 230
Tel: (056) 232 241
Ica's much-loved Italian restaurant does great pizzas and pastas, plus fine Ica wines. **$$**

## Nazca

### Las Cañas

Bolognesi 279
Tel: (056) 806 891
Peruvian and international dishes, including great ceviche, good salads, pastas, and excellent hamburgers. **$**

### El Huarango

Jr. Arica 602
Tel: (056) 521 287
Amongst the best restaurants in Nazca. There's a lovely rooftop garden, and the meals are great value. **$**

### La Taberna

Jr. Lima 321
Tel: (056) 521 411
Popular with *gringos*; offers a diverse international menu. There's often live music. **$**

## Paracas

### Brisa Marina

Boulevard Turístico, El Chaco
Tel: (054) 545 125
Breezy seaside place – just the spot to visit after an Islas Ballestas cruise, for a warming coffee in winter or mouthwatering ceviche in the warmer months. **$**

## Pisco

### El Dorado

Jr. Progreso 171, Plaza de Armas
Tel: (056) 311 740
Good BBQ chicken, and excellent fresh fish and seafood. One of the few places on the plaza to survive the 2007 earthquake, and well worth a visit. **$**

### Geno's

Jr. Progreso 294
Tel: (056) 507 058
This simple place does excellent *pollo a la braza* with chips and salad. **$**

### La Posada Hispana

Jr. Bolognesi 222
Tel: (056) 536 363
The Spanish owners here serve excellent Peruvian menus at unbelievably low prices, and the decor is a cozy, ethnic/Spanish mix. They bar produces some of the best pisco sours in town. **$**

### La Vina de Huber

Prolongación Cerro Azul
Tel: (056) 533 199
The best restaurant in Pisco, serving fantastic seafood in gargantuan portions. There's live music Saturday and Sunday, and the prices are great value. **$**

**RIGHT:** lobster soup.

*Recommended Restaurants and Cafés on page 263*

# AREQUIPA

Arequipa, the intellectual capital of modern Peru, is a proud and prosperous city with some of the most beautiful colonial architecture in the country

Lima

Arequipa

**F**ar from Lima, isolated in a fertile valley tucked between desert and mountains and crowned by turquoise skies, **Arequipa** ⑬ was a key stop on the cargo route linking the abundant silver mines of Bolivia to the coast. Built from the white sillar rock that spewed out from **Volcán Misti**, one of a trio of imposing volcanoes looming behind it, this is Peru's second-largest urban area and one of the country's most prosperous. In colonial days it had the largest Spanish population and the strongest European traditions; cattle and farming industries dating from that period remain principal sources of income for the region. *Arequipeños* are proud and fiercely independent people, and like to think of their city as a place separate from – and superior to – the rest of the country.

In 1541 the king of Spain granted this oasis at the foot of the snow-capped volcano the title "Most Noble, Most Loyal and Faithful City of the Assumption of Our Lady of the Beautiful Valley of Arequipa." Aymara people living here beside the **Río Chili** more concisely called it Ariquepa (sic), "the place behind the pointed mountain." Another legend has it that the Inca Mayta Capac was so moved by the beauty of the valley during one of his journeys that he ordered his entourage to stop. His exact words were said to be "*Ari quipay*" – "Yes, stay" in Quechua. Whatever the truth, Arequipa has grown into a magnificent city and the intellectual capital of modern Peru.

There are many ways of getting here: there are frequent flights from Lima, Cusco, Juliaca, and Tacna (on the Chilean border); and there are buses from Lima, Nazca, Cusco, and Puno. How you travel will depend on your budget, time scale, the degree of comfort you require, and how much of the country you want to see.

## The heart of the city

Arequipa's **Plaza de Armas** Ⓐ is one of the most beautiful in Peru. Wander around it before you start your tour of the

### Main attractions
PLAZA DE ARMAS
LA COMPAÑIA
CATEDRAL
MONASTERIO DE
  SANTA CATALINA
MUSEO SANTUARIOS ANDINOS
COLCA CANYON
COTAHUASI CANYON

**LEFT:** Arequipa's grand cathedral. **BELOW:** colonial balconies on the Plaza de Armas.

**TIP**

Calle Jerusalén, to the northeast of the Plaza de Armas, is a good place to change foreign currency, as it has several exchange bureaux.

city, taking in the facade of the cathedral and the two-story arcades that grace the other three sides of the plaza, with its palm trees, old gas lamps, and a white stone fountain nestling in an English-style garden. *Arequipeños* congregate here for political rallies, protests, or fiestas. The plaza's thick stone buildings with busily carved portals, their Moorish touches evident, breathe 460 years of history. An earthquake in 2002 caused considerable damage, but most of the main historical buildings have now been restored.

Head toward **La Compañía** **B** (open 9am–noon and 3–6pm; entrance fee), on the southeast of the plaza. The frontispiece of this two-story Jesuit church is a compilation of columns, zigzags, spirals, laurel crowns, flowers, birds, and grapevines, into which is embroidered in rock abbreviations of the Good Friday Masses, the city's coat-of-arms, and the date the massive work was completed: 1698. But a careful look shows that the European influence had its limits. The angels have Indian faces – one face is even crowned with feathers.

What lies inside La Compañía is equally impressive. The gilded main altar is the apogee of Peruvian baroque, and the sacristy's ceiling is covered with miniature paintings and carvings of crimson and gold. The view from the steeple is fabulous, especially at sunset when the late light casts a pink, then mauve, glow on the city's gracious white buildings. On the Calle Morán side of the church is the cloister, where stark architectural lines are broken by detailed columns, demonstrating the high level that stone carving reached during the 17th century. The Capilla de San Ignacio (St Ignatius's Chapel) is also worth a look, but check the visiting hours because they are different from those of the church.

Now retrace your steps to the massive twin-towered **Catedral** **C** (open daily 7.30–11.30am and 4.30–7.30pm; free admission), rebuilt twice in the 1800s after it was destroyed by fire and earthquake – which La Compañía escaped. The cathedral's ornate exterior is misleading because the interior is unusually bare and simple, except for an elaborate chandelier. The church's organ hails from Belgium, and its elaborately carved wooden pulpit, the work

**BELOW:** fountain in the Plaza de Armas.

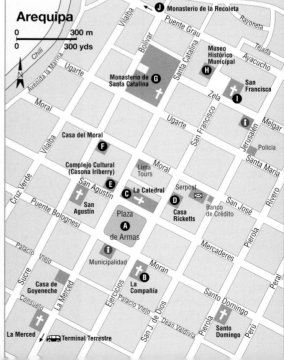

*Recommended Restaurants and Cafés on page 263*

of French artist Rigot in 1879, was brought to the city a century ago by a local aristocrat's daughter.

## Colonial mansions

Arequipa is a delight for those interested in secular colonial architecture, for this city is full of dignified patricians' homes built in the 18th century, which have somehow withstood the tremors that regularly shake this city. The single-story structures are replete with massive carved wooden doors, French windows with ornate grilles, and high-ceilinged rooms clustered around spacious central patios.

To see some of the best of them, cross Calle San Francisco to **Casa Ricketts D**. Built as a seminary in 1738, this is now the Banco Continental, but there is a small museum and art gallery inside (open 9am–1pm and 4–6pm). Next, take the street round the back of the cathedral to the **Casona Iriberry**, built in the late 18th century, which houses the **Complejo Cultural Chaves la Rosa E**. There is often something on at the complex: films, art exhibitions, and concerts. A few meters away, on the corner of Moral and Bolívar, is the **Casa del Moral F** (open 9am–5pm; entrance fee), which is also a bank, the Banco Sur, and originally named, like the street, after the venerable mulberry tree on its patio. The carvings above the door depict pumas from whose mouths snakes are slithering – the same designs found on the ceramics and fabrics of the Nazca people. Another interesting colonial house that is open to the public is the **Goyeneche Palace**.

## Convents and churches

From Casa Moral turn right along Calle Moral, then left into Calle Santa Catalina to the 16th-century **Monasterio de Santa Catalina G** (open 8am–5pm; entrance fee), the most astonishing site in Arequipa, which was opened to the public in 1970 after almost 400 years as a cloister. Despite the closed doors, little heed was paid to the vows of poverty and silence, at least in the early days. During

its heyday this convent's sleeping cells were luxurious, with English carpets, silk curtains, cambric and delicate lace sheets, and tapestry-covered stools. As for silence, French feminist Flora Tristan, visiting the convent in 1832, said that the nuns – daughters of aristocrats – were nearly as good at talking as they were at spending huge sums of money. Each had her own servants, and dined off porcelain plates, with damask tablecloths and silver cutlery.

Santa Catalina takes visitors back four centuries. Entering the cloister you see the spacious patios, the kitchen and slave quarters, and stone washtubs of this convent, where entrance requirements were among the strictest in Peru. Novices had to prove Spanish origin and come up with a dowry of at least 1,000 gold pesos. The narrow streets, arches, and gardens of the convent bear their original names: Calle Córdoba, its whitewashed walls stark against the pots of bright red gera-

*Decorative arched ceiling in the Monasterio de Santa Catalina.*

**BELOW:** Casa Ricketts, now home to the Banco Continental.

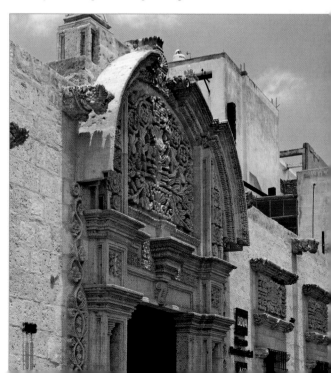

*Strolling through the peaceful alleys of Santa Catalina.*

niums; Plaza Zocodober with a granite fountain; Calle Sevilla with archways and steps. There is also an impressive collection of paintings from the 17th and 18th centuries in what was formerly the community dormitory. About 30 nuns still live in the convent, which once housed up to 500.

When the convent opened its doors to the public, its anecdotes and scandals were resurrected, among them the story of Sister Dominga, the 16-year-old who entered the convent when her betrothed left her for a rich widow. The religious life did not agree with this beautiful young woman, and she staged her own death to escape. Dominga really did place the body of a deceased Indian woman in her bed one night and set the room on fire, but it actually happened in the **Convento de Santa Rosa**, seven blocks from Arequipa's main square, which remains cloistered. It was founded in 1747 by four nuns from Santa Catalina; nearly two dozen members of the religious Order still reside there.

Close to Santa Catalina is the **Museo Histórico Municipal ◍** (open Mon– Sat 9am–5pm; entrance fee), which is interesting for an overview of the city's history. From here it is only a few yards to the **Iglesia de San Francisco ◑** (open daily 9am–12pm and 4–5.30pm), the focus of attention every December 8 during the Feast of the Immaculate Conception. A fairy-tale coach topped with the image of the Virgin Mary sur- rounded by angels and saints, usually stored in the small chapel of the Sor- rowful Virgin, is paraded through the streets in a colorful procession of pil- grims carrying flowers and candles.

To reach the most interesting museum in the city, the **Monasterio de la Reco- leta ◑** (open 9am–noon and 3–5pm), you must cross the Río Chili, by either the Puente Grau or the Puente Bolognesi. The monastery has a vast library of 20,000 books, many of them very old, and a collection of religious art. There is also a new museum, the **Museo de Arte Contemporáneo** (Tacna y Aríca 201; open Mon–Fri 10am–4.45pm, Sat and Sun until 1.45pm; entrance fee), housed in the railway manager's house opposite the train station.

## Seceding from the north

As already mentioned, *arequipeños* are a proud, even haughty lot, and their perennial attempts to secede from the rest of the country are a source of entertain- ment for *limeños*. They once designed their own passport and flag in a futile attempt at separatism. From Arequipa's well-educated and politically passionate ranks have come two of the country's best-known figures: the former President Fernando Belaúnde Terry, and the inter- nationally known novelist and failed presidential hopeful, Mario Vargas Llosa.

This regionalist passion peaks at the an- nual celebrations marking the anniversary of the city's foundation. Every August 15, *arequipeños* cut loose with parades, bull- fights, and night-time revelry highlighted by fireworks. The birthday celebration is accompanied by a week-long handicrafts and folk festival. The other important fes- tival in Arequipa is a more solemn one – the traditional religious processions of *Semana Santa*, Easter.

*Recommended Restaurants and Cafés on page 263*

To unwind in Arequipa in the evening, do what the locals do: head to a *picantería* for a cold *arequipeña* beer and some spicy food – stuffed peppers, pressed rabbit, or marinated pork. If you opt for the peppers *(rocoto relleno)*, take care – they are scorchingly hot. Tourist reactions to this spicy dish are a source of amusement for other diners and concern for restaurant owners. The beer will be accompanied by a dish of *cancha* or salty fried corn which, like potato crisps, makes you even thirstier. There is no shortage of restaurants, with something to suit all pockets, serving a wide variety of food, from the local specialties already mentioned, to good *ceviche* (the typical, marinated seafood dish – Arequipa is less than two hours from the ocean), to vegetarian dishes and good pizzas.

## Excursions from Arequipa

There are some interesting trips to be made outside Arequipa. One is to **Sabandía**, about 7 km (4 miles) from the city, near the pleasant suburb of Paucarpata. Here stands a flour mill, made of volcanic rock, which was built in the 17th century and restored, stone by stone, in 1973. In 1966, architect Luis Felipe Calle had restored an old mansion in Arequipa (now the main branch of the Central Bank) when he was given the task of restoring this old ruined mill outside the city. He set up a tent beside the mill and lived there for the two and a half years it took him to finish the project, which he did by referring to old documents and conducting interviews with residents who remembered when the mill had last operated, nearly half a century earlier. After the restoration the bank put the *molina* up for sale – and Calle himself purchased it. "Architecture of Arequipa is a fusion. The big stone houses are humble but at the same time vigorous, a faithful reflection of the spirit of their people," said Calle, whose 17th-century property – open to visitors – is set in some of the area's most beautiful countryside.

A little farther out from the city are the thermal springs of **Yura**, 30 km (18 miles) from Arequipa in the foothills of the extinct **Volcán Chachani**. Crude cement pools fed by the sulfurous waters are open for bathing, and lunch is

*Best served chilled: Arequipa's local brew.*

**BELOW:** the mummified remains of Juanita the Ice Maiden.

## Juanita the Ice Maiden

In September 1995 a fascinating discovery was made at the summit of the volcano Ampato (6288 meters/20,750 ft), near Arequipa. The heat from the eruption of a nearby volcano melted Ampato's normally ice-bound peak, which allowed a team of archeologists from Arequipa's Catholic University of Santa Maria (UCSM) to look for the remains of human sacrifices ritually made by the Incas to their Apus (mountain gods). These high-altitude sacrifices were the culmination of lengthy ceremonies made every few years, and through their sacrifice, the victims were thought to attain divinity.

The archeologists found a perfectly preserved 550-year-old sacrifice, mummified by the aridity and cold. Dressed in finely worked ceremonial robes, and surrounded by spiritually significant objects, this young victim turned out to be a delicate 12-year-old girl who soon became known to researchers as Juanita, the Ice Maiden. For research and preservation, Juanita was brought down to the University of Arequipa where she and her retinue of ceremonial objects have since shed much light on Inca beliefs. Juanita, frozen to below zero and encased in glass, is now the centerpiece of a captivating exhibition at the **Museo Santuarios Andinos** at the UCSM, which elaborates on the Inca rituals of sacrifice to the mountain gods. (Calle La Merced 110; open Mon–Sat 9am–6pm and Sun 9–3; entrance fee.)

**BELOW:** colonial church in the town of Pinchollo.

available at the Hotel Libertador. Two hours from the city, on the road to Lima, are the **Toro Muerto petroglyphs**, hundreds of volcanic rocks believed to have been engraved and painted more than 1,000 years ago by Wari (Huari) people living in the region. The petroglyphs show realistic depictions of llamas, condors, pumas, guanacos, dancers, and warriors.

## Peru's Grand Canyon

Four hours away from Arequipa, and drawing almost as much tourist attention these days, is the **Cañón del Colca** , one of the world's deepest gorges, cut 3,182 meters (10,607 ft) into the earth's crust. Deeper than the Grand Canyon, the Colca is shadowed by snow-topped peaks – many of them volcanoes – and sliced by the silvery Río Colca. The base of this canyon is cold and windy and draws only daredevil kayak enthusiasts and researchers. Above, at the brink of the chasm, Quechua-speaking farmers irrigate narrow terraces of rich volcanic earth in much the same way as their ancestors did centuries ago.

Though isolated, the Colca was a productive farming area even before the

Incas claimed it, and when the Spanish reached the 64-km (40-mile) long valley where this canyon lies, they found terraced fields and herds of llamas and alpacas. When the canyon became part of the route between the silver mines of Bolivia and the coast, the Colca farmers were snatched from their homes and forced to work in the mines. Later, when the railroad reached as far as Arequipa, the Colca valley was forgotten.

When a multinational consortium began investigating the possibility of diverting the Río Colca for a desert irrigation project, eyes turned once again to this valley and its gorge. From a lost chasm trapped in a time warp, the Colca has become one of the hottest tourist attractions in southwestern Peru. There has been a modification in the valley's crops as it has more contact with the outside world. One innovation is barley, which is now grown on some terraces for use in the brewery that makes some of the rather good *arequipeña* beer.

The canyon is an average of 900 meters (3,000 ft) deep. Perhaps the most popular section of the canyon is the **Cruz del Cóndor** (Condor Crossing), where visitors scan the skies for a glimpse of the majestic birds soaring above in pairs. They use the thermal air currents produced in the early morning or the early evening, and few who visit at those times in the hope of spotting them are disappointed.

The Cruz del Cóndor is included in a variety of one- and two-day trips, which can be organized in Arequipa. En route, many of the tours take in the **Reserva Nacional Salinas y Aguada Blanca** (at 3,900 meters/12,800 ft you'll notice how thin the air seems), where groups of shy vicuñas can often be seen. Even more remote than Colca, the **Cotahuasi canyon** has only recently been exposed to tourism. Now believed by many to exceed Colca in depth, making it the world's deepest canyon, it is a pristine area of great natural beauty ideal for adventurers and nature lovers. Accommodations can be found in the small town of Cotahuasi. ❏

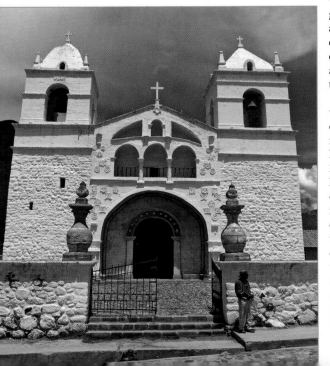

# RESTAURANTS AND CAFÉS

## Restaurants

Prices are per person for a two-course meal, excluding wine:
**$** less than US$10
**$$** US$10–20
**$$$** more than US$20

Arequipa has maintained a reputation for style and affluence. There are a number of good restaurants around the Plaza de Armas, and cafés can be found in the first block of San Francisco.

### Café Casa Verde
Jerusalén 406
Tel: (054) 226 376
Visit this pretty, quiet place not just for its good breakfasts, light meals, and snacks, but because the cost of your meal goes towards supporting a home for abandoned children. **$**

### Café Forum
San Francisco 156
A popular meeting place. **$**

### La Cantarilla
Tahuaycani 106, Sachaca
Tel: (054) 251 515
Traditional *arequipeña* and international food. Sit outside for lunch of freshwater shrimps. A 20-minute taxi ride from the center. **$$**

### Lakshmivan
Jerusalén 408
Tel: (054) 228 768
Can't take all the meat? Then this is the best spot to head to in Arequipa. There's an all-vegetarian menu featuring lots of tofu, good salads, and delicious desserts. **$**

### Ras el Hanout y los 40 Sabores
San Francisco 227
Tel: (054) 227 779
This lovely restaurant with a peaceful inner courtyard plies you with the heady flavors of Moroccan and Mediterranean cooking. On a hot afternoon, a sweet mint tea in the shade is a delight. **$$**

### Sol de Mayo
Jerusalén 207
Tel: (054) 254 148
Good lunchtime menu of Peruvian specialties such as *rocoto relleno* (stuffed hot peppers), and *ocopa* (potatoes in a spicy sauce with melted cheese). **$$**

### Tradición Arequipeña
Av. Dolores 111, J.L. Bustamante y Rivero
Tel: (054) 426 467
Serves good *arequipeña* food and occasionally has live music and dancing. **$$**

### La Trattoria del Monasterio
Calle Santa Catalina 309
Tel: (054) 204 062
A beautifully stylish Italian restaurant within the walls of the Santa Catalina monastery, run by Gastón Arcurio, Peru's most distinguished chef. There's a serene atmosphere, and amongst Arequipa's smart set, this is the place to be seen. **$$**

### Wara Wara
Av. Dolores 18, J.L. Bustamente y Rivero
Tel: (054) 420 950
Succulent meat from the grill. There are melt-in-the-mouth steaks, or try the *piqueos* (tapas) and the excellent *anticuchos* (kebabs) – and there's a good wine list to go with them. **$$**

### Wayrana
Calle Santa Catalina 210
Tel: (054) 285 641
Funky interior design and a breezy outdoor courtyard give this place a cool edge. *Cuy* is the specialty here, and if you don't fancy eating your guinea pig whole, then try the fillet of *cuy* in asparagus, mushroom, and malt beer sauce. Yum! **$$**

**RIGHT:** *rocoto relleno* (stuffed peppers).

# COLONIAL ART AND ARCHITECTURE

**Once the Spaniards laid aside the sword and the musket, they began building. Wonderful examples of their architecture still grace Peru's oldest cities**

After subduing the indigenous peoples, one of the conquistadors' first acts was to start building splendid churches. This symbolized their power and confidence, glorified God and provided places of worship for new converts. The earliest churches were built by the Franciscans: the first cathedral in Lima was completed in 1555, but only a decade later they considered it too small and began another. In Cusco, the church of El Triunfo was founded in 1536, the year the Spanish vanquished Manco Inca's forces at Sacsayhuamán. The first stones for Cusco's cathedral were laid in 1559. Not to be outdone, the Dominican order founded Santo Domingo on the site of the Inca Temple of the Sun, which the Spaniards had stripped of its vast wealth.

When the Jesuits, the most zealous of the missionaries, arrived, they started their own building program. La Compañía in Cusco, begun in 1571, rivaled the cathedral in splendor. It was virtually destroyed by an earthquake less than a century later, but rebuilt with an ornate baroque facade. La Compañía in Arequipa was initiated only in the late 17th century, by which time baroque influences were prevalent. It was predated by the cathedral and the exquisite Monastery of Santa Catalina. All were built in imitation of the great churches of Spain, with massive towers and cupolas, and arched, shady cloisters. Many had strong Mudéjar influences, blending with the innovative School of Cusco style *(see opposite)*. Around the churches were the great Plazas de Armas – the one in Cusco is a magnificent example – and in the late 17th and the 18th century elegant town houses were constructed in the colonial style in all the major cities.

**ABOVE:** the beautifully preserved Santa Catalina monastery in Arequipa. Its shady streets and cloisters were built in imitation of Mudéjar buildings in 17th-century Spain.

**BELOW:** the cathedral in Cusco contains several ornate altars, including this one which is covered with gold leaf and features paintings by artists from the School of Cusco.

**LEFT**: a statue in the Chapel of Saint Anne in Lima Cathedral.

## THE SCHOOL OF CUSCO

The School of Cusco was a 17th-century movement which blended European and indigenous motifs to create a New World art form. Paintings were religious in nature, and the costumes worn by the archangels were in the sumptuous style of the Spanish court. The colors were rich and dark, and the themes had their dark side too, depicting martyrs' horrific deaths. The master of this school was the *indígeno* artist Diego Quispe Tito, examples of whose work hang in the Museo de Arte Religioso and Cusco's cathedral, where his *Signs of the Zodiac* series *(above)* can be seen. Each painting in the series depicts a scene from the life of Christ.

**RIGHT:** San Francisco is one of the best-preserved colonial churches in Lima. There are extensive catacombs underneath the church and its interior has strong Mudéjar influences mingled with the Baroque.

**ABOVE:** the town of Julí on Lake Titicaca is home to several colonial churches, including San Juan Bautista which contains paintings depicting the life of Saint John the Baptist.

Recommended Restaurants and Cafés on page 281

# CUSCO

The ancient capital of the Inca empire is the city most tourists want to visit, a jewel of Inca and colonial architecture standing 3,330 meters (10,900 ft) above sea level

Indigenous vendors speak Spanish to tourists and Quechua to each other. Catholic nuns live in buildings once inhabited by Inca "chosen women." The Marcos Zapata painting of the Last Supper in the cathedral shows Christ and his Apostles dining on Andean cheese, hot peppers, and roast guinea pig. **Cusco** ⑮ is a city where past and present collide in an intriguing mix.

When Francisco Pizarro and his soldiers arrived nearly five centuries ago, Cusco, the capital of the Inca empire, served as home to an estimated 15,000 nobles, priests, and servants. Where now daily rail, plane, and bus services connect this city to the rest of the country, long-distance relay runners called *chasquis* once linked it to the rest of Tahuantinsuyo, as the empire was called. Today, local residents have attempted to recall those glory days, relabeling streets with their original Quechua names and even calling the city Qosqo, a pronunciation closer to its original Inca name.

## Center of the world

For the Incas, Qosqo meant "navel of the world," and they believed their splendid city was the source of life. Legend has it Cusco was founded by Manco Capac and his sister-consort Mama Ocllo, sent by the sun god Inti with the divine task of finding a spot where the gold staff they carried would sink easily into the ground. That place was Cusco, and there Manco Capac taught the men to farm and Mama Ocllo taught the women to weave.

The Inca empire came into being during the reign of Inca Pachacutec Yupanqui, who began a great expansion, imposing Quechua as the common language, conquering other Indian nations, creating a state religion, and turning Cusco into a glittering capital as large as any European city. It was Pachacutec who transformed Cusco from a city of clay and straw into a thriving metropolis with grand stone buildings in the second half of the 15th century.

A modern stone statue of Pachacutec on the south side of Cusco pays tribute to

**Main attractions**
PLAZA DE ARMAS
CATEDRAL
CALLE HATUNRUMIYOC
ARTISANS' STORES, CUESTA
SAN BLAS
LA COMPAÑÍA DE JESÚS
QORICANCHA

**PRECEDING PAGES:** *cusqueñas* in traditional dress. **LEFT:** colonial street. **BELOW:** tiled roofs.

*A water fountain in the Plaza de Armas.*

the king who ruled for 40 years and was one of the empire's greatest warriors, innovators, and unifiers of Andean civilizations. His son, Inca Tupac Yupanqui, continued his work, expanding the empire's boundaries even farther .

Some of the best-loved Inca legends have been transferred to the Peruvian theater. Among them is *Ollantay* – the story of Pachacutec's most famous general. Under Ollantay's military leadership, the empire was extended into what is now Ecuador, Bolivia, Colombia, Chile, and portions of Argentina. A grateful Pachacutec promised to grant him any wish. Ollantay boldly asked for the hand of Kusi Kuyur, the monarch's daughter. But the Inca, the son of the sun, could not allow a member of the monarchy to marry a commoner even though the daughter professed her love for the military leader. Ollantay rebelled against Pachacutec and was eventually ordered to be imprisoned for the remainder of his life. Kusi Kuyur refused to marry anyone else and was sent to be a Chosen Woman, dedicating her life to serving the sun god.

The story does not end there, however, because years later an unforeseen occurrence brought the couple together again for a happy ending. The play is staged frequently in Cusco and Lima, and is worth seeing by those who understand some Spanish.

## A brief moment of glory

At its peak, Cusco, built in the shape of a puma, was a city with sophisticated water systems, paved streets, and no poverty. But it had been an imposing urban center for only about 70 years before the Spanish arrived. Of course, since the Incas left no written records, and the Spanish explanations of what they found are contradictory, theories about Cusco's design are numerous. One specialist in archeology and astronomy even speculates that one city boundary was warped to make it coincide with the mid-point in the Milky Way, reflecting the Indian sensitivity to astronomy and the movements of the heavenly bodies.

The Spaniards were certainly impressed by the order and magnificence of Cusco, and wrote back to Spain that it was the most marvelous city of the New World. But the Incas' cultural achievements were merely a minor distraction

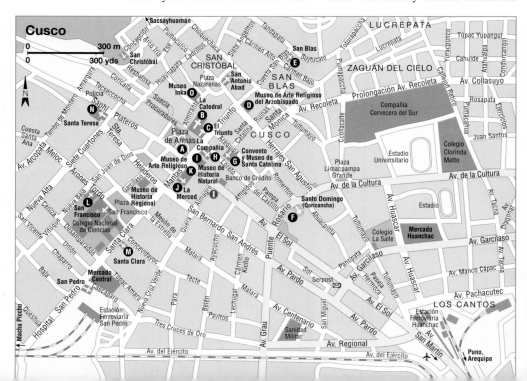

*Recommended Restaurants and Cafés on page 281*

in comparison with the lure of their treasures: conquistadors greedily pushed their way into ancient temples and seized their gold and silver artworks, which they promptly melted into bullion.

In addition to palaces and gold-filled temples, indestructible buildings, and advanced medical techniques, the Spanish soldiers found the Inca society full of skilled artisans. A storehouse of delicate, brightly colored feathers from tropical birds was used solely for the weaving of fine capes for the Inca and his priests. Rescued examples of the capes or *mantas*, which reflect the most extreme test of patience and handiwork, are found in museums in Lima. These survived because the Spanish thirst for gold was so great that they overlooked many of the empire's other treasures.

Cusco retained a level of importance for the first few decades after the Spanish conquest. It was here that Diego de Almagro's faction of Spanish soldiers attempted to wrest control from Pizarro, and for his treachery the leader was executed on the city's main plaza. It was also here that the Spanish struggled against Manco Inca as the Indians made an ill-fated attempt to stop the European conquest through gallant guerrilla warfare. But by 1535 the capital of this new Spanish colony had been set up in Lima, Cusco's wealth had been stripped, and silver from Bolivia had turned attention away from this valley.

After centuries of provincial obscurity, Hiram Bingham's discovery of Machu Picchu in 1911 and the subsequent construction of a road up to that mountain-top citadel in 1948 transformed Cusco into the jumping-off point for visits to one of South America's best-known tourist attractions.

*Detail on an Inca-Spanish wall.*

## The architecture of Cusco

The most startling and curious characteristic of Cusco at first glance is its architecture. Huge walls of intricately laid stone pay testimony to the civilization that 500 years ago controlled much of this continent. The Spaniards' attempts to eradicate every trace of the "pagan" Inca civilization proved too ambitious a task; the Europeans ended up putting

**BELOW:** Plaza de Armas.

*A painting from the school of Cusco.*

their own buildings on the mammoth foundations of the Inca ones, often using the same stones that had been cut and rounded by Inca masons. When a massive earthquake shook the city in March 1650, the colonial walls came crashing down but the Inca foundations remained intact.

## Plaza de Armas

Before you start to explore this intriguing city, remember that it is more than 3,330 meters (10,900 ft) above sea level, so take it easy until you get acclimatized. Also, don't forget to buy a Cusco Visitor Ticket *(see page 274)*, which is essential for visits to historic sites in Cusco and the Sacred Valley. Bearing these two things in mind, the **Plaza de Armas** Ⓐ is a perfect place to start. In Inca times it was not only the exact center of the empire known as Tahuantinsuyo – or The Four Quarters of the Earth – but was also twice as large as it is now. Samples of soil from each of the

conquered areas of the empire were joined at this spot, and the plaza itself, flanked by Inca palaces, was surfaced with white sand mixed with tiny shells, bits of gold, silver, and coral.

This was the spot where important Inca religious and military ceremonies were staged. Some claim the section that remains today was a portion of Aucaypata, the Square of War, featuring a stone covered in sheets of gold where offerings were made before military actions. However, other experts disagree, and suggest it was called Huacaypata – or Weeping Square – because it was here that deceased Incas were mourned. During the early days of Spanish control, the plaza was the scene of much violence and blood-letting, such as the execution of the rebel leader Tupac Amaru II in 1781. Captured while trying to flee with his pregnant wife, Tupac Amaru was a mestizo whose real name was José Gabriel Condorcanqui.

These days, things are quieter on the plaza, which is one of the most superb colonial squares in Latin America. Tourists study the handicrafts for sale as insistent local women sitting under blan-

**BELOW:** Cusco's mighty cathedral.

kets beneath the colonial arcades chant "*cómprame*," or "buy from me." Quality varies, but good bargains can be found. However, don't believe it when vendors claim their rugs and weavings are antique: wool does not endure indefinitely in the damp highlands. The centuries-old textiles displayed in Peru's museums were rescued from the arid coast. In any case, it is forbidden to buy antique textiles or take them out of the country.

## Cusco's cathedral

The most spectacular view of the plaza comes after nightfall when dramatic lighting transforms the square. But while the night is best for outside photos, the interior of Cusco's magnificent **Catedral ❸** can only be seen during the day (open daily 10am–6pm, Mass at 10am; entrance fee). It is flanked by the church of Jesús María, to the right – also known as the Iglesia de la Santísima Trinidad – and El Triunfo *(see page 274)* to the left. Jesús María was built in the mid-18th century, which makes it one of the newer structures.

Rather confusingly, visitors are normally channeled through the main doors of El Triunfo, then turn right into the cathedral itself. Built on what once was the palace of Inca Wiracocha, and made in part from stones hauled from the fortress of Sacsayhuamán outside the city, the cathedral mixes Spanish Renaissance architecture with Inca stonework. Begun in 1559, it took a century to build. The altar is of solid silver.

The cathedral also contains magnificent examples of Escuela Cusqueña (School of Cusco) paintings, including some by Diego Quispe Tito, the 17th-century Indian painter widely regarded as the master of the school. In the corner next to the sacristy is a painting by Marcos Zapata of the Last Supper, with Christ and his Apostles dining on roast guinea pig *(cuy)*, hot peppers, and Andean cheese. A painting of Christ's crucifixion is the subject of many theories: some believe it is a 17th-century work by a member of the Cusco School; others hold that it is the work of Flemish painter Sir Anthony van Dyck;

still others believe it was by a Spanish artist, Alonzo Ocano; while a final theory proposes that it is the work of various artists, because the head is out of proportion with the body. The third side-altar from the left contains a curious painting of a pregnant Virgin Mary.

The city's most venerated statue is the crucified Christ known as *Nuestro Señor de los Temblores* (Our Lord of the Earthquakes), which is depicted in a painting beside the main altar. The statue was paraded around the city during the 1650 earthquake, and after the tremors eventually stopped it was credited with miraculously bringing about the end of seismic activity. Borne on a silver litter, this gift to the New World from Spain, sent by Holy Roman Emperor Charles V, is still paraded around Cusco during Easter. For the rest of the year it remains in an alcove inside the cathedral.

*The Chapel of the Holy Family, next to the cathedral.*

**BELOW:** chatting on the cathedral steps.

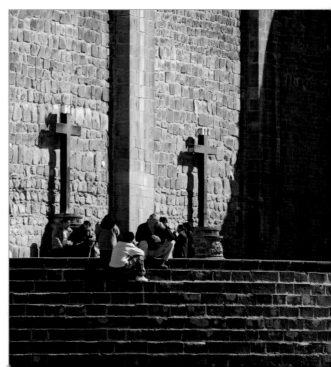

**TIP**

The **Cusco Visitor Ticket** covers many of the must-see sites in Cusco and the Sacred Valley and is valid for 10 days. A separate **Religious Circuit Ticket** allows entrance to most of Cusco's churches. Both tickets provide good value for money if you intend to visit several sights and can be purchased at the Tourist Information Office on Avenida Sol 103.

**BELOW:** a busy back street.

It is blackened by the smoke of candles perpetually burning beneath it, though these have now been replaced by artificial ones.

The cathedral's María Angola bell in the north tower can be heard up to 40 km (25 miles) away. Made of a ton of gold, silver, and bronze, the bell, which is more than 300 years old, is reportedly the continent's largest. But when it was cast it had a partner – the Magdalena, which was dropped by workers during a storm at the edge of Lake Titicaca, where the bells were made. *Cusqueños* now say that the echoes from the first peals of the María Angola each morning are actually the tolling of the Magdalena on the bottom of the lake.

## Cusco's first church

**El Triunfo ⓒ** (opening hours as for the cathedral) means "the triumph," and it was built in honor of the Spanish victory over the Indians in the great rebellion of 1536, when Cusco was under siege for many months. The uprising was led by Manco Inca, a descendant of an Inca leader, who the Spaniards assumed would be their political puppet. They were surprised, then, to find Manco surrounding the city with some 200,000 followers – against the Spaniards' 200 men and loyal Indians.

The turning-point of the siege was a great attack on the city, with Manco's men slinging red-hot stones to set the thatched roofs alight. The Spaniards were gathered in the old Inca armory of Suntur Huasi when it was pelted with fiery rocks. When the building did not catch fire, priests declared that the Virgin of the Assumption had appeared to put out the flames and inspire the Spaniards to defend the city. El Triunfo – the city's first Christian church – was built on the site. The tomb containing the ashes of the indigenous historian Garcilaso de la Vega, who died in Spain in 1616 but whose remains were returned to Cusco a few years ago, can be found in this church.

## Religious art

If you turn left when you emerge from El Triunfo and walk one block up to the corner of **Calle Hatunrumiyoc**, literally "the Street of the Big Stones," and Calle Palacio, you will come to the **Museo de Arte Religioso del Arzobispado ⓓ** (open Mon–Sat 8am–6pm, Sun from 10am; entrance fee). This Moorish building with complicated carvings on its doors and balconies was constructed on the site of the 15th-century palace of Inca Roca, under whose rule Cusco's schools were initiated. It used to be the Archbishop's Palace, and that is what people sometimes still call it. Just outside is the famous **Twelve-Angled Stone**. A "fitting" tribute to the skill of Inca masons, this masonry masterpiece was left by Inca architects seemingly anxious to prove that no piece of granite was too irregular to be fitted without mortar. The museum houses an impressive collection of religious paintings of the Cusco School, including some by Diego Quispe Tito.

Head straight up Calle Hatunrumiyoc, and on your right you will find the **Iglesia de San Blas ⓔ**. Apart from its ornate altar, San Blas is a simple church by Latin American standards, and has a

*Recommended Restaurants and Cafés on page 281*

beautifully carved pulpit, said to be one of the world's finest pieces of woodwork. There is some dispute about who produced it; some say it was an Indian leper who initiated the work after he was miraculously cured (open Mon–Sat 8am–6pm, Sun from 10am; entrance fee). The streets around San Blas form Cusco's artists' quarter, with galleries, studios, and small shops, hostels and restaurants, and the workshops of the prolific Mendival family.

## Temple of the Sun

Take any of the streets leading south from the Plaza de Armas and you will find your way to the most important place of worship in the Inca empire. Now a church, the **Iglesia Santo Domingo ➏** (open Mon–Sat 8.30am–5.30pm, Sun 2–5pm; entrance fee), was once **El Templo del Qoricancha** – the Temple of the Sun, and the most magnificent complex in Cusco. Walls there were covered in 700 sheets of gold studded with emeralds and turquoise, and windows were constructed so the sun would enter and cast a nearly blinding reflection off the precious metals inside.

The mummified bodies of deceased Inca leaders, dressed in fine clothing and adornments, were kept on thrones of gold, tended by women selected for that honor. In the same room, a huge gold disk representing the sun covered one full wall while a sister disk of silver, to reflect the moonlight, was positioned on another.

Spanish chronicles recall the Europeans' astonishment when they saw - Qoricancha's patio filled with life-size gold and silver statues of llamas, trees, flowers, and handcrafted butterflies. According to legend, Atahualpa's ransom included 20 of Qoricancha's life-size golden statues of beautiful women.

*Colonial arches in the Hotel Libertador.*

**BELOW:** Iglesia Santo Domingo.

*The recently refurbished Teatro Garcilaso on Calle Unión 117 is a good place to see contemporary Peruvian theater.*

**BELOW:** rush hour in Cusco.

The Spanish historian Pedro de Cieza de León wrote a description of the patio "in which the earth was lumps of fine gold … with stalks of corn that were of gold-stalks, leaves and ears… so well planted that no matter how hard the wind blew it could not uproot them. Aside from this there were more than 20 sheep of gold with their lambs and the shepherds who guarded them, all of this metal."

Although the temple's wealth can only be imagined, its Inca architecture can still be appreciated. Visible from inside is the perfectly fitted curved stone wall that has survived at least two major earthquakes.

Spanish chronicles also describe a fabulous Hall of the Sun in Qoricancha and four chapels dedicated to lesser gods, including the moon, stars, thunder, and the rainbow. The rainbow had special significance for the Incas, which was why the Inca flag displayed all the colors of the *arco iris*, and it remains a good omen today. Any Peruvian child asked to draw a picture of the Sierra will invariably sketch a house with mountains in the background and a rainbow arching the sky. Current excavations at the Temple of the Sun promise to reveal more of its mysteries.

## Chosen Women

Retrace your steps toward the Plaza de Armas, and on Calle Arequipa you will find another Christian enclave that was formerly an Inca holy place. This is the **Museo de Arte y Monasterio de Santa Catalina** Ⓖ (open Mon–Thur 9am–5pm, Fri until 5.30pm, Sat 9am–5pm; entrance fee), which centuries ago housed a different group of cloistered females, some 3,000 Chosen Women who dedicated their lives to the sun god. Foremost among these were the *mamaconas*, consecrated women who taught religion to selected virgins – called *acllas*. The *acllas* were taught to prepare *chicha* for use in religious ceremonies, to weave, and to pray. They made the fine robes that the Inca wore – only once – out of vicuña, alpaca, and even a silky fabric that was made from bat skins.

Attached to the convent is a museum containing works of religious art. An important contribution to the art world grew out of Cusco's mixing of the Indian and Spanish cultures in the often violent and bloody paintings of the School of Cusco (*see page 265*). In many of these paintings archangels are

*Recommended Restaurants and Cafés on page 281*

dressed as Spaniards carrying European guns, but surrounded by cherubs with Indian faces, or Christ is accompanied by indigenous Apostles. The Virgin Mary wears local Peruvian dress, and Christ hangs on a cross decorated with Indian symbols.

## The most beautiful church

In a city with so many churches, it is an honor to be dubbed the "most beautiful." That distinction belongs to **La Compañía de Jesús** ❶ (open Sun–Thur 9–11.30am and 1–5.30pm, Fri and Sat 9–11.30 and 1–3.30pm; entrance fee), sitting on the southeast corner of the Plaza de Armas where once stood Inca Huayna Capac's palace. The Jesuit church, with its baroque facade, intricate interior, finely carved balconies, and altars covered in gold leaf, was started in 1571 and took nearly 100 years to complete, in part because of damage in the 1650 earthquake. During its construction, this splendid building drew so much attention that the bishop of Cusco complained it outshone the cathedral. But by the time Pope Paul III had been called in to mediate, and had ruled in favor of the cathedral, La Compañía's construction had been completed.

To the right of La Compañía, also on the main plaza, is the university-owned **Museo de Historia Natural** ❶ (open Mon–Fri 9.30am–12pm and 3–6pm), with good examples of local fauna.

A few yards down the street, just past the Plaza de Armas, is the **Iglesia de la Merced** ❶ (open Mon–Sat 8am–12.30pm and 2–5.30pm; entrance fee), one of the most important churches in the city. Destroyed by the massive earthquake in 1650, this church was erected for a second time four years later. It contains the remains of Francisco Pizarro's brother Gonzalo, and of Pizarro's fellow conquistador Diego de Almagro, who returned to Peru after an unsuccessful search for riches in Chile, and was executed here after his failed coup attempt.

There is a connected monastery and another **Museo de Arte Religioso** ❶ (opening hours as for the church), not to be confused with the museum of the same name in the Archbishop's Palace. This one contains several fine paintings, including a Rubens, and gold and silver altarpieces, the most ostentatious of which is a jewel-studded, solid gold monstrance.

**DRINK**

Most bars on or near the plaza offer 2 for 1 drinks during "happy hour." Many of them also show free films, usually in English with Spanish subtitles.

**LEFT:** La Compañía de Jesús.
**BELOW:** flying the Inca flag in the Plaza de Armas.

*One of the many fascinating artifacts in the Museo Inka.*

**BELOW:** the five-star Libertador hotel. **RIGHT:** under the eaves.

## Garden square

Continue a couple of blocks down the same street – Calle Marqués – and you will come to the **Plaza San Francisco**. This square has been planted entirely with Andean flora, including amaranth grain. Here, too, is Cusco's coat-of-arms, featuring a castle surrounded by eight condors. The castle represents Sacsay-huamán, and the emblem refers to the bloody battle fought there in 1536 as the Incas tried to defeat the Spanish conquerors. The condors flying over the castle vividly recall the scores of flesh-eating birds that, according to legend, circled over the Inca fort as the bodies of the dead piled up.

Flanking one side of the plaza is the 16th-century church and monastery, the **Iglesia de San Francisco ❶** (open Mon–Sat 9am–3.30pm). Simple in comparison with other houses of worship in the city, it has an extensive collection of colonial art, including a painting – said to be one of the largest canvases in South America – showing the family tree of St Francis of Assisi.

There are two more churches that are well worth seeing, but rather difficult to get into, because both are the homes of closed orders of nuns. To see the first, turn down Calle Santa Clara, leading from the Plaza San Francisco, and you will find the 16th-century **Iglesia de Santa Clara ❿** (open daily for Mass 7pm). The tiny mirrors that cover the interior are the most impressive sight in this building. In order to see the second beautiful but usually inaccessible church, the **Iglesia de Santa Teresa ❷** (open daily for Mass 7am and 7pm), you must go a couple of blocks past the Plaza San Francisco, then turn right on Calle Siete Cuartones. The cloistered nuns sit at the back of the church, behind a grill, and form the church's choir. If you can't be here at these times you will have to be content with a look at the exterior of this lovely building.

Circling round behind the Plaza de Armas, on the corner of Calle Tucumán and Calle Ataúd you will find the **Museo Inka ❷** (open Mon–Fri 8am–5pm Sat 9am–4pm; entrance fee), also known as the **Admiral's Palace** because it was once the home of Admiral Francisco Aldrete Maldonado. A coat-of-arms over its doorway belongs to a subsequent owner, the

*Recommended Restaurants and Cafés on page 281*

arrogant and self-important Count of Laguna, who died under mysterious circumstances. His body was found hanging in the mansion's courtyard shortly after he mistreated a priest who had complained about the count's behavior. In the same courtyard are miniature profiles of Pizarro and Spain's Queen Isabela.

There are some strange architectural features: an optical illusion is found in a corner window column, which looks like a bearded man from the inside and a nude woman from the outside, and there are mythical creatures guarding the main stairway. The building is well worth seeing for itself, as well as for the museum's newly expanded collection of pottery, textiles, and gold artifacts. Another splendid museum has opened at the Casa Cabrera in Plaza Nazarenas, the **Museo de Arte Precolumbino** (open daily 9am–11pm; entrance fee).

## Travelers' rest

Before leaving Cusco and heading for landmarks outside the city, stop by the Cross Keys Pub, which is at a second-floor location at Portal Confitura 233, facing the cathedral on the Plaza de Armas. In this city of contrasts, what could be more natural than a British-owned watering-hole for travelers, cartographers, self-styled pioneers, eccentric scientists, and birdwatchers? Join them at the bar to consult them on out-of-the-way tourist stops. The owner, ornithologist Barry Walker, runs Manu Expeditions (*see Travel Tips, page 331*), which organizes nature tours in Manu National Park.

There is a wide selection of restaurants in Cusco, serving both Peruvian and international food. If you are looking for night-time entertainment as well as food, it can be found at the restaurants from which lively Andean music emanates. One of the finest floorshows takes place nightly at El Truco, where the *pisco sours* pack a hefty punch and the musicians and dancers are first-rate. Eating a plate of *anticuchos*, a delicious shish-kebab of beef heart, while watching the traditionally garbed performers singing in Quechua and playing reed flutes, will make visitors

temporarily forget that the Incas lost their showdown with the Spanish.

Eventually the dance songs will be replaced by much quieter mountain music. Locals will tell you that it was when the Spanish killed the last Inca and the sun god turned his back on his children that Andean songs became melancholy. If you are looking for something more contemporary, there are several video bars in Cusco where weary tourists can select a video, order drinks, and settle down in comfort to enjoy American or other foreign movies.

## Cusco's fiestas

Cusco holds a number of very colorful festivals; the best-known of them are in June, but there are several exceptions. One is the Christmas Eve festival called *Santorantikuy* (which means the buying of saints), when crafts and nativity sets are sold in the Plaza de Armas. Another is the celebration in Easter when *Nuestro Señor de los Temblores* (Our Lord of the Earthquakes), the image of Christ on the cross that is credited with saving the city from destruction during the earthquake of 1650, and which stands in the cath-

*You may be surprised to see some signs in Cusco's tourist areas translated into Hebrew. This is because so many young Israelis travel to Peru when they come out of the army.*

## Bringing Back the Sun

**M**any travelers come to Cusco for *Inti Raymi* (the Festival of the Sun) on June 24. *Inti Raymi* was the Inca winter solstice celebration held on June 21 or 22, which the Spanish moved to June 24, the Catholic feast of St John the Baptist. In the 1940s a group of Cusco intellectuals revived *Inti Raymi*, basing their fiesta on colonial accounts of the Inca festival.

*Campesinos*, townspeople, and travelers follow the Inca's procession from Qoricancha, via the Plaza de Armas, to the fortress of Sacsayhuamán. The regal Inca-for-a-day is borne on a litter, dressed in aluminum foil and glittering gold, his guard consisting of costumed Peruvian army troops. The fires of the empire are ceremonially relit, a llama is "sacrificed" to the sun, and music and dance groups perform, wearing hand-woven clothes that would have made Pachacutec proud. The pageant lasts for about three hours, but the city becomes a giant fair for a couple of days, full of energy and color. It's fascinating, but do watch out for pickpockets in the crowd.

**EAT**

There is always a new eating establishment to be found within the main plaza's portals, and many good restaurants also provide exciting Andean music and dance. Sample the succulent pink trout, prepared in many Peruvian and international restaurants. On chilly nights, head to one of the cafés on the plaza for *mate de coca*, chocolate cake, and hot milk with rum.

**BELOW:** view over the city.

edral, is paraded through the streets on a silver litter. Red flower petals are thrown in its wake, symbolizing the blood of Christ, and thousands of *cusqueños* turn out along with the civic, religious, and military hierarchies of the city.

A third exception is International Workers' Day (May 1), when workers parade through the square, each group lined up behind its respective banners – from the organization of transportation workers to the union of informal street vendors *(ambulantes)*, which is made up mostly of women with their babies. Like many ceremonies in Cusco, it opens with the raising of both the red and white Peruvian flag and the rainbow-colored standard of the Inca empire.

Corpus Christi (in honor of the Eucharist) is a movable feast, held on the Thursday after Trinity Sunday – usually in early to mid-June. Effigies of St Sebastian and St Jeronimo race into Cusco from the little towns named after them, borne on enormous litters by their devotees and led by a brass band and people carrying banners and candles. Accompanied by other statues of saints and the Virgin, brought from Cusco's

barrios and suburbs, they are taken to the church of Santa Clara. The Plaza de Armas comes alive: large altars decorated with flowers, tin, mirrors, crosses, and images of the sun are erected, and vendors set up booths with food prepared especially for Corpus Christi. These treats, well worth sampling, include *chiri-uchu*, made with guinea pig, chicken, corn, cheese, eggs, and peppers; and baked *achira*, a variety of Peruvian tuber.

After High Mass, the statues are paraded around the plaza, stopping to bow at each altar – no mean feat when some of the gilded and silver-covered figures weigh up to a ton. Each parish has its own brass band, costumed dance groups and devotees, and the plaza is a mélange of color and sound. At the end of the procession comes the priest bearing the Eucharist, almost forgotten in the crush. Slip inside the cathedral if you can, because some of the old women remain there to sing Quechua hymns in the high, bird-like voices typical of traditional music. The day gets more lively as it goes on: generous quantities of alcohol are consumed, and masked devil-dancers frolic among the shrubberies. ❏

# RESTAURANTS AND CAFÉS

## Restaurants

Prices are per person for a two-course meal, excluding wine:
**$** less than US$10
**$$** US$10–20
**$$$** more than US$20

### El Ayllu
Portal de Carnes 203, Plaza de Armas
Tel: (084) 232 357
A Cusco institution popular with older *cusqueños*, with tasteful decor and background classical and jazz music. Excellent breakfasts, cakes, and coffees. **$**

### Cross Keys Pub
Calle Triunfo 350
Tel: (084) 229 727
Typical British pub with pub grub. Great meeting place. **$**

### Granja Heidi
Cuesta San Blas 525
Tel: (084) 238 383
Excellent soups, salads, quiches, and pastas, mostly organic and homemade, with dairy products from the restaurant's own farm. **$**

### Al Grano
Santa Catalina Ancha 398
Tel: (084) 228 332
Good Asian food including vegetarian curry amidst exposed Inca stonework. Also great cookies. **$**

### Greens Organic
Santa Catalina Angosta 135
Tel: (084) 243 379
Upstairs from Incanto, this is the best place in town for vegetarians. Beautiful, natural food served by friendly staff. Try the Peruvian-style mushroom stir-fry. **$$**

### Incanto Ristorante
Santa Catalina Angosta 135
Tel: (084) 254 475
Smart Italian restaurant with a Peruvian twist, just off the Plaza de Armas. The *carpaccio de lomo* is highly recommended. **$$$**

### Inka Grill
Portal de Panes 115, Plaza de Armas
Tel: (084) 262 992
Upmarket international restaurant. Excellent food and service. **$$**

### Kin Taro
Heladeros 149
Tel: (084) 226 181
Cheap, excellent Japanese food. Sit upstairs on floor with cable TV. **$**

### Kusikuy
Suecia 339
Tel: (084) 262 870
Typical local food, including roast guinea pig. **$**

### Pachapapa
120 Plazoleta San Blas
Tel: (084) 241 318
Serves traditional Peruvian food. **$**

### Santu
Siete Angelitos 618, San Blas
Tel: (084) 224 314
This restaurant's Inca recipes will help you "discover the secret strength of the Andes." Whether that's true or not, they do great lamb ribs, alpaca steaks, and good trout ceviche. **$**

### Trotamundos
Portal de Comercio 177 (2nd floor)
Tel: (084) 239 590
Good coffee, snacks and meals, plus a fine view of the cathedral. **$**

### El Truco
Plaza Regocijo 261
Tel: (084) 232 441
Catering to large tour groups, this nightly dinner and show is the most elaborate in Cusco and good value. **$$**

### Velluto
Tandapata 700, San Blas
Tel: (084) 240 966
For its candlelit ambience and great music, this crêperie is hard to beat. Sweet and savory on the menu. **$**

### La Yunta
Portal de Carnes 214
Tel: (084) 235 103
Great juices, salads, and pizzas. **$**

**RIGHT:** fine dining in an upmarket restaurant.

Recommended Restaurants and Cafés on page 289

# THE SACRED VALLEY

The heartland of the last Incas, the Sacred Valley is home
to the awe-inspiring fortresses of Sacsayhuamán and
Ollantaytambo, and the colorful Sunday market at Pisac

Lima

**Main attractions**
SACSAYHUAMÁN
QENKO
TAMBO MACHAY
CHINCHERO
PISAC MARKET
URUBAMBA
OLLANTAYTAMBO

**LEFT:** view along
the Sacred Valley.
**BELOW:** market day
in Pisac.

efore visiting Sacsayhuamán, the best-known of the ruins outside Cusco, and continuing to Pisac and the Sacred Valley, try going east of Cusco toward Urcos – there are frequent buses which leave from near the Puno railway station. **Pikillacta** ⓰, some 30 km (18 miles) from Cusco, pre-dates the Incas: it is a large, unrestored Wari (or Huari) ruin, probably constructed early in the 12th century, with rough stone walls more than 3 meters (10 ft) high. About 1 km (⅔ mile) farther on is **Rumicolca**, the Inca gateway to the Cusco valley. In order to control access to the city, the Incas built, on Wari foundations, a wall of stone at the point where the valley narrows.

About 8 km (5 miles) farther on is **Andahuaylillas** ⓱, a little village with some interesting colonial houses and a 17th-century Jesuit church, extraordinarily ornate for such a small backwater, which contains some particularly fine murals. Opening hours vary but it is usually possible to find someone with a key to let you in. **Huaro**, a little farther on, is another tiny village whose church has some marvelous 17th-century murals.

## Sacsayhuamán

After this detour, it's time to explore the Inca ruins closest to Cusco. You can walk or take a bus from the city to the first four sites, or you could use Pisac as a base. All Sacred Valley sites are open daily 7am–6pm. The overwhelming fortress of **Sacsayhuamán** ⓲ is a bold demonstration of ancient construction skills. Made of massive stones weighing up to 17,000 kg (125 tons), this military complex overlooking Cusco has a double wall in a zigzag shape – some say to imitate the teeth of the puma figure whose head the fort may have formed. Others say it represents the god of lightning. The fort also once had at least three fabulously huge towers, and a labyrinth of rooms large enough for a garrison of 5,000 Inca soldiers. It marks the birthplace of the river that runs under Cusco, channeled through stone conduits cut to give the city an invisible water supply.

*The Inca fortress of Sacsayhuamán, the scene of bloody battles between the Incas and the Spanish.*

sands of workers labored on this massive structure for up to seven decades, hauling the immense stone blocks that make up its double outside walls, and erecting the nearly indestructible buildings that transformed the complex into one of the most wondrous in all the empire. Although the outer walls remain intact, the buildings in the complex have been destroyed – in part to provide building stones for many of the structures in Cusco. Even so, visitors to the fortress can still see the so-called **Inca's Throne** from which it is said that parading troops were reviewed.

This is one of the area's most spectacular spots at which to take dawn photos, and, like much of Cusco, it provides a startling contrast of Indian and Christian cultures. Beside this complex, built during the reign of Inca Pachacutec, is a giant white statue of Christ donated to the city in 1944 by grateful Palestinian refugees, his arms outstretched over Cusco in the valley below. It's a good place for a picnic lunch, too: perched on almost any stone you'll have an amazing view of the red-tiled roofs of Cusco and the lush fields of the surrounding valley. The gaily decorated llamas wandering

Sacsayhuamán was the focus of the Great Rebellion led by Manco Inca against the Spanish in 1536. From here, the Incas besieged Cusco for 10 months. Historians say that if Manco Inca had defeated the Spanish in Cusco, he might have saved the empire. But, no matter how valiantly his troops fought and died, the Spanish eventually wrested back control of the fort, of the old Inca capital of Cusco, and ultimately of all Peru.

Archeologists estimate that tens of thou-

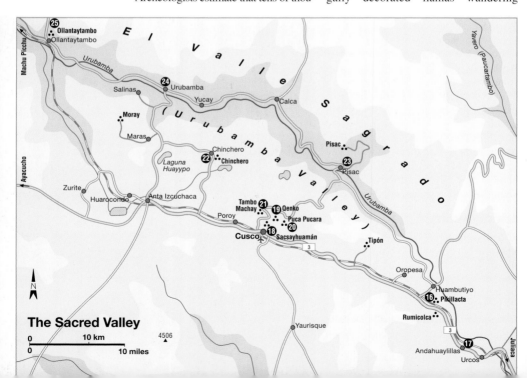

**The Sacred Valley**

0          10 km

0          10 miles

Recommended Restaurants and Cafés on page 289

through the ruins are smelly but harmless, and the giggling children tending them will almost certainly ask you to take a photograph – be sure to give them a tip.

In response to claims by Peruvian archeologists and Inca scholars who said that Sacsayhuamán was in danger from the 100,000 tourists and Peruvians who annually attend the colorful *Inti Raymi* festival *(see page 279)* to celebrate the winter solstice, the celebrations were moved to the esplanade facing the great walls. The move has satisfied conservationists and those who insist that Cusco's largest celebration each year must be held in the Inca stronghold.

## Qenko and Puca Pucara

Some 7 km (4 miles) from Sacsayhuamán is **Qenko** ⓙ, an Inca shrine with a circular amphitheater and a 5-meter (18-ft) stone block that is said to represent a puma. Its name means "zigzag," and this ceremonial center – dedicated to the worship of Mother Earth (Pacha Mama) – includes water canals cut into solid rock, and a subterranean room. Unlike Sacsayhuamán, which is a complex made up of huge stone blocks transported to the spot

and assembled there, Quenko was carved from a huge limestone formation found at the site. Into its walls were carved typical Inca-style niches and alcoves used to display gold and holy items in pre-Hispanic times. The shrine also contains drawings etched laboriously into its stone, among them a puma, a condor, and a llama.

Farther along the road to Pisac is a smaller fortress, **Puca Pucara** ⓴, believed to have guarded the road to the Sacred Valley of the Incas. Like Machu Picchu, this pink stone complex has hillside terraces, stairways, tunnels, and towers. To the north is **Tambo Machay** ㉑, the sacred bathing place for the Inca rulers and the royal women. A hydraulic engineering marvel, its aqueduct system still feeds crystalline water into a series of showers where once water rituals were held by worshipers of the sun. The ruins now consist of three massive walls of Inca stonework tucked into a hillside. There are Peruvian historians who say that this was used by Inca Tupac Yupanqui as a hunting lodge, in addition to being a shrine. Some claim that it was where Pachacutec received a prophetic vision of the Incas as conquerors. Others

*In 2007, archeologists discovered an ancient temple near Sacsayhuamán. Its irrigation systems bear the hallmarks of the Ayarmarca people who inhabited the region from 900 to 1,200 AD, but it is thought that the temple was later used and modified by the Incas.*

**LEFT:** hanging out at the Pisac ruins.
**BELOW:** the church at Andahuaylillas.

**TIP**

Many of the Sacred Valley ruins, including Sacsayhuaman, Pisac, and Ollantaytambo, are covered by the Cusco Visitor Ticket *(see page 274)* which can be purchased in Cusco.

**BELOW:** fresh produce at Pisac market. **RIGHT:** the steep slopes of the Sacred Valley.

say that the water running through the aqueduct came from a holy spring, and this may have been one of the rare spots where sacrifices of children were made.

## Market village

**Chinchero** ㉒ is an attractive village with Inca ruins, which can be visited by bus from Cusco. It has a lively market on Tuesday, Thursday, and Sunday – the last being the best day to go. It is said that Chinchero was one of the favorite spots of Inca Tupac Yupanqui, who built a palace and had agricultural terraces cultivated here at the mouth of the Río Vilcanota. Other historians say it was an important population center in Inca times and that Tupac Inca, the son of Pachacutec, had an estate here. If the Inca royalty were lured to Chinchero, it might have been by the view of snow-capped mountains and the river below. If you are here for the Sunday market, you will notice that local people use it as an opportunity to socialize as much as to buy goods. This "town of the rainbow," as it was known in pre-Hispanic days, has kept many of its ancient customs, and its inhabitants still live in a traditional way.

## Pisac

**Pisac** ㉓ makes a good base for exploring the Sacred Valley. The valley is a delightful place: the climate is pleasant, the people are agreeable, the agricultural terracing is a marvel, and there are a number of welcoming little *hostales* in which to spend the night. Pisac is a friendly village known for its good fishing, busy Sunday market, and the ruins above the town; and it lies about 32 km (20 miles) from Cusco on a curving but decent road. There is a road up to the ruins, and you can sometimes get a ride in a taxi, but otherwise you can climb there past the mountainside terraces (local children will serve as guides for a small fee) or hire a horse from beside the village church. At this high altitude, even the fittest travelers find themselves winded and their hearts pounding, so they are grateful when they round the bend on an isolated trail to find themselves face to face with one of the many Inca Kola vendors at the site.

Steep terraces and dramatic architecture mark this one-time fortress city, whose many features include ritual baths fed by aqueducts and one of the largest

known Inca cemeteries. The stones making up Pisac's buildings are smaller than those at Sacsayhuamán, but the precision with which they are cut is amazing.

In fact, in some respects the stone-masonry is more awesome than that of the more famous ruins at Machu Picchu. There are residential buildings and towers that some scientists say may have been astronomical observation spots. Higher up, there is a second set of ruins. Owing to the style – smaller stones more haphazardly arranged – a number of theories have arisen to explain the origin of this section. Some say that it was used by servants or other community members with low social standing; another, less likely theory is that it pre-dates the main part of the complex.

Pisac's **Sunday market** is a riotous affair in a town where the people work hard and – apparently – play hard. The beer tent is the favorite haunt of the motley brass band that adds an increasingly out-of-tune touch to the town's festivities. Sometimes it seems that the beer tent is the favorite stop for most of the other villagers, too. For that reason, the later in the day visitors arrive, the better their chances for some congenial bargaining for the fine alpaca blankets and sweaters available. There is a less touristy market held on Tuesday and Thursday.

## Urubamba

From Pisac, follow the road and the river about 40 km (25 miles) through the picturesque village of Yucay to **Urubamba** ㉔, which lies at the center of the valley. In recent years this has become a popular place to stay. The weather is milder than in Cusco, it is closer to Machu Picchu, and it makes a good center for visiting other places of interest. There are a number of hotels, cheap and not so cheap, in Urubamba itself and scattered along the valley. Urubamba is a bustling place with a strong Indian flavor. The coat-of-arms on the City Hall is sufficient evidence of this; no Spanish symbols are found in the emblem, which bears pumas, snakes, and trees. It was the beauty and calm of this village in former times that prompted the

18th-century naturalist Antonio de León Pinelo to expound on his theory that Urubamba was the biblical Eden. From here you can make trips to the salt pans at **Salinas** and the circular Inca agricultural terracing at **Moray**. You can take a bus for the first part of the way, but after that it's a hike.

## Ollantaytambo

Continuing along the valley, you come to the great fortress of **Ollantaytambo** ㉕, a place of great sacred and military importance to the Incas. (For details about the story of Ollantay, Pachacutec's most famous general, *see page 269*.) Here, travelers find themselves facing an elegant and intricate walled complex containing seven rose-colored granite monoliths which puzzle scientists, who say that the stone is not mined in the valley. A steep stairway enters the group of buildings, among which the best-known is the so-called **Temple of the Sun** – an unfinished construction in front of a wall of enormous boulders. Portions of the original carvings on these huge worn stones can still be seen, although it is unclear if they really are pumas, as some claim. Specialists say

*Market trader wearing a traditional embroidered skirt at the Pisac market.*

## Too Much Tourism?

Cusco, the Sacred Valley, and Machu Picchu see more tourists than any other part of Peru. While people have certainly benefited greatly from tourism, the rise in tourist numbers has its downsides, too. Huge numbers of tourists means a huge demand for resources such as water, and there has been a surge in road traffic. Thousands of feet walk on the Sacred Valley ruins each day, and Machu Picchu itself is considered one of the most endangered Unesco World Heritage Sites. In this part of Peru, village children beg for sweets from tourists, pickpockets are rife, and Peruvians, normally so friendly and helpful, can tend towards abruptly rude.

At its worst, tourism here can feel exploitative for both sides of the equation, a trend that could be disastrous for a region that depends so heavily on the tourist dollar. You can help by picking your guides and tours carefully, patronising grassroots tourist operators, and those that give something back. Lastly, be friendly, and you'll likely receive the same in return.

*The Princess's Bath
at Ollantaytambo.*

**BELOW:** the
imposing ruins of
Ollantaytambo.

that the unfinished condition of the temple has less to do with the Spanish destruction of Ollantaytambo than with the fact that it was simply never completed.

Ollantaytambo, strategically placed at the northern end of the Sacred Valley, also has plazas with sacred niches, shrines, an area of stone stocks where prisoners were tied by their hands, and ritual shower areas, including the **Princess's Bath**, or Baño de la Ñusta.

The village's military fortification was so well planned that it took the Spanish by surprise when they arrived in search of Manco Inca during the 1536 uprising. Hernando Pizarro (a brother of Francisco) led a contingent of about 100 Spaniards and a number of local Indians to the fort with the intention of capturing and executing the rebel leader. Chronicles say that as the Spaniards sneaked up to the fort just before dawn, they looked up to see the silhouettes of Inca warriors ready to take them on. It is even said they saw Manco Inca himself, directing troops from inside the Ollantaytambo complex, mounted on a captured horse. In fact, Manco Inca's men had diverted the Patacancha River through some canals, and

now they opened barriers that allowed the water to flood the plain that the Europeans were crossing. However, the Spaniards managed to escape to Cusco, where they recruited a force of 300 cavalrymen to return and confront Manco Inca. Outnumbered, he abandoned the walled city and fled to Vilcabamba, where he was killed.

Ollantaytambo is perhaps the best preserved of all the Inca settlements. The old walls of the houses are still standing, and water still runs through original channels in narrow streets that are believed to date from the 15th century. In the nearby river stand the remains of an Inca bridge, and *campesinos* around the settlement live in houses that have changed very little since Pizarro's arrival. The CATCCO **Museum** has information about local history, culture, and architecture (open daily 9am–7pm; entrance fee).

After exploring the Sacred Valley, most visitors hear for the **Inca Trail** and **Machu Picchu**. You can get a train from Ollantaytambo (either the tourist train or the local one), or take a train from Cusco and get off at Aguas Calientes (Machu Picchu Pueblo). Machu Picchu, of course, merits a chapter all to itself. ❑

# RESTAURANTS AND CAFÉS

## Restaurants

Prices are per person for a two-course meal, excluding wine:
**$** less than US$10
**$$** US$10–20
**$$$** more than US$20

### Ollantaytambo

#### Café Alcazar

Calle del Medio (Chaupi-calle) s/n
Tel: (084) 204 034
A small, laid-back café in the old Inca heart of Ollantaytambo. Serves vegetarian options, as well as meaty Peruvian staples and pasta dishes. Good fresh juices and excellent pisco sours. **$**

#### Il Capuccino

Calle Ventiderio s/n
Run by the people who own the Kusicoylloy restaurant, this pleasant café serves good coffee, great breakfasts, and tasty cakes and desserts. **$**

#### Kusicoylloy

Plaza Aracama s/n
Tel: (084) 204 114
This restaurant, right by the Ollantaytambo ruins, has a wide menu, featuring Peruvian and international dishes. There's great decor inside, making it just the place to hide away on a cold winter's evening. **$$**

#### Panaka Grill

Plaza de Armas s/n
Tel: (084) 204 047
Situated right on Ollantaytambo's pretty Plaza de Armas, this restaurant serves excellent meat grills and tasty oven-baked pizzas. **$$**

### Pisac

#### Mullu

Plaza Constitución s/n
Tel: (084) 203 033
Overlooking the plaza, this artsy, avant-garde café is just the place to hang out while sipping a refreshing juice or one of their excellent coffees. They also serve good light meals and snacks. **$**

### Urubamba

#### Casa Orihuela

Ctra Pisac–Ollantaytambo, Km 64
Tel: (084) 226 241
Located at the Hacienda Huayoccari, this is a great place to stop on the journey between Pisac and Ollantaytambo. The menu features good Peruvian staples and the restaurant has a lovely countryside atmosphere. **$**

#### El Huacatay

Jr. Arica 620
Tel: (084) 201 790/ 967 6876
A quiet and appealing place with a garden for outdoor dining on mild evenings. The chef makes excellent food – a fusion of Mediterranean and Asian cuisine – cooked with the best local ingredients. **$$**

#### Killa Wasi

Hotel Sol y Luna, Calle Huincho s/n
Tel: (084) 201 621
The fabulous poolside restaurant under terracotta tiles at this smart country hotel just ½ mile outside Urubamba is open to the public. Its varied menu features *novo andino* specialties such as curried alpaca and fried yucca, as well as tasty chicken, trout, and seafood dishes. **$$$**

#### Picantería La Chepita

Av. 1 Mayo 6, Pintacha
Tel: (084) 201 387
This small, simple place serves great food. *Picanterías* are known for their spicy food, and this is without doubt the best one in town. **$**

**RIGHT:** roast alpaca meat, which is considered a delicacy in Peru.

# MACHU PICCHU

Hidden from the world until 1911, this Inca refuge
in the mountains is breathtaking in every sense.
Trekkers can choose the hard way up, via
the Inca Trail; others may opt for the train

**O**f all the popular treks in South America, the three- to five-day Inca Trail is the one that most travelers want to do. The adventure begins with a four-hour train ride along the Río Urubamba, a region known to the Incas as the Sacred Valley. Legions of early-rising *campesinos*, loading and unloading their marketable goods at every station along the way, crowd together in what begins to look more like a cattle car than a passenger train. At Qorihuayrachina, **Kilometer 88**, the hikers' trail begins. It is no longer possible to walk the Inca Trail independently; you must pre-arrange the trip either at home or in Cusco. (If you want to avoid several days of arduous trekking, the train leaving from Cusco also stops at Chalcabamba, **Kilometer 104**, 8 km/5 miles from the lost city, and you can get off there, but you will miss out on some stunning scenery.)

The first 11 km (7 miles) meander through easy terrain of dusty scrub bushes, low-lying hills, and a few rustic huts. Conserve your strength on this stretch, because it will soon get tougher. The first barrier is the **Warmiwañusqu pass**. Beyond lies a wealth of Inca ruins, but struggling to the top of this 4,000-meter (13,000-ft) pass is no small challenge. Laboring up the seemingly endless trail, the hiker soon identifies with its name. In English it translates literally as "Dead Woman's" pass.

From here, Inca history begins to unfold. The small guard-post of **Runkuraqay**, overlooking the valley and often shrouded in mist in the morning, is the first

reward offered by the Inca Trail. Farther along, the more elaborately constructed site of **Sayajmarka** (Dominant Town) perches atop a narrow cliff. The fine stonework for which the Incas were justly famous is apparent here. Snaking along the valley below is an incredible "paved highway" made of neatly fitted stone, masterfully constructed by a culture the Spanish conquistadors considered uncivilized.

## Stunning ruins

As the trek progresses, the archeological sites become more stunning and complex.

**Main attractions**
PUYAPATAMARKA
HUIÑAY HUAYNA
INTIPUNKU
MACHU PICCHU
HUAYNA PICCHU

**PRECEDING PAGES:**
the lost city of the
Incas.
**LEFT:** Intihuatana.
**BELOW:**
Chachabamba.

**TIP**

Due to concern over erosion of the Inca Trail, the Peruvian government decided to limit the numbers of trekkers to 500 per day. Visitors must hike with an organized tour and it is vital to book ahead in high season (June–August).

**Puyapatamarka** (Cloud-Level Town) is fascinating for its circular walls and the finely engineered aqueduct system, which still provides spring water to the ancient ceremonial baths. Below, the trail offers yet another delight to the trekker.

Huge steps, a virtual stone stairway almost half a mile in length, lead down into high jungle vegetation where wild orchids and other exotic flowers bloom. Curiously, this section of the trail lay undiscovered until 1984. Until then, a modern footpath connected this interrupted section of the Inca highway.

Tenaciously clinging to the side of a steep ravine is the last set of ruins, and the most stunning. **Huiñay Huayna** presents an unbelievable picture when first seen in the distance. The ability of the Incas to construct something so complex in an area so vertical defies comprehension, yet the series of ritual baths, long stretches of terracing, and intricate stonework certainly prove what would appear to be impossible.

About two hours away lies the jewel in the crown – **Machu Picchu**. From the high pass of **Intipunku**, the Sun Gate, you get the first glimpse of the fabled city. This is the culmination of days of walking; the immersion into an ancient culture is complete. Arriving as the Incas did centuries ago, the trekker begins the final descent into Machu Picchu, sharing a path with history.

## Discovering the ruins

When Hiram Bingham and his party discovered **Machu Picchu** ㉖ in July 1911, Bingham was actually searching for the ruins of Vilcabamba, the remote stronghold of the last Incas. Today we know that he had almost certainly found Vilcabamba, without realizing it, when he stumbled across the jungle-covered ruins of Espíritu Pampa, some 100 km (60 miles) west of Machu Picchu, two months before making his spectacular find on the Urubamba gorge. But Bingham saw only a small section of Espíritu Pampa, and dismissed it as insignificant. It was left to Gene Savoy, another American explorer, to investigate Espíritu Pampa when he came looking for the lost city of the Incas more than 50 years later (see page 55).

Bingham was a Yale graduate, later a US senator, who became fascinated with Inca archeology in 1909 while in Peru studying Simón de Bolívar's independence struggle. He returned with the Yale Peruvian expedition in 1911, and took the narrow mule trail down the Urubamba gorge in July of that year. Melchor Arteaga, a local *campesino* whom he met by chance while camping on the river banks, led him to the jungle-covered ruins.

Machu Picchu – Ancient Peak – was what the local people called the mountain above the saddle-ridge where the ruins were located, and its sister mountain was Huayna Picchu – Young Peak. Not only did Bingham want to call these ruins Vilcabamba, because he believed he had discovered Manco Capac's gilded city, but he also speculated that the mountain refuge was Tampu Tocco, the mythical birthplace of the Ayar brothers, the first of the Incas.

Bingham's mistake in thinking that he had found the location of Vilcabamba is

**BELOW:** a waterfall on the Inca Trail.

understandable. Who would have imagined that there were not one, but two,
lost cities in the jungle north of Cusco?
But overwhelming evidence against the
Machu-Picchu-as-Vilcabamba hypothesis emerged, and Bingham was presented with an enigma: if Machu Picchu
was not the last refuge of the Incas, then
what on earth was it?

## Outpost in a lost province

Bingham carried out further explorations
between 1911 and 1915, discovering a
string of other ruins and a major Inca
highway (now known as the Inca Trail)
to the south of Machu Picchu. Later still,
in 1941, the Viking Fund expedition led
by Paul Fejos discovered the important
ruins of Huiñay Huayna above the
Urubamba gorge, about 4.5 km (3 miles)
due south of Machu Picchu. This proved
that Machu Picchu was not merely a lost
city, but part of an entire lost region – a
fact generally ignored by popular histo-
ries. The usual account portrays Machu
Picchu as a secret refuge known only to a
select few, and concealed from the
Spaniards. But this would have been
impossible; the location of an entire active

and populated region could not have been
concealed from the Spaniards, who had
many allies among the Indian peoples.

And yet the Spaniards did not
know of Machu Picchu's existence. The only possible conclusion is that the Incas and Indians
at the time of the conquest did not
know of it either. Somehow the
city and its region were abandoned
and depopulated before the conquistadors arrived, and the memory was lost even to the Incas themselves.
Perhaps the area was devastated by
plague, or overrun by the Antis, the hostile jungle tribesmen. But why would
there be total amnesia about its location?
This cannot have been accidental. The
Incas had a caste of *quipucamayocs* – oral
history recorders – who kept detailed
accounts of the Inca past, but this was
official history, and the Incas were notorious for wiping inconvenient details off
the record. Perhaps this was Machu Picchu's fate: a province that rebelled and
was dealt with so ruthlessly that its existence was erased from official memory.

That is merely one theory that fits the
known facts. Here is another: according

*The lone hut above
Machu Picchu offers
a spectacular view of
the ruins.*

**BELOW:** Huiñay
Huayna.

*A porter on the Inca Trail looking across at the Cordillera Vilcabamba.*

**BELOW:** the ruins of Choquesuysuy, near Machu Picchu.

to new evidence unearthed from Spanish colonial archives, and recently presented by the archeologist J.H. Rowe, there was a "royal estate" (a rather Western concept, but the most intelligible way to put it) of the Inca Pachacutec at a place called "Picchu," north of Cusco. This leads to an interpretation that Machu Picchu was built and populated by the *panaca* (royal house) of Pachacutec, and that the eventual disappearance of the *panaca*, a generation or so after the ninth Inca's death, led to the depopulation and abandonment of the whole region.

Signs of a pre-Inca occupation at Machu Picchu, going back 2,000 years, have recently been discovered, but there was certainly no pre-Inca city of any consequence here. If we accept that Machu Picchu was built for Pachacutec, we can speak of the construction dates of Machu Picchu with reasonable confidence. According to a widely accepted chronology, the Inca expansion began in the year 1438, after Pachacutec had defeated the Chanca invasion from the north. Various chronicles tell us that for strategic reasons (mainly to keep the retreating Chancas out) this mountain-

ous area was the first to be settled in the headlong rush toward empire.

The building style of Machu Picchu is "late imperial Inca," which supports this thesis, and there are no signs of post-conquest occupation. So the whole settlement was built, occupied, and abandoned in the space of less than 100 years. The rest is speculation. And who can resist speculating when faced with something as affecting and impenetrable as the mystery of these silent stones?

## Piecing together the past

What kind of settlement was Machu Picchu? John Hemming, author of *The Conquest of the Incas* – probably the best book on the subject – states that the site has only 200 habitation structures, leading him to estimate a permanent population of about 1,000 people. It is interesting that the agricultural output of the area would have greatly exceeded the needs of the population, for, beside the large extension of agricultural terracing at Machu Picchu itself, there were also much larger terraced areas at Inti Pata (just behind Machu Picchu peak to the southwest), and Huiñay Huayna, along the Inca Trail. More than one archeologist has proposed that the principal material function of the Machu Picchu region was to create a reliable supply of coca leaves for the priests and royals of Cusco.

Hiram Bingham called the ruin a "citadel," existing for strategic and defensive purposes. But beside its outer walls and moat, Machu Picchu contains an unusually high proportion and quality of religious architecture. Modern opinion leans more to the view that Machu Picchu was essentially a site of spiritual and ceremonial significance, with important agricultural functions. Its strategic purposes, if any, were secondary.

Bingham's fortress idea did not prevent him from speculating that the city was a refuge of Cusco's Virgins of the Sun, an idea inspired by the revelation that more than 75 percent of the skeletal remains found there were female. This exciting piece of news has been on the lips of tour guides ever since. Yet there is one

difficulty with this hypothesis: the Yale expedition found only skulls, the other bones having disintegrated in the humid climate. It is hard to pronounce on the gender of a skull, particularly if, like the expedition's medical authority Dr Eaton, you are not very familiar with bones of the racial sub-group it comes from. Dr Eaton pronounced most of the skulls "gracile," and therefore, he assumed, female. But they could as easily have been young men, or men of small stature. The skulls still exist, and could be studied again by modern experts, but so far no one has done so.

It is alleged that the terms of Bingham's permission to excavate at the site of Machu Picchu were unclear. This led to vague accusations of smuggling after he shipped all the relics back to Yale University. In late 2007, following negotiations with the Peruvian government, Yale finally agreed to return the majority of the artifacts to Peru. A new museum is planned in Cusco to house them.

## New discoveries

Since 1985 an astonishing number of new discoveries have been made around Machu Picchu. Taken as a whole they support and expand the emerging view of Machu Picchu as the ceremonial and possibly administrative center of a huge and quite populous region. The alluring myth of Machu Picchu as some kind of Andean Shangri-la perched alone on its remote crag must now be laid to rest.

The most extensive finds have been made across the river to the northeast, on a sloping plateau known as Mandorpampa about 100 meters (330 ft) above the railroad. Its outstanding feature is an enormous wall about 3.5 meters high by 2.5 meters wide (11½ by 8¼ ft), and more than a kilometer long, which runs straight up the mountainside toward a pointed peak known as Yanantin. It was apparently built to protect the adjacent agricultural terraces from erosion, and may also have served to demarcate two areas with separate functions.

A road running along its top heads off northeast into densely forested mountains toward Amaybamba, or perhaps some other Inca settlement as yet undiscovered. Other finds on the *pampa* include quarries, circular buildings, a large number of stone mortars, and a big observation platform.

**TIP**

Tickets for Machu Picchu can be bought in Aguas Calientes or at the ruins themselves. The bus fare is separate and can be bought at the counter by the bus stop in Aguas Calientes immediately before you board.

**LEFT:** camping on the Inca Trail.

## Riding the Rails to Machu Picchu

Unless you walk the Inca Trail, your journey to Machu Picchu will be by train, and there are various ways to do this, depending on your budget. PeruRail runs efficient daily services from Wanchac train station on Av. Pachacutec in Cusco. Buy your ticket at the station a few days beforehand, if possible, as services usually fill up. You'll need to show your passport.

If you're keen to see Machu Picchu in the early morning mist, the first services are the 6am and 6.15am Vistadome trains, which offer spectacular views, and the Backpacker service which leaves at 7am. You can also board these services at Ollantaytambo. For truly five-star travel, take the Hiram Bingham from Poroy station, just outside Cusco, at 9am. With elegant meals, top-notch guiding, and live entertainment on the return journey, this Pullman-style experience is worth the extra cost. Once passengers from all trains arrive in Aguas Calientes, buses whisk them up the switchback to the ruins. For all enquiries about trains to Machu Picchu, contact PeruRail in Cusco on 084-238 722 or see www.perurail.com.

Closer to Machu Picchu itself, the sector on the north slope of Huayna Picchu, which is known as the "Temple of the Moon," has been cleared to reveal a subterranean temple, a fine wall with an imposing gateway, and an observatory directed toward the Yanantin peak.

Farther upriver, two important burial sites known as Killipata and Ch'askapata have been discovered, and the ruins of Choquesuysuy, just upstream from where the hydroelectric power station used to stand, now appear to be much larger than had been previously believed. Of all these sites only the Temple of the Moon has been opened to the public so far.

In the years following Bingham's discovery the ruins were cleared of vegetation, excavations were made, and later a railroad was blasted out of the sheer granite cliffs of the imposing canyon. Visitors began to arrive. Pablo Neruda came in 1942, and was inspired to write his most famous poem, *The Heights of Machu Picchu*. In 1948 a sinuous 12-km (7-mile) road from the river banks to the ruins was inaugurated by Hiram Bingham himself.

## A walking tour of the ruins

To understand the ruins best, you can hire one of the certified multilingual guides who offer their services at the entrance to the ruins. Otherwise, use this walking tour as an interpretive aid. Bingham classified the ruins into sectors, naming some of the buildings. But some of his conclusions appear wide of the mark to modern archeologists; others seem too arbitrary, resting on minimal evidence. However, for the sake of clear directions we need to name different sectors, and, since nobody has come up with a better system than Bingham's, we will use the following. Enter the ruins through the **House of the Terrace Caretakers Ⓐ**, which flanks the **Agricultural Sector Ⓑ**. This great area of terracing was undoubtedly for agricultural purposes, and may have made the city self-sufficient in crops. The terraces end in a **Dry Moat Ⓒ**, beyond which lies the city itself.

If you continue straight ahead you come to the **Fountains Ⓓ**, which are actually small waterfalls, in a chain of 16 little "baths," varying in the quality of their construction. These were probably for ritual, religious purposes relating

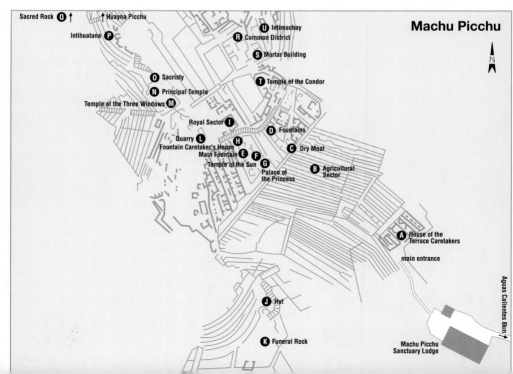

to the worship of water. Bingham speculated that Machu Picchu might have been abandoned because this water supply dried up, or became inadequate to irrigate the terraces. The hotel near the ruins consumes most of this spring water today. The **Main Fountain** ❺ is so called because it has the finest stonework and the most important location; it is just above you to the left as you arrive from the terraces.

Here, too, is the **Temple of the Sun** ❻. This round, tapering tower features the most perfect stonework to be found in Machu Picchu. It contains sacred niches for holding idols or offerings, and the centerpiece is a great rock, part of the actual outcrop on which the temple is built. The base of this rock forms a grotto that is casually referred to as the Royal Tomb, although no bones were found there.

Recent archeo-astronomical studies have demonstrated how this temple would have served as an astronomical observatory. The rock in the center of the tower has a straight edge cut into it. This is precisely aligned through the adjacent window to the rising point of the sun on the morning of the June solstice. The pegs on the outside of the window may have been used to support a shadow-casting device, which would have made observation simpler.

The temple's entrance doorway has holes drilled about the jamb, less complex than those on a similar doorway at the Coricancha in Cusco. The adjacent building has two stories and was obviously the house of someone important. Bingham named it the **Palace of the Princess** ❼.

Next to the Sun Temple, just above the main fountain, is a three-walled house, which has been restored and had its roof thatched as an example of how these structures looked in Inca times. It is usually called the **Fountain Caretaker's House** ❽ – but it is unlikely to have been a house at all, since it is open to the elements on one side. The thick stone pegs fixed high up in the wall are thought to have served as hangers for heavy objects.

Students of the more esoteric aspects of the Inca culture have suggested that this complex of adjacent structures forms a temple to the four elements: the Temple of the Sun (Fire), the "Royal Tomb" (Earth), the open-fronted Foun-

**TIP**

The site opens at 6am, and this is a wonderful time to visit, when the ruins are bathed in the early light. You can enter until 3pm, but you must leave the site by 5pm.

**BELOW:** the Temple of the Sun.

tain Caretaker's House (Air), and the Principal Fountain (Water).

The structures directly opposite the Sun Temple, across the staircase, have been classified as the **Royal Sector ❶** because of the roominess of the buildings, and also for the huge rock lintels (weighing up to 3,050 kg or 3 tons) that in Inca architecture generally characterized the homes of the mighty.

At the top of the agricultural terraces, standing high above the city, is a lone **hut ❶**, which is a great place for an overall view of the ruins. It backs onto a gently sloping area known as the cemetery, because Bingham discovered numerous bones and mummies at this spot. Just a few meters from the hut lies a curiously shaped carved rock, called the **Funeral Rock ❶**. Bingham speculated that this had been used as a place of lying-in-state for the dead, or as a kind of mortician's slab, on which bodies were eviscerated and then left to be dried by the sun for mummification.

## Mysterious stone

At the top of the staircase leading up from the fountains you come to a great jumble of **rocks ❶** that served as a quarry for the Inca masons. There is a fascinating discovery in this sector – a partially split rock that seems to show precisely how the builders cut stone from the quarry. The rock bears a line of wedge-shaped cuts where tools were hammered in to form a crack. The problem with this rock, though, is that it was reportedly cut by a 20th-century archeologist, Dr Manuel Chávez Ballón.

Follow the ridge away from the quarry with your back to the staircase, and you come to one of the most interesting areas of the city. Here is the **Temple of the Three Windows ❶**. Its east wall is built on a single huge rock; the trapezoidal windows are partly cut into it. On the empty side of this three-walled building stands a stone pillar that once supported the roof. On the ground by this pillar is a rock bearing the sacred step-motif common to many other Inca and pre-Inca temples.

Next to this site stands the **Principal Temple ❶**, another three-walled building with immense foundation rocks and artfully cut masonry. It is named for its size and quality, and also because it is the only temple with a kind of sub-temple attached to it. This is generally called the **Sacristy ❶**, because it seems a suitable place for the priests to have prepared themselves before sacred rites. The stone that forms part of the lefthand door-jamb has 32 corners in its separate faces.

Ascending the mound beyond this temple leads you to what was probably the most important of all the many shrines at Machu Picchu, the **Intihuatana ❶**, the so-called "Hitching Post of the Sun." This term was popularized by the American traveler Ephraim Squier in the 19th century, but nobody has ever unraveled the mystery of how this stone and others like it were used. Every major Inca center had one. It seems likely that the stones somehow served for making astronomical observations and calculating the passing seasons. There was at least one other "Intihuatana" in the vicinity, located near the site of the old hydroelectric power station in the valley below, to the west. The second stone was

The Salcantay to Santa Teresa trek *(see pages 123–4)* is a good alternative to the "classic" Inca Trail which is often fully booked.

**TIP**

**BELOW:** looking down on Machu Picchu.

probably situated to make a specific astronomical alignment with the main one. The main Intihuatana is a sculpture of surpassing beauty. It is the only one in all Peru to have escaped the diligent attention of the Spanish "extirpators of idolatry," and luckily has survived in its original condition.

The group of buildings across the large grassy plaza below forms another, more utilitarian sector of the city. At the north end, farthest from the entrance to the ruins, you find two three-sided buildings opening onto a small plaza, which is backed by a huge rock generally called the **Sacred Rock Q**. An intriguing aspect of this plaza is that the outline of the great flat rock erected at the northeast edge is shaped to form a visual tracing of the mountain skyline behind it. Then, if you step behind the *masma* (three-sided hut) on the southeast edge and look northwest, you find another rock that echoes in the same way the skyline of the small outcrop named **Uña Huayna Picchu**. In 2000, an enormous scandal broke out in Peru after a lighting crane being used during the filming of a commercial fell and broke part of

the sacred stone. Since then, all visitors must visit the site with an official guide.

Walking back toward the main entrance along the east flank of the ridge, you pass through a large district of cruder constructions that has been labeled the **Common District R**. At the end of this sector you reach a building with two curious disk-shapes **S** cut into the stone of the floor. Each is about 30 cm (1 ft) in diameter, flat, with a low rim carved around the edge. Bingham thought these were mortars for grinding corn, but this is doubtful. True, he did find some pestle stones in the same building, but the normal mortar used by the Quechua people today is much deeper and more rounded within; also it is portable, not fixed in one spot. These "mortars" would not have served well for that function. However, nobody has suggested a more plausible explanation for these enigmatic cavities.

Just across the next staircase you come to a deep hollow, surrounded by walls and niches, which is known as the **Temple of the Condor T**. Bingham called this the Prison Group, because there are vaults below ground, and man-size niches with holes that might have been

*Visitors climbing the steps towards the Sacred Rock.*

**BELOW:** guided tour of the ruins.

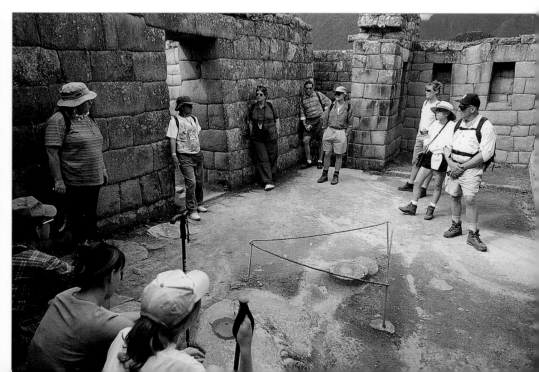

*The main street in Aguas Calientes.*

used for binding wrists. But the concept of "prison" probably did not exist in Inca society; punishments tended to involve loss of privileges, or physical suffering, or death. Some early Spaniards reported pits full of snakes or pumas into which offenders were dropped to see if they would survive, but that is hardly a prison. The complex was probably a temple. A rock at the bottom of this hollow bears a stylized carving, apparently a condor, with the shape of the head and the ruff at the neck clearly discernible.

There is a small cave known as **Intimachay** ⓤ above and to the east of the Condor Temple, which has been identified as a solar observatory for marking the December solstice. The cave is faced with coursed masonry and features a window carved out of a boulder that forms part of the front wall. This window is precisely aligned with the winter solstice sunrise, so that morning light falls on the back wall of the cave for 10 days before and after that date.

## Three walks

**BELOW:**
a resident llama.

If you arrived at Machu Picchu via Aguas Calientes rather than by the Inca Trail, there are three walks that are worth attempting. First, above the ruins to the southeast you can see a pass scooped out of the ridge, with a small ruin at the center. This is **Intipunku**, the Sun Gate. You can actually see the sun rise in this gateway from the western heights of the ruins at certain times of year. The trail traversing the mountainside from this point was the main Inca highway from Huiñay Huayna and other sites farther south. It is well preserved, and makes for a fairly easy climb, taking about an hour and a half there and back. The view of Machu Picchu from Intipunku is magnificent.

The second walk is to the **Inca Drawbridge**. A trail winds back from the heights of the ruins, by the cemetery, leading along the west flank of the mountain behind Machu Picchu. This trail grows narrower until it is cut into the side of a sheer precipice, and you find yourself taking each step with care. Follow it until you come to a spot so abrupt that the ancients had to build a huge stone buttress to create a ledge for the path to cross. They left a strategic gap in the middle of the buttress, bridged by

logs which could be withdrawn. Beyond this point the trail quickly peters out, becoming unstable and extremely dangerous. The path has been fenced off shortly before the bridge, ever since one walker tried to hike beyond it and fell to his death. To the bridge and back is an exciting one-hour walk demanding a cool head for heights.

Hardy visitors also like to climb **Huayna Picchu**, the towering granite peak that overlooks Machu Picchu from the north. It is the original Inca path, very steep, and stepped in places. Approach it with caution – but don't be put off by the peak's fearsome appearance. You don't have to be a mountaineer. If you are reasonably active and healthy you will get to the top – and back. Everyone planning to climb Huayna Picchu must sign in at the control point along the trail leaving the principal ruins.

As you near the top of Huayna Picchu you pass through ancient terraces so inaccessible and so narrow that their value for agricultural purposes would have been negligible. It is thought that they were probably ornamental gardens, to be admired from the city

below. About an hour and a half gets the average person to the peak for a stupendous view.

The **Temple of the Moon** stands inside a cavern halfway down the north face of Huayna Picchu. It was discovered in 1936 and contains some of the finest stonework of the entire Machu Picchu complex. The Inca pathway that leads to the temple forks off the main trail to the left about one third of the way up to the peak of Huayna Picchu.

## Huiñay Huayna

Physically active people staying overnight at Machu Picchu can also take the **Inca Trail** to **Huiñay Huayna** *(see page 294)*. The round-trip takes about four hours, including some time to look at the ruins. Note that the Inca Trail fee, minus the entrance fee to Machu Picchu, is charged for this hike.

The journey itself is rewarding, since the trail passes through exotic tropical forest, and is well worth the effort. It is also possible to spend the night at the basic hostel at Huiñay Huayna, and return to Machu Picchu the following morning. ❑

**TIP**

The climb to Huayna Picchu is a great way to see the famous ruins from a different angle. Take plenty of water as there are hundreds of steps to climb. Admission is from 7am to 1pm, or until 400 people have passed through the control post, so arrive early.

**LEFT:** the entrance to Huayna Picchu.
**BELOW:** hot springs in Aguas Calientes.

# LAKE TITICACA

The highest navigable lake in the world
is the legendary birthplace of the first Inca and
the site of some fascinating island communities

Lima

**L**ake Titicaca is the world's highest navigable lake and the center of a region where thousands of subsistence farmers eke out a living fishing in its icy waters, growing potatoes in the rocky land at its edge, or herding llama and alpaca at altitudes that leave Europeans and North Americans gasping for air. It is also where traces of the rich pre-Indian past still stubbornly cling, resisting in past centuries the Spanish conquistadors' aggressive campaign to erase Inca and pre-Inca cultures and, in recent times, the lure of modernization.

The turquoise-blue lake was the most sacred body of water in the Inca empire, and is now the natural separation between Peru and Bolivia; it has a surface area exceeding 8,000 sq km (3,100 sq miles), not counting its more than 30 islands. At 3,856 meters (12,725 ft) above sea level, it has two climates: chilly and rainy or chilly and dry. It gets cold in the evenings, dropping below freezing from June through August. During the day the sun is intense and sunburn is common, so take care.

## Birthplace of the Incas

According to legend, this lake gave birth to the Inca civilization. Before the Incas, the lake and its islands were holy places for the Aymara people, whose civilization was centered at Tiahuanaco, now a complex of ruins on the Bolivian side of Titicaca but once a revered temple site with advanced irrigation techniques. Geologically, Titicaca's origins are dis-

puted, although it was probably a glacial lake. Some scientists claim that it had a volcanic start; a century ago, it was popularly believed to be an immense mountain-top crater. There are a few diehards today who stick to the notion that the lake was part of a massive river system from the Pacific Ocean – but then, there are those who insist that the earth is flat.

Indian legend says the sun god had his children, Manco Capac and his sister-consort Mama Ocllo, spring from the freezing waters of the lake to found Cusco and the beginning of the Inca

**Main attractions**
PUNO CATHEDRAL
YAVARI STEAMSHIP
UROS ISLANDS
TAQUILE ISLAND
AMANTANÍ ISLAND
JULI

**PRECEDING PAGES:**
view over Lake
Titicaca.
**LEFT:** Candelaria
festival, Puno.
**BELOW:** navigating
Lake Titicaca.

*One of the elaborate flower carpets created for Puno's Virgen de la Candelaria festival.*

**BELOW:** a side street in Puno.

dynasty. Later, during the Spanish conquest, the lake allegedly became a secret repository for the empire's gold. Recent aquatic expeditions have found gold figurines and other items, most notably around the Islands of the Sun and Moon in Bolivia, but these were most probably thrown into the lake as ritual sacrifices.

In 1961, the oceanographer Jacques-Yves Cousteau used mini-submarines to explore the depths of the lake, but found no gold. What he did discover, to the amazement of the scientific world, was a 60-cm (24-in) tri-colored frog that apparently never surfaces. Visitors today find a region unlike anywhere else: a place of floating reed islands, ancient lifestyles, and crumbling churches, where women wear bowler hats and the men knit their own brightly colored headgear.

## Urban base

If you are approaching the area from Cusco you will probably take the train to Juliaca ㉗, although some tour groups travel in minibuses and there are plenty of good bus services for independent travelers. Be forewarned that flights from Cusco are sometimes discontinued for no apparent reason. Juliaca is a busy town, with the largest railway terminus in the country, a good airport, and plenty of places to eat, but not much else going for it except for a lively Sunday market.

## Capital of the Altiplano

From here you can continue by train or minibus to **Puno** ㉘, a commercial center settled as a Spanish community in 1668 by the Count of Lemos. During the colonial period it was one of the continent's richest cities because of its proximity to the Laykakota silver mines discovered by brothers Gaspar and José Salcedo in 1657. The mining boom drew 10,000 people to an area not far from what is now Puno. It also brought a bloody rivalry that ended only when the count ordered José Salcedo to be executed, and transferred Laykakota's residents to Puno.

At an altitude of 3,830 meters (12,630 ft), Puno is the capital of Peru's Altiplano

– the harsh highland region much better suited to roaming vicuñas and alpacas than to people. It is also Peru's folklore center, with a rich array of handicrafts, costumes, fiestas, legends, and, most importantly, more than 300 different ethnic dances. Among the latter, the most famous is the *Diablada* (Devil Dance), performed during the feast of the Virgen de la Candelaria during the first two weeks in February. Dancers compete fiercely to outdo one another in this dance, notable for its profusion of costly and grotesque masks. The origins of the dance have become lost over the centuries, but it is believed to have started with pre-Inca cultures, surviving through the Inca conquest and the Spanish takeover of the country, with the costumes being modified each time.

The lavish outfits the dancers wear are as varied as the dances themselves. They range from multi-hued *polleras* (layered skirts), worn by barefoot female dancers, to the short skirts, fringed shawls and bowler hats used in the highland version of the *marinera* dance *(see page 109)*. For centuries people living in the Altiplano were accustomed to

working hard, then celebrating their special days with gusto. Many of the dances incorporate features of the most repressive times, with dancers dressed as mine overseers or as cruel landowners – characters who are mocked during the festivities.

## Puno's sights

Little of Puno's colonial heritage is visible, but there remains a handful of buildings worth seeing. The **Catedral** is a magnificent stone structure, dating back to 1757, with a weather-beaten baroque-style exterior and a surprisingly spartan interior – except for its center altar of carved marble, which is plated in silver. Over a side altar to the right side of the church is the icon of The Lord of Agony, commonly known as El Señor de la Bala. Beside the Cathedral is the Balcony of the Count of Lemos found on an old house on the corners of Deústua and Conde de Lemos streets. It is said that Peru's Viceroy Don Pedro Antonio Fernández de Castro Andrade y Portugal stayed here when he first arrived in the city he later named "San Carlos de Puno."

**TIP**

Taking the Andean Explorer train from Cusco is a wonderful way to arrive in Puno. Trains depart three times a week and tickets can be purchased at Wanchac station in Cusco or from PeruRail (tel: 084-238 722, www.perurail.com). The luxurious first-class service includes meals and entertainment.

**BELOW:** Puno's Plaza de Armas.

On the **Plaza de Armas** are the **Biblioteca** (Library) and the municipal **Pinacoteca** (Art Gallery), and half a block off the plaza is the **Museo Carlos Dreyer**, displaying a collection of Nazca, Tiahuanaco, Paracas, Chimu, and Inca artifacts bequeathed to the city on the death of their owner, for whom the museum is named. One of the museum's most valuable pieces is an Aymara *aribalo*, the delicate pointed-bottomed pottery whose wide belly curves up to a narrow neck. Throughout the South American continent, the *aribalo* is a symbol of Andean culture.

Three blocks uphill from the plaza is the **Parque Huajsapata**, a hill that figures in the lyrics of local songs, and an excellent spot for a panoramic view of Puno. Huajsapata is topped by a huge white statue of Manco Capac gazing down at the lake from which he sprang. Another lookout point is found beside **Parque Pino**, at the city's north side, in the plaza four blocks up Calle Lima from the Plaza de Armas, in which stands the Arco Deústua, a monument honoring those killed in the decisive independence battles of Junín and Ayacucho.

The park is also called Parque San Juan, after the San Juan Bautista church within its limits; at its main altar is a statue of the patron saint of Puno, the Virgin of Candelaria. Also in the park is the Colegio Nacional de San Carlos, a grade school founded by a decree signed by Simón de Bolívar in 1825. It was later converted into a university and later used as a military barracks.

## Puno's market

Two blocks down Calle F. Arbul from Parque Pino is the city market, a colorful collection of people, goods, and food. Tourists should keep their eyes on their money and cameras, but it is worth a stop to see the wide selection of products – especially the amazing variety of potatoes, ranging from the hard, freeze-dried *papa seca* that looks like gravel, to the purple potatoes and yellow and orange speckled *olluco* tubers. Woolen goods, colorful blankets, and ponchos are on sale here, along with miniature versions of the reed boats that ply Lake Titicaca. Among the more intriguing trinkets are the *Ekekos*, the ceramic statues of stout jolly men laden with good luck-charms, ranging from fake money to little bags of coca leaves. Believers say that the *Ekekos* like to smoke, and they are often found with lit cigarettes hanging from their mouths. It is also said that these images only bring luck if they are received as gifts – not purchased.

## Exploring the lake

The real reason for coming to Puno is that it is the stepping-off point for exploring Lake Titicaca and its amazing array of islands, Indian inhabitants, and colorful traditions. Small motorboats can be hired for island visits or fishing trips – although fish stocks have declined in recent years and most lake trout is now farmed. Another fascinating relic of a different era is the **Yavari steamship**. Built by the British in 1862, it plied the lake until 1975, and is now a floating museum (open daily 8am–5pm; www.yavari.org) moored by the Sonesta Posada del Inca.

*Puno Week – the first week in November – when the town goes wild, is a celebration of Manco Capac's emergence from Lake Titicaca.*

**BELOW:** making handicrafts on the Uros Islands.

Map on pages 238–9

*Recommended Restaurants on page 315*

# Floating islands

The best-known of the islands dotting Titicaca are the **Islas de los Uros** ㉙, artificial floating islands of reed named after the Indians who inhabited them, but often known as the Islas Flotantes. Legends described the Uro islanders as people incapable of drowning, "like the fish and the birds of the water." The last full-blooded Uro was a woman who died in 1959. The people who live on the islands today are physically indistinguishable from mainlanders, having intermarried with Aymara- and Quechua-speaking Indians, and they now speak Aymara.

Poverty has prompted more and more of the people to move to Puno, and has caused those who remain to take a hard-sell approach to tourists on those islands that are most visited. But why not? They certainly need the money. Take some fresh fruit as gifts when you visit, as the islanders' diet is very basic. There is some criticism that tourism has not only opened the Uros Islands to the stares of insensitive tourists but has also destroyed much of the culture, as the islanders modify their handicrafts to appeal to outsiders, or abandon traditional practices

to dedicate more time to the influx of outsiders, but in fact many of the floating islands are not visited, and therefore remain untouched by tourism.

Many traditional customs and crafts remain unchanged, and the islanders are still quite different from other Peruvians. They fish, hunt birds, and live off lake plants, and the most important element in their lives is the lake reeds they use to make their houses and boats and even as the base of their islands – the largest of which are **Toranipata**, **Huaca Huacani**, and **Santa María**. The lower layers of the reed islands decay in the water and are replaced from the top with new layers, making a spongy surface that is a bit difficult to walk on. Even the walls of the schools on the bigger islands are made of *totora*. The soft roots of the reed are eaten, too, making it a pretty handy thing.

Another island that lures tourists is **Isla Taquile** ㉚, the home of skilled weavers and a spot where travelers can buy well-made woolen and alpaca goods, as well as colorful garments whose patterns and designs bear hidden messages about the wearer's social standing or marital status. Prices of these goods may

*The Yavari steamship still has many of its original features.*

**BELOW:** the Yavari steamship.

*A Taquile woman wearing a traditional black shawl.*

**BELOW:** terraced fields on Isla Amantaní.

be higher than on the mainland, but the quality is very good. The residents of this island run their own tourism operations in the hope of maintaining a degree of control over tourism and ensuring that the visits of outsiders do not destroy their delicate culture *(see page 317)*. There are no hotels on Taquile, but the Quechua-speaking islanders open their homes to tourists interested in an overnight stay. Arrangements for such accommodations can be made with local people, who wait at the top of the steep stone staircase where the boats dock. You will find several places to eat, mostly serving simple but tasty fish and rice dishes. You can visit Taquile in one day, but it means spending much of the day on a boat, and an overnight stay is recommended.

### Isla Amantaní

Handicrafts also play an important role in life on **Isla Amantaní**, a lovely, peaceful island even farther away from Puno than Taquile. Amantaní was once part of the Inca empire, as attested to by local ruins, and was reputedly once a prison island, before the Spanish invaded and slaughtered the islanders. The Spaniard who was granted a concession to the island used the native population in forced labor, and his descendants were still in control after Peru's independence from Spain. But eventually an island fiesta turned violent, and the islanders attacked their landlord with hoes and subsequently split up the island into communally held fields.

Amantaní has opened its doors to outsiders who are willing to live for a few days as the Aymara-speaking islanders do – and that means sleeping on beds made of long hard reeds and eating potatoes for every meal. There is no running water, and night-time temperatures drop to freezing even in the summer. But those happy to rough it catch a glimpse of an Andean agricultural community that has maintained the same traditions for centuries. Some Amantaní residents live and die without ever leaving the island.

Journeys to Amantaní and Taquile commence at the Puno docks aboard spluttering wooden motorboats that are operated by the islanders. At the end of the three-hour trip, visitors are registered as guests and then assigned to a host

*Recommended Restaurants on page 315*

family, which shows the way to its mud-brick or reed home set around an open courtyard decorated with white pebbles spelling out the family's name. The socializing begins when a family member who may speak a little English offers a guided walk around the island, from where the views are absolutely spectacular. Women from the island wearing traditional black and white lace dresses pass by with slingshots in their hands to kill scavenging birds.

Another island, **Isla Esteves**, is connected to Puno by a causeway and is best-known for the luxurious but ugly Hotel Libertador Isla Esteves, which stands out like a sore thumb. It's a far cry from what used to be the main construction on the island – a prison that accommodated the patriots captured by the Spanish during Peru's War of Independence. James Orton, a naturalist and explorer who died crossing Titicaca on a steamship in 1877, is buried here; his memorial sits beside one honoring the liberation fighters who perished in the war with Spain. Orton, a professor of natural history from Vassar University, was on his third expedition to explore the Beni River in the Amazon area. The Beni's link to the Mamore River – both crucial conduits during the jungle's 19th-century rubber boom – was named the Orton in honor of the great explorer.

## Excursions from Puno

Some 35 km (20 miles) from Puno is **Sillustani**, with its circular burial towers or *chullpas* overlooking **Lago Umayo**. The age of the funeral towers, which are up to 12 meters (40 ft) high, remains a puzzle. A Spanish chronicler described them as "recently finished" in 1549, although some look as if they were never completed. They were built by people of the Colla civilization, who spoke Aymara, and whose architecture was considered more sophisticated than that of the Incas, but who had been conquered by the Incas about a century before the Spanish arrived. The *chullpas* were apparently used as burial chambers for members of the nobility, who were entombed together with their entire families and possessions to take with them to the next world. This is a stunningly beautiful spot with a wealth of birdlife, and guinea pigs scuttling across the paths.

*On the island of Taquile, men can be seen knitting wherever they go.*

**LEFT:** Amantaní woman.
**BELOW:** a stone archway on Isla Amantaní.

Not far away (about 20 km/12 miles from Puno) is **Chucuito**, an Altiplano village that sits upon what was once an Inca settlement and which has an Inca sundial in the plaza. Close to the village stands the ancient fertility temple of the same name, whose most notable feature is an enclosure of giant stone phalluses. Have a look at the **Iglesia Santo Domingo** with its small museum; the church of **La Asunción** is also worth visiting.

**Juli** (about 80 km/50 miles from Puno), and once the capital of the lake area, has four beautiful colonial churches. Although it now appears a little strange to see so many large churches so close together, at the time when the Spanish had them built they were hoping to convert huge numbers of Indians to Catholicism. In addition, the Spanish were accustomed to providing one church for Europeans, one for mixed-raced Christians and yet another for Indians. The largest – and oldest – of Juli's ornate churches is **San Juan Bautista**, with rich colonial paintings tracing the life of its patron saint, John the Baptist.

From the courtyard of the **Iglesia La Asunción** there is a captivating view of the lake. The other churches in the city are **San Pedro**, once the principal place of worship, in which a 400-strong Indian choir used to sing on Sunday, and **Santa Cruz**, which is just beside the city's old cemetery, and is currently in the worst state of repair. Santa Cruz was originally a Jesuit church upon the front of which indigenous stonemasons carved a huge sun – the Inca god – along with more traditional Christian symbols. From Juli, the Transturin hydrofoils leave for Bolivia. The timetable is a bit erratic, and it is best to make arrangements in Puno, rather than wait until you get to Juli.

The road from Juli hugs the shore, and about 25 km (15 miles) farther on you come to the little village of **Pomata**, with its granite church of **Santiago Apóstol**.

## Pilgrimage site

**Copacabana**, a pleasant and friendly little town on the Bolivian side of the lake, can be reached by taking a minibus ride from Puno (via Yunguyo) around the side of the lake, passing the reeds waving in the wind, shy but curious children at the bends in the road, and the ever-present brilliant blue of

**BELOW AND RIGHT:** ruined and restored churches at Juli.

Titicaca. This pleasant trip sometimes involves a short ferry ride at the **Strait of Tiquina**. As a pilgrimage site, Copacabana is accustomed to tourists and has a number of modest but clean restaurants and hotels, and a couple of very comfortable ones, newly built by the lakeside. It is most famous for its Cathedral containing a 16th-century carved wooden figure of the Virgin of Copacabana, the Christian guardian of the lake. The statue, finished in 1853, was the work of Indian sculptor Francisco Tito Yupanqui, nephew of Inca Huayna Capac. Except during Mass, the statue stands with its back to the congregation – but facing the lake so that it can keep an eye out for any approaching storms and earthquakes. One of the loveliest outings in Copacabana is a dawn or dusk walk along the waterfront, watching the sky explode into color with sunrise, or slip into the blue-black of night at sunset.

## Getting to Bolivia

From Copacabana, launches can be hired to visit the Bolivian islands on Lake Titicaca – the **Isla del Sol** and the **Isla de la Luna** (the Island of the Sun and the Island of the Moon). The former (also accessible via a public ferry) has a sacred Inca rock at one end and the ruins of Pilko Caima, with a portal dedicated to the sun god at the other. The Island of the Moon, which is also known as Coati, has ruins of an Inca temple and a cloister for Chosen Women.

The bus from Puno to La Paz takes about eight hours on a newly paved road via Copacabana in Bolivia; an impressive route with great views of snowy peaks over the lake. Most buses stop for lunch in Copacabana, which has a beautiful Cathedral. You can also reach Bolivia by taking a bus from Puno around the other side of the lake, via Desaguadero, a scruffy border town. This route is shorter, but is not as scenic as going via Copacabana. ❑

*Baroque stonework on the Iglesia Santa Cruz in Juli.*

### Restaurants

#### Puno

**La Casa del Corregidor**
Av. Deustua 576
Tel: (051) 351 921
A great place to hang out for coffee and cake and light meals. Casa del Corregidor is set in a beautiful 17th-century home, and you can just drink in the atmosphere. **$**

**Don Piero**
Jr. Lima 364
Popular restaurant with locals and *gringos*. Live music some evenings. **$**

**Mojsa**
Jr. Lima 635
Tel: (051) 363 182
*Mojsa* is an Aymara word that means sweet or delicious. Good breakfasts and excellent-value meals right through the day, including noteworthy pizzas. **$**

**Pizzeria del Buho**
Jr. Libertad 386
Tel: (051) 356 223
Cozy small restaurant specializing in wood oven-baked pizzas. **$**

**Restaurant Giorgio**
Jr. Lima 430
Tel: (051) 367 771
This large restaurant serves an extensive menu fusing Peruvian and international cuisine, like guinea pig with Greek-style potatoes and *ocopa* sauce. Most nights it also has floorshows of traditional dancing from the Altiplano. **$$**

**El Trabuco**
Jr. Libertad 172
Tel: (051) 365 076
All the staples of Andean cuisine are served in this small, cozy spot. Good lake trout ceviche. **$**

**Tradiciones del Lago**
Jr. Lima 418
Tel: (051) 368 140
As the name suggests, this restaurant offers food according to local recipes. Lake fish features big on the menu, and there's a cozy atmosphere. **$**

**Ukuku's**
Pasaje Grau 172, 2nd floor
Tel: (051) 367 373
With huge portions of Peruvian and international fare, this is truly good value for money. There's an interesting exhibition of photos of the area on the walls. **$$**

• • • • • • • • • • • • • • • •
*Prices are per person for two courses, excluding wine.*
**$** = less than US$10
**$$** = US$10–US$20
**$$$** = more than US$20

# TAQUILE ISLAND

**Lake Titicaca's Taquile Island is a harshly beautiful place whose people have retained their traditional lifestyle and values**

In the 16th century Taquile was a colonial hacienda. After Peru's independence in 1821 it became a prison island, but the people of Taquile gradually regained control of their lands and today they are a closely integrated community. Their language sets them aside from other Titicaca Amerindians: they speak Quechua rather than the more common Aymara.

Taquile is a very special place: the earth is a rich, reddish brown, a color that predominates in the women's clothes, and the lake a glorious vivid blue. Life seems to have changed little over the centuries: the earth is farmed with traditional implements, and crop diversification is unknown. Plenty of potatoes but few fresh vegetables or fruits are grown. Trout, the best in Peru, are fished from the lake and served in the few basic restaurants. On the hillsides stand the remains of Inca terracing.

The Taquile weaving cooperative is renowned for the quality of its garments, and the people habitually look as if they are dressed for a fiesta. The women wear layers of multi-colored skirts and embroidered blouses; the men sport smart waistcoats and black trousers along with the little pointed hats that they knit themselves.

The islanders have a passion for fiestas, too, and whether they are celebrating Santiago (St James), which falls on July 25 or Pacha Mama (Mother Earth) in early August, high spirits, music, and plenty of *chicha* are always very much in evidence.

**ABOVE:** music is one of the ways in which islanders preserve their heritage. The men's embroidered belts contain coded calendars giving information about crops and marriage dates.

**BELOW:** island agriculture is largely based on fishing and terraced horticulture. Small herds of cattle can be seen grazing on the steep slopes of the island.

**LEFT:** wherever you go on Taquile, you will see men knitting the brightly colored stocking hats they wear. Colors denote marital status and social standing.

## CONTROLLING THE FLOW

When visitors first arrived on Taquile during the early 1970s, ferried across the lake by enterprising Puno boat-owners, the islanders decided that if change was on the way they wanted to control it. They began operating their own passenger boats, and regulating the number of people who visit the island.

There are no hotels on the island, but some families open their homes to visitors, who can spend the night and share their meal for a very reasonable charge. If you want to sample their hospitality, remember that the accommodations will be pretty basic. Realizing that their woven goods are also of interest to outsiders, the islanders now sell them on the main plaza. Prices are higher than on the mainland, but the quality is superb. It seems that the people of Taquile are making a very good job of managing tourism: enjoying the economic benefits without allowing it to erode their culture.

**ABOVE:** Taquile islanders file out of church after Sunday morning Mass. As elsewhere in Peru, Christian observances co-exist with indigenous rites.

**RIGHT:** children growing up on Taquile today will inevitably find their lives affected – for good and ill – by the influx of foreign tourists. However, their parents' generation is trying hard to make tourism work while preserving the traditional ways.

# INSIGHT GUIDES

## TRAVEL TIPS

# PERU

# TRAVEL TIPS

# **T**RANSPORTATION

# GETTING THERE
# AND GETTING AROUND

## GETTING THERE

### By Air

Peru is well connected by international flights, which arrive at the Jorge Chávez International Airport in Lima *(see Getting Around, opposite)*.

### *Flights from Europe*

Direct flights to Lima are available from Amsterdam with KLM and from Madrid with Iberia or the budget airline Air Comet. There are numerous connecting flights from other European cities to these airports. Other non-direct flights to Lima make connections in Brazil or the USA.

### *Flights from the US and Canada*

American Airlines, Continental Airlines, and LAN fly direct to Lima from major US cities including Miami, Houston, Los Angeles, and New York. Delta operates direct flights from Los Angeles, Atlanta, and Salt Lake City.

American Airlines also makes daily flights from Canada via Miami, and Air Canada flies direct from Toronto to Lima.

### *Flights from Australasia*

The best route from Australia or New Zealand is probably with LAN to Santiago de Chile, and then continuing with LAN to Lima.

### *Flights from South Africa*

Flights from South Africa usually make connections in Buenos Aires, Argentina, or São Paulo, Brazil.

### *Flights within Latin America*

There is no shortage of flights to Peru from other South American countries. Lloyd Aero Boliviano flies between Cusco and La Paz, Bolivia, twice a week. LAN operates an

## Airline Offices in Lima

**Aero Cóndor**
Av. José Pardo 562, Miraflores
Tel: (01) 614 6014
www.aerocondor.com.pe

**Aeroméxico**
Av. Pardo y Aliaga 699, Of. 501,
San Isidro
Tel: (01) 421 3500
www.aeromexico.com

**Air Canada**
Calle Italia 389, Of. 101, Edificio
Mar Azul, Miraflores
Tel: (01) 421 1457
www.aircanada.com

**Air France**
Av. Alvarez Calderón 185, Of. 601,
San Isidro
Tel: (01) 213 0200
www.airfrance.com

**Alitalia**
Av. José Pardo 601, Miraflores
Tel: (01) 444 9285
www.alitalia.com

**American Airlines**
Av. Canaval y Moreyra 380, 14th
floor, San Isidro
Tel: (01) 211 7000/211 7739

www.aa.com

**Continental Airlines**
Víctor Andrés Belaúnde 147,
Of. 110, San Isidro
Av. Larco 1315, Miraflores
Tel: (01) 441 6837/440 3110
www.continental.com

**Copa Airlines**
Dos de Mayo 741, Miraflores
Tel: (01) 444 7815
www.copaair.com

**Delta**
Av. Víctor Andrés Belaúnde 147,
San Isidro
Tel: (01) 421 1275
www.delta.com

**Iberia**
Av. Camino Real 390, Of. 902, Torre
Central del Centro Camino Real,
San Isidro
Tel: (01) 411 7800/421 7394
www.iberia.com

**KLM**
Av. Alvarez Calderón 185, Of. 601,
San Isidro
Tel: (01) 213 0200
www.klm.com

**LAN**
José Pardo 513, Miraflores
Tel: (01) 710 8300
www.lan.com

**LC Busre**
Calle Los Tulipanes 218,
Urb. San Eugenio
Tel: (01) 619 1300
www.lcbusre.com

**Lloyd Aereo Boliviano**
Av. José Pardo 231, Miraflores
Tel: (01) 447 0166/241 5514
www.labairlines.com.bo

**Lufthansa**
Av. Jorge Basadre 1330,
San Isidro
Tel: (01) 212 5113/212 5749
www.lufthansa.com

**Star Perú**
Av. José Pardo 485, Miraflores
Tel: (01) 705 9000
www.starperu.com

**TACA Perú**
Comandante Espinar 331,
Miraflores
Tel: (01) 213 7000
www.taca.com

## Flight Information

For general information about **Jorge Chávez International Airport** in Lima, or to check international and domestic flight times, visit their website, www.lap.com.pe, or call the flight center on (01) 511 6055.

extensive network of flights across the continent, including direct flights from Lima to Buenos Aires, Argentina; Santiago de Chile; Quito, Ecuador; and Caracas, Venezuela. TACA Perú operates flights from Lima to numerous cities in South and Central America.

For travel to and from Mexico, Aeroméxico, Mexicana, and Copa Airlines operate regular flights.

## Travel Agents

The following travel agents specialize in travel to South America and can arrange flights, accommodations, and transportation. They may also be able to provide information on air passes, offered by airlines such as LAN, for travel within the continent.

### UK
**Journey Latin America**
12 and 13 Heathfield Terrace, Chiswick, London W4 4JE
Tel: (020) 8747 8315
Fax: (020) 8742 1312
www.journeylatinamerica.co.uk
**South American Experience**
Welby House, 96 Wilton Road, Victoria, London SW1V 1DW
Tel: (0845) 277 3366
Fax: (020) 7821 4001
www.southamericanexperience.co.uk

### USA
**Exito**
108 Rutgers Street, Fort Collins, Colorado, CO80525
Tel: (800) 655 4053
Fax: (510) 655 4566
www.exitotravel.com

### Canada
**Inti Travel**
Box 1586, Banff, AB, T1L 1B5
Tel: (403) 760 3565
Fax: (403) 760 3566
www.intitravel.ca

### Australia
**World Expeditions**
Level 5, 71 York Street, Sydney, NSW 2000
Tel: (02) 8270 8400
Fax: (02) 8270 8401
Toll-free: 1300 720 000
www.worldexpeditions.com

## Overland

Peru has borders with Chile, Bolivia, Colombia, Brazil, and Ecuador. The border crossing with Chile is at Tacna on the Peruvian side, and Arica on the Chilean; taxis regularly make the crossing, and some long-distance buses operate between Lima, Quito, Santiago de Chile, and Buenos Aires. Tickets for such marathon journeys sometimes include food and overnight accommodations.

From Bolivia, efficient minibus services will take you from La Paz to Puno. The journey from Ecuador is also straightforward: take a bus to the border at Huaquillas and walk through to Tumbes. Other buses operate from there, but note that the "international service" advertised in Quito still requires a

change of bus at the border, unless you are traveling with the Ormeño bus company *(see Long-distance Buses, page 324)*, so it is actually more expensive and occasionally much less convenient than doing the trip in stages.

All cross-border rail links have been closed due to a lack of profitability.

## By Sea

Few people arrive at Lima's port of Callao by ocean liner or freight ship. The limited services available are expensive and inconvenient in comparison to flying.

## GETTING AROUND

### From the Airport

Jorge Chávez International Airport lies around 16 km (10 miles) from the center of Lima.

The most reliable bus service to and from the airport is Shuttle Bus Urbanito, Jr. Manoa 391, Breña, tel: (01) 424-3650/425 1202, www.urbanito.com.pe (in Spanish). A fare to central Lima is around US$15, and to Miraflores or San Isidro, US$20.

There is an official taxi desk outside the Arrivals area (before going through the barrier). Otherwise, once past the Arrivals barrier, there are plenty of taxi drivers waiting, but be prepared to bargain. Alternatively you can pre-book a taxi *(See box, page 324, for a list of recommended taxi companies)*. A fare to the center of Lima is US$10–15, and to Miraflores or San Isidro, about US$20–25. *Ejecutivo* taxis charge a little more.

In Cusco and other cities, taxis from the airport into the center are very cheap, but make sure you agree on a price before starting your journey.

## On Departure

Don't forget to hang on to the tourist card that you fill out when you arrive in Peru. You'll need to hand it in to immigration when you leave. And don't spend the last of your money on souvenirs before making for the plane: remember that airport departure tax of US$30.25 is payable on international flights, and US$6.05 is necessary on domestic flights.

**BELOW:** keeping the traffic moving in Trujillo.

## Orientation in Lima

Lima is divided into districts, each with its own distinctive character. Downtown Lima has grandiose plazas, mansions, and the restored historical Plaza Mayor, although there is a certain amount of street crime.

In the more glitzy suburbs of Miraflores and San Isidro, there is better security. New shopping complexes and landscaped gardens make this a complete contrast to the rest of the city.

Barranco is an upmarket beach suburb where some artists have their workshops, giving it a bohemian reputation. Open-air cafés and restaurants have live jazz and creole music, while the crumbling old mansions give the tree-lined streets a relaxed ambience.

## By Bus

### Local Buses

Lima's public buses can only really be recommended for a one-time cultural experience. Flagging one down is a feat in itself – then you must survive the jostling crowds and pickpockets.

There are thousands of privately run minibuses stopping and starting every few seconds, but taxis *(see box, right)* are relatively cheap and much quicker. Just make sure you agree on the fare before entering the taxi.

Between small towns and villages in Peru there are regular local buses. You can also travel by *taxi colectivo*: a car acting as a taxi service for four or five passengers. *Colectivos* leave whenever they are full. In more remote parts, most travel is by pick-up truck. If you have a long journey ahead, insist upon a seat inside. It's

**BELOW:** rush hour in the capital.

## Taxis

Taxis in Peru have no meters – you flag a car down and simply bargain on a rate, preferably before even getting in. There have been some incidents of hijacking involving taxis in the past, so it is best to use a registered one where possible. In smaller cities you may prefer to walk, but in Lima taxis are often essential and very cheap.

Note that your hotel will arrange taxis for you if you ask. This is more expensive, but very secure. If you don't speak much Spanish and don't fancy bargaining on the street, this can be the best option.

standing room only on top and you'll be smothered by dust – or drenched in the rainy season.

### Long-Distance Buses

Between cities, there are excellent, comfortable bus services. Numerous companies operate morning and evening departures from Lima to most cities. There is no central bus station in Lima, as each company has its own terminal. Always check the departure point for the journey you are making when buying tickets. Reliable bus companies include:
**Civa**
Av. 28 de Julio, esq. Paseo de la República, La Vitoria
Tel: (01) 332 5236/5264 or (01) 418 1111
www.civa.com.pe (in Spanish)
**Cruz del Sur**
Jr. Quilca 531
Tel: (01) 431 5125
Av. Javier Prado Este 1109, San Isidro
Tel: (01) 225 5748

Reliable taxi services in Lima include the following:
**CMV Taxi Remisse Ejecutivo**
Tel: (01) 422 4838
**Mitsui Taxi Remisse Ejecutivo**
Tel: (01) 349 7722
**Taxi Amigo**
Tel: (01) 349 1077
**Taxi Green**
Tel: (01) 484 4001
**Taxi Movil**
Tel: (01) 422 6890
**Taxi Real**
Tel: (01) 470 6205
**Taxi Seguro**
Tel: (01) 241 9292

Call center tel: (01) 311 5050
www.cruzdelsur.com.pe
There is a free delivery service for tickets purchased through the call center. Luxury buses leave from the San Isidro terminal.
**Ormeño**
Paseo de la República 801, La Vitoria
Tel: (01) 427 5679
www.grupo-ormeno.com.pe (in Spanish)
**Tepsa**
Jr. Lampa 1237
Tel: (01) 427 5642/3
Call center tel: (01) 470 6666
www.tepsa.com.pe (in Spanish)

## By Car

Driving in Lima is a nightmare: road conditions are chaotic, the local style of driving is aggressive, signposting is rare, and theft from cars is a constant danger, particularly at night. Taking all of this into consideration, the best way to travel is by taxi. However, outside the capital driving gets easier and the main hazard is the state of the roads – apart from the Pan American Highway, many are unpaved. Certain regions are better appreciated with your own mode of transport, such as the Callejón de Huaylas, a 200-km (125-mile) long valley nicknamed the "Peruvian Switzerland" for its glaciers, lakes, and snowy peaks. The town of Huaraz is a 6-hour drive from Lima on well-surfaced roads.

For stays of up to 30 days, you don't need an international driving license to rent a car: just a valid driving license from your own country, a passport, and credit card. For longer stays, contact the **Touring y Automóvil Club del Perú (TACP)**, César Vallejo 699, Lince, Lima, tel: (01) 211 9977, www.touringperu.com.pe (in Spanish), to obtain an inter-national driving permit.

### Car Rental Agencies

In addition to their branches in Lima (listed below), most car rental companies have branches in Arequipa and Cusco, and some regional airports.

**Avis**
Av. Javier Prado Este 5235, Camacho, La Molina
Tel: (01) 434 1111
Jorge Chávez International Airport
Tel: (01) 517 3214
www.avisworld.com

**Budget**
Av. Canaval y Moyeyra 569, San Isidro
Tel: (01) 442 8703/6
Av. Larco 998, Miraflores
Tel: (01) 444 4546
Jorge Chávez International Airport
Tel: (01) 575 1674 (24 hours)
www.budgetperu.com (in Spanish)

**Dollar Rent a Car**
Av. Cantuarias 341, Miraflores
Tel: (01) 444 3050
www.dollarpe.com (in Spanish)

**Hertz**
Av. Cantuarias 160, Miraflores
Tel: (01) 445 5716
Av. Salaverry 2599, San Isidro
Tel: (01) 421 0282
Jorge Chávez International Airport
Tel: (01) 517 2402 (24 hours)
www.hertz.com.pe

**Inka's Rent A Car**
Cantuarias 160, Miraflores
Tel: (01) 447 2129/445 5716
Jorge Chávez International Airport
Tel: (01) 417 2402

**National Car Rental**
Av. Costanera 1380, San Miguel
Tel: (01) 578 7878/517 2555
(24 hours)
Jorge Chávez International Airport
Tel: (01) 517 2555
www.nationalcar.com.pe

### By Air

Lima is the gateway to the rest of the country, although there are a handful of international flights from Cusco and Iquitos. There are domestic flights between all major cities and several domestic airlines, including Aero Cóndor, Star Perú, and LC Busre, providing daily services to most cities. There is little qualitative or price difference between them. LAN operates domestic flights to destinations throughout the country, and TACA Perú has flights from Lima to Cusco. *(See box on page 322 for addresses of airline offices in Lima.)*

Domestic airlines are sadly unreliable in meeting their flight schedules. Times are often changed and, in the case of remote destinations, occasionally canceled

**ABOVE:** crossing Lake Titicaca on a *totora* boat.

due to lack of interest; you will often not find out until you are at the airport. Other small, new airlines that operate for a while and then close down, fly to smaller places and remote jungle airstrips.

It's best to book in person at the reservations office, or through a good travel agent who will confirm your tickets. Tales of travelers being bumped off flights are legion: it is best to reconfirm your ticket 72 hours in advance. LAN now has an online check-in facility, and you can print your boarding pass to bring with you to the airport.

For domestic flights there is an airport tax of US$6.05 at all airports.

### By Rail

Train journeys in Peru are very popular with all types of travelers. Well-serviced "first-class" or Pullman carriages are the most comfortable; "backpacker" seats are also available, but they are less comfortable and you need to watch your luggage at all times. The trips provide valuable glimpses of rural life and views of magnificent landscapes.

The popular 10-hour journey between Puno and Cusco, which goes via Juliaca, is a wonderful experience. The Andean Explorer service, operated by PeruRail, runs three times a week in both directions. *(See page 309 for information on tickets.)*

The Lima–Huancayo passenger service *(see box, page 210),* the world's highest train journey, runs approximately twice a month. It is operated by Ferrocarril Central Andino (FCCA), tel: (01) 226 6363 ext 222, www.ferrocarrilcentral.com.pe. Visit

www.incasdelperu.org for up-to-date information and schedules. There is also a scenic section of railway connecting Huancayo to the pretty town of Huancavelica.

To reach the ruins at Machu Picchu by train, there are several trains which make the journey from Cusco to Aguas Calientes, from where you can catch a shuttle bus to the ruins. PeruRail operates a daily service from Wanchac station in Cusco, which also stops at Ollantaytambo. There are several types of train to choose from, including the Vistadome and Backpacker trains, and the five-star Hiram Bingham service *(see box, page 297).*

### By Boat

Boats can be taken from the bay of Paracas to the Ballestas Islands, home of sea lions, Humboldt penguins, and various seabirds.

From Puno, there are tranquil excursions by boat across Lake Titicaca to the islands of Taquile and Amantaní, and the floating islands of Uros, which are made entirely of reeds. Simply go to the dock where boats leave at regular intervals. It is a three-hour boat ride to Taquile or Amantaní and boats usually depart between 8 and 9am. Boats return from Taquile late afternoon, although many visitors choose to stay overnight. Boats to Amantaní are less frequent so visitors usually stay at least one night on the island.

In the Amazon, passenger and cargo boats, and motorized canoes are the only way to travel along the winding, muddy waterways. *(See page 224 for details of Amazon river boats.)*

# **A** CCOMMODATIONS

# HOTELS, HACIENDAS, AND LODGES

### Hotels and Lodges

Accommodations in Peru can be as sophisticated or as simple as you wish. There's everything from the smartest five-star hotels imaginable to village home-stays where bed is a mattress on an earthen floor. In between there's a plethora of sleeping options, from colonial mansions to simple and welcoming hostels. For longer stays, many cities now offer rental apartments. Some of the loveliest places to stay in Peru are the country haciendas and lodges, away from the big towns.

These often offer activities such as trekking and horseback riding, and are sometimes built near hot springs.

Most hotels in Peru are clean, efficient, friendly, and surprisingly good value. Excluding the most budget variety, the majority have en suite bathrooms, comfortable beds, and are serviced every day. Hot water is not always reliable, however (even in the smarter places), so it's worth checking whether the taps run warm 24 hours a day.

The majority of hotel rooms have two (or even three) single beds, so if you want a double bed specify a *cama*

*matrimonial.* One bane of Peruvian hotel rooms is street noise, so you may wish to ask for *la habitación más tranquila* (the quietest room).

Most hotels include continental breakfasts in their rates and many, particularly in Lima and Cusco, offer a free airport pick-up and internet connection. Staff are generally happy to help with advice on sightseeing and information on the local area.

Though security is not a great problem in the more upmarket hotels, it's a good idea to hide your valuables inside your luggage, or make use of the hotel's safe, if there is one.

ACCOMMODATIONS LISTINGS

## LIMA

### Downtown Area

**Gran Hotel Bolívar**
Jr. de la Unión 958, Plaza
San Martín
Tel: (01) 619 7171
Fax: (01) 619 7170
www.granhotelbolivarperu.com
Opulent, old-style comfort.
Within easy walking distance
of historic sites, but not a
safe area at night. **$$$**

**Hostal Las Artes**
Jr. Chota 1460
Tel: (01) 433 0331
http://arteswelcome.tripod.com
Good budget hotel located
in an old restored
mansion. Rooms with or
without bathroom. **$**

**Hotel España**
Jr. Azángaro 105
Tel: (01) 428 5546/427 9196
www.hotelespanaperu.com

Clean, with shared
bathrooms. A fun
atmosphere for
backpackers. **$**

**Hotel Kamana**
Camana 547
Tel: (01) 426 7204
Fax: (01) 426 0790
www.hotelkamana.com
Comfortable and modern
rooms with private bath-
rooms, in the heart of
downtown Lima. **$**

**Hotel Residencial Europa**
Jr. Ancash 376,
Plaza San Francisco
Tel: (01) 427 3351
Budget hotel popular with
backpackers in the heart
of downtown Lima. Clean,
with shared bathrooms. **$**

**La Posada del Parque**
Parque Hernán Velarde 60
Tel: (01) 433 2412

Fax: (01) 332 6927
www.incacountry.com
Old mansion in quiet
cul-de-sac, with antiques
and artworks; big rooms
with private bathroom. **$**

**Sheraton Lima Hotel
& Towers**
Paseo de la República 170
Tel: (01) 315 5000
Fax: (01) 315 5015
www.sheraton.com.pe
A comfortable, modern
hotel, with the usual
Sheraton good service.
At the edge of downtown
Lima – not a safe area
to walk at night. **$$$**

### Miraflores

Miraflores suburb is the
commercial center of
Lima and home to affluent

Peruvians. Shops, night-
clubs, and restaurants
abound.

**Las Américas**
Av. Benavides 415
Tel: (01) 241 2820
Fax: (01) 444 7272
www.thunderbirdresorts.com/peru
A hotel for executives.
Well placed in the
heart of Miraflores.
**$$$**

**B&B Tradiciones**
Av. Ricardo Palma 955
Tel: (01) 445 6742/628 1222
Email: bbtradiciones@hotmail.com
This small, family-run guesthouse is a real find. The owners speak numerous languages and are an endless source of kindness and information. You'll feel less like a tourist and more like a guest in a Peruvian home. Free WiFi access. **$**

**Casa de los Sánchez**
Av. Diagonal 354, Parque Kennedy
Tel: (01) 446 4944
Fax: (01) 445 2738
www.lacasadesanchez.com
Upper end of budget accommodation in heart of Miraflores. Rooms with private bathroom. **$**

**Flying Dog Backpackers Bed & Breakfast**
Jr. Diez Canseco 117
Tel: (01) 445 6745
Fax: (01) 445 0940
www.flyingdogperu.com
Friendly hostel close to Parque Kennedy. **$**

**Hostal El Patio**
Diez Canseco 341
Tel: (01) 444 2107
Fax: (01) 444 1663
www.hostalelpatio.net
Very nice colonial-style hotel in the heart of Miraflores. Includes breakfast and free wireless internet connection. **$**

**Hostal José Luis**
Francisco de Paula de Ugarriza 727
Tel: (01) 444 1015
Fax: (01) 446 7177
www.hoteljoseluis.com
Private house in safe neighborhood. Most rooms with private bathroom and refrigerator. Excellent value. Must reserve in advance. **$**

**Hostal Señorial**
José González 567
Tel/fax: (01) 444 5755
www.senorial.com
Colonial-style house in quiet street, with garden and patio. Comfortable rooms and friendly atmosphere. **$$**

**Hotel Antigua Miraflores**
Av. Grau 350
Tel: (01) 241 6116
Fax: (01) 241 6115
www.peru-hotels-inns.com
Attractive colonial house, with restaurant, bar, gym, sauna, jacuzzi, and conference rooms. **$$**

**Hotel La Castellana**
Grimaldo del Solar 222
Tel: (01) 444 3530
Fax: (01) 446 8030
www.hotel-lacastellana.com
Conveniently located colonial house, with restaurant and courtyard; comfortable rooms. **$$**

**Hotel San Antonio Abad**
Av. Ramón Ribeyro 301
Tel: (01) 447 6766/444 5475
Fax: (01) 446 4208
www.hotelsanantonioabad.com
This breezy place has a lovely colonial feel, with friendly staff and pleasingly simple rooms. Some have balconies overlooking the interior courtyard. Free WiFi access and good breakfasts included. **$**

**Lima Travel Lodge**
Jr. Pataz 1213, Covida, 39
Tel: (01) 9728 3336
www.limatravelodge.com
If you're looking for somewhere in the real Lima, rather than the glitz of Miraflores, try this simple, clean hostel close to the airport. The friendly owners arrange interesting tours of the less touristy side of the city and also give Spanish lessons. **$**

**Marriot Hotel Lima**
Malecón de la Reserva 615
Tel: (01) 217 7000
Fax: (01) 217 7002
www.marriott.com
This 25-story, ultra-modern glass tower has a superb location right on the Pacific waterfront, opposite the Larcomar shopping and entertainment center. **$$$**

**Miraflores Park Hotel**
Av. Malecón de la Reserva 1035
Tel: (01) 242 3000
Fax: (01) 242 3393
www.mira-park.com
The most luxurious hotel in Miraflores, with ocean view. **$$$**

**Miramar Ischia**
Malecón Cisneros 1244
Tel: (01) 444 6969
Fax: (01) 445 0851
Email: ischia@bellnet.com.pe
Attractive, friendly hotel, with sea view. Near downtown Miraflores. **$$**

**Peruflat**
Calle Francisco del Castillo 523
Tel: (01) 9751 0055/9741 7603
www.peruflat.com
For longer stays in Lima these beautifully equipped

and spotless one- and two-bedroom apartments in a prime location in Miraflores are ideal. Weekly and monthly rates available. Great value for money. **$**

## San Isidro

The residential "garden" of Lima and the home of its prestigious golf and country clubs.

**Hotel los Delfines**
Calle los Eucaliptus 555
Tel: (01) 215 7000
Fax: (01) 215 7071
www.losdelfineshotel.com
Luxury hotel with casino and nightclub. The two resident dolphins are the hotel's most special guests. **$$$**

**Hotel San Isidro**
Av. Pezet 1765
Tel: (01) 264 2019
Fax: (01) 264 3434
www.sanisidroinn.com.pe
A quiet, traditional hotel in the garden neighborhood. **$**

**Sonesta Posada del Inca El Olivar**
Pancho Fierro 194
Tel: (01) 712 6000
Fax: (01) 712 6099
www.sonesta.com/lima
Quiet location in one of Lima's last wooded areas; with a pool, coffee shop, and restaurant. **$$$**

**Swissôtel**
Via Central 150, Centro Empresarial Camino Real
Tel: (01) 421 4400
Fax: (01) 421 4422
www.swissotel.com
Very elegant, with a Swiss-style restaurant. **$$$**

**Youth Hostel Malka**
Los Lirios 165
Tel: (01) 442 0162
Fax: (01) 222 5589
www.youthhostelperu.com
Open 24 hours. Shared and private rooms with or without bathroom. **$**

## Barranco

Attractive residential suburb beyond Miraflores with many beaches, and colonial buildings around its social hub.

**Mochilero's Backpackers Hostel**
Pedro de Osma 135
Tel: (01) 477 4506
Fax: (01) 477 0302
Email: backpacker@amauta.rcp.net.pe

**ABOVE:** Hotel España.

Dormitories in beautiful colonial building, just off Plaza Barranco and near to all the bars. Great value. **$**

**The Point**
Malecón Junín 300
Tel: (01) 247 7997/247 7709
www.thepointhostels.com
Definitely of the backpacker variety, this fun hostel has dorms and some private rooms with en suite bathrooms. A lively place to be, right by the ocean. **$**

**La Quinta de Allison**
28 de Julio 281
Tel: (01) 247 1515
Fax: (01) 247 6430
Private bathrooms, cable TV, near Plaza de Barranco. **$**

**Second Home Peru**
Calle Domeyer 366
Tel: (01) 477 5021
Fax: (01) 247 1042
www.secondhomeperu.com
This lovely guesthouse, once an artist's mansion, has five beautiful rooms, some with wide Pacific views. A peaceful haven in the heart of Barranco. **$$**

**La Villa Barranquina**
Av. Martínez de Pinillo 129
Tel: (01) 499 0772
Fax: (01) 477 9660
Beautifully located close to central Barranco in a late 19th-century building, these prettily furnished mini apartments are a great place to stay in this part of town. Ask for a room with sea views. **$$**

TRANSPORTATION · ACCOMMODATIONS · SHOPPING · ACTIVITIES · A – Z · LANGUAGE

# NORTH COAST

## Trujillo

**Casa De Clara Guest House**
Cahuide 495, Santa María
Tel: (044) 299 997/966 2710
Email: casadeclara@yahoo.com
Economical, multilingual backpackers' guesthouse just seven blocks from the Plaza de Armas in a peaceful area overlooking a park. All mod cons, including free wireless internet, library, and tours. **$**

**Los Conquistadores**
Diego de Almagro 586
Tel: (044) 203 350
Fax: (044) 235 917
www.losconquistadoreshotel.com
Comfortable hotel, with bar and restaurant. **$$**

**Gran Bolívar Hotel**
Jr. Bolivar 957
Tel: (044) 222 090
Fax: (044) 262 200
www.perunorte.com/granbolivar
This breezy hotel has good, clean rooms (some with attractive artworks) and pleasant communal areas. There's free WiFi access, too. **$$**

**Gran Hotel El Golf**
Los Cocoteros 500, Urb. El Golf
Tel: (044) 282 515
www.perunorte.com/granhotelgolf
This resort-type establishment has recently been totally renovated. Rooms overlook the gardens and swimming pool, and the hotel can arrange for guests to play golf, of course. **$$**

**El Gran Marqués**
Díaz de Cienfuegos 145, Urb. La Merced
Tel: (044) 249 366/223 990
Fax: (044) 249 161
Email: hotel@elgranmarques.com
Smart, comfortable hotel that's one of the nicest places to stay in Trujillo. The friendly staff give helpful advice on arranging trips to the region's attractions. **$$**

**Hostal Trujillo**
Grau 581
Tel: (044) 258 271
Budget hotel, clean, rooms with private bathroom. **$**

**Hotel Peregrino**
Jr. Independencia 978
Tel: (044) 203 989/203 990
www.peregrinohotel.com (in Spanish)
Clean simple rooms, good food, and helpful staff. Prices include breakfast and free pick-up from your point of arrival. **$**

**Los Jardines Bungalows Hotel**
América Norte 1245
Tel: (044) 222 258
Reservations in Lima:
Tel: (01) 463 2056
Large hotel with bungalow accommodations and pool, on the outskirts of town. Good for families with young children. **$$**

**Libertador Plaza Mayor Trujillo**
Jr. Independencia 485, Plaza de Armas
Tel: (044) 232 741
Fax: (044) 235 641

www.libertador.com.pe
Good-value accommodation in a beautiful building in central location, with an excellent Sunday buffet. **$$**

**Real Hotel**
Jr. Pizarro 651
Tel: (044) 257 416
The clean, breezy rooms here are a haven in the midst of the busiest part of Trujillo. Bring your earplugs, though, as the location can be noisy. **$**

## Huanchaco

**Hostal Bracamonte**
Los Olivos 503
Tel: (044) 461 162
Fax: (044) 461 266
www.hostalbracamonte.com
Family-run hotel, with 15 rooms. Pool, games room, and restaurant. **$**

**Las Palmeras de Huanchaco**
Av. Larco 1150
Tel/fax: (044) 461 199
www.laspalmerasdehuanchaco.com
In summer this sunrise-yellow beach-side hotel, with a nice pool, really comes alive. **$$**

## Chiclayo

**Garza Hotel**
Av. Bolognesi 756
Tel: (074) 228 172
Fax: (074) 228 171
www.garzahotel.com
Modern and efficient, with a swimming pool. **$$**

**Gran Hotel Chiclayo**
Av. Federico Villareal 115
Tel: (074) 234 911
Fax: (074) 223 961
www.granhotelchiclayo.com.pe
Business hotel close to town center. Air conditioning, hot tub, cable TV, business center, casino. **$$**

**Hotel El Sol**
Jr. Aguirre 119
Tel: (074) 232 120/231 020
Fax: (074) 231 070
A sparklingly clean place that's cool, efficient, and friendly. The double rooms have comfortable beds. Twenty-four hour hot water and TV. **$**

**Tumi de Oro**
L. Prado 1145
Tel: (074) 237 767
Clean budget hotel; rooms

with or without bathroom; hot water. **$**

## Piura

**Los Portales Hotel**
Libertad 875
Tel: (073) 321 161
www.hotelportalespiura.com
Historic building right on the main square, with restaurant, pool, casino, and business center. **$$**

## Máncora

**Hotel del Wawa**
Av. Piura
Tel: (073) 258 427
www.delwawa.com (in Spanish)
*Wawa* comes from the Quechua for little child, a nickname given to the owner, who's now one of Peru's premier surf hunks. These air-conditioned cabins with palm-leaf roofs are located right on the beach. There's also a surf school and a good restaurant. **$$**

## Punta Sal

**Punta Sal Club Hotel**
Crta Sullana, Km 173, Tumbes
Tel: (072) 540 088
Reservations in Lima:
Tel: (01) 422 7855/442 5992
Resort hotel with smart beach bungalows; deep-sea fishing trips available. **$$**

## Tumbes

**Costa Azul**
Balneario de Zorritos, Zorritos
Tel: (072) 544 268
Reservations in Lima:
Tel: (01) 9823 8040
www.costaazulperu.com
Small resort by the beach in the lovely seaside village of Zorritos just outside Tumbes. Great value. **$**

**BELOW:** breakfast alfresco at the Libertador Trujillo.

## Cajamarca

**Hostal Los Balcones de la Recoleta**
Jr. Amalia Puga 1050
Tel: (076) 363 302
Built around a central garden, this atmospheric old building is a clean, friendly, and welcoming place to stay. There's a good restaurant, too. One of the nicest in Cajamarca and great value. **$**

**Hotel Laguna Seca**
Av. Manco Cápac 1098,
Baños del Inca
Tel: (076) 594 600
Fax: (076) 594 646
www.lagunaseca.com.pe
Renovated hacienda 6 km (4 miles) from Cajamarca. The bathtubs in each room are filled directly from the nearby Baños del Inca thermal springs. **$$$**

**Hotel el Portal del Marques**
Jr. del Comercio 644
Tel: (076) 368 464/343 339
Reservations in Lima:
(01) 9880 5440
www.portaldelmarques.com
Pleasant hotel just a block away from the Plaza de Armas. Staff are friendly and efficient, and there's an excellent restaurant on site. **$$**

**El Ingenio**
Av. Via de Evitamiento 1611–1709
Tel: (076) 827 121
Fax: (076) 828 733
www.elingenio.com
Tranquil hotel just outside town with a relaxed atmosphere and attractive interior patios. **$$**

**Posada del Puruay**
Crta Porcon–Hualgayoc, Km 4.5
Tel: (076) 367 928
Reservations in Lima:
(01) 336 7869

**BELOW:** El Ingenio in Cajamarca.

www.posadapuruay.com.pe
This superbly renovated hacienda just outside Cajamarca has a lovely central courtyard with a fountain, acres of terracotta tiles, and beautifully decorated rooms. A peaceful place to stay, close to the hot springs of the Baños del Inca. **$$**

**Sierra Galana**
Jr. Comercio 773
Tel/fax: (076) 82 2470
Well located and comfortable hotel in the center of town, furnished with heavy wooden antiques. **$$**

## Huaraz

**Albergue Churup**
Jr. Amadeo Figueroa 1257
Tel: (043) 422 584
www.churup.com
This small, family-run hotel looks like something out of the Swiss Alps and is beautifully furnished inside. There's a roaring log fire on winter nights. **$**

**B&B Mi Casa**
Av. Tarapacá 773
Tel: (043) 423 375
www.aventuraquechua.com
Small guesthouse run by friendly owners with simple rooms set around an interior courtyard. Good breakfasts served. Plenty of travel and mountain advice available. **$**

**La Casa de Zarela**
Jr. Julio Arguedas 1263
Tel/fax: (043) 421 694
www.lacasadezarela.com
A quiet, small hotel with lovely decoration, interior courtyards, and terraces, plus a great café. En suite double and triple rooms available. Zarela is endlessly knowledgeable about the area and will help arrange climbing and trekking trips. **$**

**Casablanca**
Tarapaca 138
Tel: (043) 422 602
Fax: (043) 424 801
www.huaraz.com/casablanca
Characterful, modern, and clean; good service. **$**

**Edward's Inn**
Bolognesi 121
Tel/fax: (043) 422 692
www.edwardsinn.com
Friendly family-run place. Edward is a good source of information on climbing and trekking. **$**

**Hostal El Patio**
Av. Monterrey
Crta Huaraz Caraz, Km 6
Tel: (043) 424 965
Fax: (043) 426 967
Reservations in Lima:
Fax: (01) 448 0254
www.elpatio.com.pe
Beautiful hacienda-style hotel in a peaceful country setting – just down the road from the thermal baths. **$**

**Hotel Andino**
Pedro Cochachín 357
Tel: (043) 421 662
Fax: (043) 422 830
www.hotelandino.com
Comfortable hotel with excellent service and stunning views. **$$–$$$**

**Llanganuco Lodge**
Lake Keushu (at the entrance of the Llanganuco valley)
Reservations in Huaraz:
Jr. Amadeo Figueroa 1244
Tel: (043) 967 2949
www.llanganucolodge.com
This new lodge in the mountains outside Huaraz is perfect as a luxury base for day adventures, or for a few days' acclimatization before a climb. **$$**

**Olaza's Guest House**
Jr. Julio Arguedas 1242
Tel: (043) 422 529
www.andeanexplorer.com/olaza
Set around a peaceful central courtyard, this is a clean, pleasant guesthouse with lovely rooftop terraces and amazing views of the mountains. The owners are specialists in mountain bike adventures. **$**

**El Tumi**
Jr. San Martín 1121
Tel/fax: (043) 421 784/852
www.hoteleltumi.com
A comfortable modern hotel. Excellent value for money. **$$$**

### PRICE CATEGORIES

Prices are all for double rooms:
**$** = under US$50
**$$** = US$51–100
**$$$** = over US$100

## CENTRAL SIERRA

### Ayacucho

**Ayacucho Hotel Plaza**
Jr. 9 de Diciembre 184
Tel: (066) 312 202
Fax: (066) 312 314
Built round a courtyard on the Plaza de Armas, perhaps the best hotel Ayacucho has to offer. **$$**

**Hostal La Florida**
Jr. Cusco 310
Tel: (066) 312 565
This hotel's pretty courtyard gives it a tranquil air. The rooms are plain but clean and comfortable, with good rooftop views from the upper levels. **$**

**Hostal Santa Rosa**
Jr. Lima 166
Tel: (066) 812 083
Centrally situated, with good service. **$**

**Hotel Crillonesa**
Calle Zazareo 56
Tel: (066) 312 350
Comfortable and clean, with good views of the city from rooftop. **$$**

**Márquez de Valdelirios**
Alameda Bolognesi 720
Tel: (066) 318 944
In a lovely colonial house, close to the center of town, this peaceful place is stylishly furnished and comfortable. There's a good restaurant, too. **$**

### Huancayo

**Hotel Presidente**
Calle Real 1138
Tel: (064) 231 275
Situated in the heart of Huancayo, this business-like hotel is smart, clean, and efficient, with good facilities. **$$**

### Huancavelica

**Hotel Presidente**
Plaza de Armas
Tel: (067) 452 760

Set in an old stone building with wooden balconies, this is Huancavelica's top choice. Simple rooms, but there's reliable hot water and a range of facilities, including a laundry service. **$$**

## NORTHERN AMAZON

### Iquitos

**Acosta Hotel**
Corner of Huallga and Calvo de Araujo
Tel/fax: (065) 231 761
Reservations in Lima:
Tel: (01) 421 9195
Fax: (01) 442 4515
Has a swimming pool and a good restaurant. **$$**

**El Dorado Plaza Hotel**
Jr. Napo 258,
Plaza de Armas
Tel: (065) 222 555
Fax: (065) 224 304
www.eldoradoplazahotel.com
This amazing, glitzy place looks like it's just stepped out of Las Vegas. Good food, good rooms, good service, and above all, air conditioned to positively arctic degrees. **$$$**

**Hobo Hideout**
Putumayo 437
Tel: (065) 234 099
Popular place for backpackers. **$**

**Hostal La Casona**
Av. Fitzcarrald 147
Tel: (065) 234 394
www.lacasonadeiquitos.com
This may be a classic backpacker place, but if you're after peace, ask for one of their lower-level rooms on the interior courtyard – possibly the quietest rooms in the city. A quaint little hotel that will also help you arrange jungle trips. **$**

**Hostal El Colibri**
Jr. Nauta 172
Tel: (065) 241 737
Email: hostalelcolibri@hotmail.com
A short distance from the boulevard which runs along the Amazon waterfront, this simple hotel offers comfortable rooms with fans, private bathrooms, and cable TV. **$**

**Hospedaje La Pascana**
Calle Pevas 133
Tel: (065) 233 466
www.pascana.com
This simple little place is set around a quiet garden. The rooms have cold water and powerful fans. An excellent in-house agency, Pascana Amazon Services, arranges off-the-beaten-track Amazon adventures and visits to lodges. **$**

**Hotel El Dorado**
Jr. Napo 362
Tel: (065) 232 574
Fax: (065) 232 203
Modern hotel with swimming pool close to Plaza de Armas. **$$**

**Hotel Marañón**
Fitzcarrald and Nauta 285–289
Tel: (065) 242 673
Fax: (065) 231 737
Email: hotelmaranon@terra.com.pe
This cool, air-conditioned place is efficient and friendly and close to the Plaza de Armas. It can suffer from street noise, so ask for their quietest room or pack your earplugs. **$**

**Real Hotel Iquitos**
Malecón Tarapaca s/n
Tel/fax: (065) 231 011
Some of the rooms are large, with amazing views of the Amazon; other rooms are smaller, and half the price. **$–$$**

## LODGES

See Jungle Lodges *(page 230)* for more information on staying in a lodge in the Peruvian Amazon.

**Amazonia Expeditions**
Av. La Marina 100, Iquitos
Tel: (065) 242 792
Reservations in the US:
10305 Riverburn Drive, Tampa, Florida 33647
Tel: (800) 262 9669
Fax: (813) 907 8475
www.perujungle.com
Amazonia Expeditions runs Tahuayo Lodge close to the Tamshiyacu-Tahuayo Reserve. Many researchers choose to visit this beautiful, remote lodge, so the guides are absolutely top rate. The area that constitutes the Tamshiyacu-Tahuayo reserve is thought to be a Pleistocene refugia (an area that remained forested during the last Ice Age, when most of the Amazon was dry savanna). Many species here exist nowhere else in the world.

There are 15 suitably rustic but comfortable cabins right on the River Tahuayo.

**Asiendes**
Pascana Amazon Services
Calle Pevas 113, Iquitos
Tel: (065) 233 466
Email: reservas@pascana.com
For an Amazon trip that is full adventure as well as cultural immersion, this is the experience of a lifetime. Right in the heart of the Pacaya-Samiria Reserve lies the village of San Martín de Tipishca. Villagers here of the Cocama-Cocamilla people have built a house where they accommodate small groups of visiting tourists. The venture is run by the villagers themselves, and they know the forest and its wildlife intimately. There are walks and boat trips, as well as experience of life in an isolated village deep in the Amazon. You'll need at least six days here, and longer trips can be arranged.

## Explorama Lodges

Av. La Marina 340, Iquitos
Tel: (065) 252 530
Fax: (065) 252 533
Reservations in the US/Canada:
Tel: (1800) 707 5275
Fax: (781) 581 3714
www.explorama.com

Explorama Lodges have been around for over 40 years and are one of the best-known and most recommended tour operators. They now run four lodges as well as the renowned Canopy Walkway that allows guests to walk above the tops of the rainforest trees: an unforgettable experience. Itineraries of varying lengths run to: Ceibatops Luxury Lodge, just 40 km (25 miles) from Iquitos; the rustic Explorama Lodge downriver from Iquitos; ExplorNapo Lodge on the Sucusari Reserve; and the adventure-camping style ExplorTambos Camp. The amazing Canopy Walkway is run in conjunction with the Amazon Conservatory of Tropical Studies (ACTS). Thirty-five meters (115 ft)

high and 500 meters (⅓ mile) long, the walkway is suspended between 14 of the area's largest trees and is a thrilling vantage point for observing rainforest fauna and flora. Guests can also visit Renuperu ethnobotanical medicinal plant garden adjacent to ExplorNapo Lodge, where the secrets of the Amazon's healing plants are studied.

## Paseos Amazónicos

Pevas 260, Iquitos
Tel: (065) 233 110
Fax: (065) 231 618
Reservations in Lima:
Tel: (01) 241 7576
Fax: (01) 446 7946
www.paseosamazonicos.com

Three lodges 32, 60, and 185 km (20, 38, and 115 miles) from Iquitos. Sinchicuy Lodge (the closest to Iquitos) is adapted for wheelchair access. Various excursions offered, including three suitable for disabled travelers.

## Yacumama Lodge

Reservations in the US:
Eco-Expeditions, 12973 SW 112th St, Miami, FL 33186
www.yacumamalodge.com

**ABOVE:** Explorama Lodge in the Northern Amazon.

Comfortable lodge on Río Yarapa, 177 km (110 miles) upriver from Iquitos; three-night/four-day and one-week itineraries.

## Yarapa River Lodge

Reservations in Iquitos:
Av. La Marina 124
Tel: (065) 993 1172
Reservations in the US:
Tel: (315) 952 6771
www.yarapa.com

This beautiful award-winning lodge on the Yarapa River offers three-night and longer itineraries with activities

that include wildlife spotting, piranha fishing, rainforest walks, lake swimming (not in the same place that you fish for piranhas), and visits to local villages. Excellent food, and guides that know the rainforest inside out. Accommodations in fully mosquito-netted rooms. There are rescued and orphaned animals that choose to stay close to the lodge, making this feel sometimes like a wonderful open-air zoo.

# SOUTHERN AMAZON

## Parque Nacional Manu

### Manu Nature Tours

Reservations in Cusco: Pardo 1046
Tel: (084) 252 721
Fax: (084) 234 793
www.manuperu.com

Manu Lodge is only lodge inside the Parque Nacional El Manu. Manu Cloud Forest Lodge also available. More expensive than some of the lodges, but it's comfortable, and an excellent spot for birdwatching.

### Manu Expeditions

Calle Humberto Vidal Unda G-5, Segunda Etapa, Urb. Magisterial, Cusco
Tel: (084) 226 671/239 974
Fax: (084) 236 706
www.manuexpeditions.com

Run by ornithologist Barry Walker. Camping trips into the reserve, led by knowledgeable guides. Offer customized trips into other areas/lodges in the southern jungle.

## Reserva Nacional Tambopata

### Eco Amazonia Lodge

Bajo Río Madre de Dios, Km 30, Puerto Maldonado
Reservations in Cusco:
Garcilazo 210, Of. 206
Tel: (084) 236 159/242 244
Fax: (084) 225 068
Reservations in Lima:
Calle Enrique Palacios 292, Miraflores
Tel: (01) 242 2708
Fax: (01) 446 5223
www.ecoamazonia.com.pe
(in Spanish)

Two hours downriver from Puerto Maldonado, with oxbow lakes and tree canopy access.

### Explorers' Inn

Reservations in Lima:
Alcanfores 459, Miraflores
Tel: (01) 447 8888
Fax: (01) 241 8427
www.peruviansafaris.com

Good chance of observing wildlife from this location, about 60 km (38 miles)

from Puerto Maldonado on the Tambopata River.

### Libertador Tambopata Lodge

Reservations in Puerto Maldonado:
Prada 269
Tel: (082) 571 726
Fax: (082) 571 397
Reservations in Cusco:
Nueva Baja 432
Tel: (084) 245 695
www.tambopatalodge.com

Offers a good chance of observing wildlife. Situated 4 hours upriver from Puerto Maldonado.

### Reserva Amazónica

Reservations in Lima:
Tel: (01) 610 0400
Reservations in the US/Canada:
Tel: (800) 442 5042
Reservations in the UK:
Tel: (0800) 458 7506
www.inkaterra.com

Luxury lodge on the Río Madre de Dios, 15 km (9 miles) from Puerto Maldonado. Package includes trekking in the lodge's private reserve.

### Tambopata Research Center

Reservations in Lima:
Rainforest Expeditions, Av. Aramburú 166, 4B, Miraflores
Tel: (01) 421 8347
Fax: (01) 421 8183
Reservations in the US/Canada:
Tel: (877) 870 0578
www.perunature.com

Six–seven hours upriver from Puerto Maldonado on Tambopata River. Simple accommodation, low-impact native architecture; 15 minutes' walk from one of the world's largest macaw clay licks.

# SOUTH COAST

## Pisco

**Hostal Posada Hispana**
Av. Bolognesi 222
Tel/fax: (056) 536 363
www.posadahispana.com
Clean, characterful, and good-value budget hotel. Rooms with private bathroom and hot water. Also has a travel agency. **$**

**Hostal Tambo Colorado**
Av. Bolognesi 159
Tel: (056) 531 379
www.hostaltambocolorado.com
A pleasant, quiet place looking onto an interior coutyard and café. The rooms are painted bold colors and each has a sparkling en suite bathroom. The friendly owners will help with Pisco tours. **$**

**Hosteria del Monasterio**
Av. Bolognesi 326
Tel: (056) 531 383
This pleasant place is run by the same owners as Posada Hispana. Imaginatively decorated, comfortable, and welcoming. **$**

## Paracas

**El Carmelo**
Crta Panamericana Sur, Km 301.2
Tel/fax: (056) 232 191/232 553
www.elcarmelohotelhacienda.com
Lovely hacienda-style country hotel built around a sunny garden and swimming pool. Close to Ica on the Panamericana Sur. **$$**

**Hotel El Mirador**
Crta Paracas, Km 20
Tel: (056) 545 086
www.elmiradorhotel.com
Set on the hill just above Paracas, this roomy old hotel is breezy and cool, with a large beautiful garden and pool at the rear. Some rooms have a view of the sea. **$**

## Ica

**Las Dunas**
Av. La Angostura 400
Tel: (056) 256 224
Reservations in Lima: Invertur
Tel: (01) 241 8000

Fax: (01) 446 6280
www.lasdunashotel.com
A holiday resort, complete with horseback riding and private airstrip for Nazca Lines flights. **$$$**

**Hotel Mossone**
Balneario de Huacachina s/n
Tel: (056) 213 630
Attractive colonial-style hotel over-looking the lagoon. Good service and excellent food. **$$**

## Nazca

**Hostal Alegría**
Jr. Lima 168
Tel: (056) 522 702
Fax: (056) 523 431
Email: hotel_alegria@hotmail.com
Simple but good bungalows with private bathroom; quiet garden; popular with backpackers. **$**

**Hotel Las Líneas**
Jr. Arica 299
Tel: (056) 522 488/522 066
Email: laslineas@hotmail.com
Just off Plaza de Armas. Small rooms, hot showers;

restaurant has a surprisingly varied menu. **$$**

**Hotel Majoro**
Panamericana Sur, Km 452
Tel/fax: (056) 522 750
Email: reservas@hotelmajoro.com
Near the airfield, hacienda with garden, swimming pools, hot showers, and friendly service. **$**

**Nazca Lines Hotel**
Jr. Bolognesi s/n
Tel: (056) 522 293
Fax: (056) 522 112
Most upscale option in Nazca: clean and comfortable, with a pool. **$$**

# AREQUIPA AND THE COLCA CANYON

## Arequipa

**La Casa de Margott**
Calle Jerusalén 304
Tel: (054) 229 517
Fax: (054) 283 022
www.lacasademargott.com
A huge palm gives shade in the middle of the colonial courtyard that this hotel is built around. Good, plain rooms and

sunny terraces. Very close to Arequipa's main attractions. **$**

**La Casa de Melgar**
Calle Melgar 108
Tel/fax: (054) 222 459
www.lacasademelgar.com
This lovely hotel is situated within the walls of the bishop of Arequipa's 18th-century home. There are several interior courtyards

and quiet gardens, and the rooms are thoughtfully decorated with antiques. Although not luxurious, this is probably the most beautiful place to stay in Arequipa. **$**

**Casa Grande**
Luna Pizarro 202, Vallecito
Tel: (054) 214 000
Fax: (054) 214 021
Email: casagrande@planet.com.pe
Old house with a good family atmosphere. In a quiet area. **$$**

**Hostal La Casa de Mi Abuela**
Jerusalén 606
Tel: (054) 241 206
Fax: (054) 242 761
www.lacasademiabuela.com
Constantly receives rave reviews. Large complex of bungalow-style rooms in garden setting. **$**

**Hostal Belén**
Av. Bolognesi 132
Tel: (054) 253 625
Fax: (054) 201 419
Simple but fun hotel; rooms give onto central patio. **$**

**Hotel Conquistador**
Mercaderes 409
Tel: (054) 212 916
Fax: (054) 218 987
Pleasant colonial building and friendly service. **$**

**Hotel El Balcón**
García Calderón 202, Vallecito
Tel: (054) 286 998
Comfortable colonial-style hotel, just outside the center of town. Pleasant and good value. **$**

**Hotel El Lago**
Camino al Molino de Sabandía s/n, Sabandía
Tel/fax: (054) 448 417
www.hotelesellago.com
Set on a lakeside 15 minutes from Arequipa, this

**BELOW:** the poolside at the Libertador in Arequipa.

TRANSPORTATION
ACCOMMODATIONS
SHOPPING
ACTIVITIES
A – Z
LANGUAGE

brightly painted hotel is hardly an architectural delight, but the rooms are comfortable. Recently renovated and redecorated, this is a modern four-star hotel. **$$**

**Hotel Libertador Ciudad Blanca Arequipa**
Plaza Bolívar s/n, Selva Alegre
Tel: (054) 215 110
Fax: (054) 241 933
www.libertador.com.pe
The most traditional hotel in Arequipa, just out of town, by Parque Selva Alegre. Great breakfast on the terrace; pool, soccer, jacuzzi, sauna, gym. **$$$**

**Lula's B&B**
Urb. Las Condes, Cayma
Tel: (054) 272 517/934 2660
www.bbaqpe.com

If you've had enough of hotels and you'd like somewhere that feels more like home, the lovely B&B run by multilingual Juana Lourdes Díaz Oviedo de Seelhofer, otherwise known as Lula, not far from the center, is a great option. As well as comfortable lodgings, Lula offers meals and Spanish lessons and is brimming with information on her city. **$**

**La Posada del Monasterio**
Santa Catalina 300
Tel: (054) 405 728
Fax: (054) 206 565
Colonial building with modern extension, opposite Santa Catalina convent. Great view of city. Pleasant living room with

open fire. Garden and patio. **$$**

**Posada del Puente**
Av. Bolognesi 101
Tel: (054) 253 132
Fax: (054) 253 576
www.posadadelpuente.com
Friendly and small *posada*, with river views, a lovely garden, and a good restaurant. **$$**

**Sonesta Posada del Inca**
Portal de Flores 116
Tel: (054) 215 530
www.sonesta.com
On the Plaza de Armas, with excellent views and rooftop pool. **$$**

### Colca Canyon

**Casa Andina Classic**
Huayna Cápac s/n, Chivay

Tel: (054) 531 020
Fax: (054) 531 098
www.casa-andina.com
Part of a chain of bed and breakfast hotels. Free wireless internet plus planetarium show in the observatory every night. **$$**

**Colca Lodge**
Fundo Puye-Yanque-Calloma
Tel: (054) 531 191
Fax: (054) 531 056
www.colca-lodge.com
This delightful country lodge is built of stone, mud-bricks, and thatch, and is right in the heart of the Colca valley, on the banks of the Colca River and next to wonderful hot springs. Stay here a night and you'll want to stay a week. **$$**

# CUSCO AND THE SACRED VALLEY

**ABOVE:** a warm welcome at Cusco's Hotel Libertador.

### Cusco

Don't be daunted by the number of hotels in Cusco. The competition is high and so is the quality. However, even with the large number of mid-range to budget accommodations, it is wise to book in advance, especially in June and August. When choosing a room, bear in mind that the traffic in Cusco is noisy; car horns start honking around 5.30am.

**Amaru Hostal I**
Cuesta San Blas 541
Tel/fax: (084) 225 933
www.amaruhostal.com

Clean and friendly hotel. Rooms with or without private bathroom. **$**

**Amaru Hostal II**
Calle Chihuampata 642, San Blas
Tel: (084) 223 521
Fax: (084) 225 933
www.amaruhostal.com
This is a very pretty hotel set in an old house and built around a green garden. Good views over the rooftops of Cusco. Rooms are rustic and comfortable. The place looks gorgeous lit up at night. **$**

**Hostal Corihuasi**
Suecia 561
Tel/fax: (084) 232 233
www.corihuasi.com
Attractive colonial-style house near the Plaza de Armas, with warm and quiet rooms. Friendly service; hot water. **$**

**Hostal El Balcón**
Tambo de Montero 222
Tel: (084) 236 738
Fax: (084) 225 352
www.balconcusco.com
This beautiful old house has been converted into a wonderful, rustic hotel, set around a garden with lovely views of Cusco. There's a cozy restaurant and WiFi access. **$**

**Hostal Monarca**
Recoleta and Pumapaccha 290
Tel: (084) 226 145
Fax: (084) 229 934

www.hostalmonarca.com
Close to the center of Cusco, just three blocks from the Plaza de Armas, in a pretty, historic building with sunny terraces. Rooms are modern, cozy, and carpeted. There's also a good restaurant. **$**

**Hostería de Anita**
Calle Alabado 525
Tel: (084) 225 933
www.hosteriadeanita.com
Staying at this lovely, quiet, small hotel feels more like staying in the home of the friendly owners. There's a pretty, semi-tropical courtyard garden, hot water in the bathrooms, and great breakfasts. **$**

**Hotel El Dorado Inn**
Av. El Sol 395
Tel: (084) 231 232
Tel: (084) 240 995
Email: hotelessanaugustin.com.pe
Reservations in Lima:
Tel: (01) 472 1415
Pleasant if a bit noisy. Good service and restaurant. **$$**

**Hotel Libertador Palacio del Inka Cusco**
Plazoleta Santo Domingo 259
Tel: (084) 231 961
Fax: (084) 233 152
www.libertador.com.pe
A top-class hotel in a 380-year-old building; well furnished and efficient. The Inti Raymi restaurant

Lima

serves good *novoandino* food. **$$$**

**Hotel Los Andes de América**
Calle Garcilaso 150
Tel: (084) 222 253/666 060
www.cuscoandes.com
Centrally heated, comfortable rooms arranged around an interior courtyard. Helpful staff; excellent buffet breakfast included. **$$**

**Hotel Los Niños**
Meloq 442
Tel/fax: (084) 231 424
www.ninoshotel.com
Attractive renovated colonial building with courtyard. Friendly, clean, comfortable and very popular – so book well in

### PRICE CATEGORIES

Prices are all for double rooms:
**$** = under US$50
**$$** = US$51–100
**$$$** = over US$100

advance. There is a sister hotel and apartments in Cusco, plus a comfortable hacienda just outside the city. All profits fund projects to help street children. **$**

**Hotel Royal Inka I**
Plaza Regocijo 299
Tel: (084) 231 067
Fax: (084) 234 221
www.royalinkahotel.com
Close to the main plaza, and housed in a National Historical Monument. **$$**

**Hotel Royal Inka II**
Calle Santa Teresa 335
Tel: (084) 222 284/231 067
Fax: (084) 234 221
www.royalinkahotel.com
Attractively situated on the upper plaza, with good service. More comfortable than Royal Inka I. **$$**

**Hotel Ruinas**
Calle Ruinas 472
Tel: (084) 260 644
Fax: (084) 236 391
www.hotelruinas.com
Comfortable hotel, some rooms with great view of Nevado Ausangate. **$$**

**Hotel Sueños del Inka**
Calle Alabado 119, San Blas
Tel: (084) 242 2999
Fax: (084) 223 583
www.suenosdelinka.com
Located in the artists' quarter of San Blas, this hillside hotel had panoramic views over Cusco. Rooms are slightly dated, but warm and comfortable. Friendly service. **$**

**Monasterio de Cusco**
Calle Palacio 136, Plazoleta Nazarenas

Tel: (084) 241 777
Fax: (084) 246 983
www.monasterio.orient-express.com
Elegant colonial building with two restaurants and a bar; immaculate service. **$$$**

**Sonesta Posada del Inca**
Portal Espinar 142
Tel: (084) 227 061
Fax: (084) 248 484
www.sonesta.com
Comfortable, with excellent service, restaurant; rooms have soundproofed windows and individually controlled heating. **$$**

## Machu Picchu

**Machu Picchu Sanctuary Lodge**
By Machu Picchu ruins
Tel: (084) 610 8300
http://machupicchu.orient-express.com
Luxurious modern hotel next to the entrance to the ruins. Extremely expensive. Used by many large tour groups. **$$$**

## Aguas Calientes

**Gringo Bill's**
Calle Colla Raymi 104
Just off Plaza de Armas
Tel/fax: (084) 211 046
www.gringobills.com
Friendly, relaxed hotel. Rooms with or without private bathroom. **$$**

**Hatuchay Tower Machu Picchu Hotel**
Crta Puente Ruinas Mz 4
Tel: (084) 211 201
Reservations in Lima:

**ABOVE:** Sol y Luna Lodge and Spa.

Tel: (01) 447 8170
www.hatuchaytower.com
This new hotel has 42 modern rooms and the suites have jacuzzis. The Machu Picchu bus stop is practically at the hotel's door. **$$$**

**Hostal Machu Picchu**
Av. Emperio de los Inkas 127
Tel: (084) 244 598
Email: presidente@terra.com.pe
Good, basic, and clean. Private bathrooms with hot water. Next to the railway line. **$**

**Inkaterra Machu Picchu**
Just outside Aguas Calientes
Tel: (084) 211 122
www.inkaterra.com
Lovely boutique hotel with a series of luxurious bungalow cottages set in a large garden. There are also spa services and a good restaurant. **$$$**

**Inti Inn Machu Picchu**

Pachacutec and Viracocha
Tel: (084) 234 312
www.grupointi.com
Close to the Plaza de Armas, this hotel has clean, light-filled rooms with wrought-iron bedheads, terracotta floor tiles, and en suite bathrooms with plenty of hot water. **$$**

## Urubamba

**Hostal Los Jardines**
Jr. Convención 459
Tel: (084) 201331/201884
www.machawasi.com
Set in a quiet corner of Urubamba, this simple but welcoming hostel has lovely sunny gardens, and the owners also run mountain bike tours in the Sacred Valley. **$**

**Incaland**
Av. Ferrocarril s/n
Reservations in Lima:
Tel: (01) 495 1283
Large hotel with comfortable rooms, reliable hot water, and a swimming pool. **$$**

**Monasterio de la Recoleta**
Jr. la Recoleta s/n
Tel: (084) 201 666
Fax: (084) 201 004
www.hotelessanagustin.com.pe
Rooms in a 17th-century monastery situated just outside Urubamba, with a restaurant and bar. **$$**

**Sol y Luna Lodge and Spa**
Calle Huicho s/n (1 km (½ mile) outside Urubamba)
Tel: (084) 201 620
www.hotelsolyluna.com
This lovely lodge is made up of comfortable round

**BELOW:** the secluded retreat of Inkaterra Machu Picchu.

bungalows set around a large and burgeoning garden. There's a spa on site, t'ai chi and yoga lessons are offered, and the lodge arranges all manner of activities, including trekking, mountain biking, and horseback riding. **$$$**

### Pisac

**Hotel Pisaq**
Plaza de Armas

Tel/fax: (084) 203 062
www.hotelpisaq.com
This delightful hotel overlooking Pisac's main square is brightly decorated with hand-painted murals and has a friendly, family atmosphere. There's a café which serves simple Peruvian fare, a hot rock sauna, a massage service, a pizza oven, and a laundry service. **$**

### Yucay

**Sonesta Posada del Inca**
Plaza Manco II 123
Tel: (084) 201 107
Fax: (084) 201 345
www.sonesta.com
Luxurious former monastery, with a museum, spa and fitness center, and gardens. **$$**

### Ollantaytambo

**El Albergue**

Next to Ollantaytambo rail station
Tel/fax: (084) 204 014/204 029
www.elalbergue.com
Ollantaytambo's oldest hostal is also known as the "train station hotel" on account of its handy location. Simple and relaxing hostal, with eight rooms stylishly decorated by the artist-owner. Has a sauna and very pretty gardens. Staff can organize activities in the area. **$–$$**

# LAKE TITICACA

### Puno

**Casa Andina Classic – Puno Plaza**
Jr. Grau 270
Tel: (051) 367 520
Fax: (051) 363 712
www.casa-andina.com
A modern hotel near Puno's main square, with 35 rooms offering bed and breakfast facilities. **$$**
**Casa Andina Classic – Puno Tikarani**
Jr. Independencia 185
Tel: (051) 367 803
Fax: (051) 365 333
www.casa-andina.com
Just five minutes away from the shores of Lake Titicaca, but still close to the center of Puno. This hotel has simple, comfortable rooms and a roaring log fire to keep you warm on those cold Titicaca nights. **$$**
**Colón Inn**
Jr. Tacna 290

Tel: (051) 351 432
Fax: (051) 357 090
www.coloninn.com
Warm and comfortable with a pleasant restaurant. **$–$$**
**Hostal Europa**
Alfonso Ugarte 112
Tel: (051) 353 026
Popular with backpackers despite problematic showers. **$**
**Hostal Hacienda**
Jr. Deústua 297
Tel/fax: (051) 356 109
www.lahaciendapuno.com
Attractive hotel with the feel of an old colonial house. Well decorated and comfortable, with good service. **$$**
**Hostal Pukara**
Jr. Libertad 328
Tel/fax: (051) 368 448
Email: pukara@terra.com.pe
Friendly, comfortable, family-owned small hotel in the center of Puno. **$**

**Hotel Libertador Lago Titicaca Puno**
Isla Esteves s/n
Tel: (051) 367 780
Fax: (051) 367 879
www.libertador.com.pe
Large and luxurious hotel on the shores of Lake Titicaca, with a private jetty. **$$$**
**Hotel Sillustani**
Jr. Tarapaca 305
Tel: (051) 361 881
Fax: (051) 356 111
www.sillustani.com
Clean and friendly. All rooms have 24-hour heating and hot water. **$$**
**Isla Suasi**
Calle Deustua 576
Tel: (051) 365 968/962 2709
www.islasuasi.com
A privately owned island on the northeast shore of Lake Titicaca in the district of Conima. **$$$**
**Miski Wasi Inn**
Jr. Santiago Giraldo 117
Tel: (051) 365 861

Email: miskiwasiinn@hotmail.com
This is a quiet, friendly, family-run hotel, not far from the Plaza de Armas. There's plenty of hot water 24 hours a day, and good heating to keep you warm through cold nights. **$**
**Sonesta Posada del Inca**
Sesqui Centenario 610, Sector Huaje-Puno
Tel: (051) 364 111
www.sonesta.com
Located 5 km (3 miles) outside Puno, on Lake Titicaca. Part of the same chain as the Sonesta Posadas del Inca in Lima, Cusco, and Yungay. **$$$**
**Totorani Inn**
Av. La Torre 463
Tel: (051) 364 535
www.totorani.com
Whilst this hotel is no great thing of beauty, the rooms are comfortable, and the owners are kind and helpful and will help arrange tours. Free internet access and laundry service. **$**

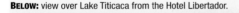

**BELOW:** view over Lake Titicaca from the Hotel Libertador.

### PRICE CATEGORIES

Prices are all for double rooms:
**$** = under US$50
**$$** = US$51–100
**$$$** = over US$100

# S HOPPING

## SHOPS AND MARKETS

### What to Buy

In Lima, as well as in the many regional marketplaces, the best quality and value lies in handcrafted products *(see pages 98–103, for more information)*. This particularly applies to gold, silver, and copper work, as well as Peru's rich textile goods – such as alpaca garments and woven tapestries. Many tourists also take home reproductions of pre-Columbian ceramics, with gourds being a great favorite.

Visitors to the jungle may have the opportunity to purchase traditional handicrafts, including adornments (necklaces worn for tribal dances), utensils (baskets, food bowls, hunting bags), and weapons (bows, arrows, spears). However, never be tempted to buy skins, live animals, or arrows decorated with parrot feathers. This trade is largely illegal and has direct consequences in

destroying wildlife populations.

Apart from *artesanías*, quality shopping goods can only be found in the commercial streets of Miraflores and San Isidro, where suppliers for international brands keep a limited stock at very high prices. For bargains in electronics, you would do better to cross the southern border into northern Chile and its *Zona Franca* (Duty Free) complexes.

### Where to Shop

Each region has its own distinctive crafts, but if your time is limited, you'll find that many cultures are well represented in Lima. There are a number of shops within an attractive courtyard at "1900," Belén 1030, just down from Plaza San Martín. Two other recognized centers of quality merchandise are El Alamo, 5th block of La Paz, Miraflores, and El Suche, the 6th block of La Paz in Miraflores.

### Fine Alpaca

Alpaca products are well worth buying, as long as you are prepared to hand-wash them with great care. Vendors will often tell you their goods are made from alpaca "bebé." This does not mean baby alpacas, but refers to the wool taken from the throat of the animal, where it is at its finest and softest.

Most woolen jumpers sold as alpaca are usually a more hard-wearing mix of llama wool and synthetic fibers.

#### *Markets*

Outdoor markets offer the best bargains, although quality varies and one needs to be wary of pickpockets. The best ones in Lima are to be found on the first four blocks of Avenida Petit Thouars. There is also a pleasant artists' market with canvases of varying quality on Parque Kennedy in the heart of Miraflores.

Outside Lima, Pisac market is renowned for its woolen rugs, blankets, and bags, and beautifully soft alpaca sweaters. The Sunday market in Huancayo is packed with stalls selling woven blankets and knitted jumpers, hats and bags, and is also known for its carved pumpkin gourds.

### Handicrafts

#### *Lima*

**Artesanía Cusco**
Jr. Camana 200
Tel: (01) 427 1760
**Silver Llama**
Calle Loma Rica 210, Santiago de Surco
Tel: (01) 275 3553
www.silverllama.com

**BELOW:** Andean scenes for sale in Parque Kennedy, Miraflores.

**ABOVE:** traditional Peruvian textiles.

**Artesanías Urin Huanca**
Ricardo Palma 205, Miraflores
Tel: (01) 241 9780
**Kunturwasi**
Ocharán 182, Miraflores
Tel: (01) 447 7173
Mon–Fri 10am–8pm, Sat
10.30am–7pm.
**Mercado Artesanal**
Av. Petit Thouars Block 52,
Miraflores
**Peru Artcrafts**
Centro Comercial Larcomar,
Miraflores
Tel: (01) 445 311
**Killawasi**
Av. Larco 812, Miraflores
**Iskay**
Pedro de Osma 106, Barranco
Tel: (01) 247 2102

*Cusco*
**Centro de Textiles Tradicionales
Cusco (CTTC)**
Av. Sol 603
Tel: (084) 228 117
www.textilescusco.org
**La Casa Ecológica**
Triunfo 393
Tel: (084) 255 646
www.casaecologicacusco.com
Sells fairly traded art and crafts,
and organic food.
**Timoteo Ccarita**
Punto de Encuentro (next to La
Compañía), Plaza de Armas

## Alpaca, Leather, and Fur

*Lima*
**Alpaca 111**
Av. Larco 671, Miraflores
Tel: (01) 447 1623
Store 107, Centro Comercial
Larcomar, Miraflores
**Royal Alpaca**
Juanalfa 266, Miraflores

Tel: (01) 445 9372
Mon–Fri 8am–5pm.

*Arequipa*
**Alpaca 111**
Calle Mercaderes 141
Tel: (054) 225 550
**Michael y Compañia**
Santa Catalina 120
Tel: (054) 202 2525

*Cusco*
**Alpaca's Best**
Plaza Nazarenas 197
Tel: (084) 245 331
Mon–Sat 9am–9pm.
**Alpaca 111**
Plaza Regocijo 202
Tel: (084) 243 233
**La Casa de la Llama**
Calle Palacio 121
Tel: (084) 240 813
Daily 9am–10pm.

## Gold and Jewelry

*Lima*
**Cabuchón**
Libertadores 715, San Isidro
Tel: (01) 440 7800
Mon–Fri 10am–7pm, Sat until 6pm.
**Camusso**
Pancho Fierro 194, San Isidro
Tel: (01) 421 9525/221 2121
Mon–Fri 9am–1pm and 3–7pm,
Sat 9am–1pm.
    The major hotels in Lima often
house exclusive jewelry and *artesanía*
stores, such as H. Stern Jewelers,
with outlets at the Hotel Gran Bolívar,
the Sheraton *(see page 326)*, the
Gold Museum *(see page 159)*, and
the International Airport.

## Books

There is not much in the way of good
English-language bookshops in Peru.
The following will have titles in
English and are the best bets:

*Lima*
**ABC**
Centro Comercial San Isidro,
Paseo de la República 3440

## Souvenir Drinks

Pick up a bottle of *pisco* to take
home and make *pisco sour*
cocktails to remind you of your trip
*(see recipe on page 247)*. Peru's
national drink is sold all over the
country, but the best stuff comes
from *bodegas* near Ica. Or, if you
fancy something non-alcoholic,
why not tuck a bottle of the super-
sweet Inca Kola into your bag?
There's nothing quite like it.

Sells newspapers, magazines, guidebooks, and coffee-table books in
English, French, and German. Keep
in mind these items will be more
expensive than at home.
**El Virrey**
Miguel Dasso, 147, San Isidro
Tel: (01) 440 0607
An excellent bookshop where
politicians and intellectuals go
shopping. It has a great stock of
publications on Peru plus a small
section of books in English.
**Zeta Bookstore**
Comandante Espinar 219, Miraflores,
Tel: (01) 446 5139
www.zetabook.com (in Spanish)
General bookstore which stocks
some titles in English.
**Special Book Services**
Av. Angamos Oeste 301, Miraflores
Tel: (01) 241 8490
www.sbs.com.pe (in Spanish)
Good general bookstore with
branches in most major cities.
**Ibero Librería**
Av. Oscar R. Benavides 500,
Miraflores
Tel: (01) 242 2798
Email: diagonal@iberolibros.com
General bookstore which also has
branches in the Larcomar shopping
center and on Calle Real, Huancayo.

*Cusco*
**Special Book Services**
Av. El Sol 781A
Tel: (084) 248 106
www.sbs.com.pe (in Spanish)

*Arequipa*
**Special Book Services**
Calle San Francisco 125
Tel: (054) 205 317
www.sbs.com.pe (in Spanish)

**BELOW:** Taquile Island is renowned for
its knitted goods.

# A CTIVITIES

# THE ARTS, NIGHTLIFE, FESTIVALS, CINEMA, SPORTS, OUTDOOR ACTIVITIES, AND TOURS

## THE ARTS

From music and song to a huge spectrum of handicrafts, Peru has one of the most diverse arts scenes in South America.

You can't leave Peru without spending an evening at a *peña*, where you'll experience some of the country's hundreds of musical genres. Peru's identity is as much bound to the haunting strains of the pan pipes and the melodious Andean harp, as it is to the rhythms of Afro-Peruvian drumming. At any festive gathering in the Andes, you'll see people dance the *huayno*, and in the coastal north, the coquettish *marinera* is performed with gusto.

In Lima's theaters, you'll find everything from plays of Inca origin to distinctly avant-garde productions. Theaters and art galleries are

**BELOW:** backstage at a theater in Cusco.

concentrated in Lima *(see below)*. Check the Cultural section of *El Comercio* newspaper for performances and exhibitions.

### Theaters

**Teatro Larco**
Av. Larco 1036, Miraflores
Tel: (01) 248 0567
**Teatro Británico**
Bellavista 527, Miraflores
Tel: (01) 447 1135
**Teatro Municipal**
Ica 377
Tel: (01) 428 2303/462 7576

### Cultural Centers

**Instituto Cultural Peruano Norteamericano (ICPNA)**
Av. Angamos Oeste 160, Miraflores
Tel: (01) 706 7000
www.icpna.edu.pe
**Centro Cultural de la Pontificia Universidad Católica del Perú (CCPUCP)**
Av. Camino Real 1075, San Isidro
Tel: (01) 616 1616
http://cultural.pucp.edu.pe (in Spanish)

### Art Galleries

The best art and antique establishments are in the areas of San Isidro, Miraflores, and Barranco.
**Forum**, Larco 1150, Miraflores
Tel: (01) 446 1313
**Full Art Peru**
Calle los Manzanos 355, San Isidro
Tel: (01) 264 0268
www.fullartperu.com (in Spanish)
**Galería de la Municipalidad de Miraflores**
Av. Larco, 3rd block
Tel: (01) 444 0540

### Concerts

The Philharmonic Society in Lima presents celebrated international orchestras and soloists from April to November. For further information check the cultural section of *El Comercio*, or contact: Sociedad Filarmónica de Lima, Porta 170, Of. 307, Miraflores, tel: (01) 445 7395/242 6396, www.socfillimaperu.com.pe (in Spanish).

**Galeria Municipal Pancho Fierro**
Pasaje Santa Rosa 114
Tel: (01) 315 1543
**Museo de Arte**
Paseo Colón 125
Tel: (01) 423 4732
http://museoarte.perucultural.org.pe (in Spanish)
*(See page 159.)*

## NIGHTLIFE

### Live Music

*Lima*

Lima offers some of the best music from all over Peru. Not only are there good groups performing Andean folk music, but there are Afro-Peruvian bands, salsa, *techno-cumbia* dance music, and some jazz bands. The *peñas* which put on Andean folk music get very crowded at the weekends, as do the *salsadromos* where young Peruvians love to dance the night away. Most venues are located in Barranco, Lima's Bohemian suburb of cafés, bars, and live music.
**Manos Morenas**
Av. Pedro de Osma 409, Barranco
Tel: (01) 467 0421

## Calendar of Festivals and Holidays

### January

**January 1** New Year's Day (national holiday).
**January 18** Anniversary of the founding of Lima. Official anniversary of the founding of Lima by the Spanish conquistador Francisco Pizarro on January 18, 1535.
**End January** *Festival de la Marinera*, Trujillo. Annual traditional dance competitions.

### February

**February 1–15** *Cruz de Chalpon*, Chiclayo. Handicraft and commercial fair in the nearby prilgrimage center of Motupe.
**Early February** *Virgen de la Candelaria*, Puno. "La Mamita Candicha," the patron of Puno, is honored with folklore demonstrations. Thousands participate in the parades, dances, fireworks, and music of this important religious event.
**Mid-February** Carnival, Puno and Cajamarca. Pre-Lent carnival is celebrated throughout Peru, but especially in these cities, with *La Pandilla* dancing and traditional festivities.

### March/April

**Early March** *Fiesta de la Vendimia*, Ica. The grape harvest of the Ica valley is celebrated with parades, dances, and revelry.
**March/April** *Semana Santa* (Easter/Holy Week). Among the nationwide commemorations is the spectacular procession in Cusco in honor of *El Señor de los Temblores,* held on Holy Monday and Thursday. The people of Tarma make carpets of flowers to cover the streets for their evening processions. (Half-day holiday on Maundy Thursday, full-day holiday on Good Friday.)
**Third week April** National Contest of *Caballos de Paso*, Lima. This exhibition and contest in Mamacona, 30 km (18 miles) south of Lima, involves horse breeders from the most important regions of Peru.

### May

**May 1** Labor Day and *San José* (St Joseph's Day) (national holiday).
**May 2** *Cruz Velacuy*, Cusco. The crosses in all the churches of Cusco are veiled, and festivities take place.
**May 2–4** *Las Alasitas*, Puno. Important exhibition and sale of miniature handicrafts.

### June

**First week** Mountaineering Week in the Andes, particularly in Huaraz. The Callejón de Huaylas and the Cordillera Blanca provide the majestic settings for the National and International Ski Championships, as well as many other adventurous activities.
**Mid-June** Corpus Christi, Cusco. One of the most beautiful displays of religious folklore, the Procession of the Consecrated Host is accompanied by statues of saints from churches all over Cusco.
**June 24** *Inti Raymi* (Festival of the Sun), Cusco. This ancient festival is staged at the Sacsayhuamán fortress, and involves Inca rituals, parades, folk dances, and contests. *San Juan* (St John's Day) is also celebrated throughout the Andes.
**June 29** *San Pedro y San Pablo* (St Peter's and St Paul's Day; national holiday).

### July

**July 15–17** *La Virgen del Carmen*, Cusco. Festivities are held throughout the highlands and are especially colorful in Paucartambo, 255 km (160 miles) from Cusco.
**July 28–9** Peru's Independence celebrations (national holiday).

### August

**August 15** Arequipa Day, the city's most important annual event. Festivities include folkloric dances and handicraft markets, and climax with a fireworks display in the Plaza de Armas.
**August 30** – *Santa Rosa de Lima* (national holiday).

### October

**October 8** Commemoration of the Battle of Angamos (national holiday).
**October 7–20** *El Señor de Luren*, Ica. Thousands of pilgrims pay homage to the town patron, with the main procession on the 17th.
**October 18, 19, and 28** *El Señor de los Milagros*, Lima. A massive procession in honor of Lima's patron saint, on the 18th.
**October 19** Unu Urco Festival, Urcos and Calca (near Cusco). Ceremonies, Andean music, dancing, and parades.

### November

**November 1** *Día de Todos los Santos* (All Saints' Day; national holiday).
**November 1–7** Puno Jubilee Week. Puno celebrates its founding by the Spanish, followed by a re-enactment of the emergence of the legendary founders of the Inca empire, Manco Capac and Mama Ocllo, from the waters of Lake Titicaca. This week sees the best of Puno's folkloric festivities.
**November 29** Zaña Week, Chiclayo. Week of celebrations for the foundation of Zaña include folklore shows, sporting events, and exhibitions of *Caballos de Paso*.

### December

**December 8** *La Concepción Inmaculada* (Immaculate Conception; national holiday).
**December 24** Festival of *Santu Rantikuy*, Cusco. Andean toy and handicrafts fair in the main plaza.
**December 24–5** Christmas (half-day national holiday on 24th, full day on 25th).

**BELOW:** flag-bearers at the Virgen de la Candelaria festival in Puno.

Set in a beautiful early 20th-century house in the most happening part of Barranco. Folk music from about 10pm until late every day except Sunday and Monday, as well as as excellent criollo cuisine.

**Brisas del Titicaca**
Jr. Walkuski 168
Tel: (01) 332 1901/1881
www.brisasdeltiticaca.com
One of the best-known *peñas* in Lima, with spectacular folkloric nights Tue–Sat showcasing the dance and music of Puno and other regions. Specialties from the Altiplano served.

**La Candelaria**, Av. Bolognesi 292, Barranco, tel: (01) 247 2186. In the heart of Barranco, La Candelaria has live music and a lively folkloric floorshow every weekend from 10pm and serves exotic cocktails and snacks.

**La Estación de Barranco**
Pedro de Osma 112, Barranco
Tel: (01) 247 0344
Tue–Sat, shows at 11pm.

**Peña Hatuchay**
Mariscal Miller 883, Jesús María
Tel: (01) 332 8860
The best night out for budget-conscious travelers and anyone else who is willing to get into the informal spirit. Colorful decor and a great variety show. Shows on Friday and Saturday at 9pm.

**Sachún**
Av. del Ejército 657, Miraflores
Tel: (01) 441 0123/441 4465
Tue–Sat traditional Andean and Afro-Peruvian dances.
For jazz, latin jazz, and rock performances, try the following venues:

**El Dragón**
Av. Nicolás de Piérola 166, block 1, Barranco
Tel: (01) 477 5420

**La Casona de Barranco**
Av. Grau 329, Barranco

**Jazz Zone**
Av. La Paz 656, Pasaje El Suche, Miraflores
Tel: (01) 241 8139

**Cocodrilo Verde**
Francisco de Paula 226, Miraflores
Tel: (01) 242 7583

### Cusco

Cusco has some of the best *peñas* in South America, with a range of Andean styles (some of the bands are internationally known). They're mostly around the Plaza de Armas and easy to find because of the blaring music. Two *peñas* sharing the same staircase on the southwestern side of the plaza are probably the best place to start.
Several restaurants around the plaza, such as El Truco, also have live music – just stroll around and

## Cinema

Peru's film industry is very small, but going to the cinema (*el cine*) is popular, and there are movie houses in all the larger towns, often showing US films in English, with Spanish subtitles. Sometimes the Spanish language wins out, though, and it's the *gringos* who have to be content with subtitles. Cinemas in Lima include:

**Multicines StarVision El Pacífico**, Av. Diagonal (esq. Av. José Pardo), Miraflores, tel: (01) 444 9964.

**Cinemark** has cinemas at the Jockey Plaza (Av. Javier Prado Este, block 42, Monterrico, Surco) and Megaplaza shopping malls

listen. Many of the larger hotels also stage folkloric shows. Folkloric venues include:

**Ukukus**
Calle Plateros 316
Tel: (084) 242 951

**El Truco**
Plaza Regocijo 261
Tel: (084) 235 295

## Bars and Nightclubs

### Lima

**O'Murphy's Irish Pub**, Schell 627, tel: (01) 242 1212. Pub grub and good atmosphere.

**La Noche**, Av. Bolognesi 307, Barranco, tel: (01) 247 2186. La Noche has the reputation for being the best spot for live music in Lima. It occupies a large multi-level house and does mainly jazz, indie rock, and electronic gigs. The jam sessions on Monday nights are a Lima classic.

**Discoteca Gótica**, Centro Comercial Larcomar, Miraflores. One of Lima's best nightclubs.

### Cusco

**Los Perros**, Tecsecocha 436. Trendy bar for cocktails and beers, with couches. Great mix of music.

**Rosie O'Grady's**, Santa Catalina Ancha 360, tel: (084) 243 514. Attractive, smart Irish Bar with good food and Guinness.

**Cross Keys Pub**, Plaza de Armas. Typical British pub, with darts.

**Ukukus**, Plateros 316. Late afternoon movies, live local bands, followed by disco.

**Mama Africa**, Portal de Harinas 191. Movies, internet café, hip music.

**Kamikaze**, Plaza Regocijo 274. Live band around 11pm followed by rock/pop, reggae and salsa music. There is a happy hour before the live band performs.

(Av. Alfredo Mendiola and Av. Pacífico), as well as one in San Miguel and one in Chorrillos. Tel: (01) 437 0081/437 5244, www.cinemark-peru.com.

**Cineplanet**, Av. Santa Cruz 814, Miraflores, tel: (01) 452 7000.

**Multicines Larco**, Centro Comercial Larcomar, Miraflores, tel: (01) 446 7558.

**Romeo y Julieta**, Pasaje Porta 132, Miraflores, tel: (01) 444 0135.

**Filmoteca de Lima**, Museo de Arte, Colón 123, tel: (01) 444 0135.

**El Cine**, Centro Cultural PUCP, Camino Real 1075, San Isidro, tel: (01) 616 1616.

## SPORTS

### Spectator

The main spectator sports in Peru are soccer (football), horse racing, and, to a lesser extent, bullfighting.
Association football matches take place at the National Stadium (Estadio Nacional), Paseo de la República in downtown Lima, which seats 45,000.
Horse racing takes place most weekends and some summer evenings at the Monterrico Racetrack at the junction of the Panamerican Highway South with Avenida Javier Prado in Lima. Take your passport to get access to the members' stand.

### Participant

Lima Tours (*see Trips and Tours, opposite*) can arrange visits to **El Pueblo Inn**, a country club 11 km

**BELOW:** hiking the ancient Inca Trail to Machu Picchu.

(7 miles) east of Lima, specifically for sporting activities such as tennis, golf, horseback riding, and swimming. Other 18-hole golf courses in Lima include the Country Club de Villa, Granja Azul, and La Planicie.

For ten-pin bowling and pool-playing, go to the **Brunswick Bowl**, Balta 135, in Miraflores.

## OUTDOOR ACTIVITIES

A great variety of activities is available to tourists outside Lima, from spectacular mountain treks to whitewater rafting excursions. See Andean Adventures *(pages 120–9)* for more information.

### Horseback Riding

Horseback riding is popular in the Sierra, where horses can easily be hired. Check the condition of the horses, however, as not all are well treated. Agencies in Cusco can arrange excursions in the Sacred Valley, and it is also possible to arrange rides in the Colca canyon from Arequipa.

### Trekking

Trekking is one of Peru's great attractions, and best undertaken in the dry season, May through October. Most famous is the four-day Inca Trail to Machu Picchu. This excursion is very popular, so it's wise to book before you arrive in Cusco (it is forbidden to walk the trail independently). Restrictions on the numbers of people allowed on the Inca Trail have led to the promotion of other routes in the region, such as the Salcantay to Santa Teresa Loop *(see page 123)*. The Inka Porter Project (www.peruweb.org/porters) based in Cusco can provide details of trekking agencies who treat their porters and the environment well.

The Ausangate Loop which starts near Cusco is five-seven day hike which circles Mount Ausangate. Tour operators can also arrange shorter and less tiring walking tours in the Sacred Valley and around Cusco.

The other main center for trekking is Huaraz (a short flight or eight-hour bus journey north of Lima), the starting point for treks in the Cordillera Blanca, including the Llanganuco to Santa Cruz Loop *(see page 197)*. The Cordillera Huayhuash *(see page 200)* is an increasingly popular destination for trekkers, and is often less crowded than treks in the Cordillera Blanca.

Members of the South American Explorer's club can find other trekking companions through the notice boards at the Lima and Cusco club houses *(see page 348)*.

### Climbing

The Cordillera Blanca is home to Peru's highest peak, Mount Huascarán *(see page 197)* and 30 other summits over 6,000 meters (19,680 ft). The Cordillera Huayhuash also attracts many climbers but has fewer facilities.

The **Peruvian Mountain Guide Association**, based in the Casa de Guias in Huaraz (Plaza Ginebra 28, tel: 043-421 811) is a useful source of information and can recommend certified guides.

### Mountain Biking

Peru's hilly terrain offers numerous opportunities for mountain biking, particularly around Cusco, Arequipa, and Huaraz. **Mountain Bike Adventures** in Huaraz (tel: 043-424 259, www.chakinaniperu.com) operate biking trips of varying lengths in the Cordillera Blanca.

The organizers of the annual **Megavalanche** bike race near Cusco *(see page 127)* organize bike races and other extreme sports all over Peru. See www.megavalanche.com.

### Rafting and Kayaking

Peru offers some spectacular whitewater rafting and kayaking on the Apurimac and Tambopata rivers and there are other, smaller excursions near Lima, Arequipa, and Huaraz *(see page 129)*. **Amazonas Explorer**, based in Cusco, organize rafting and kayaking trips on the Apurimac River and to the Colca canyon *(see below)*.

## TRIPS AND TOURS

Tours to sights all over the country can be arranged through agencies in Lima. Some companies, such as Lima Tours, Inka Natura Travel, and Condor Travel, also have regional offices.

**Lima Tours**
Jr. de la Unión 1040
Tel: (01) 619 6900
Fax: (01) 619 6921
www.limatours.com.pe
One of the largest tour organizers in Peru, with branches in every tourist region. Lima Tours has exclusive rights on visits to some colonial houses in Lima, including evening dinners in 17th-century mansions.

**ABOVE:** a knowledgeable tour guide can offer a useful insight into a destination.

**Class Adventure Travel (CAT)**
Calle San Martín 800, Miraflores
Tel: (01) 444 2220/1652
US/Canada: (877) 240 4770
UK: (0800) 975 5573
www.cat-travel.com
Well-organized tours and private groups throughout Peru.

**Aracari Travel Consulting SAC**
Av. José Pardo 610 # 802, Miraflores
Tel: (01) 242 6673/243 0522
Fax: (01) 242 4856
www.aracari.com
Specializes in arranging escorted group tours and accommodations in the Sacred Valley, Chachapoyas, and the northwest of the country.

**Condor Travel**
Armando Blondet 249
Tel: (01) 615 300
www.condortravel.com
Organizes tours throughout Peru, including trips to Cusco, Machu Picchu, and the Colca canyon.

**Inka Natura Travel**
Manuel Bañon 461, San Isidro
Tel: (01) 440 2022/422 8114
Fax: (01) 422 9225
www.inkanatura.com
Organizes archeological tours in northern Peru and Cusco, and nature tours to Manu national park and the Tambopata national reserve.

**AndesTrek**
Av. Larco 101, Of. 213 Miraflores
Tel: (01) 797 7660
Fax: (01) 221 5023
www.andestrek.net
Organizes mountaineering, trekking, and other tours throughout Peru.

### Nazca

For flights over the Nazca Lines in light aircraft, reservations can be made with several companies at Nazca airport or in town, or in Lima,

TRANSPORTATION · ACCOMMODATIONS · SHOPPING · ACTIVITIES · A – Z · LANGUAGE

including the following:
**Aero Cóndor**
Panamericana Sur, Km 447, Hostal
Nido del Condor, Nazca
Tel: (056) 256 230
Av. José Pardo 562, Miraflores, Lima
Tel: (01) 614 6014
Information after office hours,
tel: (01) 441 8484
www.aerocondor.com.pe
**Aeroica**
In Nazca airport or at Hotel La
Maison Suisse, Panamericana Sur,
Km 447, Nazca
Tel: (056) 522 434
Trips and Travel SRL, Diez Canseco
480B, Miraflores, Lima
Tel: (01) 445 0859
Fax: (01) 444 2140
www.aeroica.net
**Aero Paracas**
Av. Santa Fé 274, Lima
Tel: (01) 271 6941/273 0507
Fax: (01) 449 4768
www.aeroparacas.com

## Arequipa

Most attractions in Arequipa are
accessible on foot and easily
appreciated as an independent
traveler, although if you don't have
much time, city tours are available,
which include the Santa Catalina
monastery and other points of
interest. Day tours into the
mountainous terrain include the
Colca canyon, climbing the El Misti
volcano, viewing the petroglyphs at El
Toro, bathing in local thermal springs,
and visiting the Cotahuasi canyon.
The following companies offer
traditional and adventure tours around
Arequipa and to the Colca Canyon:
**Lima Tours**
Calle Mercaderes 193, Of. D-4
Tel: (054) 225 759
Fax: (054) 285 922
www.limatours.com.pe

**Ideal Travels**
Urb. San Isidro F-2, Vallecito
Tel: (054) 244 439
Fax: (054) 245 199
Email: idealperu@terra.com.pe
**Giardino Tours**
Jerusalén 604A
Tel: (054) 221 345
Fax: (054) 242 761
www.giardinotours.com
**Maravillas Peruanas Travel**
Santa Catalina 102
Tel: (054) 227 297
Fax: (054) 200 970
Email: maravillasperuanas@hotmail.com
**Condor Travel**
Calle Santa Catalina 210
Tel: (054) 237 821
www.condortravel.com
**Sky Viajes y Turismo**
Calle Zela 301A
Tel: (054) 281 731
www.skyperu.com
**Holley's Unusual Excursions**
Tel/fax: (054) 258 459
Email: anthonygch@star.com.pe
An interesting option: English
owner Anthony Holley knows the
area inside out and runs four-
wheel-drive excursions for up to
six people.
**Amazonas Explorer**
PO Box 333, Arequipa
Tel: (054) 212 813
Fax: (054) 220 147
www.amazonas-explorer.com
First-class rafting and mountain-
biking expeditions, including
rafting and canoeing trips in the
Colca canyon. The English/Swiss
owners are experts in alternative
adventure.

## Puno

Tours can be taken around the lake,
to the ruins at Sillustani, Chucuito,
and the town of Juli, with the
following agencies.

**Turpuno**
Jr. Lima 208, Of. 1B
Tel: (051) 352 001
Fax: (051) 351 431
www.turpuno.com
**Edgar Adventures**
Jr. Lima 328
Tel: (051) 353 444
Fax: (051) 354 811
www.edgaradventures.com
**Käfer Viajes y Turismo**
Jr. Arequipa 179
Tel: (051) 354 742
Fax: (051) 352 701
www.kafer-titicaca.com
**Solmar Tours**
Jr. Arequipa 140
Tel: (051) 352 701

## Cusco

On arrival in Cusco, the first thing
to do is to purchase a Visitor Ticket
*(see page 276)*, a combination
entry pass to all the historic
buildings of note in Cusco and the
Sacred Valley.
Tour operators in Cusco fall into
two categories: those offering
standard tours of Cusco and the
surrounding ruins and market villages;
and those operating adventure tours
such as trekking, climbing, river
running, and jungle expeditions.

### Cultural Tours
**Lima Tours**
Jr. Machu Picchu D24,
Urb. Manuel Prado
Tel: (084) 228 431
Fax: (084) 221 266
www.limatours.com.pe
**Condor Travel**
Calle Saphi 848A
Tel: (084) 248 181
www.condortravel.com
**Inka Natura Travel**
Calle Ricardo Palma J-1,
Urb. Santa Mónica
Tel: (084) 255 255
Fax (084) 245 973
www.inkanatura.com

### Adventure Tours
**Trekperu**
Jr. Ricardo Palma N-9,
Urb. Santa Mónica
Tel: (084) 239 988
Fax: (084) 261 501
www.trekperu.com
**Peruvian Andean Treks**
Av. Pardo 705
Tel: (084) 225 701
Fax: (084) 238 911
Email: postmaster@patcusco.com.pe
**Explorandes**
Av. Garcilazo 316A
Tel: (084) 238 380
Fax: (084) 233 784
www.explorandes.com

**BELOW:** a tour group at the Huaca del Dragón in northern Peru.

**Amazonas Explorer**
Av. Collasuyo 910, Urb. Miravalle
Tel/fax: (084) 252 846
www.amazonas-explorer.com
Organizes first-class rafting and
mountain biking expeditions. The
English/Swiss owners are experts in
alternative adventure.

## Manu

The following tour companies
organize trips into Manu National
Park from Cusco. (See Accommo-
dations, page 331, for details of
lodges in the Southern Amazon.)
**Manu Expeditions**
Calle Humberto Vidal Unda G-5,
Segunda Etapa, Urb. Magisterial,
Cusco
Tel: (084) 226 671
Fax: (084) 236 706
www.manuexpeditions.com
**Manu Nature Tours**
Av. Pardo 1046, Cusco
Tel: (084) 252 721
Fax: (084) 234 793
www.manuperu.com
**Pantiacolla Tours (Manu Biosphere
Reserve)**
Calle Saphi 554, Cusco
Tel: (084) 238 323
Fax: (084) 252 696
www.pantiacolla.com

## Tambopata Reserve

The following companies based in
Lima organize trips into Tambopata
national reserve from Puerto
Maldonado. (See Accommodations,
page 331, for details of lodges in
the Southern Amazon.)
**Peruvian Safaris**
Alcanflores 459,
Miraflores, Lima
Tel: (084) 447 8888
Fax: (084) 241 8427
www.peruviansafaris.com
**Rainforest Expeditions**
Av. Aramburú 166, Dep. 4B,
Miraflores, Lima
Tel: (01) 421 8347
Fax: (01) 421 8183
www.perunature.com

## Huaraz

For tours to Chavín, Pastoruri, other
day trips, and longer treks:
**Huaraz Chavín Tours**
Av. Luzuriaga 502
Tel: (043) 421 578
Fax: (043) 424 801
www.chavintours.com.pe
**Explorandes**
Av. Centenario 489
Tel: (043) 421 960
Fax: (043) 428 051
www.explorandes.com

**Montañero Aventura y Turismo**
Parque Ginebra 30B
Tel: (043) 426 386
Fax: (043) 422 306
www.trekkingperu.com
**Andean Sport Tours**
Av. Luzuriaga 571
Tel: (043) 721 612

## Trujillo

Tours to any of the major archeo-
logical sites (Sechín, Huacas del Sol
y de la Luna, Huaca del Dragón, and
Chan Chan) can be arranged in
Trujillo.
**Contour**
Jr. Francisco Pizarro 478, Of. 101
Tel: (044) 200 412
Email: rfeire@contour.com.pe
**Guía Tours**
Independencia 580
Tel: (044) 245 170
Fax: (044) 246 353
**Trujillo Tours**
Jr. Diego de Almagro 301
Tel/fax: (044) 233 091/233 069
**VIP Tours**
Calle Argentina 159, Urb. 2,
El Recreo
Tel: (044) 257 515
Email: viptourser@millicon.com.pe
**Condor Travel**
Tours in and around Trujillo should
be organized with the Lima office
(see page 339).

## Chachapoyas

**Vilaya Tours**
Jr. Grau 624
Tel: (041) 477 506
Fax: (041) 478 154
www.vilayatours.com
Runs tours and treks in the
Northern Sierra, including trips to
the Kuélap ruins.

## Chiclayo

Important archeological sites such
as Sipán can be reached with:
**Inka Natura Travel**
Gran Hotel Chiclayo, Av. Federico
Villareal 115
Tel: (074) 209 948
Fax: (074) 270 797
www.inkanatura.com

## Cajamarca

Tours of the city include numerous
colonial churches, the thermal
baths at Baños del Inca, and the
Ventanillas de Otuzco, and can
be arranged with the following
agencies:
**Cumbe Mayo Tours**
Jr. Amalia Puga 635
Tel/fax: (076) 362 938

**ABOVE:** Amazonian transport.

**Clarín Tours**
Jr. Del Batán 161
Tel/fax: (076) 366 829
www.clarintours.com
**Atahualpa Inca Tours**
Jr. Amazonas 760, Of. 01
Tel/fax: (076) 367 041
**Cajamarca Travel**
Jr. Dos de Mayo 570
Tel: (076) 365 460
Fax: (076) 368 642
Email: cajamarcatravel@terra.com.pe

## Iquitos

There are many interesting sights in
and around the city as well as jungle
expeditions. (See Accommodations,
pages 330–1, for details of lodges in
the Northern Amazon.)
**Amazon Tours and Cruises**
Requeña 336
Tel: (065) 231 611
Fax: (065) 231 265
www.amazontours.net
**Amazon Cruises**
Av. Gen. Rumiñahui and 1er Tranversal
221, San Rafael, Quito, Ecuador
Tel: (5932) 286 6898
Tel: (5932) 286 7832
www.amazoncruise.net
This Quito-based company is a one-
stop shop for boat-based tours in the
northern Amazon, including trips from
Yurimaguas to Iquitos and into the
Pacaya-Samiria national reserve.
(See page 224 for details of river
boat excursions in the Amazon).

## Ayacucho

For tours in the Central Sierra,
contact: **Morochucos Tours**
Portal Constitución 41
Tel: (066) 818 908
Jr. Cusco 349
Tel: (066) 312 542
www.morochucos.com

TRANSPORTATION

ACCOMMODATIONS

SHOPPING

ACTIVITIES

A – Z

LANGUAGE

# A – Z

## A HANDY SUMMARY OF PRACTICAL INFORMATION, ARRANGED ALPHABETICALLY

## Addresses

The following will help you find your way around the addresses listed in this book:
Av. *(Avenida)* = avenue
Calle = street
Crta *(Carretera)* = highway
Edificio = building
Esq. *(Esquina)* = corner
Hostal = cheap hotel (not a hostel)
Jr. *(Jirón)* = way/street
Of. *(Oficina)* = office
Pasaje = passage/alley
Piso = floor/story
s/n *(sin numéro)* = no number
Urb. *(Urbanización)* = area or neighborhood

## Admission Charges

All tourist attractions, apart from some churches and a handful of museums, charge admission. Most expensive of all is Machu Picchu, but when you've come all this way, it's

worth the price. There are usually discounts for children and students, and family tickets are sometimes available. If you're claiming a student discount, be sure to carry your International Student Identity Card (ISIC; *see page 350*). Entrance fees are usually quoted in soles, although larger attractions may give them in dollars as well. Be sure to keep your ticket after you enter a site, as it may be checked. In Cusco, the Cusco Visitor Ticket is the way to see the city's main attractions *(see page 274).*

## Budgeting for Your Trip

You can get by in Peru on US$30 a day – but that would be just getting by at rock bottom prices, and why would you want to stint when there's so much enjoyment to be had? A more reasonable budget is US$60 per day for a comfortable and enjoyable holiday. This includes comfortable accommodations at US$20–40 per night and meals at

less touristy restaurants which are amazingly cheap. The best value is the daily *menú*, which rarely costs more than five soles.
If you stay in four- and five-star hotels and eat in restaurants designed for tourists, your budget will need to be several hundred dollars per day. Long-distance transport by bus is cheap, and taxis in town likewise *(see page 324).* Handicrafts are more expensive in the big city craft markets; try to buy in the villages instead.

## Business Hours

In Lima office hours are Mon–Fri 9am–5pm with a lunch break at noon. Shops are generally open from 10 or 11am until about 8 or 9pm. Larger shopping centers open earlier and stay open later. Banks are generally open Mon–Fri 9am–6pm (and some until 7 or even 10pm). Weekend banking hours depend on the bank, although most are open on Saturday. Outside Lima and the larger cities,

## CLIMATE CHART

### Lima

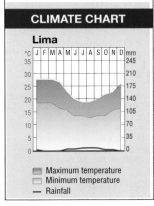

- Maximum temperature
- Minimum temperature
- Rainfall

## CLIMATE CHART

### Cusco

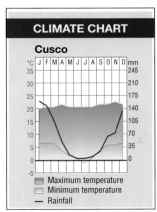

- Maximum temperature
- Minimum temperature
- Rainfall

## CLIMATE CHART

### Iquitos

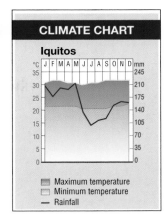

- Maximum temperature
- Minimum temperature
- Rainfall

shops and banks usually close for lunch between 12 or 1pm and 3.30 or 4pm. Money changers are on the streets, especially in Lima, almost 24 hours a day.

### Business Travelers

All of the five-star hotels, and many of the four-star hotels, have business centers. Most hotels have computers with internet connection for guests' use, and a large number now have a wireless internet connection too. Mobile phone SIM cards can be bought in any telecommunications shop *(see page 350)*. Most better hotel rooms have phones, and the rates are often reasonable, but check at the reception before you dial.

### **C**hildren

Peruvians love children, and your child will receive much positive

attention while traveling in Peru. In Lima and the bigger cities there are parks with children's playgrounds, and older children will enjoy many of the regular tourist attractions.

Shops sell babies' diapers (nappies), baby food, and formula milk. Be very careful with the food your children eat. Avoid uncooked vegetables, salads, and unpeeled fruits. Make sure all water is bottled, filtered, or at least well boiled. Children become especially tired at high altitude: take it easy. Bring a car seat if you are hiring a car, as these are hard to come by. Better restaurants have chidren's high chairs. Peruvian children's clothes and shoes are beautiful and cheap: make sure their suitcases are just half full!

### Climate

Peru has wet and dry seasons, although on the coastal desert strip it is always dry. However, Lima suffers

a bizarre weather condition prevailing from April to November called the *garúa*, a damp cold mist which obliterates the sun and sours everyone's mood. August is the worst month for this, with temperatures around 13–17°C (55–62°F). The rest of the year, Lima enjoys sunshine and moderate temperatures from 21–26°C (69–79°F).

Towns like Nazca on the western slopes of the Andes are dry and hot all year round, but the central Andes experience distinct wet and dry seasons. The best time to visit the highlands is between May and September, when views of the mountains are crystal clear. Although the days are bright and clear, nights can be bitterly cold, and temperatures can fall to 0°C (32°F). During the rest of the year, the weather is warmer but wetter, and the Andes are often obscured.

In the Amazon basin, the wet season lasts from January to April, when landslides and flooding are a constant problem. During the dry season, May to October, it might not rain for weeks at a time (although there might be short showers every day). Daytime temperatures average 27–32°C (81–90°F), with night-time lows averaging 21–26°C (69–79°F).

However, unexpected cold fronts called *friajes,* which come up from the south, are unique to the southern rainforests and can bring a few days of wind and rain with spring-like daytime temperatures of 13–18°C

**BELOW:** children are often doted on in Peru.

### Electricity

Peru uses 220 volts, 60 cycles AC, except Arequipa which is on 50 cycles. The major hotels provide 110-volt outlets in bathrooms for the use of shavers only.

(55–65°F) and night-time lows of 10°C (50°F). Although this weather condition is unusual, it is said to have a beneficial effect on the wildlife of the region.

### Crime and Security

As Peru's urban centers have swollen, so has petty crime. Pickpockets and thieves have become more and more common in Lima and Cusco. It is recommended that tourists do not wear costly jewelry and that watches be covered by a sleeve. Thieves are amazingly adept at slitting open shoulder bags, camera cases, and knapsacks; keep an eye on your belongings.

All kind of confidence tricksters pull ever more imaginative ruses; some pose as policemen, others work together with bus and taxi drivers or use diversionary tactics to get hold of your valuables. Special care is needed at railway stations and airports. Should you have anything stolen, you will need to fill out a report with the Tourist Police *(see below)*.

Go out at night in small groups if possible. Visits to the shantytowns *(pueblos jóvenes)* on the outskirts of the cities are very dangerous without a guide.

Officials also warn against dealing with anyone calling your hotel room or approaching you in the lobby or on the street, claiming to represent a travel agency or specialty shop. Avoid contact with over-friendly strangers who may want to involve you in criminal deals. Be aware that drug dealing is a crime that results in a long prison sentence.

Driving alone and after dusk is not advisable. Don't hitchhike. For journeys overland choose only well-known and established bus companies and take care that you

**ABOVE:** tourist police on patrol in Arequipa's main square.

are always able to identify yourself: carry your passport at all times.

There is little or no activity by rebel groups these days, and incidents of violence involving foreign tourists are few and far between. There is army activity in the coca-growing regions of the Andes, but these are extremely remote.

Expeditions and trekking tours should ideally be undertaken in larger groups and accompanied by a local and experienced mountain guide. It is a good idea to notify a reliable third party of your destination and home address before leaving for a long trekking tour. For more specific inquiries, contact your embassy or the **South American Explorers' Club** *(see page 348)*.

### Tourist Police

Peru's tourist police, known as DIRTURE (Dirección de Turismo Ecología) can be found in downtown Lima and other tourist centers.

Recognizable by their white shirts, they are very helpful, and have special English-speakers on duty. They can also be contacted at the following addresses:

**Lima:** Comisaría Especial de Turismo Lima Sur, Malecón de la Marina 1120, Miraflores, tel: (01) 424 2053.

**Cusco:** Calle Saphi in the Delegación de Policía (two blocks from the Plaza), tel: (084) 249 654.

**Arequipa:** Calle Jerusalén 315–16, tel: (054) 201 258.

**Iquitos:** Calle Santiago Lores 834, tel: (065) 242 081.

### Customs Regulations

Visas are not required by citizens of other South American countries, the European Union, the US, Canada, Japan, South Africa, Australia, or New Zealand.

All visitors, however, must have a passport and are issued with an entry stamp and tourist card on arrival in Peru. These are valid for 90 days (check you have been given the full amount), and the card must be surrendered to immigration on departure. These tourist cards can be extended for 30 days, for a fee of US$20 and presentation of a return ticket, at the Dirección Nacional de Migraciones in the Oficina de Migración, Prolongación Av. España 734, Breña, Lima, tel: (01) 330 4114/4020/4074.

### Disabled Travelers

Unfortunately, there isn't much in the way of facilities for disabled travelers in Peru. Hotels, except for the more upmarket, five-star variety, don't tend to have accessible rooms or bathrooms. However, the following companies in Lima offer transport facilities for disabled travelers:

## Conversion Tables

| LENGTH | | WEIGHT | | VOLUME | |
|---|---|---|---|---|---|
| **Inches** | **Centimeters** | **Pounds** | **Kilograms** | **US Pints** | **Liters** |
| 1 | 2.54 | 1 | 0.45 | 1 | 0.47 |
| 2 | 5.08 | 2 | 0.90 | 2 | 0.95 |
| 3 | 7.62 | 3 | 1.36 | 3 | 1.42 |
| 6 | 15.24 | 4 | 1.81 | 4 | 1.89 |
| 9 | 22.86 | 5 | 2.27 | | |
| | | 6 | 2.72 | **US Gallons** | **Liters** |
| **Feet** | **Centimeters** | 7 | 3.18 | 1 | 3.78 |
| 1 | 30.48 | 8 | 3.63 | 2 | 7.57 |
| 2 | 60.96 | 9 | 4.08 | 3 | 11.36 |
| 3 | 91.44 | 10 | 4.53 | 5 | 18.93 |
| 6 | 182.88 | 20 | 9.07 | 10 | 37.85 |
| 9 | 274.32 | 50 | 22.68 | 20 | 75.71 |
| 12 | 365.76 | 100 | 45.36 | 50 | 189.27 |

A – Z ◆ 3 4 7

TRANSPORTATION
ACCOMMODATIONS
SHOPPING
ACTIVITIES
A – Z
LANGUAGE

## Emergencies

In case of an accident, attack, emergency, etc., call:
- **General emergency** 105; 103 general information; 116 fire emergencies *(see also page 348 for medical services)*
- **Escuadron de Emergencias** (police radio control and emergency service). In Lima, tel: (01) 431 3040/431 3117/431 3076.
- **Dirección Nacional Contra El Terrorismo** (DINCOTE; terrorism and hijacking). In Lima, tel: (01) 431 5865. In Callao, tel: (01) 465 0910.

**CM Tours & Representaciones**, Calle Los Molinos 306, Urb. San Ignacio de Monterrico, Surco
Tel: (01) 275 0612
Fax: (01) 275 0676
Email: cmtours@amauta.rcp.net.pe
Runs vehicles with platform lifts which can accommodate up to 15 wheelchairs.
**Pro Peru Travel**
Av. Camino Real 445, San Isidro
Tel: (01) 221 0110
Fax: (01) 221 3271
Email: pro-peru@terra.com.pe
Travel agency which specializes in tours for disabled travelers.

## E mbassies and Consulates

### Foreign Embassies in Lima

**Argentina**
Pablo Bermúdez 143, 2nd floor, Santa Beatriz
Tel: (01) 433 5704
**Australia**
Víctor A. Belaúnde 147, Edificio Real 3, Of. 1301, San Isidro
Tel: (01) 222 8281
**Bolivia**
Los Castaños 235, San Isidro
Tel: (01) 442 8231
**Brazil**
Av. José Pardo 850, Miraflores
Tel: (01) 421 5650
**Canada**
Libertad 130, Miraflores
Tel: (01) 444 4015
**Chile**
Av. Javier Prado Oeste 790, San Isidro
Tel: (01) 221 2080
**Colombia**
Av. Jorge Basadre 1580, San Isidro
Tel: (01) 442 9648
**Ecuador**
Las Palmeras 356, San Isidro
Tel: (01) 212 4171
**Ireland**
Av. Angamos Oeste 340, Miraflores
Tel: (01) 446 3878

**South Africa**
Víctor A. Belaúnde 147, Edificio Real 3, Of. 801, San Isidro
Tel: (01) 440 9996
**UK**
Torre Parque-Mar, 22nd floor, Av. José Larco 1301, Miraflores
Tel: (01) 617 3000
British Consulate, Cusco:
Tel: (084) 239 974
**United States**
Av. La Encalada s/n, cuadra 17, Santiago de Surco
Tel: (01) 434 3000
US Consulate, Cusco:
Tel: (084) 224 112

### Peruvian Embassies Abroad

**Australia**
40 Brisbane Avenue, Level 2
Barton Act 2600
Tel: (02) 6273 7351
www.embaperu.org.au
**Canada**
130 Albert Street, Suite 1901
Ottawa, Ontario K1P 5G4
Tel: (613) 238 1777
www.embassyofperu.ca
**New Zealand**
Level 8, Cigna House, 40 Mercer Street, Wellington
Tel: (04) 499 8087/499 8057
www.embassyofperu.org.nz
**UK**
52 Sloane Street, London SW1X 9SP
Tel: (020) 7235 1917
www.peruembassy-uk.com
**US**
1700 Massachusetts Avenue, N.W., Washington D.C. 20036
Tel: (202) 833 9860
www.peruvianembassy.us

## Etiquette

Peruvians are polite and call each other *Señor* (Sir), *Señora* (Madam), or *Señorita* (Miss). Say *joven* to attract the attention of a young boy or young man.

Always greet someone with *buenos días* (good morning), *buenas tardes* (good afternoon/evening), *or buenas noches* (good night) before starting a conversation. Men shake hands when meeting for the first time and women usually kiss when they are introduced to men or women for the first time. Say *mucho gusto* (pleased to meet you) when you first meet someone. Men usually open doors for women or stand aside to let them go first.

Before starting a meal, wish others *buen provecho (bon appétit)*. Toast others with *salud* – and you can also say this when someone sneezes. *(See pages 352–7 for other useful words and phrases.)*

**ABOVE:** Peru is a popular destination for gap year travelers.

## G ay and Lesbian Travelers

Homosexuality is rarely openly talked about or revealed in Peru. Gay men are derisively called *maricón* or *mariposa* (butterfly), and lesbian women are barely heard of. The rainbow Inca flag should not be confused with the gay-friendly rainbow seen in other parts of the world. That said, there is a gay community, particularly in Lima, and information on gay venues in the city can be found at www.gayperu.com (in Spanish). The same organisation runs a travel agency operating tours to major tourist destinations in Peru: www.gayperutravel.com.

## H ealth and Medical Care

The most serious illnesses to guard against are **yellow fever** and **malaria**, which both occur in jungle areas of the North and South Amazon, and malaria on parts of the coast. There have been outbreaks of yellow fever in Puerto Maldonado, so visitors should ensure they are vaccinated. Visitors are advised to consult their physician

## Heat of the Sun

The tropical sun might feel very gentle but it can burn you to a crisp. Ultraviolet rays are particularly powerful at high altitudes; wearing a brimmed hat as well as sunglasses, and using a high-factor sunscreen will all help protect you from the glare. High humidity dehydrates the body; drink plenty of liquid and add salt to your food.

about anti-malarial drugs before leaving home. Malarial mosquitoes only bite at night, so always use a mosquito net when sleeping in jungle towns and keep covered up as much as possible between dusk and dawn. **Cholera** is not a great threat to tourists. It is caused by the bacterium Vibrio cholerae; the main symptom is diarrhea and the best treatment is rehydration. Vaccination is possible, but the best protection is to take elementary hygiene precautions such as avoiding unclean water and raw or poorly cooked food (particularly seafood), and steering clear of dirty accommodations and swimming pools.

**Hepatitis A** is caught by ingesting contaminated food or water. Be cautious about seafood; stick to bottled drinks, peeled fruit and good-quality restaurants, thereby ensuring your standard of hygiene. Two shots taken six months apart should protect against Hepatitis A for ten years (one shot works for six months).

A less serious and much more common condition for travelers in Peru is upset stomach and **diarrhea** – often caused by a change in culture and diet, unclean water or utensils, or simply the change of place. Traveling itself places extra pressure on the immune system, so take it easy until you feel stronger. In most cases, the symptoms will improve after a day or so of fasting and drinking plenty of fluids (hot tea without milk is ideal). If the more serious condition of dysentery develops (ie any blood or pus in the stool), you should see a doctor.

Don't be surprised if your exaltation at flying into Andean mountain cities is followed by a less pleasant sensation called *soroche* or **altitude sickness**. In most cases the symptoms are very mild – fatigue, shortness of breath, slight nausea, and headache. The best prevention and cure is to lie down for a few hours upon arrival at your hotel and then slowly introduce yourself to physical activity. Coca tea, available in all highland hotels and restaurants, is also said to help. If it doesn't, medication (which among other things contains aspirin and caffeine) is available without

prescription at pharmacies. If the symptoms are severe – i.e. vomiting, rapid irregular pulse, insomnia – take it seriously and descend immediately to a lower altitude (although this usually happens only to mountain climbers).

Travel insurance which covers the cost of an air ambulance should be taken out before you start your trip.

### Medical Services

Good hotels will have reliable doctors on call. The following clinics in Lima have 24-hour emergency service and an English-speaking staff member on duty:

**Clínica Anglo Americana**
Alfredo Salazar 350, San Isidro
Tel: (01) 712 3000
**Clínica Internacional**
Jr. Washington 1471, Lima
Tel: (01) 619 6161
**Clínica Javier Prado**
Av. Javier Prado Este 499, San Isidro
Tel: (01) 440 2000
**Clínica San Felipe**
Av. Javier Prado Este 4841
Tel: (01) 219 0000
**Clínica Tezza**
Av. El Polo 570, Monterrico, Surco
Tel: (01) 610 5050
**Emergency Hospital Casimiro Ulloa**
Av. República de Panamá 6355, San Antonio, Miraflores
Tel: (01) 445 5096

A recommended English-speaking dentist is Victor Manuel Aste, Calle Antero Aspillaga 415, Dpto 101, San Isidro, tel: (01) 441 7502.

### **I**nternet

There are hundreds of internet cafés (used mainly by tourists) and *cabinas* (set up with locals in mind) all over Peru. You can surf the internet for around US$1 per hour and make cheap international phone calls.

### **M**aps

The **Touring y Automóvil Club del Perú (TACP)**, César Vallejo 699, Lince, Lima, tel: (01) 211 9977, www.touringperu.com.pe (in Spanish), is the best source for maps and information. General maps are available from **The South American**

**ABOVE:** there are good mobile phone networks in most of Peru.

Explorers' Club *(see below)* and the **Instituto Geográfico Nacional**, Aramburú 1190, Surquillo, tel: (01) 475 3030, ext 122; open Mon–Fri 8am–5.30pm. Maps and street plans can also be bought at kiosks and bookshops. Telefónica's Yellow Pages *(Páginas Amarillas)* includes street maps of Lima Metropolitana and Callao.

The tourist offices of iPeru *(see page 350)* give out good maps of Peru, Lima, and other cities for free. Bookshops, particularly Ibero Librerías (Av. Larco 199, Miraflores) near Parque Kennedy in Lima, stock useful driving maps of Peru.

### Media
#### Newspapers and Magazines

Peru has an enormous, unbridled, and ever-changing media scene. Newspapers and magazines – mostly of the tabloid variety – come and go, and there's a large television network with nine terrestrial channels and dozens of cable channels. TVs and satellite dishes are ubiquitous, even in the remotest settings, while radio is the medium of choice for local news. Panamericana is Peru's top TV and radio station (the radio found at 101.1FM on the dial).

Of the Peruvian print media, Lima-based *El Comercio* (www.elcomercioperu. com.pe; in Spanish) is the largest and most serious. *Expreso* (www.expreso.com.pe; in Spanish) is considered right-leaning and has a good listings section for goings-on in Lima. Another leading daily is the high-circulation sensationalist tabloid *La República* (www.larepublica.com.pe; in Spanish). The weekly news magazine

---

### South American Explorers

This organization offers its members many useful services, including information on all aspects of trekking, and is a useful contact point for meeting other people to travel with. It also has a library and a book exchange service.

There are two SAE clubhouses in Peru:
Lima: Calle Piura 135, Miraflores, tel/fax: (01) 445 3306.
Cusco: Choquechaca 188, Apt. 4, tel/fax: (084) 245 484
www.saexplorers.org

*Caretas* (www.caretas.com.pe; in Spanish) has excellent in-depth features on current affairs.

Outside the capital, there's the well-regarded *El Diaro del Cusco*, the Arequipa-based weekly news magazine *El Búho*, which is thought of as an independent voice for the nation, and a wide range of small regional papers which report chiefly on the areas they pertain to.

For travelers, most of the better hotels have cable TV with English-language news networks. English-language newspapers are available in some news agencies in Lima and Cusco, but not always reliably. With the wide availability of internet connections, the web is your best bet for up-to-date news.

## Money

Since 1986 Peru has twice introduced a new currency to stop depreciation. In 1991 the nuevo sol (s/) replaced the shrinking inti at a ratio of 1 to 1 million. The annual inflation rate steadied during the 1990s after the hyperinflation of the 1980s.

There is no shortage of money-changing facilities in Lima, formal and otherwise – if you don't mind haggling on street corners. On the Plaza San Martín, in downtown Lima, hundreds of outdoor bankers run alongside the traffic – the rate is usually a little better than in the banks. It is legal to change with these *cambistas*, who generally wear a blue jacket and carry a calculator, and usually quite safe – although if you don't feel comfortable with it, there are plenty of alternatives. Banks will change your currency at the slightly inflated "official" rate, and good hotels have exchange services or will send a hotel courier to one of the *casas de cambio* for a better rate (remember to give him a tip). Travel agents accept payment in some foreign currencies and exchange small amounts.

The Banco de Crédito and the Banco de la Nación are recommended for any international banking business such as receiving US dollars from overseas. Ask for a *liquidación por canje de moneda extranjera* (cash in exchange for foreign currency).

It is convenient to carry some US cash as well as your travelers' checks, credit cards, or cash advance card (although Lima, Cusco, Arequipa, and Iquitos have every money-changing facility). It is not always possible to change checks, and cash dollars get a better rate, although you run the risk of theft.

American Express will replace lost travelers' checks only in Lima.

Make sure that you don't carry more cash than your insurance policy covers you for, or you will be penalized for being under-insured in the event of a claim.

Local currency can be obtained using Visa, Cirrus, Plus, and Mastercard at the ATM machines of most banks, including Banco de Crédito, Banco Latino, Banco de la Nación, Interbank, and Scotiabank.

### Credit Cards

Credit cards such as Diners Club, Visa, American Express, and MasterCard are accepted by good hotels and restaurants. There are branches of Diners, MasterCard and Visa in Lima.

To report credit card loss in Lima, call:
**Visa:** 108 Operator Collect Call: (001) 410 581 9754/0120
**Diners Club:** (01) 615 1111
**MasterCard:** 108 Operator Collect Call: (001) 636 722 7111
**American Express:** (01) 221 8204/ 221 8207

**Offices in Cusco:**
**MasterCard:** Banco Latino, Calle Almagro 125
**Visa:** Banco de Crédito, Av. Sol 189

## P hotography

There are so many wonderful things and interesting-looking people to photograph in Peru, you'll want to just keep clicking. But do be respectful about photography and ask people before taking pictures of them, unless it's from a good distance. People usually oblige, often for a tip. Taking pictures of airports and military installations is prohibited. If you are shooting film, you can get this dev-

## Time Zones

Lima is five hours behind Greenwich Mean Time and therefore coincides with Eastern Standard Time in the USA.

eloped in most of the larger towns and cities, and most photographic shops and even hotels will download digital photos to disk for a fee. Take care to protect your camera from dust in the highlands in the dry season, and from the extreme humidity of the rainforest.

## Postal Services

The central Post Office in Lima, operated by Serpost (www.serpost.com.pe), at Jr. Junín and Jr. de la Unión, opens Mon–Sat 8.15am–1pm and 2–7.30pm, Sun 8am–1pm.

To have mail sent to you in Lima or any other city, it should be addressed, with your surname in capital letters, to Poste Restante, Lista de Correos, Correo Central, followed by the name of the city. Take your passport for identification when you go to collect it. There is a parcel collection office at Tomás Valle Cuadra 7, Los Olivos (near the airport), tel: (01) 533 1340. There are branch post offices throughout Lima, including:
**Airport office:** Jorge Chávez International Airport; open 24 hours.
**Miraflores:** Av. José Pardo 715; Mon–Sat 8am–8.45pm, Sun 9am–2pm.
**San Isidro:** Libertadores 325; Mon–Fri 8am–7pm, Sat 9am–2pm, Sun closed.

### Courier Services

**DHL International**
Los Castaños 225, San Isidro
Tel: (01) 517 2500

**BELOW:** Peru is a predominantly Catholic country.

**ABOVE:** the helpful tourist information service has offices in all major towns.

Fax: (01) 614 2500
www.dhl.com.pe
**Federal Express**
Pasaje Mártir José Olaya 260, Miraflores
Tel: (01) 242 2280
www.fedex.com/pe
**OLVA Courier**
Calle Porta 161, Miraflores
Tel: (01) 719 8026 (Lima); (01) 614 0909 (call center)
www.olvacourier.com
**SkyNet**
Natalio Sánchez 125, 2nd floor, Lima
Tel: (01) 433 1717
www.skynetlim.com.pe
**TNT International Express**
Av. Libertadores 199, San Isidro
Tel: (01) 222 0555

**UPS**
Av. de Ejército 2107, San Isidro
Tel: (01) 264 0105
www.ups.com
**World Courier**
Av. Camino Real 390, Of. 1002, San Isidro
Tel: (01) 442 8080
www.worldcourier.com.pe

### *American Express*

American Express clients can have mail sent to: Amex, c/o Lima Tours, Av. Pardo y Aliaga 698, San Isidro, tel: (01) 441 4744. Non-Amex members can also use this service but may have to pay a small fee. You will need to take your passport as identification.

### Public Holidays

Peru has numerous national holidays as well as some regional ones *(see Holidays and Festivals, page 339).*

### **R** eligious Services

Catholic services are held daily in larger churches and on Sundays in most smaller parishes. The conveniently located Iglesia de La Virgen Milagrosa in Miraflores, Lima, has regular daily services. Visitors of other Christian denominations will now find churches of most branches in Peru, but other religions are less well served.

### **S** tudent Travelers

Full-time students traveling in Peru are eligible for many discounts if they produce their International Student Identity Card (ISIC). See the Peru section of the website (www.isic.org) for details of discounts on attractions in Peru and recommended points of interest for student travelers.

### **T** elecommunications

There are public phone boxes on just about every corner on Lima, charging varying rates. You can call from these using coins, telephone cards, and in some cases credit cards. A disproportionately high number of phone boxes in Peru seem to swallow coins without letting you call, so it's better to use one of the many *locutorios* found in cities, towns, and even small villages throughout Peru. Here there is a series of phone booths for local, long-distance, and international calls, as well as calls to mobiles. Show the number you want to call and you will be directed to a glass-walled booth. Charges are calculated on the central computer, and you pay after you have made your calls. It's convenient, cheap, and private.

There are also mobile *locutorio* services in the street: people dressed in an apron bearing the logo of the mobile service provider offer calls which are charged by the minute. There are a variety of phone cards *(tarjetas telefónicas)* available from corner stores and supermarkets for cheap local, national, and international calls.

Mobile phones *(cellulares)* are ubiquitous in Peru, and signal coverage is good. SIM cards can be purchased at booths in the airport on arrival, or phone shops in major towns and cities. Alternatively, buy a new handset and SIM card: both the hardware and the calls are extremely cheap.

## Tourist Information

Peru has an excellent tourist information infrastructure provided by iPeru. Their offices and information booths are in central locations in all the bigger towns and tourist attractions of Peru. iPeru staff provide general (though comprehensive) information, but cannot recommend particular companies services. For this there are travel agencies in all the major tourist areas that can advise on activities and book hotels. The 24-hour number for enquries is (01) 574 8000. See also www.peru.info.

**Lima**: Jorge Chávez International Airport, main hall, tel: (01) 574 8000.
Jorge Basadre 610, San Isidro,

tel: (01) 421 1627.
Larcomar Entertainment Center, Module 14, Plaza Gourmet, Miraflores, tel: (01) 445 9400.
**Arequipa**: Rodríguez Ballón Airport, 1st floor, main hall, tel: (054) 444 564.
Santa Catalina 210, tel: (054) 221 227.
Portal de la Municipalidad 100, Plaza de Armas, tel: (054) 223 265.
**Ayacucho**: Municipalidad de Huamanga (town hall), Plaza Mayor, tel: (066) 318 305.
**Chachapoyas**: Jr. Ortiz Arrieta 588, Plaza de Armas, tel: (041) 477 292.
**Chiclayo**: Sáenz Peña 838, tel: (041) 205 703.
**Cusco**: Velasco Astete Airport, main hall, tel: (084) 237 364.

Av. Sol 103, Of. 102, tel: (084) 234 498.
There is also a complaints office in the city: Indecopi, Portal de Carrizos 250, tel: (084) 252 974/234 498.
**Huaraz**: Pasaje Atusparia, Of. 1, Plaza de Armas, tel: (043) 428 812.
**Iquitos**: Francisco Secada Vignetta Airport, main hall, tel: (065) 260 251.
Centro de Iquitos, Calle Loreto 201, tel: (065) 236 144.
**Puno**: Calle Lima y Deustua (on the north corner of Plaza de Armas), tel: (051) 365 088.
**Tacna**: San Martín 491, tel: (052) 425 514.
**Trujillo**: Municipalidad de Trujillo (town hall), Plaza Mayor de Trujillo, Jr. Pizarro 402, tel: (044) 294 561.

Calls from hotel phones range from reasonable to expensive. Check before you call – phone cards can sometimes be used in conjunction with hotel phones.

### Telephone codes

The international code for Peru is 00 51. Below are the codes for the principal cities. You only need to include the area code when dialing between areas (long-distance calls).

Arequipa: 054
Ayacucho: 066
Cajamarca: 076
Chachapoyas: 041
Chiclayo: 074
Cusco: 084
Huancavelica: 067
Huancayo: 064
Huaraz: 043
Ica: 056
Iquitos: 065
Lima: 01
Piura: 073
Puerto Maldonado: 082
Puno: 051
Tacna: 052
Trujillo: 044

## Tipping

At some of the smartest hotels and restaurants, service charges are sometimes included, and this will be stated on the bill. Otherwise tipping is up to the customer. Peruvians themselves rarely leave tips in restaurants, and tipping is not routinely expected, but you can leave a few soles. Tipping seems to be most customary in Cusco, where there are the most tourists. It's not customary to tip taxi drivers, but you should tip people who help you with your luggage. If you stay any length of time in a hotel, you can, if you are happy with the service, leave a tip for the people who have serviced your room. On the conclusion of trekking, climbing, and other outdoor adventure activities, it's usual to leave a generous tip for your guide.

## Toilets

Unfortunately, toilets in Peru leave much to be desired. Apart from in the smarter parts of Lima and at the main tourist attractions, it's rare to find public toilets. Outside these areas, you often have to use a restaurant or bus station toilet, and in smaller towns toilets are often of the squat variety. Carry your own toilet paper as this is rarely provided, but remember to dispose of it in the bin provided as the drains are not

built to cope with toilet paper. When trekking in areas where there are no drop toilets, dig a 20-cm (8-inch) deep hole at least 100 meters (330 ft) away from water and bury your waste. Burn toilet paper if you can.

## Websites

**www.peru-hotels.com**
Hotel listings and bookings, plus transport and flight information in English.
**http://travel.peru.com/travel/english**
News, general information, and listings in English and Spanish; also a travel agency.
**www.peru-travel.net**
Online hotel bookings, and an excellent range of articles on places of interest. In English.
**www.andeantravelweb.com/peru**
Full of useful information about tour companies, adventure activities, hotels, and the best destinations.

## What to Wear

Good traveling clothes should be comfortable and durable and preferably made of natural fiber, although one or two synthetics in the form of evening wear that won't wrinkle in your suitcase come in handy for those formal nightspots. Take some good walking shoes that won't look too out of place in a casual restaurant.

One rarely regrets traveling light, especially in a land where clothes shopping is a dream. Remember all those alpaca sweaters and leather goods – you can buy as many warm clothes as you like when you arrive. However, it is almost impossible to get shoes in large sizes.

**BELOW:** a service charge may be added to the bill in upmarket restaurants.

## Weights and Measures

Peru uses the metric system. Here's a table to help you convert to the imperial system (see chart on page 246).

| To Convert: | Multiply By: |
|---|---|
| centimeters to inches | 0.4 |
| meters to feet | 3.3 |
| kilometers to miles | 0.6 |
| kilograms to pounds | 2.2 |

Bring warm clothes for the Sierra, light clothes for the jungle, and a combination for the coastal deserts, which are warm by day and cool at night (see also Climate, page 345). The most appropriate clothing for a jungle trip is a long-sleeved shirt and trousers of close-woven material. These protect the wearer from most biting insects. A hat gives valuable protection while traveling on the river or birdwatching on the lakes. Mountaineers and hikers should not forget to bring good walking shoes, warm clothes, and equipment, because there is a shortage of trekking supplies in Peru. Avoid olive-green trousers and military-style jackets; Peruvians could get the wrong idea.

## When to Go

It is possible to visit Peru all year round, but the most popular time of year is between May and September as this coincides with the dry season in the highlands and the jungle (see Climate, page 345).

## Women Travelers

Apart from the usual sensible precautions, lone female travelers can feel safe in Peru. Don't walk alone late at night in questionable areas, watch out for your handbag, and keep money in inside pockets or a body pouch. Peruvians are generally very polite, helpful, and respectful of women: you will be helped with bags and have doors held open for you – enjoy it. If you are traveling alone, the most common reaction amongst Peruvians is a welcoming and protective one. They may ask you if you're single or married which is not meant to be any kind of advance, they are just intrigued to see a woman unaccompanied. If you do have to fend off unwanted advances say soy casada (I'm married) or you could consider putting a ring on your right index finger. Feminine hygiene products can be bought in most supermarkets and chemists.

# L ANGUAGE

# UNDERSTANDING THE LANGUAGE

## Language

Understanding a little Spanish will help you get the most of your stay in Peru. There are a few g local variations of the Spanish *(castillano)* familiar to many. An expression you will hear everywhere, and which is difficult to translate, is *no más. Siga no más* for example, means "Go ahead." *Come no más* means "Just eat it (It'll get cold/it's nicer than it looks, etc.)." You will soon get the hang of it.

In the Andes, *indígenas* all speak Spanish, but you will hear Quechua (also spelt Quichua) words that have crept into the language: wambras translates as "guys," and cheveré means "cool." Another indigenous language, Aymara, is spoken around Lake Titicaca.

Berlitz publishes an excellent Latin American Spanish Phrase Book and Dictionary, containing vocabulary and phrases for every situation.

It would be impossible for us to give a complete language guide here, but the following are some useful words, phrases, and tips that will hopefully ease understanding.

## Pronunciation

### Vowels

**a** as in apple
**e** as in bed
**i** as in police
**o** as in got
**u** as in rude

### Consonants

Consonants are approximately like those in English, the main exceptions being:
**c** is hard before **a**, **o**, or **u** (as in English), and is soft before **e** or **i**, when it sounds like **s** (as opposed to the

pronunciation of **th** as in think used in Spain). Thus, *censo* (census) sounds like senso.
**g** is hard before **a**, **o**, or **u** (as in English), but where English **g** sounds like **j** – before **e** or **i** – Spanish **g** sounds like a guttural **h**. **g** before **ua** is often soft or silent, so that *agua* sounds more like awa, and Guadalajara like Wadalajara.
**h** is silent.
**j** sounds like a gutteral h.
**ll** sounds like y.
**ñ** sounds like ni, as in onion.
**q** is followed by u as in English, but the combination sounds like k instead of like kw. **¿Qué quiere Usted?** is pronounced: Keh kee-ehr-eh oostehd?
**r** is often rolled.
**x** between vowels sounds like a guttural h, e.g. in México or Oaxaca.
**y** alone, as the word meaning "and", is pronounced **ee**.

Note that **ch** and **ll** are each a separate letter of the Spanish alphabet; if looking in a phone book or dictionary for a word beginning with **ch**, you will find it after the final **c** entry. A name or word beginning with **ll** will be listed after the final **l** entry.

## Basics

**yes** *sí*
**no** *no*
**thank you** *gracias*
**you're welcome** *de nada*
**okay** *está bien*
**please** *por favor*
**Excuse me** (to get attention) *¡Perdón! ¡Por favor!*
**Excuse me** (to get through a crowd) *¡Permiso!*
**Excuse me** (sorry) *Perdóneme*
**Wait a minute!** *¡Un momento!*
**Can you help me?** *¿Me puede ayudar?*

**Do you speak English?** (formal) *¿Habla inglés?*
**Please speak more slowly** *Hable más despacio, por favor*
**Could you repeat that please** *¿Podría repetírmelo, por favor?*
**I (don't) understand** *(No) entiendo*
**Show me the word in the book** *Muéstreme la palabra en el libro*
**I'm sorry** *Lo siento/Perdone*
**I don't know** *No lo se*
**No problem** *No hay problema*
**Where is...?** *¿Dónde está...?*
**I am looking for...** *Estoy buscando*
**That's it** *Ese es*
**Here it is** *Aquí está*
**There it is** *Allí está*
**Let's go** *Vámonos*
**At what time?** *¿A qué hora?*
**late** *tarde*
**early** *temprano*
**yesterday** *ayer*
**today** *hoy*
**tomorrow** *mañana*

**BELOW:** some basic Spanish comes in very handy when traveling in Peru.

## Greetings

**Hello** ¡Hola!
**good morning** buenos días
**good afternoon** buenas tardes
**welcome** bienvenido
**How are you?** (formal/informal)
¿Cómo está?/¿Qué tal?
**Very well** Muy bien
**And you?** (formal/informal)
¿Y usted?/¿Y tú?
**What is your name?** ¿Como se
llama?
**My name is...** Me llamo...
**Mr/Miss/Mrs**
Señor/Señorita/Señora
**Pleased to meet you** ¡Mucho gusto!
**I am British/American** Soy
británico(a)/norteamericano(a)
**See you tomorrow** Hasta mañana
**See you soon** Hasta pronto
**See you later** Hasta luego
**goodbye** adiós
**good night** buenas noches

## Telephone Calls

**The area code** El código de área
**Where can I buy telephone cards?**
¿Dónde puedo comprar tarjetas
telefónicas?
**May I use your telephone to make
a local call?** ¿Puedo usar su teléfono
para hacer una llamada local?
**Of course you may** ¡Claro!
**Hello (on the phone)** ¡Hola!
**May I speak to...?** ¿Puedo hablar
con... (name), por favor?
**Sorry, he/she isn't in**
Lo siento, no se encuentra
**Can he/she call you back?**
¿Puede devolver la llamada?
**Yes, he/she can reach me at...**
Sí, él/ella puede llamarme a
[number]
**I'll try again later** Voy a intentar
más tarde
**Can I leave a message?**
¿Puedo dejar un mensaje?
**Please tell him/her I called**
Por favor avisarle que llamé
**Hold on** Un momento, por favor
**Can you speak up, please?**
¿Puede hablar más fuerte,
por favor?

## Finding Your Way

**Where is the lavatory (men's/
women's)?** ¿Dónde está el baño
(de caballeros/de damas)?
**Where is the (tourist office)?**
¿Dónde está la (oficina de turismo)?
**I am lost** Estoy perdido/a
**Is it near/far from here?** ¿Está
cerca/lejos de aquí?
**on the right** a la derecha
**on the left** a la izquierda
**straight ahead** derecho
**near** cerca de

## The Alphabet

Learning the pronunciation of the
Spanish alphabet is a good idea.
In particular, learn how to spell
out your own name. Spanish has
three letters in its alphabet that
don't exist in English: the "ñ",
the "ch" and the "ll".

| | |
|---|---|
| **a** = ah | **ñ** = enyay |
| **b** = bay | **o** = oh |
| **c** = say | **p** = pay |
| **ch** = chay | **q** = koo |
| **d** = day | **r** = erray |
| **e** = ay | **s** = essay |
| **f** = effay | **t** = tay |
| **g** = hay | **u** = oo |
| **h** = ah-chay | **v** = oovay |
| **i** = ee | **w** = oovay |
| **j** = hotah | doe-blay |
| **k** = kah | **x** = ek-kiss |
| **l** = ellay | **y** = ee gree- |
| **ll** = ell-yay | ay-gah |
| **m** = emmay | **z** = say-tah |
| **n** = ennay | |

**in front of** en frente de/frente
de/frente a
**beside** al lado de
**above** arriba
**below** abajo
**behind** atrás de
**around** alrededor de
**in, on, at** en
**between** entre
**avenue** avenida (Av.)
**street** calle
**main street** calle principal
**corner** esquina (Esq.)
**building** edificio (Edif.)
**penthouse** PH – penthouse
**ground floor** PB – planta baja
**upper floor (of two)** PA – planta alta
**mezzanine** mezanina
**basement** sótano
**small pension** residencia (Res.)
**a block** una cuadra
**town square** plaza
**bank** banco
**post office** correos
**library** biblioteca
**town hall** ayuntamiento
**theater** teatro
**cinema** cine
**disco** discoteca/boliche
**sports ground** polideportivo
**stadium** estadio
**bus stop** parada de autobús
**bus station** estación de autobuses
**train station** estación de tren
**taxi stand** parada de taxi
**pharmacy** farmacia
**hospital** hospital
**police station** estación de policía
**hotel** hotel
**youth hostel** albergue
**camping** camping
**parking** playa de estacionamiento

## In the Hotel

**Do you have a vacant room?**
¿Tiene una habitación disponible?
**I have a reservation**
Tengo una reserva
**I'd like...** Quisiera...
**a single/double (with double bed)/
a room with twin beds** una
habitación individual (sencilla)/
una habitación matrimonial/una
habitación doble
**for one night/two nights**
por una noche/dos noches
**with a sea view** con vista al mar
**Does the room have a private
bathroom or shared bathroom?**
¿Tiene la habitación baño privado
o baño compartido?
**Does it have hot water?**
¿Tiene agua caliente?
**Could you show me another room,
please?** ¿Puede mostrarme otra
habitación, por favor?
**What time do you close (lock)
the doors?**
¿A qué hora se cierran las puertas?
**I would like to change rooms**
Quisiera cambiar la habitación
**How much is it?**
¿Cuánto cuesta?/¿Cuánto sale?
**Do you accept credit cards/
travelers' checks/dollars?**
¿Se aceptan tarjetas de crédito/
cheques de viajeros/dólares?
**What time is breakfast/
lunch/dinner?** ¿A qué hora es el
desayuno/el almuerzo/la cena?
**Please wake me at...**
Por favor despertarme a...
**Come in!** ¡Pase!/¡Adelante!
**I'd like to pay the bill now, please**
Quisiera cancelar la cuenta ahora,
por favor

## In the Restaurant

**I'd like to book a table** Quisiera
reservar una mesa, por favor
**Do you have a table for...?**
¿Tiene una mesa para...?
**breakfast** desayuno
**lunch** almuerzo
**dinner** cena
**I'm a vegetarian** Soy vegetariano(a)
**May we have the menu?** ¿Puede
traernos la carta/el menú?
**wine list** la carta de vinos
**What would you recommend?**
¿Qué recomienda?
**fixed-price menu** el menú fijo
**special of the day**
plato del día/sugerencia del chef
**waiter** mozo
**What would you like to drink?**
¿Qué quiere tomar?
**a bottle of...** una botella de...
**a glass of...** un vaso/una copa de...
**Is service included?**
¿Incluye el servicio?

## Menu Decoder

### Entremeses/Primer Plato (First Course)

**sopa/crema** *soup/cream soup*
**sopa de ajo** *garlic soup*
**sopa de cebolla** *onion soup*
**ensalada mixta** *mixed salad*
**ensalada de palta con tomate** *avocado and tomato salad*
**pan con ajo** *garlic bread*

### La Carne (Meat)

**crudo** *raw*
**jugoso(a)** *rare*
**término medio** *medium rare*
**a punto** *medium*
**bien hecho** *well done*
**a la brasa/a la parrilla** *charcoal grilled*
**a la plancha** *grilled*
**al horno** *baked*
**ahumado(a)** *smoked*
**alas** *wings*
**albóndigas** *meat balls*
**asado(a)/horneado(a)** *roasted*
**aves** *poultry*
**cerdo/chancho/puerco** *pork*
**chivito** *goat*
**chorizo** *Spanish-style sausage*
**chuleta** *chop*
**conejo** *rabbit*
**cordero** *lamb*
**costillas** *ribs*
**empanizado(a)** *breaded*
**frito(a)** *fried*
**guisado(a)** *stewed*
**hamburguesa** *hamburger*
**hígado de res** *beef liver*
**jamón** *ham*
**lengua** *tongue*
**lomito** *tenderloin*
**milanesa** *breaded and fried thin cut of meat*
**morcilla** *blood sausage*
**muslo** *thigh*
**pato** *duck*
**pavo** *turkey*
**pechuga** *breast*
**pernil** *leg of pork*
**piernas** *legs*
**pollo** *chicken*
**rebozado(a)** *batter fried*
**riñones** *kidneys*
**salchichas/panchos** *sausages or hot dogs*
**ternera** *veal*
**chicharrón de pollo** *chicken cut up in small pieces and deep fried*

### Pescado/Mariscos (Fish/Seafood)

**almejas** *clams*
**anchoa** *anchovy*
**atún** *tuna*
**bacalao** *cod*
**calamares** *squid*
**camarones** *shrimp*
**cangrejo** *crab*
**centolla** *kingcrab*

**langosta** *lobster*
**langostinos** *prawns*
**lenguado** *sole or flounder*
**mariscos** *shellfish*
**mejillones** *mussels*
**mero** *grouper, sea bass*
**ostras** *oysters*
**pulpo** *octopus*
**salmón** *salmon*
**sardinas** *sardines*
**trucha** *trout*
**vieiras** *scallops*

### Vegetales (Vegetables)

**ajo** *garlic*
**alcaucil** *artichoke*
**arvejas** *peas*
**batata** *sweet potato*
**berenjena** *eggplant/aubergine*
**brócoli** *broccoli*
**calabaza** *pumpkin or yellow squash*
**cebolla** *onion*
**chauchas** *green beans*
**choclo** *corn (on the cob)*
**coliflor** *cauliflower*
**espárrago** *asparagus*
**espinaca** *spinach*
**hongos, champiñones** *mushrooms*
**lechuga** *lettuce*
**papa** *potato*
**pepino** *cucumber*
**pimentón** *green (bell) pepper*
**porotos** *Lima beans*
**puerro** *leeks*
**remolacha** *beets/beetroot*
**repollo** *cabbage*
**zanahorias** *carrots*
**zapallo** *yellow squash*
**zapallito** *green squash*
**zapallito largo** *zucchini/courgette*

### Frutas (Fruit)

**banana** *banana*
**palta** *avocado*
**plátano** *green banana*
**cereza** *cherry*

**BELOW:** *salsa picante* made from chiles is often served in Peruvian restaurants.

**ciruela** *plum*
**dátil** *date*
**durazno** *peach*
**frambuesa** *raspberry*
**fresa** *strawberry*
**guayaba** *guava*
**higo** *fig*
**papaya** *papaya*
**lima** *lime*
**limón** *lemon*
**mandarina** *tangerine*
**manzana** *apple*
**melón** *cantelope/melon*
**mora** *blackberry*
**naranja** *orange*
**parchita** *passion fruit*
**sandía** *watermelon*
**pera** *pear*
**piña** *pineapple*
**pomelo** *grapefruit*
**uvas** *grapes*

### Drinks

**agua mineral con/sin gas** *carbonated/non-carbonated mineral water*
**café** *coffee*
**cerveza** *beer*
**chocolate caliente** *hot chocolate*
**coca** *cola*
**mate de coca** *coca-leaf tea*
**jugo de fruta** *fruit juice*
**jugo de naranja** *orange juice*
**limonada** *lemonade*
**té (con leche)** *tea (with milk)*
**té manzanilla** *camomile tea*
**tonica con ginebra** *gin and tonic*
**vino blanco** *white wine*
**vino tinto** *red wine*
**vodka** *vodka*
**whisky** *whisky*

### Miscellaneous

**arroz** *rice*
**azúcar** *sugar*
**empanada** *savory turnover*
**fideos** *spaghetti*

## Money

**money** *dinero*
**credit card** *tarjeta de crédito*
**bank** *banco*
**cash machine/ATM** *cajero automático*
**currency exchange bureau** *casa de cambio*
**I'd like to change some dollars/pounds into soles** *Quisiera cambiar unos dólares/libras esterlinas por soles*
**I'd like to change some traveler's cheques** *Quisiera cambiar unos cheques de viajero*
**What is the exchange rate?** *¿Cuál es la tasa de cambio?*
**How much commission do you charge?** *¿Cuál es la comisión?*

**huevos (revueltos/fritos/hervidos)**
*eggs (scrambled/fried/boiled)*
**ice cream** *helado*
**manteca** *butter*
**margarina** *margarine*
**mermelada** *jam*
**mostaza** *mustard*
**pan** *bread*
**pan integral** *wholewheat bread*
**pan tostado/tostadas** *toast*
**pimienta negra** *black pepper*
**queso** *cheese*
**sal** *salt*
**salsa picante** *spicy sauce*
**sandwich** *sandwich*
**panceta** *bacon*
**tortilla** *omelet*

## Shopping

**I'd like...** *Quisiera...*
**I'm just looking** *Sólo estoy mirando, gracias*
**How much is this?** *¿Cuanto cuesta/sale?*
**Do you have it in another color?**
*¿Tiene en otro color?*
**Do you have it in another size?**
*¿Tiene en otro talle/número?*
**smaller/larger**
*más pequeño/más grande*
**trousers** *pantalones*
**skirt** *falda*
**dress** *vestido*
**shirt** *camisa*
**jacket** *chaqueta*
**suit** *traje*
**coat** *abrigo*
**underpants** *calzoncillos*
**socks** *calcetines*
**shoes** *zapatos*
**hat** *sombrero*
**swimsuit** *traje de baño*
**I would like some of that...**
*Quisiera un poco de eso...*
**I would like a kilo of...**
*Quisiera un kilo de...*
**I would like half a kilo of...**
*Quisiera un medio kilo de...*

## Colors

**light** *claro*
**dark** *oscuro*
**red** *rojo*
**blue** *azul*
**green** *verde*
**yellow** *amarillo*
**brown** *marrón*
**cream** *color crema*
**beige** *beige*
**gray** *gris*
**orange** *naranja*
**pink** *rosado*
**purple** *púrpura*
**white** *blanco*
**black** *negro*
**silver** *plateado*
**gold** *dorado*

**A little more/less**
*Un poco más/menos*
**That's enough/no more**
*Está bien/nada más*
**Would you like anything else?**
*¿Quiere algo más?*
**expensive** *caro*
**cheap** *barato*
**clothes store** *tienda de ropa*
**bookstore** *librería*
**hairdressers** *peluquería*
**bakery** *panadería*
**cake shop** *pastelería*
**butcher's** *carnicería*
**fishmonger's** *pescadería*
**green grocery** *verdulería*
**market** *mercado*
**supermarket** *supermercado*
**grocery store** *tienda de abarrotes*
**newsstand** *kiosco*
**shopping center** *centro comercial*

## Tourist Attractions

**tourist office** *oficina de turismo*
**postcard** *postal*
**handicrafts** *artesanía*
**market** *mercado*
**winery** *bodega*
**museum** *museo*
**art gallery** *sala de exposiciones*
**indigenous community** *comunidad indígena*
**old town** *ciudad vieja*
**ruins** *ruinas*
**bridge** *puente*
**tower** *torre*
**monument** *monumento*
**statue** *estatua*
**fort** *castillo/fuerte*
**palace** *palacio*
**chapel** *capilla*
**church** *iglesia*
**cathedral** *catedral*
**convent** *convento*
**park** *parque*
**playground** *parque infantil*
**botanical garden** *jardín botánico*
**zoo** *zoológico*
**cable car** *teleférico*
**viewpoint** *mirador*
**hill** *cerro*
**mountain** *montaña*
**(mountain) peak** *pico*
**stream** *quebrada*
**river** *río*
**lagoon** *laguna*
**lake** *lago*
**sea** *mar*
**Pacific Ocean** *Océano Pacífico*
**island** *isla*
**glacier** *glaciar*
**beach** *playa*
**hot springs** *aguas termales*
**swimming pool** *piscina*

## Airport/Travel Agency

**airport** *aeropuerto*
**airline** *línea aérea*

**ABOVE:** it's worth learning the names of some local dishes.

**flight** *vuelo*
**arrivals** *llegadas*
**departures** *salidas*
**connection** *conexión*
**customs and immigration**
*aduana y migraciones*
**travel/tour agency** *agencia de viajes/de turismo*
**ticket** *boleto pasaje*
**I would like to purchase a ticket for...** *Quisiera comprar un boleto (pasaje) para...*
**When is the next/last flight/ departure for...?** *¿Cuándo es el próximo/último vuelo/para...?*
**How long is the flight?**
*¿Cuánto tiempo dura el vuelo?*
**What time do I have to be at the airport?** *¿A qué hora tengo que estar en el aeropuerto?*
**Is the tax included?**
*¿Se incluye el impuesto?*
**What is included in the price?**
*¿Qué está incluido en el precio?*
**departure tax**
*el impuesto de salida*
**I would like a seat in first class/ business class/tourist class**
*Quisiera un asiento en primera clase/ejecutivo/clase de turista*
**I need to change my ticket**
*Necesito cambiar mi boleto*
**lost-luggage office**
*oficina de reclamos*
**on time** *a tiempo*
**late** *atrasado*

## Transportation

**luggage, bag(s)** *equipaje, valija(s)*
**bus** *colectivo* (urban), *micro*
(long distance)
**bus stop** *parada (de colectivo/micro)*

TRANSPORTATION · ACCOMMODATIONS · SHOPPING · ACTIVITIES · A-Z · LANGUAGE

**bus terminal** *terminal de pasajeros*
**first class** *primera clase*
**second class** *segunda clase*
**tourist class** *clase de turista*
**one-way ticket** *boleto de ida*
**round-trip, return ticket**
*boleto de ida y vuelta*
**What time does the bus/boat/
ferry [leave/return?]** *¿A qué
hora [sale/regresa] el autobús/
la lancha/el ferry?*
**Which is the stop closest to...?**
*¿Cuál es la parada más cerca de...?*
**Is this seat taken?**
*¿Está ocupado este asiento?*
**Could you please advise me when
we reach/the stop for...?**
*¿Por favor, puede avisarme
cuando llegamos a/a la parada
para...?*
**Is this the stop for...?**
*¿Es ésta la parada para...?*
**Next stop please** *La próxima parada,
por favor*
**subway** *metro/subterráneo*
**train station** *estación de tren*
**platform** *el andén*
**sleeping car** *coche cama*
**taxi** *taxi*
**car** *coche/automóvil*
**car rental** *alquiler de coche*
**dock for small boats/large boats**
*embarcadero/muelle*
**ferry** *ferry*
**sailboat** *velero*
**yacht** *yate*
**ship** *barco*

### Driving

**Where can I rent a car?**
*¿Dónde puedo alquiler un coche?*
**Is mileage included?**
*¿Está incluido el kilometraje?*
**comprehensive insurance**
*seguros comprensivos*
**spare tire** *goma de repuesto*
**jack** *gato*
**emergency triangle** *triángulo de
emergencia*
**Where is the registration document?**

*¿Dónde está el carnet de
circulación?*
**Does the car have an alarm?**
*¿El coche tiene alarma?*
**a road map** *un mapa vial*
**a city map** *plano de la ciudad*
**How do I get to...?**
*¿Cómo se llega a...?*
**Turn right/left** *Gire a la
derecha/izquierda*
**at the next corner/street**
*en la próxima esquina/calle*
**Go straight ahead** *Siga derecho*
**You are on the wrong road**
*Esta no es la calle*
**Please show me where I am
on the map** *Por favor, indíqueme
dónde estoy en el mapa*
**Where can I find...?**
*¿Dónde hay...?*
**Where is the nearest...?**
*¿Dónde está el/la... más cerca?*
**How long does it take to get
there?** *¿Cuánto tiempo lleva
para llegar?*
**driver's license**
*licencia de conducir/manejar*
**service/gasoline station** *estación
de servicio*
**My car won't start**
*Mi coche no arranca*
**My car is overheating**
*Mi coche está recalentando*
**My car has broken down**
*Mi coche se rompió/no anda*
**tow truck** *una grúa*
**Where can I find a car repair shop?**
*¿Dónde hay un taller mecánico?*
**Can you check the...?**
*¿Puede revisar/chequear...?*
**There's something wrong with
the...** *Hay un problema con...*
**oil** *aceite*
**water** *agua*
**air** *aire*
**brake fluid** *líquido de frenos*
**light bulb** *bombita*
**trunk** *maletín*
**hood** *capó*
**door** *puerta*
**window** *ventana*

**ABOVE:** taxis don't usually have meters
so you'll need to barter with the driver.

### Road Signs

**autopista** *freeway*
**bajada/subida peligrosa**
*dangerous downgrade/incline*
**calle sin salida** *dead-end street*
**calle flechada/de una sola mano**
*one-way street*
**carril derecho** *right lane*
**carril izquierdo** *left lane*
**carretera** *highway, road*
**gomería** *tire repair shop*
**cede el paso** *yield/give way*
**circunvalación** *by-pass road/ringroad*
**conserve su derecha**
*keep to the right*
**conserve su carril**
*do not change lanes*
**cruce de ferrocarril (sin señal)**
*railway crossing (without signal)*
**despacio** *slow*
**desvío** *detour*
**distribuidor** *freeway interchange*
**doble vía** *two-way traffic*

## Numbers

| | | | |
|---|---|---|---|
| **1** *uno* | **16** *dieciséis* | **101** *ciento uno* | **first** *primer(o)/a* |
| **2** *dos* | **17** *diecisiete* | **200** *doscientos* | **second** *segund(o)/a* |
| **3** *tres* | **18** *dieciocho* | **300** *trescientos* | **third** *tercer(o)/a* |
| **4** *cuatro* | **19** *diecinueve* | **400** *cuatrocientos* | **fourth** *cuart(o)/a* |
| **5** *cinco* | **20** *veinte* | **500** *quinientos* | |
| **6** *seis* | **21** *veintiuno* | **600** *seiscientos* | **NOTE** |
| **7** *siete* | **25** *veinticinco* | **700** *setecientos* | In Spanish, in numbers, |
| **8** *ocho* | **30** *treinta* | **800** *ochocientos* | commas are used where |
| **9** *nueve* | **40** *cuarenta* | **900** *novecientos* | decimal points are used |
| **10** *diez* | **50** *cincuenta* | **1,000** *mil* | in English and vice versa. |
| **11** *once* | **60** *sesenta* | **2,000** *dos mil* | For example: |
| **12** *doce* | **70** *setenta* | **10,000** *diez mil* | **English** **Spanish** |
| **13** *trece* | **80** *ochenta* | **100,000** *cien mil* | $19.30 $19,30 |
| **14** *catorce* | **90** *noventa* | **1,000,000** *un millón* | 1,000 m 1.000 m |
| **15** *quince* | **100** *cien* | **2,000,000** *dos millones* | 9.5 % 9,5 % |

## Days of the Week

Note that the Spanish form takes a lower-case initial letter.
**Monday** *lunes*
**Tuesday** *martes*
**Wednesday** *miércoles*
**Thursday** *jueves*
**Friday** *viernes*
**Saturday** *sábado*
**Sunday** *domingo*

**enciende luces en el túnel**
*turn on lights in the tunnel*
**encrucijada** *crossroads*
**entrada prohibida** *no entry*
**estacionamiento** *parking lot*
**fuera de servicio** *not in service*
**hundimiento** *sunken road*
**intercomunal** *interconnecting freeway between two close towns*
**no estacione/prohibido estacionar**
*no parking*
**no gire en U** *no U-turn*
**no hay paso, vía cerrada**
*road blocked*
**sin salida** *no exit*
**no pare** *no stopping here*
**no toque la bocina** *no horn honking*
**¡ojo!** *watch out!*
**pare** *stop*
**paso de ganado** *cattle crossing*
**paso de peatones** *pedestrian crossing*
**peaje** *toll booth*
**peligro** *danger*
**pendiente fuerte, curva fuerte** *steep hill, sharp curve*
**rotonda** *traffic circle/roundabout*
**lomo de burro, reductor de velocidad, obstáculos en la vía, muros en la vía, policia acostada**
*speed bump(s)*
**resbaladizo al humedecerse**
*slippery when wet*
**ruta** *highway*
**salida** *exit*
**semáforo** *traffic light*
**sólo tránsito local** *local traffic only*
**tome precauciones** *caution*
**un solo carril** *single lane*
**velocidad controlada**
*speed controlled or restricted*
**vía en reparación/en recuperación**
*road under repair*
**zona de construcción**
*construction zone*
**zona de derrumbes** *landslide zone*

**zona de niebla (neblina)** *fog zone*
**zona de remolque** *tow zone*
**zona escolar** *school zone*
**zona militar** *military zone*

## Emergencies

**Help!** *¡Socorro! ¡Auxilio!*
**Stop!** *¡Pare!*
**Watch out!** *¡Cuidado! ¡Ojo!*
**I've had an accident** *He tenido un accidente/Sufrí un accidente*
**Call a doctor** *Llame a un médico*
**Call an ambulance**
*Llame una ambulancia*
**Call the...** *Llame a...*
**...police** *la policía* (for minor accidents)
**...transit police** *la policía de tránsito* (for traffic accidents)
**the fire brigade** *los bomberos*
**This is an emergency, where is a telephone?** *Esto es una emergencia. ¿Dónde hay un teléfono?*
**Where is the nearest hospital?**
*¿Dónde queda el hospital más cercano?*
**I want to report an assault/ a robbery**
*Quisiera reportar un asalto/ un robo*
**Thank you very much for your help**
*Muchísimas gracias por su ayuda*

## Health

**shift duty pharmacy**
*farmacia de turno*
**hospital/clinic** *hospital/clínica*
**I need a doctor/dentist** *Necesito un médico/dentista (odontólogo)*
**I don't feel well** *Me siento mal*
**I am sick** *Estoy enfermo(a)*
**It hurts here** *Duele aquí*
**I have a headache/stomachache/ cramps** *Tengo dolor de cabeza/de estómago/de vientre*
**I feel dizzy** *Me siento mareado(a)*
**Do you have (something for)...?**
*¿Tiene (algo para)...?*
**cold** *resfrío*
**flu** *gripe*
**cough** *tos*
**sore throat** *dolor de gargantua*
**diarrhea** *diarrea*
**constipation** *estreñimiento*
**fever** *fiebre*
**heartburn** *acidez*
**aspirin** *aspirina*

**antiseptic cream** *crema antiséptica*
**insect/mosquito bites**
*picaduras de insectos/mosquitos*
**insect repellent** *repelente contra insectos*
**sun block** *bloqueador solar*
**toothpaste** *pasta de dientes*
**toilet paper** *papel higiénico*
**tampons** *tampones*
**condoms** *condones*

## Months of the Year

Note that the Spanish form takes a lower-case initial letter.
**January** *enero*
**February** *febrero*
**March** *marzo*
**April** *abril*
**May** *mayo*
**June** *junio*
**July** *julio*
**August** *agosto*
**September** *septiembre*
**October** *octubre*
**November** *noviembre*
**December** *diciembre*

## Seasons

**spring** *primavera*
**summer** *verano*
**fall (autumn)** *otoño*
**winter** *invierno*

## Time

Note that times are usually followed by *de la mañana* (in the morning) or *de la tarde* (in the afternoon). Transport schedules are often given using the 24-hour clock.
**at nine o'clock** *a las nueve*
**at a quarter past ten** *a las diez y cuarto*
**at half past one/one thirty** *a la una y media*
**at a quarter to two** *a las dos menos cuarto*
**at midday/noon** *a mediodía*
**at midnight** *a medianoche*
**it is five past three** *son las tres y cinco*
**it is twenty five past seven** *son las siete y veinticinco*
**it is ten to eight** *son las ocho menos diez*
**in five minutes** *en cinco minutos*
**does it take long?** *¿tarda mucho?*

TRANSPORTATION
ACCOMMODATIONS
SHOPPING
ACTIVITIES
A – Z
LANGUAGE

# FURTHER READING

## General

The novels of Peru's high-profile writer and former presidential candidate, Mario Vargas Llosa, provide an interesting insight into the country's psyche. **Aunt Julia and the Scriptwriter**, which has also been made into a film, and **The Time of the Hero** are probably the most readable. **The Green House** is set in Peru's Amazon and **Death in the Andes**, explores the effects of terrorism on various rural communities.
**Eight Feet in the Andes**, by Dervla Murphy. John Murray, 2003. Describes Murphy's extraordinary journey from Cajamarca to Cusco.
**The Dancer Upstairs**, by Nicholas Shakespeare. Picador, 1997. A fascinating account of Shining Path leader Abimael Guzmán's final attempt to avoid capture.
**Inca Kola**, by Matthew Parris. Orion, 1993. Entertaining account of backpacking in Peru.
**Touching the Void**, by Joe Simpson. Vintage, 1998. Gripping account of an ill-fated ascent of Siula Grande.
**Exploring Cusco**, by Peter Frost. Nuevas Imágenes S.A., 1999 (fifth edition). Comprehensive coverage of the Cusco region by a longtime resident. Frost's **Machu Picchu Historical Sanctuary** makes for a beautiful companion piece.
**Martín Chambi: 1920–1950**, by Martín Chambi. Lunwerg 1990. A collection of pictures by Peru's most famous photographer.
**The White Rock, An Exploration of the Inca Heartland**, by Hugh Thomson. Weidenfeld and Nicolson 2001. How the lost cities of the Incas have been re-discovered.
**The Peru Reader: History, Culture, Politics**, by Orin Starn, Carlos Degregori, Robin Kirk (eds). Duke University Press, 2006. A collection of essays and extracts that gives a portrait of Peru's social history through the 20th century.

## History

**Chavin: and the Origins of Andean Civilization**, by Richard Burger (ed.), Thames and Hudson, 1995. A thorough study by British

archeologists of one of Peru's most fascinating pre-Inca cultures.
**Nazca: Eighth Wonder of the World?** by Anthony Aveni. British Museum Press, 2000.
**The Conquest of the Incas**, by John Hemming. Penguin, 1983. The best modern account of the fall of the Inca Empire. Extremely readable style, brings the history of Peru to life. Hemming has also written a coffee-table book called **Monuments of the Incas** with black and white photography by Edward Ranney. Both are classic introductions to understanding Peru.
**The Incas and their Ancestors**, by Michael E. Moseley. Thames and Hudson, 1991. Fascinating research into how the Inca empire flourished.
**Antisuyo**, by Gene Savoy. New York, 1970. Fascinating book, long out of print, by a man with an incredible nose for lost cities.
**Lost City of the Incas**, by Hiram Bingham. New York, 1972. Classic account of Bingham's explorations. Outdated theories, but a great read.
**The Ancient Kingdoms of Peru**, by Nigel Davies. Penguin, 1997. Peru's ancient civilizations, from the Moche to the Incas.

## Amazon Jungle

**The Cloud Forest**, by Peter Matthiesson. Penguin, 1987. Account of travel on the Amazon and through the cloud forest of Peru.
**A Guide to the Birds of Colombia**, by Steve Hilty. Princeton Press, 1986. The most useful identification guidebook for birds in this area.
**At Play in the Fields of the Lord**, by Peter Matthiesson. Matthiesson's novel of uncontacted tribes and missionaries set in the department of Madre de Díos.
**The Jivaro: People of the Sacred Waterfall**, by Michael Harner. University of California Press, 1992. Harner's celebrated ethnography of the head-shrinking Jivaro Amerindians in northeast Peru.
**The Wizard of the Upper Amazon**, by Ralph Lamb. His true account of a boy captured by Amerindians in northern Peru and his apprenticeship as a shaman.

## Other Insight Guides

Insight Guides cover nearly 200 destinations, providing information on culture and all the top sights, as well as superb photography.
**Insight Guide: South America** covers the whole subcontinent, from Colombia to Tierra del Fuego. Other Insight Guides on South America include: Argentina, Brazil, Chile and Easter Island, Ecuador and the Galápagos, Rio de Janeiro, and Venezuela. Rainforest enthusiasts will be interested in **Insight Guide: Amazon Wildlife**, which vividly captures in expert text and glorious photography the flora and fauna of the region.

Insight Pocket Guides contain personal recommendations from a local host, a program of carefully timed itineraries and a fold-out map. They are particularly useful for the short-stay visitor intent on making the best use of every moment. Titles covering this region include Ecuador and the Galápagos, Peru, and Rio de Janeiro.

Insight FlexiMaps are designed to complement our guidebooks. They provide full mapping of major destinations, and their easy-to-fold, laminated finish gives them ease of use and durability. The range of titles features the following destinations: Argentina, Buenos Aires, Ecuador and the Galápagos, Peru, Rio de Janeiro, and Sao Paolo.

# ART AND PHOTO CREDITS

**AKG Images** 25CR&B, 51C, 58C
**AP/PA Photos** 27T&CL, 68L&R, 71, 72, 73
**The Art Archive** 45, 54, 61L
**Axiom** 236/237
**Alejandro Balaguer/ Biosfera/Latinphoto** 187T
**Bettmann/Corbis** 26C&BR, 33B, 55L, 67
**Rachael Bowes/Alamy** 250B
**The Bridgeman Art Library** 52, 61R, 65
**Brooklyn Museum/Corbis** 25TL
**Danilo Donadoni/Dinodia** 186, 189
**Endos/Alamy** 190
**Mary Evans Picture Library** 26TL, 46, 48R, 49
**Explorama Lodge** 331
**Ferrocarril Central Andino** 210L
**Michael and Patricia Fogden/Corbis** 249B
**Peter Frost/APA** 21, 38, 39, 42, 43B, 88C, 109B, 123, 154T, 194T, 196, 229, 231, 232, 233, 243T, 245T&B, 246T, 247L, 248, 249T, 254, 271T, 272T&B, 275B, 278T, 279, 284, 285R, 288T&B, 293, 294, 295T&B, 296T&B, 297L&R, 301B, 302T, 303L&R, 340, 343
**Peter Frost** 88B
**Howie Garber/Mira.com** 217
**Nicholas Gill/Alamy** 30B
**Diego Goldberg/Sygma/Corbis** 64C
**Urban Golob/Alamy** 194B
**Miquel Gonzalez/laif/Camerapress** 183
**Jeremy Horner/Hoa-Qui/Camerapress** 184B
**Hotel El Ingenio** 329
**Hulton-Deutsch Collection/Corbis** 62C
**IFC Films/Everett/Rex Features** 128B
**The Image Works/TopFoto** 216
**iStockphoto.com** 7BL, 107B, 132C, 135
**jonarnoldimages** 92
**Wolfgang Kaehler/Corbis** 64B
**Frans Lanting/Frans Lanting Photography** 9CL
**Rachel Lawrence** 210R, 211T, 212B
**Eric Lawrie** 7CRT, 43C, 51B, 87C, 192, 193, 197, 198, 199T&B, 202, 206T, 207, 250T, 253
**Leonardo** 334B
**J Marshall-Tribaleye Images/Alamy** 185, 187B
**Michael Maslan Historic Photographs/Corbis** 63

**Jenny Matthews/Panos** 94
**Megavalanche Peru** 127
**Max Milligan/John Warburton-Lee Photography** 222L
**Gabi Mocatta** 27BR, 120, 159, 195, 200, 201, 221, 222R, 223, 224L&R, 226, 230, 244
**National Geographic/Getty Images** 261B
**North Wind Picture Archives** 56
**Abraham Nowitz/APA** 1, 2/3, 3BR, 4T&B, 5, 6 (all), 7TR, TL, CL, CRB&BR, 8C, BL&BR, 9TR&B, 10 (all), 11 (all), 12/13, 14/15, 16/17, 18, 19L&R, 20, 22, 23, 24 (all), 28, 29, 30C, 31C&B, 32C&B, 33C, 34C&B, 35, 36, 37, 41, 50L, 55R, 57C&B, 58B, 59R, 61B, 62B, 66, 74/75, 76, 77, 78C&B, 79, 80, 81, 82C&B, 83, 84, 85C&B, 86CL&CR, 87B, 89L&R, 96/97, 98, 99, 100 (all), 101, 102C&B, 103L&R, 104, 105, 106C&B, 107C, 108L&R, 109C, 112, 113, 114C&B, 115C&B, 116C&B, 117C&B, 118/119, 126B (all), 128C, 130, 131, 132B, 134B, 136/137, 138/139, 140/141, 142, 143 (all), 148, 149, 151T&B, 152T&B, 153, 154B, 155, 156T&B, 157T&B, 158T&B, 161 (all), 162L&R, 163 (all), 164, 165, 166/167, 170, 171, 172, 173T&B, 174T&B, 175T&B, 176 (all), 177T&B, 178, 179, 188, 203, 212T, 213, 227, 247R, 255, 256, 257, 258, 259T&B, 260T&B, 261T, 262, 263, 266/267, 268, 269, 270, 271B, 273T&B, 274, 275T, 276T&B, 277L&R, 278BL&BR, 280, 281, 282, 283, 285L, 286L&R, 287T&B, 289, 290/291, 292, 300, 301T, 302B, 304/305, 306, 307, 308T&B, 309, 310, 311T&B, 312T&B, 313 (all), 314L&R, 315T, 318, 323, 324, 325, 327, 328, 332, 333, 335, 336, 337T&B, 338, 339, 341, 342, 345, 346, 347, 348, 349, 350, 351, 352, 354, 355, 356
**NPL/Rex Features** 228
**Oronoz** 53, 60
**Pete Oxford/Minden Pictures/Getty** 134
**Peter Oxford/NPL/Rex Features** 90, 91, 93, 218, 219T&B, 220T&B
**Beren Patterson/Alamy** 299
**Claus Possberg/Latinphoto** 124
**Karl-Heinz Raach/laif/Camerapress** 252
**Jaime Razuri/AFP/Getty Images** 69

**Bert de Ruiter/Alamy** 182
**Tui de Roy/Minden Pictures/Getty** 133
**Galen Rowell/Mountain Light/Alamy** 8TR
**Niceforo Ruiz/Latinphoto** 205, 209, 211B, 225
**Martin Shields/Alamy** 95
**Sol y Luna Lodge** 334T
**South American Explorers** 122B
**South American Pictures/Anna Bailetti** 204, 206B, 208, 242
**South American Pictures/Robert Francis** 251
**South American Pictures/Tony Morrison** 184T, 240
**South American Pictures/Luke Peters** 243B, 246B
**Paul Springett/Alamy** 241
**Superstock** 214/215
**Topham Picturepoint** 129R
**Carlos Torres/epa/Corbis** 70
**Ana Cecilia Gonzales Vigil/WpN** 160
**Renzo Uccelli/Latinphoto** 121, 125, 129L
**Werner Forman Archive** 40, 48L
**Corrie Wingate** 86B, 122C, 126C

### PICTURE SPREADS

**110/111:** Peter Frost/APA 110BR, 111CL; Eric Lawrie 111TR; Abraham Nowitz/APA 110/111C, 110TL, 111BR

**180/181:** all Abraham Nowitz/APA except 181TR Eric Lawrie

**234/235:** Ingo Arndt/Minden Pictures/Getty 235BL; M and P Fogden/Minden Pictures/Getty 234/235C; Frans Lanting/Frans Lanting Photography 235TR; Gabi Mocatta 234BR; NHPA/Photoshot 234BL; Photolibrary.com 235BR

**264/265:** all Abraham Nowitz/APA except 265TR Paul Maeyaert/AISA

**316/317:** all Abraham Nowitz/APA except 317BL Eric Lawrie

**Cartographic Editor:** Zoë Goodwin

**Map Production:** Berndtson and Berndtson Productions

© 2008 Apa Publications GmbH & Co.
Verlag KG (Singapore branch)

**Production:** Linton Donaldson

# INDEX

*Numbers in italics refer to photographs*

# Lima

0  1 km
0  1 mile

N

Aeropuerto Internacional
Jorge Chávez

Rimac

Av. del Elmer
Av. Morales Duarez
Av. Morales Duarez

Av. Elmer J. Faucett

Av. Perú
D

Av. 12 de Octubre
Av. 27 de Noviembre

Terminal
Marítima

Pl.
Fanning

Av. República Argentina

Av. Maquinarias

Av. 2 de Mayo

Pje.
Azarete

CALLAO

Av. Panamá

Av. República Argentina

Supe

Av.

Fuerte Real Felipe

Constitución

Av. Saenz Peña

Montezuma

Guardia Chalaca

Av. Benavides

Centro
Médico
Naval

Universidad
Nacional de
San Marcos

German Amezaga

Playa Chucuito

Jr. Gamarra

Buenos Aires

Paz Soldán

Loreto

Virtu

La colina

Ovalo
Saloom

Av. República de Venezuela

Av. Elmer J. Faucett

Av. José de la Riva Agüero

Pu

Playa Cantolao

Av. Bolognesi

José Galvez

Canjulo

Av. de la Marina

Av. de los Precursores

PARQUE
DE LAS
LEYENDAS

Mu
La

LA PUNTA

Escuela
Naval

Av. Grau

Playa
Carpayo

LA PERLA

Santa Rosa

Av. Costanera

Av. la Paz

Av. de los Patriotas

Manco II

SAN MIGUEL

Av.

de la M

Playa
Malecón

Colegio Militar
Leancio Prado

Av. Libertad

Av. Libertad

Av. la Paz

Lazo

Feria Internacional
del Pacífico

MAGDALENA

Av. la Paz

Av. Bertoloti

## Central Lima

Hector Garcia
Riveyro

Rimac

Casa de
Osambela

Santo
Domingo

Serpost

Estación
Desamparados

Jr. Tacna

Jr. Rufino Torrico

Jr. Callcoma

Municipalidad
de Lima

Palacio de
Gobierno

Jr. Amazonas

Camete

Huancavelica

Av. Tacna

Jr. Ica

Jr. Camaná

Plaza

Palacio
del Arzobispo

Monasterio de
San Francisco

Iglesia y Convento
de las Nazarenas

Jr. Chancay

Jr. Rufino Torrico

Callao

Mayor

La Catedral

Jr. Ancash

Teatro Municipal

Av. Emancipación

Huancavelica

Jr. de la Unión

Jr. Ica

Carabaya

Lampa

Jr. Azangaro

Universidad
Federico
Villarreal

Teatro Segura

Jr. Camaná

Jr. Moquegua

Jr. Miro Quesada

Palacio
Torre Tagle

Plaza
Bolívar

Jr. Ayacucho

Av. Tacna

Jr. Ocona

Camaná

La Merced

Lampa

L'Eau Vive

Museo de
la Inquisición

Jr. Junín

Congreso

Jr. Rufino Torrico

Jr. Nicolas de Pierola

Gran Hotel
Bolívar

Jr. de la Unión

San Pedro

Jr. Ucayali

Jr. Ucayali

Jr. Andahuaylas

Jr. Quilca

Jr. Ilo

Plaza
San Martín

Carabaya

Puno

Av. Emancipación

Jr. Miro Quesada

PACIF

Plaza
Francia

Av. Nicolas de Pierola

Contumaza

Jr. Lampa

Jr. Azangaro

Jr. Puno

Cuzco

Jr. Miro Quesada

Jr. Paruro

Jr. Cuzco

OCEA

Jr. Pachitea

Lino Cornejo

Apurimac

Av. Abancay

Jr. Ayacucho

Jr. Andahuaylas

Av. Uruguay

Jr. Lampa

Jr. Pachitea

PARQUE
UNIVERSITARIO

Ministerio de
Educación

Jacinto López

Av. Roosevelt

Av. Roosevelt

Inambari

Jr. Puno

Jr. Leticia

Av. Garcilaso de la Vega

Paseo de la República

Paseo de la República

Palacio
de Justicia

Corabambos

Jr. Sandia

Av. Nicolas de Pierola

Jr. Ayacucho

Montevideo

N

Miguel Allovin

Jr. Leticia

Museo de
Arte Italiano

Jr. Manuel Cuadros

Jr. Iquitos

Jr. Sandia

Av. 9 de Diciembre

Plaza
Grau

Av. Grau

Av. Grau

Av. Abancay

0  300 m

Museo
de Arte

Jr. Misti

0  300 yds